Where East Meets (Mid)West

Exploring an American Regional Divide

Edited by Jon K. Lauck and Gleaves Whitney

◩ The Kent State University Press   *Kent, Ohio*

© 2025 by The Kent State University Press, Kent, Ohio 44242
All rights reserved
ISBN 978-1-60635-496-4
Published in the United States of America

No part of this book may be used or reproduced, in any manner whatsoever, without written permission from the Publisher, except in the case of short quotations in critical reviews or articles.

Cataloging information for this title is available at the Library of Congress.

29 28 27 26 25   5 4 3 2 1

Where East Meets (Mid)West

Contents

Preface: Errand onto the Appalachian Plateau: Finding the Midwest's Eastern Borderlands
   Jon K. Lauck vii

Introduction
   Gleaves Whitney 1

1. Before There Was a West: Appalachian Frontiers in American Newspapers, 1763
   Mary Kupiec Cayton 20

2. How the Western Antislavery Movement Redrafted American Freedom and Democracy
   Jeanne Gillespie McDonald 45

3. Ohio: At the Heart of History
   Kevin F. Kern and Gregory S. Wilson 68

4. A Conversation of Conspiracy: Regionalism and the Unstable Politics of the Early Republic, 1787–1807
   Timothy C. Hemmis 90

5. Tippecanoe: An American Epic
   Mary Stockwell 106

6. Between Northeastern Stockholders and Southern Slaveowners: The 1856 Presidential Election and the Formation of the Midwest
   Andrew W. Wiley 123

7. German or Yankee? Defining Ohio Identity on the Pennsylvania Border
   Randall S. Gooden 139

8 Where Does the Eastern Edge of the Midwest Fall in Ohio?
   Gregory S. Rose 158
9 Italian Americans in Ohio's Mahoning Valley: Creating Identity in the Industrial Midwest
   Donna M. DeBlasio and Martha I. Pallante 176
10 "Opera Was Not Written for New York Alone": The Middling Promotion of Operas in English on the Redpath Chautauqua Circuits
   Cody A. Norling 193
11 From Crass Materialists to Missionaries of Culture: A Regional History of Cultural Ascendance and Economic Decline through the Cleveland Orchestra
   Jacob Bruggeman and Eric Michael Rhodes 215
12 Locating Cleveland: Mapping Black Activism and Art in a "Way Post" City
   Stephanie Fortado 238
13 Political Cultures in Conflict: Locating Ohio into a Region during and after the Era of the New Deal
   Kenneth J. Heineman 257
14 The Divided Battleground: Presidential Voting in Ohio and the Midwest in the Twenty-First Century
   A. Lee Hannah and Christopher J. Devine 274

Contributors 296

Index 302

Preface

Errand onto the Appalachian Plateau
Finding the Midwest's Eastern Borderlands

JON K. LAUCK

> This country has all sorts of places still to be discovered in it.
> –James Wright

Columbus is in the center of Ohio, a state that is the Heart of It All, as the saying goes, and the city is plainly midwestern. My old friend Jon Butler used to describe driving home to Minnesota (he grew up in Hector, in central Minnesota, near the Dakotas) from his academic post in New Haven, Connecticut. When he began to approach Columbus, he remembered, he knew he was in the Midwest. The lands to the east of Columbus felt like something different to him. They were certainly in the orbit of the core Midwest but also shading into something else, a borderland, the eastern edges of the midwestern pale.

On the first day of April 2024, I landed in Columbus and, after a day of meetings and meals, began a trek east the next morning, at 6:10. A storm system had rolled in overnight, and in the morning darkness the rain sloshed down in waves. Governor Mike DeWine held a news conference and said, "There's a big red blotch on the state of Ohio!" I could see the blotch on my weather app, which was also blinking "Flash Flood Warning!" Before long, despite the morning murk and the rain and the flashing red warnings, I could see what Butler meant when the land was momentarily illuminated via lightning flashes.

Columbus is in the flatter midwestern core, where the glaciers slid in and left behind glacial till and fertile soils and little lakes, but that changes when traveling east. I first passed through Hebron in Licking County. Hebron was named by Christian settlers who embraced the biblical reference or perhaps borrowed the name from Hebron, Connecticut, whose founders likely had the same idea. The Hebron massacre was in the news again as part of the debate over the deep origins of the 2023 Gaza war, which would paralyze college campuses on the coasts the following spring. Hebron, Ohio (there are also Hebrons in Illinois, Indiana, Iowa, Missouri, Nebraska, and North Dakota) sits on the eighty-second meridian, a designation I notice because back in my home state of South Dakota people often mark space vis-à-vis the hundredth meridian, which splits the state and signals the dividing line between lands where twenty inches of rain is normal and lands where it is not. West of the hundredth meridian is the arid West, as famously explained by the Midwest-born explorer and scientist John Wesley Powell. But Hebron, far from that line of aridity, gets an ample average of forty-two inches of rain per year, a large chunk of which fell during my drizzly drive. Licking County (so named by settlers for its plentiful salt licks) is bordered by Knox County, home to Centerburg, the precise geographic center of Ohio. Hebron was where the National Road intersected with the Ohio & Erie Canal, which connected the top and bottom halves of the state, so the town is dubbed the Historic Crossroads of Ohio. The deep central-ness of Ohio—the closeness to the capital, the Horseshoe, the state's geographic center—can be felt here.

Down the road east of Hebron is Zanesville, named for the once-famous Zane family. Older Americans will remember the popular western novels of its native son Zane Grey, whose books President Eisenhower of Kansas used to read in the White House to escape from the pressures of the early Cold War. As a young man, Grey took to fishing and hunting and read James Fenimore Cooper's Leatherstocking Tales of early frontier scouting, along with other accounts of pioneering. He also read the popular books by Charles Fosdick and Horatio Alger and *Our Western Border*, a chronicle of pioneers and their struggles in the early Ohio country, who included Daniel Boone, George Rogers Clark, and the Zane family. The town is named for Ebenezer Zane, an early pioneer who constructed Zane's Trace, or trail, from Wheeling, West Virginia, kitty-corner across Ohio down to Maysville, Kentucky.[1] Zanesville is where the smaller Licking River connects to the larger Muskingum River and Zane's Trace crosses the enlarged Muskingum River, which flows south, down to Marietta on the Ohio River. Johnny Appleseed knew these central byways well and used the Muskingum and the trace to extend his apple tree empire throughout the Ohio interior.[2] On this April day, the Muskingum was engorged by the insistent rain and the lowlands along the river were flooding. There used to be ferries in Zanesville, which transported people and goods across the Muskingum, but in the twenty-first century a rare Y-shaped bridge provides the path for cars navigating the Licking–Muskingum confluence. Because of its centrality to early Ohio history, Zanesville was the state's capital for a while before the final move to Columbus. Greater Zanesville—or, let us say, Muskingum County—is geographically significant for another reason. It marks the beginning of the Appalachian Plateau, or where the East meets the Midwest. Near the village of Gratiot, the land visibly begins rolling and the trees thicken through the lightning flashes.

My destination that misty morning was not Hebron or Zanesville but New Concord, Ohio, and Muskingum University, home of the Muskies. While once the real muskellunge grew long in the deeper pools of the Muskingum River, they are now rare, but the legend—and mascot—lives on, even though I am not alone in more closely connecting the great fish to northern Wisconsin than southeast Ohio. New Concord was largely a social visit. Several years ago, I came to know MU's president, Sue Hasseler, when she was a vice president at Augustana University in Sioux Falls, South Dakota, on the other end of the Midwest. But I also wanted to map out this geographical edge country. Reaching New Concord, on the far Eastern side of Muskingum County, one has definitively passed onto the Appalachian Plateau, or the obviously unglaciated eastern rim of Ohio. Muskingum University sits high on a hill, which makes the geographic point, and on the path into town there is a large bridge over Fox Creek which flows between two rounded hills.

As one approaches the plateau, the change is subtle. There is not a big escarpment announcing its arrival. This is a transition zone, not a stark line of demarcation. This is not the central spine of the Appalachians, not the highlands and hollows. This is the slow beginnings of the topography that evolves into Appalachia. But since this land is unglaciated, it lacks the glacial till and rich soils that glaciated western Ohio boasts. A friend in Columbus had said that "western Ohio is basically eastern South Dakota," or the flat farming territory where we both grew up. The topographical differences between eastern and western Ohio can be measured in corn. In Mercer County, Ohio, on the western side of the state, the farm ground totals 270,000 acres; in Jefferson County, in eastern Ohio (home to Steubenville), 77,000 acres are dedicated to farming; farms occupy 92 percent of Mercer County; 43 percent in Jefferson (while 32 percent is forested); Mercer produces 18.5 million bushels of corn a year; Jefferson produces 350,000.

On an Ohio tour threaded together by stops at some of the state's many colleges, one must note that New Concord is the birthplace of William Rainey Harper, the first president of the University of Chicago and a champion of the classics and the humanities. He was born in a cabin—which still stands on Main Street—in 1856 and attended then Muskingum College (graduating at age thirteen). I dropped by the cabin at the bottom of the hill below the college next to the village hall and across the street from Wally's Pizza and Margaret Lane Antiques. Harper earned his PhD from Yale by age eighteen and then married Ella Paul, the daughter of the president of Muskingum College, and began teaching classics at nearby Denison University in Granville. His ambitions soon had him building the University of Chicago into one of the world's great research universities.

John Glenn, a heroic figure from a now distant America, was also raised here, and a towering portrait of him graces the president's office at Muskingum University. John Glenn Sr. ran a local plumbing business, and his son delivered the *Columbus Dispatch* on his bicycle and played football and basketball at New Concord High School. John Glenn Jr. then attended Muskingum College and played football before becoming an officer and fighter pilot in the Marine Corps and flying fifty-seven combat missions in the Pacific during World War II. Glenn was an all-American from Ohio. He became an astronaut, served in the US Senate, and ran for president. He was a Mason and an elder in the Presbyterian Church. In 1943, he married Annie Castor in New Concord, and they were husband and wife for seventy-three years. Glenn is a figure from the center of Ohio—from the Heart of It All—who represented the best of the Midwest to the rest of the country and symbolized the solidity of the heartland. New Concord is part of "deep Ohio," as novelist Stephen Markley calls it.[3] On the way out of town, I tried to stop at the National Road and Zane Grey Museum, but it is closed on Tuesdays.

Before heading farther east toward Appalachia, I turned southwest toward Athens, having downloaded Tom Wolfe's classic *The Right Stuff* (1979) to listen to on the drive and reflect on the greatness of John Glenn, whom I remembered passing in the hallways as a young college intern in the US Senate and whose namesake—John Glenn International Airport—had been my gateway to Columbus. Wolfe spotlights Glenn's decency and striving and describes the scene when the national media descends on his Presbyterian church in New Concord looking for good photos to accompany their coverage of Glenn being the first American to orbit the Earth. I passed signs for The Wilds, an open air zoo with rhinoceroses and zebras, and wished my kids were along. The Wilds used to be a coal mine, a sign of the coming of Appalachia. South of I-70 I was at the mercy of GPS and began traveling down narrow winding lanes with no shoulders through thick trees and a few scattered small fields which would soon yield spring hay. The roads—Pike Road, Hicks Road, Old Wheeling Road, Fulkerson Road, Clay Pike, Miller's Lane—I likely could not find again. But they definitely took me through the Appalachian hills. This was not the gridded flat Midwest and not the drier western Midwest. Near Philo High School, Indian Run Creek flooded over the road from all the rain. I proceeded through the gushing brown water in my rental car not knowing the depth, and, happily, it worked out. On the radio, Ohio's governor had earlier warned against doing this.

I finally reached Highway 60 and the town of Duncan Falls on the raging Muskingum River. Near Lock No. 9, some guys in pickups were watching the water rise and guessing how bad the flooding would be. Highway 60 led me south with the great brown river on the right and steep cliffs on the left. A permanent "Falling Rock" sign got my attention—this is hill country—as did a temporary "High Water" sign being planted on the side of the road by Ohio DOT workers. In the town of Gaysport, the bridge across the river groaned against the mounting pressure of millions of gallons of water rushing downstream. Reaching McConnelsville, about thirty miles downstream from Zanesville, I crossed the river and headed southwest on Highway 78 while the Muskingum continued southeast toward Marietta on the Ohio River. Climbing up out of the river valley, I saw clouds settled on the hills above. The highway is dedicated to the

Seventy-Eighth Ohio Volunteer Infantry, since many of the regiment's men came from this area, part of the larger army of 240 Ohio regiments that pulverized the Confederacy. I reached the top of a small mountain where one can see the whole forest-covered valley. The GPS read Malta, Ohio, but I saw no signs saying such.

The trees here did not relent. Further south, I passed Wayne National Forest, named after Gen. "Mad Anthony" Wayne, who ably served General Washington during the Revolution and then waged a campaign in the Ohio wilderness against a confederation of tribes resisting American suzerainty over the early Midwest. I had just published an article about the complexity of this early history and imagined how it all unfolded in the territory around me.[4] The appearance of a national forest in my path was another sign that the traditional Midwest lies farther west. The nonglaciated Appalachian Plateau is heavily forested and home to many trees, including the buckeye, a contrast to my part of the Midwest, where towns take names such as "Lone Tree" for their rarity. This first week of April, the purple buds of the eastern redbud trees and the pink buds of cherry trees popped, coloring the surrounding hills. Past the impressive Wayne National Forest and two smaller state forests, one reaches Athens, home to the first college in the Midwest: Ohio University, firmly planted in the Appalachian hills. OU even offers a certificate in Appalachian studies. The previous year, it hosted AppalachiaFest, the conference of the Appalachian Studies Association. Athens had also hosted the Appalachia Rising music festival in the past. On that second day of April, I gave a talk about midwestern history at the Central Region Humanities Center at OU, and the audience and later conversations made clear that Athenians consider themselves to be living on the edges of the Midwest and Appalachia in an interstitial and academic zone that embraces music and the arts and writing. Athens, indeed. They love it here. When regionalists talk about the power of place—a power that calls one home after they leave—this is what they mean.

Athens was once tightly linked to Marietta, fifty miles to the east, farther onto the Appalachian Plateau. After the American Revolution, several veterans from New England formed the Ohio Company of Associates to buy land from Congress in the Northwest Territory and develop a settlement they called Marietta (they also created Ohio University in Athens). As veterans, they chose the name to honor the French queen and to recognize critical French assistance during the war. The Yankees located their settlement on the Ohio River at the mouth of the Muskingum River because they rightly understood that the Ohio would be the first main riverine artery into the future Midwest, a new land, one on the other side of the mountains. The Ohio River would also serve as a real and symbolic dividing line between the Midwest and the lands of deeper Appalachia across the river. Travelers frequently commented on how different the cultures on both sides of the river were and how these differences persisted over the decades.

On the morning of April 3, before a talk to a Marietta College class of history majors, I ventured across the Ohio River into an upward bulge of West Virginia which juts into Ohio and bends the river northward for several miles. I drove through Williamstown, West Virginia, saw signs for the contested mayor's race and others for a city council race, and tried to buy a cup of coffee at the State Line First West Virginia Coffee Shop, but it was closed. A candidate for city council told the local newspaper he would not put up political signs: "It's a small town. People know me or they don't. It won't hurt my feelings either way."[5] I crossed back over the river and had better luck at the Lafayette Hotel, with its coffee stand outside The Gun Room diner and next to the Rufus Putnam Room, named for the Revolutionary war general who cofounded Marietta (the Ohio University mascot is, accordingly, named Rufus). Out in the Ohio River, a large tug pushed giant barges full of gravel against the swift current under the Williamstown Bridge. The hotel is named for General Marquis de Lafayette, who aided the American revolutionaries and who visited here in 1825. Read a list of all the veterans of the Revolution who lived in the area, he responded, "I know them all. I saw them at Brandywine, Yorktown and Rhode Island. They were the bravest of the brave."[6]

West Virginia should have been given more space on this trip's itinerary. It is the only state that fully rests within the traditional boundaries of Appalachia, and the state has a particular immigration story that should not be glossed over. In the 1600s, after conquering Ireland, English authorities encouraged people from the Scottish lowlands to move across the Irish Sea and settle the province of Ulster, the upper eastern quadrant of Ireland. The Scots were Presbyterians, not English Anglican or Irish Catholic, and thus stood apart. Half of these settlers later migrated to the American colonies, especially Pennsylvania, and started making their way to the backcountry, into the Appalachian mountains. These "Wild Irish" immigrants gained a reputation for squatting, drinking, fighting, singing, and clashing with Native Americans. Stern Presbyterians founded Muskingum College as a religious institution and are the reason John Glenn became a Presbyterian elder. The people of eastern Pennsylvania did not mind having these immigrants out on the frontier serving as a buffer against Indian hostilities. The friction between the settled, wealthier parts of the colonies and the backcountry enclaves was often intense. In western Virginia (there was no West Virginia until the Civil War era), 80 percent of the population was Scots-Irish.[7] Grazing, weaving, and modest farming prevailed among the mountaineers until after the Civil War, when large timber companies bought up the rights to harvest the region's thick and varied trees. The region, one Appalachian lawyer recalled, was still "matted with an immense primeval forest, so dank and so dense as to amount to almost a jungle." A few decades later, coal mining became a major force in this area, underscoring another distinction from the core of the Midwest. By the beginning of the twentieth century, the local timber and coal supplies were mostly controlled by large corporations not based in Appalachia.[8] I do not think I am alone in tracing many of my impressions of West Virginia to the 1960 Democratic primary, won by Senator John Kennedy, which led to the creation of a specifically *regional* economic development initiative focused on the needs of this geographic space.[9]

The history majors at Marietta College had a lot to say about regions. One young woman from Dayton, in western Ohio, definitely noticed the distinction between farming Ohio and Appalachian Ohio. Another, from Columbus, said that when she drove southeast to get to Marietta she noticed how the land changes into a new topography around Hocking Hills State Park. A third woman, who grew up in northern West Virginia, felt both Appalachian and midwestern and believed Marietta inhabits a borderland. Local historian Jean Yost noted that he always said he grew up in the Ohio Valley and did not use the terms Midwestern or Appalachian. In another sign of the power of the rain storms I passed through the previous day, one young woman in the class reported that she was just given keys to a new dorm room, higher up, because the lower floors were flooding. The television news reported on "local residents saying it's the highest they've seen the river in decades." Marietta College students and local Boy Scouts were called out to help those with flooded homes. On Thursday, the river crested at 41.49 feet near Wheeling. At 42 feet, the river would have entered "major flood stage," according to the National Weather Service.[10] The director of the Jefferson County (Steubenville) Emergency Management Agency, said of the flooding, "Whatever you do, don't drive through it."[11]

After my Marietta sojourn to start day three of the trip, I followed Highway 7 northeast along the Ohio River to Steubenville. About twenty miles in, however, the Ohio DOT blocked the road with signs that said "ROAD CLOSED—HIGH WATER—Max Fine $2,000." I had to return to Marietta and get on the interstate north, which I had wanted to avoid in favor of the two lane path along the big river. I later heard that much of Marietta went underwater after I passed through. The high water even caused some barges to come loose and drift down the swollen river.[12]

The lost time was a shame; I wanted to visit Mount Pleasant on the drive. Mount Pleasant highlights the multiple migration streams into Ohio that made the state an ethnically complex place and a testing ground for American pluralism. Marietta was a Yankee New England town, at least in its early decades, before more and more migrants diluted this early influence. So was Cleveland in the north, which Connecticut Yankees settled. Down the Ohio River, past Marietta, more southerners trickled into the bottom of Ohio, especially from Kentucky, many of them Scots-Irish settlers who had passed through the Appalachian mountains farther south. But Mount Pleasant is a different story. These settlers were Quakers, some of whom came straight across from Pennsylvania into central Ohio and were joined by many of the Germans, or Pennsylvania Dutch who had settled outside of Philadelphia and were Lutheran, German Reformed, Amish, Mennonite, Schwenkfelder, Moravian, and other sects that spun out from the Protestant reformation.[13] Zane Grey's ancestors first came to the United States as Quaker immigrants in the 1600s, and Quaker immigrants established towns such as Mount Pleasant, Ohio, where the Quaker Yearly Meeting House still stands. Not coincidentally, given the Pennsylvania-heavy origins of American Quakers, there's a town named New Philadelphia nearby. These Quakers and Germans did not always love their Appalachian neighbors, and observers' "praise of the industrious Ohio farmers was lavish," while their opinions of Appalachian mountaineers were another matter.[14] The tidy and efficient German farms were frequently contrasted to the spaces on the Appalachian side of the fence.[15]

These migration streams also speak to geography and why the region that became the Midwest was seen as a separate physical space. They speak, specifically, to the imposing power of the Appalachian mountain chain. The settlers of the original thirteen colonies saw the Appalachians as the Great Barrier to the West. Using the mountains, the British tried to wall off the west via the Proclamation Line, and it generally worked. Only adventurers and ragged squatters and the Wild Irish ventured out into these hinterlands. The breakthrough came when Daniel Boone went down the Great Valley of the Appalachians and snuck through Cumberland Gap to reach Kentucky. Others rowed up the Potomac River and made the trek over the mountains via the Cumberland Road (which is not connected to Cumberland Gap—everyone wanted to flatter the Duke of Cumberland, the son of the king) until they reached a tributary of the Ohio River and could travel by canoe and flatboat. This was mostly walking or on horseback and traveling through cold mountains and thus not an appealing trip.[16] It took years for decent roads to be built, so the mountains still remained imposing. The Erie Canal, providing water access to the Great Lakes via New York, and the railroad were the real transportation breakthroughs. But each route maintained its regional ethnic orientation—Cumberland Gap: Scots-Irish southerners; Cumberland Road: Mid-Atlantic Germans and Quakers; Erie Canal: New England Yankees. These varied streams would guarantee a mixed population pool in Ohio. By the mid-nineteenth century, Ohio was the most ethnically diverse state in the country.[17]

I finally rolled into Steubenville on the Ohio River. The destination and its name remind me of how old this place is. The big river begins in Pittsburgh, where the Allegheny and Monongahela Rivers merge and over which British and French armies fought in the 1750s during the French and Indian War. A lot of these events happened nearly three centuries ago. This area was first governed by the Northwest Ordinance, passed in 1787, about the time Major Duncan, namesake of Duncan Falls, was killed by the Shawnee. Marietta was founded in 1788 and Athens in 1797. Marietta's settlers reached their destination via a newly christened flatboat named the *Mayflower*, a moniker conveying deep time and the nation's thin beginnings. While Zane Grey is known for his western novels, his early works were about the 1700s and Revolutionary War heroes. Such an interest explains the name of Steubenville, which honors Baron Friedrich Wilhelm von Steuben, the German officer who trained Washington's army. The town was first Fort Steuben, built in 1786. The mayor, Jerry Barilla, who warmly greeted me and offered a tour of the fort, told me that the town needs a statue of Steuben, and I of course agreed and was surprised there was not one already. Many of the Revolutionary War veterans, who could not be paid during the dark days of the conflict, were given deeds to lands in Ohio as compensation. The Fire Lands, or Sufferers' Lands, were part of Connecticut's Western Reserve specifically set aside for those patriots burned out by the British. They named the new Ohio counties after Generals Washington, Knox, Darke, Crawford, Greene, Hamilton, Hardin, Marion, Mercer, Preble, Putnam, Shelby, Stark, Warren, and Clark and patriots like Adams, Carroll, Franklin, Henry, Jefferson, Madison, Monroe, Van Wert, and Williams. Cincinnati was named after the Society of Cincinnati, which honored those who left their families and professions to serve in the Revolution, as the Roman general Lucius Quinctius Cincinnatus had left his farm to fight off an invader of Rome. The American Revolution, in short, left a direct imprint on Ohio in ways it did not in states farther west.

Of course the topography is old, too, the mountains and forests untouched by glacial scraping. As John Denver sang about neighboring West Virginia, "life is old there, older than the trees." In this borderland between the Appalachian Mountains and the leveled farming areas of central Ohio there are lots of hills—a middling topography between the mountains to the east and the flatness to the west. The day before, driving into Athens, I passed Hocking Hills State Park, and its presence is consistently mentioned. Above Ohio University you can find the colloquially named and locally popular Bong Hill (OU was named the nation's best party school, after all). These hills, spared from the steam-shoveling power of the glaciers, were not what the agrarian-minded early settlers had in mind. The lands of the Ohio Company around Marietta, a new history of Ohio reminds us, were "rather unfertile."[18] "Farmers found that the shallow upland soils, which eroded readily, would not continually support crops," according to one natural history.[19] The early explorer Christopher Gist found the hilly unglaciated section of eastern Ohio to have soil that was "mean stony and broken" and "not very rich."[20] Unlike in flatter Ohio, this area boasted hills that made surveying the territory much more difficult.[21]

Mayor Jerry Barilla, a Steubenville native who ran Frank and Jerry Furniture and Appliance for fifty years, is obviously Italian. While he gave his tour of Fort Steuben, I struggled not to ask questions about local boy Dino Crocetti, aka Dean Martin, because I assumed local folks are tired of this conversation (Dino does not have a statue either, like the neglected Baron von Steuben). But an old posse of friends and I love Dean and Frank Sinatra and believe they helped us survive the absurdities of graduate school, so I had to broach the topic and the mayor was happy to oblige. Every year Steubenville hosts the Dean Martin Festival, which keeps the Dino flame alive, but his boyhood home in a poor neighborhood of the city is long gone. Italians were strong in Steubenville and further north, all through the Mahoning Valley, which guides the Mahoning River down into the Beaver River, which empties into the mighty Ohio in far western Pennsylvania. Italians have a stronger presence in this area, unlike farther south, below Steubenville, where the settlers tended to be from an earlier generation and were mostly Germans and Quakers from Pennsylvania, Yankees, and some Scots-Irish from the highlands. The Italians came about a century later than these earlier settlers, part of the pre–World War I immigration wave brought in by iron and steel jobs. The people in particular places shift over time and transform the identity of towns, cities, and regions. Regional identity is not static. We adjourned for dinner at Naples, a restaurant Dino used to frequent (a student at Ohio University had insisted I also try the pizza at Capri Sausage and Meatball in town, but time was fleeting and my belt was already too tight). I could only eat about half of my massive veal parmesan. As the sun set on the river, I took some photos of the bridges pointing into West Virginia to the east and drove through the lovely campus of Franciscan University of Steubenville, perched high on a hill overlooking the Ohio River.

Before it was completely dark, I headed north along the river and fueled up in Toronto. By the time I reached East Liverpool, night had fallen. The outlines of the hills were visible from the lights of small houses and the valley below glowed with streetlights and the flashing machinery of sundry industrial plants. East Liverpool is a central notch in the rust belt. I noticed the landscape change in Martins Ferry (there is no apostrophe after Martin, for some reason), about forty miles back. It was no longer the green hills and thick forest and small farms of bucolic Appalachia. This was iron, steel, brick, cement, grease, and ash territory. Hulking smokestacks, surrounded by Goliath-size helpings of coal, had started to line the river. Cooling towers with blinking beacons and industrial tubing and rail lines and dump trucks and bridges and tugs and barges become the norm. Dilapidation is more visible. Places like Martins Ferry expose the recent hard times and the scars of the old industrial order. I drove around the town to try and find the football field by the river that the writer James Wright wrote the poem about and find lots of razor wire, collapsing houses, and an air of destitution. Some old houses tip toward the river and seem close to sliding down the hill. The story is that local boys would practice football on the field next to the Ohio River and would be covered in soot from local factories by the end of practice so they would jump into the river to clean up. Soot signaled the presence of good industrial jobs. The NFL kicker Lou Groza, whose Hungarian-immigrant father ran a bar in town, said "When there's soot on the window sill, there is prosperity." As the success of Groza and others attest, the Pittsburgh-to-Cleveland steel belt has long been known as a seedbed of gridiron talent.[22] One can bear witness to this football history at the Upper Ohio Valley Museum and Learning Center at the Lou Holtz Hall of Fame in East Liverpool.

Wright captured the local football scene, and the turning of the seasons, in his poem "Autumn Begins in Martins Ferry, Ohio" (1963). About the same time, *Life* sent a photographer and a reporter to town to document high school football in what a New York reporter smugly called a "grimy mill town." According to the magazine, misbehaving football players were swiftly dealt with, including via judicial tribunals assembled by their teammates, so they did not jeopardize the team's chances. This system of self-regulation, which the reporter uses in an apparent attempt to highlight the exaggerated importance of football, comes off sounding rather effective. Juvenile delinquency, the story reported, was "virtually unknown." The high school Latin teacher, Miss Heloise Knapp, could "drag a linebacker out of class by his ear faster than he can red dog an enemy quarterback." As a result, the coach admitted, he had players "who can call signals better in Latin than they can in English."[23]

While Wright's poem captured the salience of football in Martins Ferry, the young poet also knew his location in the surrounding topography. His father worked in glass factories along the Ohio River, and his "mother's family came from West Virginia, and they were honest-to-God hillbillies to fare-thee-well." He said Ohio was "both northern and southern; it's eastern and western; all kinds of people live there."[24] Martins Ferry was an "industrial area enclosed by the foothills of the Appalachians on both sides, near that big river." As a professor later in life, Wright ordered his students, mostly from New York, to get out and see the big country they lived in and made sure they knew that "when you've reached Pittsburgh you're not really yet at the beginning of the Middle West." That place was beyond the Appalachian foothills. He also told them to get a cup of coffee in Zanesville and to actually *see* the country. Wright is an old guide to regions and nooks and side trails and crannies who helped everyone see the fullness of the country and he was well equipped for such duties. He grew up in Martins Ferry reading the Hoosier writer James Whitcomb Riley in the town where William Dean Howells, the father of American literary realism, was born at a time when regionalist movements were strong.[25] We need more Wrights these days if we are going to understand the center of the country.

I felt like a schmuck driving around Wright's Martins Ferry since my rental car was a white BMW hybrid (the rental place was out of the bland "midsize sedan" I ordered) and it had Alabama plates. The Steubenville mayor said, "Everyone will think you're a drug dealer!" But I did not want to skip the stop in Martins Ferry, partly because it is the oldest settlement in Ohio, a place where land-seeking squatters illegally assembled in defiance of federal authority. The American army was sent in to burn them out.[26] This harsh early history does not shock. It fits the mood. The Martins Ferry–East Liverpool corridor is a place where the pain of deindustrialization can be seen and felt. Just north of East Liverpool is the now ominous sounding East Palestine, where in early 2023 a massive train derailment and toxic spill added to the air of industrial decline and menace. Government officials burned the toxic chemicals inside the wrecked train cars, sending dense black smoke through the valley. Then, a few weeks before my visit, different government officials said this "controlled burn" was not necessary.[27]

East Liverpool is where the Ohio River valley turns sharply east, so we need to part company. About ninety miles upriver is Pittsburgh, where the Ohio begins its long journey. The city sits deeper into Appalachia (the city's elevation is 1,223 feet, compared to back in Columbus in the Midwest proper at 781 feet). East Liverpool sits across from the last few miles of the little strip of West Virginia sticking up, which holds parts of Pennsylvania and Ohio apart like a boxing referee. The dwindling narrow slice of West Virginia is a sign that rural Appalachia is fading.

With the Ohio River valley turning east and departing Ohio, I headed north toward Youngstown. I stayed in the Doubletree Hotel in a building designed by architect Albert Kahn, which used to be the headquarters of Youngstown Sheet & Tube, the steel company that broke the back of the Mahoning Valley in 1977 after its Black Monday closure. The next morning over breakfast, the new president of Youngstown State University, Bill Johnson, told me that the valley is changing. The old era of New Deal Democrat domination is over. Johnson, a former area congressman, would know. He narrowly captured a seat in Congress in the district south of here as a Republican in the 2010 midterm wave and kept winning subsequent elections by larger margins. He noted that this valley was turning Republican faster than any other area of the country. The Democrats lost steam when they advocated free trade agreements; opposed new energy development, such as natural gas, in the area; and drifted to the left on cultural issues. Obama won this strip of counties in eastern Ohio in 2008. In 2016 and 2020, Trump won them all. In April 2024, the race to fill Congressman Johnson's seat was under way and the Republicans had chosen as their candidate the Italian American Michael Rulli, whose family of immigrants from Calabria, Italy ran Rulli Brothers Market, a grocery business based in Youngstown. (Rulli would go on to defeat the Democratic candidate in the special election in June.) James Pogue, a native Ohioan, has described the political consequences of the unwinding of the old industrial order in Ohio and the resulting feelings of loss and how they shape politics and signal a generational changing of the guard.[28] On April 4, I gave a talk in central Youngstown at the Butler Institute of American Art, funded by an early valley industrialist, and I saw Norman Rockwell's *Lincoln the Railsplitter* (1964) hanging there. The popular painting of the first midwestern president is the perfect centerpiece for the first museum dedicated exclusively to American art.

Youngstown was very welcoming, but the road called. I visited my friend Jeff Bilbro across the state line in Grove City, Pennsylvania; he had recently moved here from Michigan. He works at a Presbyterian college and pointed out all the Presbyterian churches in the area and is confident this is Scots-Irish Appalachia and not the Midwest. Bilbro is editor of a journal titled *Local Culture,* designed to provide an alternative to the obsessions of the national media and to highlight geographic and cultural nuances, so he understands these oft-overlooked details of local life. I headed to Kent, Ohio, to see where the 1970 shootings happened, then to Cleveland to hear a talk about Guardians baseball down in the Flats next to the Cuyahoga River. The first question the speaker was asked is whether he regrets the Cleveland Indians' 2021 decision to become the Guardians. On the drive into the city, I took a photo of the fifty-foot tall Guardians on the art deco Hope Memorial Bridge over the Cuyahoga River, which gave the old baseball team its new name. At my Beaux Arts–style hotel—which used to house the Cleveland Board of Education—I ran into some Iowa Hawkeye fans in town for the Final Four tournament and yelled, "Go Caitlin Clark!" They yelled, "Go Hawks!" The next morning, Friday, I went down to Lake Erie and took a photo of the Cleveland Cliffs freighter the SS *William G. Mather,* the "Ship That Built Cleveland," which has been permanently retired in front of Browns stadium.

Downtown Cleveland felt empty. Large American cities, especially during the morning sprint to work, once bustled and hustled. I looked for a copy of the *Cleveland Plain Dealer* but could not find one, even at my downtown hotel. My final talk of this trip was at the Rust Belt Humanities Lab at Ursuline College, in the Cleveland suburb of Pepper Pike. The final slide of my presentation was of *Gray and Gold* (1942), a mesmerizing painting by John Rogers Cox of Terre Haute, Indiana, that I visited earlier that day at the Cleveland Museum of Art (William Mather, the president of Cleveland Cliffs Iron, whose name is on the freighter in the harbor, was the president of the museum from 1933 to 1949). The darkening skies of the painting fit the mood—emptied downtown Cleveland, memories of Martins Ferry, the tourists, who began to annoy the locals, arriving to see the total eclipse. The *Wall Street Journal* reported that the Final Four and the eclipse would put Cleveland on the map and overcome a legacy of Cleveland jokes. Caitlin Clark's comment that Cleveland "felt like a larger version of Des Moines" did not help the cause.[29] I finally found a copy of the *Plain Dealer*—Caitlyn Clark was on the cover.[30]

A woman at the Rust Belt symposium raised her hand and wondered aloud where Cleveland fits into our discussion of regional identity. She went to graduate school in Columbus, and it was a different place to her.

PREFACE xxiii

She also liked the old retort, "I'm from Cleveland, bitch!"—a nice bit of regionalist defiance that I appreciate. She made the essential point here—Jon Butler was right. When one enters Ohio from the east, it changes from Appalachian hills and the Rust Belt to something different about an hour east of Columbus, something more flat, more farm-oriented, more traditionally Midwest. These are the regional boundaries and identities the people assembled that morning aimed to explore. The organizers were even launching a new journal, titled *Rust Belt Studies,* to carry the flag. An impressive young woman from Cleveland, Ursuline English professor Katharine Trostel, led the charge. Exploring the East–Midwest borderland is the purpose of the book in your hands, part of a grand enterprise designed to explore the center of this nation and its subregions and corners and sides and borderlands.

On Friday night I departed Cleveland for Sioux Falls and at 5:30 the next morning drove south through the Big Sioux River valley to Omaha to watch a spring 12U football tournament, and could see for miles in every direction. I passed Akron, Iowa, named by people who moved west in the nineteenth-century and fondly remembered Akron, Ohio, a city just south of Cleveland I was sorry to miss on my trip. I passed the exit to Vermillion, South Dakota, home to the University of South Dakota and the journal *Middle West Review* and thought about how it, along with Ursuline College's *Rust Belt Studies,* could effectively represent and chronicle both ends of the Midwest. As I pondered the USD–Ursuline alliance, the only breaks in the flat topography were the Loess Hills guiding the Big Sioux River into Sioux City and the short white cliffs on the south side of the Missouri River leading it into Omaha. I crossed the Mormon Bridge over the Big Mo passing from Iowa into Nebraska and drove by a giant grain elevator complex, and I thought about how the Missouri and Ohio Rivers form the broad outline of the Midwest. The railcars I saw near the Iowa–Nebraska border are full of corn-made ethanol, not the industrial ethylhexyl acrylate that made headlines back in East Palestine. The guys on the radio were talking about the University of Iowa women's basketball team, which for the second season in a row advanced to the national title game. Last year, the team represented the region against a southern powerhouse, Louisiana State University, and this year it played an eastern dynasty, the University of Connecticut. A prairie wind with gusts of thirty-five miles per hour undeterred by knoll or forest or valley thrashed the gridiron in Papillion, Nebraska. This is the agrarian core of the Midwest, the eastern fringes of which were seven hundred miles behind me in the Appalachian hills. In between there is a lot of America that needs to be studied and rediscovered.

Notes

I extend special thanks to Christa Adams, John Kropf, Chris Laingen, Greg Rose, and Matt Young for a thorough reading of this preface. The epigraph is taken from "James Wright: The Pure Clear Word," Wright interview with Dave Smith, *American Poetry Review* 9 (May–June 1980), 20.

1. Frank Gruber, *Zane Grey: A Biography* (Cleveland: World, 1970), 13; Charles McKnight, *Our Western Border* (Philadelphia: J. C. McCurdy, 1875). Zane Grey's mother was Josephine Alice Zane, a granddaughter of Ebenezer Zane, whom General George Washington commended for his service in the Revolution. Washington granted Ebenezer Zane ten thousand acres in the Ohio country, which caused him to build Zane's Trace. Josephine married a preacher-dentist named Lewis M. Gray, the grandson of an Irishman who settled in Muskingum County. Their son Pearl Gray dropped *Pearl* in favor of *Zane* and spelled his last name *Grey*, to become Zane Grey of Zanesville, Ohio. Gruber, *Zane Grey*, 6–7.

2. William Kerrigan, *Johnny Appleseed and the American Orchard: A Cultural History* (Baltimore: Johns Hopkins Univ. Press, 2012), 76.

3. On Markley, see Jon Lauck, "The Neo-Regionalist Moment: Hearing the Emerging Voices of the American Center," *Los Angeles Review of Books,* Mar. 28, 2019.

4. Jon Lauck, "Finding the Pre-History of the Midwest: A Note on American Indian Scholarship," *South Dakota History* 54 (Spring 2024): 59–82.

5. Kristen Hainkel, "Williamstown Mayor Faces Challenger in Election," *Parkersburg News and Sentinel,* Jan. 31, 2024.

6. David B. Baker, "Lafayette's Perilous Journey to Marietta," *Marietta Times,* Nov. 25, 2023.

7. Kevin Kenny, *The American Irish: A History* (New York: Pearson-Longman, 2000), 23–29; Maldwyn A. Jones, "The Scotch-Irish in British America," in *Strangers within the Realm: Cultural Margins of the First British Empire,* ed. Bernard Bailyn and Philip D. Morgan (Chapel Hill: Univ. of North Carolina Press, 1991), 287 (which notes that 70 percent of the Scots-Irish immigrants were Presbyterians); John Opie, "A Sense of Place: The World We Have Lost," in *An Appalachian Symposium: Essays Written in Honor of Cratis D. Williams,* ed. J. W. Williamson (Boone, NC: Appalachian State Univ., 1977), 116.

8. Harry M. Caudill, *Night Comes to the Cumberlands: A Biography of a Depressed Area* (Boston: Little, Brown, 1962), 22, 70–75.

9. Robert O. Rupp, *The Primary That Made a President: John F. Kennedy and West Virginia* (Knoxville: Univ. of Tennessee Press, 2020); Gregory Wilson, *Com-

munities Left Behind: The Area Redevelopment Administration, 1945–1965 (Knoxville: Univ. of Tennessee Press, 2009).

10. Andrew Wulfeck, "Ohio River Crests at Major Flood Status Submerging Towns in Appalachia," *Fox Weather,* Apr. 6, 2024, https://www.foxweather.com/weather-news/rainfall-flooding-ohio-kentucky-west-virginia. Kristen Hainkel, "Wild Water: Marietta and Mid-Ohio Valley Anticipating Water Receding," *Marietta Times,* Apr. 6, 2024; "Ohio River Swells to 41.49 Feet, Highest since 2005, Before Beginning Slow Retreat," *Intelligencer/Wheeling News-Register,* Apr. 5, 2024.

11. Warren Scott, "Area Officials Watch for Potential Flooding," *Herald-Star* (Steubenville), Apr. 3, 2024.

12. Cybele Mayes-Osterman, "Officials Work to Pull Out 7 Barges Trapped by Ohio River Dam after 26 Break Loose," *USA Today,* Apr. 16, 2024.

13. Ellen Starr Brinton, "The Yearly Meetinghouse of Mount Pleasant, Ohio," *Bulletin of Friends Historical Association* 41 (Autumn 1952): 93; James L. Burke and Donald E. Bensch, *Mount Pleasant and the Early Quakers of Ohio* (Columbus: Ohio Historical Society, 1975); Timothy G. Anderson, "The Creation of an Ethnic Culture Complex Region: Pennsylvania Germans in Central Ohio, 1790–1850," *Historical Geography* 29 (2001): 135–57.

14. Caudill, *Night Comes to the Cumberlands,* 17; Estyn Evans, "The Scotch-Irish in the New World: An Atlantic Heritage," *Journal of the Royal Society of Antiquaries of Ireland* 95, nos. 1–2 (1965): 40, 44.

15. Kenny, *American Irish,* 31–32.

16. John Hrastar, *Breaking the Appalachian Barrier: Maryland as the Gateway to Ohio and the West, 1750–1850* (Jefferson, NC: McFarland, 2018), 5–6.

17. Jon K. Lauck, *The Good Country: A History of the American Midwest, 1800–1900* (Norman: Univ. of Oklahoma Press, 2022), 31.

18. Brian Schoen, introduction to *Settling Ohio: First Peoples and Beyond,* ed. Timothy G. Anderson and Brian Schoen (Athens: Ohio Univ. Press, 2023), 5.

19. Michael B. Lafferty, ed., *Ohio's Natural Heritage* (Columbus: Ohio Academy of Science, 1979), 161, 177 (also noting, in keeping with Muskingum University's mascot, that of the "many fish that inhabit the waters of the hill country, probably none is more spectacular than the mighty Ohio muskellunge").

20. Mansel G. Blackford, "Pioneers and Land on the Ohio Frontier," *Ohio History* 125 (Fall 2018): 10.

21. "Quakers First Settle Ohio," *Historic Atlas of Ohio Yearly Meeting* (Barnesville: Ohio Yearly Meeting of Friends, 2012), 12.

22. *The Toe: The Lou Groza Story* (Cleveland: Gray, 2003), 13–15; John F. Rooney Jr., "Up from the Mines and Out from the Prairies: Some Geographical Implications of Football in the United States," *Geographical Review* 59 (Oct. 1969): 491.

23. John R. McDermott, "Rocky Cradle of Football," *Life,* Nov. 2, 1962. McDermott was a New York native and Columbia University graduate who began working at *Life* in 1954 and became the senior editor for sports and adventure. He later became the editor of *Golf Digest* and the *Masters Journal.* See "J. R. McDermott, 66, Publishing Executive," *New York Times,* Apr. 10, 1995.

24. *James Wright: Collected Prose,* ed. Anne Wright (Ann Arbor: Univ. of Michigan Press, 2000), 33, 155.

25. "James Wright," 20, 21; Jon K. Lauck, *From Warm Center to Ragged Edge: The Erosion of Midwestern Literary and Historical Regionalism, 1920–1965* (Iowa City: Univ. of Iowa Press, 2017).

26. Henry Howe, *Historical Collections of Ohio,* 3 vols. (Cincinnati: State of Ohio, 1907), 1:325; Archer Butler Hulbert, *The Ohio River: A Course of Empire* (New York: G. P. Putnam's Sons, 1906); 166; Kevin F. Kern and Gregory S. Wilson, *Ohio: A History of the Buckeye State* (Hoboken, NJ: Wiley-Blackwell, 2023), 113–14.

27. Liz Goodwin, "East Palestine 'Controlled Burn' Could Have Been Avoided, NTSB Chair Says," *Washington Post,* Mar. 6, 2024.

28. James Pogue, "Going Back to Cincinnati," *American Conservative,* Aug. 23, 2021.

29. Hannah Miao, "The New Center of the World Is Cleveland. Locals Say It's About Time," *Wall Street Journal,* Apr. 5, 2024.

30. Jimmy Watkins, "A Season for the Ages Is Coming to a Head in Cleveland," *Cleveland Plain Dealer,* Apr. 5, 2024.

Introduction

GLEAVES WHITNEY

The authors in this book have sought to understand the area where two great American regions meet—the East and the Midwest. To the casual observer, the obvious barrier between them is the Appalachian Mountains, a divide continental in scope that separates waters flowing toward the Atlantic Ocean from those flowing toward the Gulf of Mexico. But is the western slope of the Appalachians "midwestern"? Hardly anyone thinks so.

To most people who think about the Midwest as a region, the border between the East and the Midwest has some relation to the limits of the Corn Belt, the Great Lakes, the Allegheny Plateau, the Ohio River watershed, the Northwest Ordinance, even the debate Pittsburghers have over whether they are more midwestern or Appalachian.

More specifically, the border between the East and Midwest unfolds in the rolling landscape traversed by the Pennsylvania and Ohio turnpikes as they approach each other. Other than Pennsylvania and Ohio welcome signs, there is no verbiage hinting at a significant borderland that's being crossed. Yet, travelers can sense the changes as the miles tick by. Somewhere south of the glacial outwash plains near Lake Erie, and north of where the Ohio River cuts through the bluffs near Marietta, and east of the Cuyahoga River where Interstate 80 ascends the Allegheny Plateau, the natural and cultural landscape offers unmistakable markers of a transition.

Many of these markers are apparent to residents, geographers, and observant travelers. But what is the nature of the transition? Does the border area between the East and Midwest gently morph from one physiographic and cultural region to the other across many miles? Yes. Are there places where the boundary is more like a clash—of different geologies and ecologies, peoples and histories? To be sure. Are there locales of such contrary and confounding influences that categories fail? Indeed. Can today's border region be regarded as yesterday's "Middle Ground"?[1] Absolutely.

A few years ago, at a sports bar in Grand Rapids, Michigan, several of the authors of this collection entertained these questions. Over time, others entered the conversation and, under the wise guidance of Susan Wadsworth-Booth, Kent State University Press director, and of Jon Lauck, the author of pioneering works about the Midwest, the discussions grew into this book, which presents a variety of ways of understanding the blending, transitioning, and clashing where East meets Midwest.

Our title self-consciously plays off Rudyard Kipling's enduring line in "The Ballad of East and West." Though set in the heart of Eurasia, the poem provides an apt allusion for the heart of America. While Kipling's most quoted line insists, "Oh, East is East and West is West, and never the twain shall meet," his ballad is actually about something significant that East and West share. Thus, Kipling creates a palpable tension between what East and West have in common and what they don't. Likewise, following these introductory comments are summaries of the authors' thoughts about the in-between places that are not archetypically East Coast and not quite Midwest, places in which a similar tension is evident.

With few exceptions, this is a book whose contributors have a bent toward historical geography. And for some, the significant borders in the region under consideration run latitudinally, in a roughly east–west direction, not longitudinally, in a generally north–south direction. They share something with Colin Woodard's highly engaging book *American Nations: A History of the Eleven Rival Regional Cultures of North America*. Woodard makes a compelling argument for the political and cultural continuity of successive generations of settlers moving west. Using county data, Woodard tries to show that western migration has resulted in prominent latitudinal bands running continuously through western Pennsylvania and eastern Ohio—the state line between them being largely irrelevant. He refers to these three major east–west bands as "Yankeedom," "the Midlands," and "Greater Appalachia." So we shall tip our hats to authors like Woodard, who argue for the significance of latitudinal boundaries.[2]

Another approach to American regions has been to focus more on longitudinal boundaries. The borderland between the East and Midwest falls in this category and informs most of the authors' investigations in the current volume.

However a region is marked off, whether it is primarily latitudinal or longitudinal or both in equal measure, valuable tools of geographical and historical analysis are indispensable for the task. NASA's nighttime satellite images, NOAA's satellite images, daylight aerial photographs, and atlases provide different starting points to explore the Midwest and how it differs from surrounding regions.[3] Consider: without the aid of place-names, a person with map sense can look at nighttime satellite images and identify concentrations of city lights that align in familiar patterns. Metropolitan Cleveland, for instance, is readily identifiable because of the cluster of lights hugging the dark expanse of Lake Erie; metropolitan Pittsburgh stands out in the conspicuous concentration of city lights southeast of Cleveland; and so forth.

As Cleveland illustrates, a major geographic boundary that defines the Midwest's northern extent is apparent in satellite photographs that show the lack of light on the Great Lakes. But a subtler boundary exists, too, across the land south of the Great Lakes. Between the denser clusters of lights in the Midwest and the darker expanses "up north," there is an arc of light traceable from the Twin Cities to Green Bay to Bay City to Port Huron. Above this arc is a striking drop in light energy in the dark North Country with its extensive boreal forests and thousands of glacial lakes. Below this arc is the well-lighted Midwest, with its farms and industrial centers stretching south into the heartland of the nation.[4]

Patterns of light and dark also suggest the Midwest's western limits. There is an abrupt decline in light energy west of 97º longitude west, in a line running roughly from Fargo, North Dakota, to Wichita, Kansas. West of the meridian the land transitions into the less populated shortgrass rangelands of the Great Plains. East of the meridian the land transitions into the more populated tallgrass prairie parklands of the Corn Belt.[5]

Similarly, when we inspect nighttime satellite images of the region where the East meets the Midwest—the subject of this book—to the east there is a lack of dense city lights in the Allegheny and Appalachian Mountains. To the west, by contrast, is the glaciated interior plain where Ohio's lighted industrial cities spread out like a string of pearls. Even the casual observer must suspect a significant geographical transition between the two. The physiographic name given to the in-between places is the Allegheny Plateau. This plateau extends southwest from central New York through western Pennsylvania and eastern Ohio. Larger cities near the plateau's margins include Erie, Pittsburgh, and Cleveland.

Consulting maps and atlases, researchers can construct additional ways to suggest where the East ends and Midwest begins. One of the most usual means of doing so is by looking at US Department of Agriculture corn production data by county, a common marker of the Midwest. In his chapter, Gregory Rose does just this. He shows that the eastern extent of the Corn Belt fades east of an imaginary line running from Cleveland to Cincinnati.

Satellite and aerial photographs can also help us discern the eastern, southeastern, and southern boundaries of the Midwest. The Ohio River provides the primary marker. Downstream from its source in Pittsburgh, the Ohio flows generally south–southwest. Looking at nighttime satellite images, the practiced eye can trace a sinuous line of communities along the thousand-mile-long river from Pittsburgh to Marietta to Cincinnati to Louisville to Paducah.

Especially visible in aerial photographs are the different public land survey systems Euro-American settlers used on each side of the Ohio River. The traditional metes-and-bounds surveys used in the eastern states and Upper South led to settlement patterns along a hodgepodge of crooked lines that contrast with the straight east–west, north–south lines of the Midwest's township-and-range survey system.[6]

The Ohio River served as the nation's great trans-Appalachian highway for much of the nineteenth century, connecting markets in the East to those in the Mississippi Valley. It also was a critical cultural and political divide in US history, separating the slaveholding South from the free North.

When Alexis de Tocqueville was touring the newer western states in the Ohio Valley in 1831, he famously wrote, "The traveler who floats down the current of the Ohio ... may be said to sail between liberty and servitude." The French aristocrat noted striking cultural differences on either side of the river due to the presence of the peculiar institution to the south: "The banks of the Ohio River provided the final demonstration ... [that] time and again, in general, the [state] that had no slaves was more populous and prosperous than the one where slavery was in force." Tocqueville characterized Kentucky as the state where "society has gone to sleep ... [and] it is nature that seems active and alive, whereas man is idle." By contrast, the state to the north, Ohio, shows "evidence of comfort; man appears rich and contented; he works."[7]

Pittsburgh has been mentioned, and rightly so, since it is arguably the dominant city in the East–Midwest border region. Pittsburgh is a challenge to characterize. Historically the source of the Ohio River was located in a rich Middle Ground, noted above. More recently, it has been Exhibit A where the concept of boundaries can be confounding. Situated where the Monongahela and Allegheny rivers converge, the Steel City is also located where three major American regions collide: the Midwest (coming up from the interior plains to the west), Appalachia (coming down the surrounding mountain hollows), and East (coming across the Appalachian Mountains from America's large coastal cities).[8] Pittsburghers recognize that their city is influenced by all three.[9] They know, for instance, that most geographers locate the Commonwealth of Pennsylvania in a bloc of states variously labeled the Northeast, East Coast, or Mid-Atlantic region—none of which the Midwest claims.

And yet, these same people also know that Pittsburgh feels more like midwestern Ohio than East Coast Philadelphia.[10] Indeed, it partakes of the Midwest in a number of ways. Since the 1970s, it has shared a midwestern Rust Belt identity with Ohio's cities that are a short drive away. The fierce gridiron rivalry in the NFL between the Steelers and the Browns is more like a family feud than a foreign war. And linguists note that Pittsburghers prefer to say *pop*, which is midwestern, rather than *soda*, used in the East, or *Coke*, favored in the South.

To complicate matters, Pittsburgh is a short drive from the Mason-Dixon line, where the South begins. It is also the largest city bordering on Appalachia and has the humorous nickname "the Paris of Appalachia." Indeed, Pennsylvania has more square miles in Appalachia than any other state, including West Virginia.[11] So no discussion of the East–Midwest border region can neglect Appalachia's influence. It's why Pittsburghers are sometimes called "Yinzers." *Yinz*, a second-person plural pronoun spoken by the blue-collar Scots-Irish who settled in the Steel City, is the equivalent of *you guys* or *y'all*, spoken elsewhere.[12]

About 35 percent of Ohio is also classified as Appalachia. At first blush, this may seem counterintuitive. Historically, Ohio was recognized as the beginning of the Midwest in both time (since it was the first territory in the Old Northwest to achieve statehood, in 1803) and space (since it is the easternmost state in the Midwest). Yet, it is also Middle Ground. In the eastern and southern parts of the Buckeye State, never far from the Ohio River, there is a wide band of thirty-two counties that is officially designated as Appalachia.[13] For a variety of reasons, many of them economic, people migrated from West Virginia and Kentucky into these neighboring Ohio counties. Such migration, like the Great Migration of Blacks from the Deep South to central and northern Ohio between 1910 and 1980, tilted the Buckeye State decidedly toward the South, forever scrambling traditional notions of a neat midwestern boundary along the Ohio River.

Human migration has long made the history of the East–Midwest borderlands complex. For eighteenth-century Native Americans in the Iroquois Confederation, there were no fixed boundary lines on a map in the European sense; groups of aboriginal peoples sought to travel seasonally within, through, and around the Allegheny Plateau, Ohio River valley, and Great Lakes Basin. The region was a Middle Ground coveted for its rich resources and network of strategic portages—advantages not lost on European empire builders seeking to exploit the area.[14] From the colonial French perspective, the Great Lakes and Ohio Country—the future Midwest—comprised the core of its North American empire; the East, the periphery. From the colonial British perspective, it was just the opposite, with the East comprising the core of its North American empire while the Great Lakes and Ohio Country served as the periphery.

In early modern times, four powerful nations—the Iroquois Confederation, France, Britain, and United States—vied for control of what would become the East–Midwest borderlands. Wars would decide the fate of the land and people. First the French, then the Indians, and finally the British were all violently expelled by rival powers. After the Americans held their own against the British in their first war for independence (1775–83), then vanquished the Miami and Shawnee confederations (1790s and 1810s), then held their own again in their second war for independence (1812–15), they consolidated their hold on the region. In the pages that follow, historian Mary Kupiec Cayton observes that "East formally met the Trans-Appalachian West in British North America in 1763, when the Peace of Paris brought an end to the Seven Years War."

French historiography for many years maintained that George Washington, when still a British subject, sparked the Seven Years War—the first world war in history—when he and his band of Virginia militia fired on Native Americans allied to the French in Jumonville Glen, in southwestern Pennsylvania.[15] As a young man, George Washington had surveyed the Alleghany Plateau and Upper Ohio, and the experience left an indelible impression on him. Indeed, after the first War for Independence, Washington called the Ohio Country and its border region with Pennsylvania the "second promised land," a land "flowing with milk and honey" that beckoned immigrants from afar. The new republic brimmed with optimism.[16]

Washington was beckoning immigrants to America when the Confederation Congress was debating how to accommodate them. Out of these debates arose the Northwest ordinances of the 1780s. The ordinances of 1784, 1785, and 1787 are part and parcel of any rendering of the Midwest and constitute a major event in world history. In the first place, they provided for future states—initially, the future midwestern states of Ohio, Indiana, Illinois, Michigan, and Wisconsin—to come into the Union not as subordinate colonies but on an equal constitutional footing with existing states. Second, the ordinances sought to mitigate the sectional tensions that had arisen over the peculiar institution; they did so by giving the emerging United States north of the Ohio River a blueprint for growth that would eventually lead the North to dominate the South in congressional representation and economic muscle. Third, the states north of the Ohio would realize the dream of a free republic without slaves—a republic, in other words, that could better live up to the promises the Founders had made to the world in the Declaration of Independence.

Under the Northwest Ordinance of 1787, advocates for three different republican visions—the agrarian republic of Thomas Jefferson, the commercial republic of Alexander Hamilton, and the virtuous republic of John Adams—vied to shape the country north of the Ohio and east of the Mississippi rivers. But it was the democratic reality that brought Tocqueville and others to America, especially along its frontiers.[17] The French aristocrat believed America's democratic experiment was of world-historical importance. Not surprisingly, his book also provides a compelling starting point for inquiring into the emerging East–Midwest borderland in the Ohio Country. According to John Quincy Adams in an 1837 letter to Tocqueville, the Frenchman made a remarkable observation while on his journey from the East Coast to the interior of the new republic. The sixth president of the United States told Tocqueville that *Democracy in America* reminded him of something his father—John Adams, the second president of the United States—had written to the Abbé de Mably.[18] The senior Adams had described the political, civic, and cultural characteristics "of the British Colonies on the Continent before the American Revolution," insights into which would be "indispensable for the historian." The younger Adams continued in his letter to Tocqueville: "It is the same organization, which so impressively attracted your attention, and of which you have given so clear and interesting an account. The organization of the towns and counties, chiefly in New England, *and in the Northwestern new States, settled in part by emigrants from New England*. You are, I believe, the first foreign traveler that has noticed this element of our history."[19]

If Tocqueville noticed the influence of John Adams's virtuous republic in New England on parts of the Midwest, Walt Whitman waxed poetic about the democratic elements north of the Ohio River. In 1879 Whitman went through the very borderlands under consideration in this volume. Traveling from Philadelphia through Ohio and beyond, he ventured that "no one can begin to know what America is, or what it is destined to be in the near future, without exploring and living a while in Ohio" and other midwestern states.[20]

In this volume you will encounter a variety of viewpoints that reflect the diverse scholarship being produced around the question of the Midwest in general and its transition from the East in particular.

In chapter 1, Mary Kupiec Cayton argues that the East formally met the Trans-Appalachian West in British North America in 1763, when the Peace of Paris brought an end to the Seven Years' War. The treaty provided the European empires involved with a formal answer to the question of who would control which sectors of the vast North American continent. But it ensured no peace. Indian tribes and nations inhabiting the borderlands areas of the Great Lakes, Pennsylvania, Maryland, Virginia, and the Ohio Country, not consulted in the peace settlement, responded with violent intertribal resistance meant to terrorize prospective settlers and to repel them. We have come to call their guerilla war action Pontiac's Rebellion.

Cayton's essay focuses on the ways the day's popular newspaper presses configured and imagined the new Trans-Appalachian borderlands during the crucial transitional year of 1763. Improvements in postal roads and the proliferation of newspapers, especially from Pennsylvania northward, meant that domestic news stories were increasingly shared among newspapers during the 1750s as they had not been before. Cayton argues that sensationalized stories of Indian violence on the Pennsylvania and Virginia frontier became regional staples of American news coverage during Pontiac's War. These widely circulated accounts of Indian terror led for readers to a collapse of clear distinctions between the different tribes and confederations involved, as all Indians were conflated into one rhetorical type. In the northern popular press, the process of western expansion became viewed henceforward as one that pitted civilized white settler families against the savage Indian terrorists. In contrast, such a characterization was not salient, at least in 1763, in the Georgia and South Carolina press—not only because a different dynamic obtained in that region but because tenuous domestic communications networks with points northward meant that Pontiac's Rebellion and its attendant violence played a much smaller role in southern news coverage. The emphasis in the Deep South was on the intertribal potential for violence and on pacification as a way of maintaining trade networks.

In chapter 2, Jeanne Gillespie McDonald observes that Ohio, Indiana, Illinois, Michigan, and Wisconsin were distinctly different from the original thirteen states, and one must view the Old Northwest Territory and the conflicts between liberty and bondage preceding the Civil War to explain those differences. At the most fundamental level, frontier egalitarianism conflicted with indentured servitude and racism, and the Old Northwest became an experiment in American freedom. Illinois's abolitionists and statesmen, for example, like those from other Old Northwest states, were able to articulate how freedom was more beneficial than slavery. Abolition exerted a generative force in third-party politics that was felt nationally. As the Whig Party dissolved and the Democrats fractured, the nascent

Republican Party, for a brief, historical reset, accomplished the destruction of slavery and brought the nation back to its founding documents, upon which the Union pledged anew to build.

Like the Midwest itself, Ohio defies the popular association with blandness or "fly-over country." Instead, argue Kevin F. Kern and Gregory S. Wilson in chapter 3, Ohio has been central to major events of North American and global history from prehistoric times to the present. It was a cultural mecca during the Adena and Hopewell periods and a Middle Ground among Native peoples and Euro-Americans as they vied for control of the Great Lakes region from the 1600s through the early 1800s. Ohio was the first midwestern state carved from the public land system, and its geography helped secure its place at the center of the economic, transportation, and communication revolutions of the early and mid-nineteenth century. As part of the Midwest's industrial heartland, Ohio embodied the wrenching transformations associated with the industrial revolution of the late nineteenth and early twentieth centuries, as a haven for Black and white migrants from the South, those from Europe and elsewhere around the world, famed industrialists, labor organizers, progressive reformers, and radicals alike. Its representativeness and economic might gave Ohio status as a political bellwether, and the state sent eight men to the presidency. While aspects of Ohio's representativeness remain, its centrality faces an uncertain future. Recent trends suggest that Ohio's status as "The Heart of It All" may be in doubt.

Timothy C. Hemmis's chapter 4 explores the perceived divide that existed in the Early Republic by way of the lives of George Morgan and Aaron Burr. Hemmis focuses on two episodes: Morgan's Spanish New Madrid scheme of 1788 and the Burr-Morgan dinner meeting of 1806, which exposed Burr's larger conspiracy against the federal government. These events both illuminate the East–West regionalism that existed along the American borderlands during this transitional period. Although at different times in their lives, both men sought to exploit the East–West regionalism in the country for their own personal and political gain. Fortunately for the young republic, both men failed in their schemes. But because of their failure, the East–West divide has been overlooked by many modern scholars.

Intellectuals in the cultural centers of America's East Coast have often found much to ridicule about the Midwest. But to date, few events originating there have suffered more derision than William Henry Harrison's

1840 campaign for the White House. Commentators as diverse as Ralph Waldo Emerson, Arthur Schlesinger, and Gail Collins have been baffled, amused, and thoroughly disgusted by the commotion surrounding Harrison's run for the White House. But in chapter 5, Mary Stockwell's makes clear that these eastern thinkers have ignored the epic tale, centered in the Midwest, which lay at the heart of Harrison's campaign. In parades, songs, and stump speeches, Americans celebrated the memory of Harrison's struggle against the Shawnee chief Tecumseh for control of the vast country that lay north of the Ohio River and west to the Mississippi. They rightly recalled that if not for Harrison, who defeated Tecumseh's followers at the Battle of Tippecanoe and later Tecumseh himself at the siege of Fort Meigs and the Battle of the Thames River during the War of 1812, then the land now known as Ohio, Michigan, Indiana, Illinois, and Wisconsin would have belonged to the Indians and the British, and not the United States. After Harrison died, following his inauguration in 1841, the story of Tippecanoe, including all he had done to save America's heartland, slipped from the nation's collective memory. In contrast, Tecumseh became a sympathetic and tragic hero in a series of ever more flattering biographies. Historians, like Alvin Josephy in *The Patriot Chiefs*, have described Tecumseh as the "greatest of all American Indian leaders, a majestic human who might have given all the Indians a nation of their own."[21] As Stockwell reminds her readers, Josephy forgot to add that the price to be paid for this nation would have been the Midwest, where today over 65 million Americans live, a price that Harrison, now usually remembered only to be ridiculed, refused to pay.

In chapter 6, Andrew W. Wiley argues that divisions over slavery had divided western Americans living between the Appalachian Mountains and the Mississippi River valley before the Civil War. He shows this by using the 1856 Democratic presidential campaign. Fearing a rising Republican Party that promised to contain slavery to the South, Democrats in the region modern Americans call the Midwest crafted a political campaign that stoked western prejudices against the Northeast while allaying fears about slavery expanding to lands further west. It was a campaign tailored specifically for free-state westerners, ultimately winning over enough voters to push Democrat James Buchanan into the White House. Although the terms *Midwest* and *midwesterner* came into use decades later, the 1856 Democratic campaign shows that the Midwest was taking shape in the 1850s.

Randall S. Gooden's chapter 7 explores the struggles of settlers from different ethnic and geographic origins in the East as they shaped their new identities as midwesterners. His analysis unfolds in two adjacent Ohio townships. Poland and Springfield Townships in present-day Mahoning County, Ohio, lay right on the physical boundary between the East and West on the Pennsylvania state line. The two townships originated from two different survey regions—the Connecticut Western Reserve and the extension of the Seven Ranges—in two different counties, Trumbull and Columbiana. As such, they drew settlers from different eastern peoples. Yankees from New England and Scots-Irish from Pennsylvania came to Poland while Pennsylvania Dutch and other German Americans made their homes in Springfield. This chapter looks at the ways these different cultural groups interacted and the resulting prejudices and clashes that defined their midwestern experiences. These include the thrusting of the two townships together in the same county in the 1840s. Ethnic and religious prejudices surfaced, and attitudes toward slavery and temperance clashed as the Second Great Awakening gave way to new political movements. As the Civil War approached, Poland Township became predominantly Republican and antislavery, and Springfield clung to Jacksonian Democracy with an ambivalence to slavery. Each township sent a large number of men into the Union army in the war, but a sizeable Copperhead element existed in Springfield, as it competed with its neighbor to the north. Following the war, Springfield became a noteworthy producer of liquor, as prohibition took root across the state and held sway in Poland. Then, as both townships vied for seats in state and county government, they took opposite sides as the growing industrial town of Youngstown competed with Canfield, the historic county seat, for the location of the courthouse. As the twentieth century dawned, class rivalries marked the relationship between the two townships, as Poland—the historically more prosperous of the two—established enclaves of exclusivity, while dealing with its own changes due to immigration and industrialization. By modern times, the rivalries between the two remained as part of their midwestern, Ohio images, quite distinct from their original eastern roots.

In chapter 8, Gregory S. Rose urges us to take a closer look at where the East meets the Midwest in the usual suspect: Ohio. The line legally separating Ohio and Pennsylvania does not necessarily align with their two states' cultural, physical, and agricultural characteristics that form the basis for assigning Ohio to the midwestern region and Pennsylvania to the Middle-Atlantic region. Ohio is typically included within the Midwest when the region is defined using state borders. However, placing any or all of Ohio within the Midwest can generate controversy, as some consider the state too far east, despite it being the first state to emerge from the Old Northwest, the Midwest's precursor and lacking the Midwest's most stereotypical characteristics. A state-based outline of the Midwest does not provide the most accurate representation of the region.

Rather than relying on state borders to determine whether Ohio fits within the Midwest, a better defined eastern edge of the region within Ohio can be identified. The eastern edge of the culturally, vernacularly, or perceptually identified Midwest commonly lies west of Ohio's eastern border. While central and western Ohio's environmental characteristics tie most closely to those of the Midwest and the climate across the state is favorable for growing corn, the eastern edge of the Corn Belt, which in many ways is coterminous with the Midwest, falls across central Ohio. Further, eastern Ohio's landforms, physiography, topography, undersurface materials, soil types, and vegetation differ from those in the remainder of the state. This variety of evidence supports an assertion that the eastern boundary of the Midwest region best aligns with a transition zone that runs from Cleveland to Cincinnati rather than with the eastern border of Ohio.

In chapter 9, Donna M. DeBlasio and Martha I. Pallante argue that Ohio's Mahoning Valley, at the far eastern edge of the state's Western Reserve, is a unique place to examine immigrants in the borderlands between the Midwest and the East Coast. Italian Americans, as well as other immigrant groups, are normally not the subject of historical investigation in smaller communities like Youngstown and its environs. Most studies of these groups are focused on large cities such as New York or Baltimore on the East Coast or Chicago and Detroit in the Midwest. While there are also some studies of rural communities, small to medium-sized urban areas are largely neglected. Arriving in great numbers in the early twentieth century, Italians and Italian Americans eventually became one of the largest ethnic groups in the valley, second only to the longer-established German Americans. The Mahoning Valley is also unique because of the dominance of one industry—iron and steel—and its ancillary industries. The overwhelming presence of the steel industry meant that few women or children could find work in the mills. Thus, children usually stayed in school much longer, defying the stereotype of Italians in larger communities being either indifferent to or even hostile toward education of their young. This also meant that women and children could add to their family's income by working from home selling the fruits of their gardens, operating small stores, and working odd jobs. The increase in income allowed earlier home ownership opportunities as well as disposable income for leisure activities. By the same token, because the valley's communities were not as densely populated as older eastern cities, the trend for working-class residents was detached, single-family homes, mirroring Jon Teaford's description of Midwest cities' residential areas.[22] DeBlasio and Pallante think the Mahoning Valley provides an opportunity to aid in our understanding of the borderlands and midwestern identity.

Cody A. Norling's chapter 10 assesses the national and regional implications for the ways that the Redpath Chautauqua Bureau promoted its English-language operas across an East–Midwest divide. Though founded on the enculturating principals of the original Chautauqua Institute, midwestern chautauquas were carefully crafted pastiches of artistic and literary presentations designed to speak to the sensibilities of midwesterners while downplaying the perceived social baggage of its East Coast roots, and popular operas in English thus served as a middle ground between elite art and immodest theatrical entertainment. These productions, which nevertheless adhered to a perceived cultural superiority of European art music, were presented as a form of so-called democratization and sought to reclaim opera from the domain of Northeastern urban centers. The results of this study do not confirm a tangible, geographic border between regions, however; rather, the middling promotion of operas on the chautauqua circuits betrays a certain flexibility to the social and cultural boundaries that divide regions.

In chapter 11, Jacob Bruggeman and Eric Michael Rhodes show through a history of the Cleveland Orchestra that northeast Ohio has long straddled the cultural boundary between the Midwest and the East Coast. Having long identified as Yankees, early twentieth-century boosters founded the orchestra as a vehicle to transmute their economic capital into the cultural clout most associated with East Coast arts institutions. They were successful. By the midcentury, the orchestra had joined the ranks of the Big Five, sharing the stage with the East Coast orchestras of New York, Boston, and Philadelphia. Cleveland's reputation as industry's "best location in the nation" faded during deindustrialization. In response, postwar city branders attempted to convert cultural capital into regional economic development. Relying on the international acclaim of Cleveland's arts institutions (the type most often associated with big East Coast cities), the late-twentieth-century growth coalition adopted the tagline "The best things in life are here!"—including an orchestra to rival New York's.

Stephanie Fortado's chapter 12, "Locating Cleveland: Mapping Black Nationalism in a 'Way Post' City," situates Cleveland, Ohio, as an important and understudied location for the circulation of Black art and Black nationalist activism between Harlem and the Midwest. Noted historian of the Black arts movement James Smethurst once described Cleveland as an "an ideological and cultural way post between the Midwest and the East Coast."[23] Fortado's chapter provides and overview of some of the organizations, individuals and local spaces that contributed to Cleveland's position as this midwestern way post—including the United Negro Improvement Association and the Revolutionary Action Movement, playwright and poet Langston Hughes and activist Don Freeman, movement cofounder, and Cleveland spaces such as the Karamu House theater and the Jomo Freedom Kenyatta House youth center—to trace the importance of this city in the twentieth-century movements for Black liberation.

In chapter 13, Kenneth J. Heineman taps a common theme in this volume when he observes that a major difficulty to defining what is the Midwest comes down to one state: Ohio. The Buckeye State's demography and economy in the 1930s seemingly made it an important part of the New Deal's Industrial Heartland electoral bloc. However, the reality was more complicated. Organized labor struggled and fractured in Ohio even as it gained power in Illinois, Michigan, New York, and Pennsylvania. The 1937 Little Steel Strike illustrates this, as it exposed Ohio's demographic tensions while revealing a complex political culture. Ohio's political culture contained elements found in its Midwest, Appalachian, and Mid-Atlantic neighbors, but their sum set Ohio apart from all for the balance of the twentieth century—and into the twenty-first.

In the final chapter, A. Lee Hannah and Christopher J. Devine bring us up to recent times and tackle where Ohio has remained midwestern and where it has become something else. Using maps and voting data of relatively recent voting patterns, their analysis provides the most direct evidence for categorizing the six regions of Ohio as midwestern—or not—based on presidential election results. The authors show the difference in voting between the Midwest as a whole and each of the six major regions of Ohio during the Bush, Obama, and Trump elections. Without question, the state's band of Appalachian counties has grown increasingly distinct from its other, more midwestern parts.

From this survey we have seen that for historians, geographers, and others, there is no lack of starting points to investigate the East–Midwest divide. The Appalachian Mountains, Allegheny Plateau, Great Lakes, and Ohio River form estimable geographic boundaries. But human agency has established imposing boundaries too.

From the late eighteenth century to the early twentieth, the Midwest was recognized for its world-historical importance—a paradigm of the new republican spirit. In succession we have seen how, in early modern events and documents, the 1763 Peace of Paris tried to settle who would control the Trans-Appalachian West. One generation later, at the end of America's first War for Independence, George Washington's circulars articulated the idea that the Ohio Country was special, the stage for something dramatically new. John Adams's studies and letters chronicled the new republic's remarkable political, civic, and cultural characteristics. And new England Yankees helped produce the Northwest Ordinance of 1787 and the next year established the first formally recognized American settlement in the border region, in Marietta, Ohio.

Decades after the founding, Tocqueville's *Democracy in America* juxtaposed democratic hopes with the pathos of the Indians and Blacks who struggled to coexist with European settlers in the region.[24] After the Civil War, Whitman showed how the Midwest "distilled" America's democratic project and "foreshadowed what America would become."[25]

This last observation points to an important question that grows out of but ultimately transcends the present work. It's a question that requires readers to look at how they see the world. For a number of people who have looked at the region under consideration, the most significant "boundaries" are neither latitudinal nor longitudinal but temporal. Ideas matter. History matters. The human person in community matters. For such people, ultimately it is of little consequence whether one lives east of the Appalachians or west of them. The divides that count are those formed, over time, by the habits of the heart.

Like Tocqueville observing the differing habits of the heart on either side of the Ohio River, we are challenged to make sense of today's American divides. Our nation's social and legacy media are preoccupied by a familiar theme: progressives contra conservatives, red states versus blue states, Republicans against Democrats. Do such divides reflect the triumph of history over geography? Do they develop more as a function of time rather than as a function of space? Or do space and time, geography and history, remain inseparably linked?

Now and in the coming decades, the East and Midwest may be reshaped more by people sorting themselves on the basis of worldviews and ideologies than by many of the other factors examined in the present volume. The work of exploring new elements in our major American divides will require the rising generation to revisit the questions the authors in the present volume raise.

Notes

1. For an exploration of the term *Middle Ground* in the context of the Upper Midwest and its historic importance in the cultural, economic, and imperial encounters of different peoples, see the pioneering study by Richard White, *The Middle Ground: Indians, Empires, and Republics in the Great Lakes Region, 1650–1815*, 2nd ed. (Cambridge: Cambridge University Press, 2010).

2. Colin Woodard, *American Nations: A History of the Eleven Rival Regional Cultures of North America* (New York: Penguin, 2012).

3. NASA, "City Lights of the United States 2012," *Earth Observatory*, accessed Aug. 13, 2024, https://earthobservatory.nasa.gov/images/79800/city-lights-of-the-united-states-2012.

4. See *North Country: Essays on the Upper Midwest and Regional Identity*, edited by Jon K. Lauck and Gleaves Whitney (Norman: University of Oklahoma Press, 2023).

5. See Jon K. Lauck, ed. *The Interior Borderlands: Regional Identity in the Midwest and Great Plains* (Sioux Falls: Center for Western Studies, 2019).

6. KyFromAbove: Kentucky's Elevation Data & Aerial Photography Program website, accessed Aug. 13, 2024, https://kyfromabove.ky.gov/; Ohio Department of Transportation, Aerial Imagery Archive, accessed Aug. 13, 2024, https://gis3.dot.state.oh.us/ODOTAerialArchive/, accessed 8/13/2024.

7. Alexis de Tocqueville, *Democracy in America*, trans. and ed. Harvey C. Mansfield and Delba Winthrop (Chicago: Univ. of Chicago Press, 2000), 331–32.

8. *Confluence of the Allegheny and Monongahela Rivers, Pittsburgh, P.A.*, image scanned from original glass slide, Radford University Digital Collections, McConnell Library, https://monk.radford.edu/records/item/7193-confluence-of-the-allegheny-and-monongahela-rivers-pittsburgh-p-a?offset=18

9. Brian O'Neill, "Northeast? Midwest? Appalachia? Where Does Pittsburgh Belong?" *Pittsburgh Post-Gazette*, Aug. 8, 2018.

10. "Pittsburgh: Is It Northeastern, Midwestern, or Appalachian? (Best, Rates, America), City-Data, April 2021, https://www.city-data.com/forum/city-vs-city/3259092-pittsburgh-northeastern-midwestern-appalachian-3.html.

11. Inside Appalachia, "What Is Appalachia? Here's What People from around the Region, Including Pittsburgh, Have to Say," WESA, Dec. 11, 2021, https://www.wesa.fm/identity-community/2021-12-11/what-is-appalachia-heres-what-people-from-around-the-region-including-pittsburgh-have-to-say.

12. CP Staff, "Pittsburghese Dictionary: How to Talk Like a Yinzer," *Pittsburgh City Paper*, June 9. 2021, https://www.pghcitypaper.com/pittsburgh/pittsburghese-dictionary-how-to-talk-like-a-yinzer/Content?oid=19623370.

13. "Appalachian Countries Served by ARC," ARC website, accessed June 24, 2024, https://www.arc.gov/appalachian-counties-served-by-arc/.

14. Cutting through the East–Midwest border region is a major North American watershed that separates the Great Lakes Basin and the Ohio River valley. The portages connecting these two major drainage basins were historically important sites of commercial trade and military conflict.

15. Fred Anderson, *Crucible of War: The Seven Years' War and the Fate of Empire in British North America, 1754–1766* (New York: Knopf, 2000), 54; Francis Jennings, *Empire of Fortune: Crowns, Colonies, and Tribes in the Seven Years' War in America* (New York: Norton, 1988), 69; John Shy, interviewed by author, Ann Arbor, MI, Oct. 4, 1988.

16. George Washington quoted in Gleaves Whitney, "The Upper Midwest as the Second Promised Land," in *Finding a New Midwestern History*, ed. Jon K. Lauck, Joseph Hogan, and Gleaves Whitney (Lincoln: University of Nebraska Press, 2018), 281–82.

17. R. Douglas Hurt, *The Ohio Frontier: Crucible of the Old Northwest, 1720–1830* (Bloomington: Indiana University Press, 1996).

18. John Adams dated the letter January 15, 1783. See John Adams to the Abbé de Mably, available at *Founders Online*, National Archives, https://founders.archives.gov/documents/Adams/06-14-02-0111-0004.

19. John Quincy Adams to Alexis de Tocqueville, June 12, 1837, in *Tocqueville on America after 1840: Letters and Other Writings*, ed. and trans. Aurelian Craiutu and Jeremy Jennings (New York: Cambridge University Press, 2009), 497 (emphasis added).

20. Jon K. Lauck, *The Good Country: A History of the American Midwest, 1800–1900* (Norman: University of Oklahoma Press, 2022), 23. For Whitman's 1879 travels through and reflections on the part of the country we now call the *Midwest*,

see his *Specimen Days,* quoted in Kelly Scott Franklin, "'The Good Country' Review: The Heart of a Nation," *Wall Street Journal,* Nov. 24, 2022.

21. Alvin Josephy, *The Patriot Chiefs: A Chronicle of American Indian Resistance,* rev. ed. (New York: Penguin, 1993), 173.

22. Jon C. Teaford. *Cities of the Heartland: Rise and Fall of the Industrial Midwest* (Bloomington: Indiana Univ. Press, 1994).

23. James Edward Smethurst, *The Black Arts Movement: Literary Nationalism in the 1960s and 1970s* (Chapel Hill: Univ. of North Carolina Press, 2005), 180.

24. For a review of the historiographic turn regarding racial conflict, sparked in large measure in 1974 by the historian Gary Nash, see Jack Rakove, "Ambiguous Achievement: Northwest Ordinance," in *Northwest Ordinance: Essays on Its Formulation, Provisions, and Legacy,* ed. Frederick D. Williams (East Lansing: Michigan State University Press, 1989), 1–19.

25. Whitman, quoted in Franklin, "'The Good Country' Review."

Chapter 1

Before There Was a West

Appalachian Frontiers in American Newspapers, 1763

MARY KUPIEC CAYTON

In British North America, the year 1763 arrived on a wave of optimism. News of a major British victory at Havana reached the mainland, and the end of a great war was at hand. It had begun in a struggle over the control over trade in the Trans-Appalachian West and had eventually been fought not only on the North American continent but in the Caribbean, the continent of Europe, and the subcontinent of India. France, Britain's old foe, would see her empire broken and that of Spain, France's ally, much weakened. Negotiating a treaty extended over a period of months, as French negotiators changed midstream and the British debated the desirability of taking either sugar islands in the Caribbean or the vast northern regions of Canada as the spoils of war.[1] Beyond dispute, however, was the right of Britain to dominate trade in the vast Ohio Valley watershed. The west was to be British, or so those involved in the negotiations seem to have thought.

Whatever may have been settled on paper in Paris had only a marginal relationship to what was happening on the ground four thousand miles away. Although peoples of color, most particularly those of the dozens of Native nations who had either participated in or been affected by the late war, inhabited territory that changed hands, none were included in negotiations of the terms of the treaty. Their satisfaction with any settlement was crucial to the peace and prosperity of all others in the land who were, or were dominated by, Britons. Britain's failure to ensure that the needs and wishes of the varied indigenous peoples of the Trans-Appalachian West ensured a world of continuing problems, bloodshed, and conflict. These erupted in 1763 before the celebrations of the conclusion of the war even commenced. They would continue to bedevil the area settlers called *the back country,* then *the frontier,* for a century and a half.

The problem of the frontier, embodied in violence of Pontiac's War and accompanying fears of a pan-Indian union against the British, was the first important colonial narrative to emerge regarding the nature and fate of the new western acquisitions after the conclusion of the Seven Years' War. How newspapers in particular made sense of and portrayed the conflict had an outsized influence on how many conceived of America's moving frontier for centuries afterward. One of these was Frederick Jackson Turner, whose theory of the influence of the frontier on American national character has dominated popular sensibility since its first publication in 1893. "The existence of an area of free land, its continuous recession, and the advance of American settlement westward, explain American development," he argued. *The frontier,* as both Turner and the newspapers of 1763 came to define it, was "the meeting point between savagery and civilization."[2]

Neither this way of viewing western settlement nor of conceiving of the relationship between Native peoples and Europeans was inevitable. This chapter focuses on how this new west of the British empire became characterized and perceived through the medium of North American newspapers in the pivotal year of 1763. The story of Pontiac's Rebellion, as American newspapers configured it and as newly constructed communications networks in the North American colonies disseminated it, produced a representation of its participants that endured far beyond this particular series of encounters.[3]

Print, Newspapers, and the Flow of Information, 1763

Whatever else the news is, it is also a commodity. Someone produces some version of something that happened in a tangible form. Someone pays for its production and distribution. And someone consumes it in whatever medium it is conveyed. The news is never simply a matter of recording objectively and transparently "what happened."

Domestic news became easily transmissible between most of Britain's mainland American colonies between about 1758 and 1763. The first colonial newspaper, published in Boston in 1690, consisted of exactly one issue. Authorities rapidly suppressed it. By 1704, the more enduring of these, the

Table 1.1: British North American Newspapers Published 1704–1763

Title	Place of publication	Beg. date
[Massachusetts Gazette and] Boston News-Letter	Boston, MA	1704
Boston Gazette	Boston, MA	1719
South-Carolina Gazette	Charles-Town, SC	1732
Boston Evening Post	Boston, MA	1735
Boston Post-Boy	Boston, MA	1735
Pennsylvania Gazette	Philadelphia, PA	1736
Pennsylvania Journal	Philadelphia PA	1742
New-York Gazette, or Weekly Post-Boy	New York, NY	1747
Virginia Gazette	Williamsburg, VA	1750
Maryland Gazette	Annapolis, MD	1751
New-York Mercury	New York, NY	1752
Connecticut Gazette	New Haven, CT	1755
New-Hampshire Gazette	Portsmouth, NH	1756
New London Summary	New London, CT	1758
Newport Mercury	Newport, RI	1758
New-York Gazette	New York, NY	1759
Providence Gazette	Providence, RI	1762
Wochentliche Philadelphische Staatsbote	Philadelphia, PA	1762
Germantowner Zeitung	Germantown, PA	1762?
Georgia Gazette	Savannah, GA	1763
Connecticut Gazette	New London, CT	1763

Sources: Isaiah Thomas, *The History of Printing in America,* vol. 2 (1810; repr., New York: Burt Franklin, 1874); *Directory of US Newspapers in American Libraries,* Library of Congress, accessed March 4, 2021, http://www.loc.gov/collections/directory-of-us-newspapers-in-american-libraries/.

Note: Only eight of the newspapers that began before 1763 were still publishing in that year. Newspaper texts for all but the *Maryland Gazette* and the *South-Carolina Gazette* were accessed through America's Historical Newspapers, Readex database. The *South-Carolina Gazette* was accessed via the Accessible Archives database, the *Maryland Gazette* via the Maryland Gazette Collection, *Archives of Maryland Online,* copyright November 15, 2023, https://msa.maryland.gov/megafile/msa/speccol/sc2900/sc2908/html/mdgazette.html.

All newspapers were located in provincial capitals except those in New London and Germantown. In 1763, Connecticut had two capitals (New Haven and Hartford), as did Rhode Island (Newport and Providence). New Jersey, Delaware, and North Carolina produced no newspapers in that year. Nothing of the *Virginia Gazette* for 1763 is extant.

Boston News-Letter, began publication. By 1750, eight of the twenty-one newspapers that would exist in 1763 were actively publishing. They emanated from only four places: Boston (four), Philadelphia (two), and New York and Charles-Town, South Carolina (one apiece). Some early American newspapers had a deliberate literary quality, while others functioned as official outlets for disseminating information from provincial and imperial governments. Over time, most developed a more-or-less commercial orientation. In 1763, somewhere between a half and two-thirds of each four-page issue consisted of paid advertising. The first page generally was dominated by European news, and the second, and sometimes a portion of the third, by provincial documents and notices from elsewhere.[4]

Locations of newspapers depended on several factors: where a printer was available to set up shop and could obtain the equipment to do so; where a reliable income could be secured initially through the acquisition of government printing contracts and/or newspaper subscriptions; where news from elsewhere could be accessed easily, either by ship or by postal carrier, or both; and, in most cases, where it made sense to collect advertisements that could be disseminated to appropriate publics. Over time, networks of newspapers developed, as a consequence of the entrepreneurship of Benjamin Franklin and James Parker, his sometime business partner, who furnished money and equipment to printers in exchange for a stake in the profits.[5] Nearly all of the newspapers in 1763 were located in provincial capitals, where printers might have some hope of revenue from government contracts and postmasterships. Printing was only sustainable economically where the printer received revenue from multiple sources and activities.

Print only became widely circulated enough to capture and broadcast news across provincial boundaries with the improvement and transformation of the postal infrastructure in the 1750s. Britain, a nation that increasingly saw itself as an empire of commerce, by the late seventeenth-century understood the value of enhancing communication routes within its North American colonies. Nevertheless, imperial authorities could never quite find the right way to do so. Without a well-functioning colonial postal system, information tended to go from metropole to port city and back, but without much inter-province circulation. Imagine the news in the early days of the American newspaper as akin to information in the early days of the internet: content existed, but a broad network of users was lacking. Without an adequate infrastructure for transmitting the news, the information newspapers generated remained limited to small and fairly local or regional audiences. Extending networks through a reliable postal system generated a recursive process: the wider the possibilities for market dissemination, the larger the numbers of those generating news content to circulate. Numbers of newspapers grew as postal routes improved.

Before the improvements in inter-colonial postal service, nearly all printed news originated in Europe, delivered via articles and dispatches received at Atlantic ports. The market for domestic news boomed in 1758, when Franklin as postmaster authorized free transmission of newspapers and newspaper correspondence through the mails.[6] Franklin had become Philadelphia postmaster in 1737, eager for the job because a postmaster "had better opportunities of obtaining news; his paper was thought to be a better distributer of advertisements."[7] In 1753, Franklin had been named deputy postmaster general for the colonies, along with his friend William Hunter, a printer-publisher at Williamsburg. Franklin took major responsibility for areas north of Annapolis, Hunter for areas to the south.

Franklin had more to work with. Postal routes, however inefficient, had long been established between Boston and New York, with secondary routes between New York and Philadelphia. Mails also flowed south to Annapolis. As postmaster for the northern colonies, Franklin not only moved the colonial branch of the royal postal system to a paying basis, improving delivery speed and frequency in the area under his jurisdiction, but he also, through his newspaper connections, made it the artery of information circulation for the colonies. After experiencing the exclusion of his *Pennsylvania Gazette* from the mails in its early days, Franklin vowed to allow any newspaper to travel postage-free. Improved service between Boston and New York meant that newspapers (and the news contained therein) reliably traveled from New York to Philadelphia three times a week. Moreover, interest in printed news was also spurred by two other developments. Published stories of the Seven Years' War in North America, a major part of a worldwide contest that would play a major role in determining the continent's fate, whetted readers' appetite for more. In addition, Franklin's use of regularly scheduled stages in the North to carry the mails made the flow of distant news more regular. By 1763, readers in

Boston, New York, and Philadelphia were likely to be aware of important information circulating in any of other three cities and their hinterlands within a fortnight at most.

The southern postmastership was another story, however. Regular carriage of the mails by land was deterred by both geography and economy. Virginia had been late in establishing postal routes because the colony lacked important centers of population and commerce. Traffic flowed largely east to west on rivers, rather than north to south on land, and for a long time, Virginians relied on informal person-to-person mail delivery on river routes. South of Williamsburg, land service was dismal, even in 1763. The Virginia pattern obtained in colonies to the south similarly organized. Because travel by land was fraught and uncertain, north-to-south communication often moved over water, going first to London in order reach southern destinations. It is no surprise, then, that the southernmost colonies were tied more closely by virtue of communication patterns to Europe and the West Indies than to the colonial north.[8]

The two newspapers in the lowland south, the *South-Carolina Gazette* and the *Georgia Gazette,* existed in a different information universe than those in Franklin's postmastership. Connections to the central Philadelphia–New York information nexus were unreliable. By 1763, Maryland and Virginia were much more closely tied to northern networks than to those further south. Indeed, even a decade later, in 1773, Hugh Findlay, the Royal Surveyor of the Postal Roads for North America, found mail service between Charleston and points northward to be problematic. A roundtrip correspondence between that city and New York took ten weeks at best; at the worst, the mail never made it to its destination. Before 1764, when the royal postal service implemented changes in its shipping packet to North America, one packet shuttled directly between Falmouth and New York, while a second reached Charleston only after stops in the West Indies, Pensacola, and Fort St. Augustine.[9]

In sum, north of Williamsburg, British colonies on the North American seaboard in 1763 had become integrated into an increasingly efficient information network. The southernmost colonies had not. What that network meant was that for the first time, American domestic news could be readily circulated effectively among significant numbers of the colonies. Those in North Carolina, South Carolina, and Georgia were separated from their sister provinces in the north not only by miles but in amounts and types of information received and exchanged. The news was the news—but it differed somewhat in content and emphasis in the two North American spheres of circulation.

By the Numbers: The West and the Western Frontier in Newspapers, 1763

What did the newspapers have to say about the newly acquired British western lands in 1763? The question is hard to answer by what would seem to be the obvious approach of conducting keyword searches in series 1 and 2 of Early American Newspapers, the digitized collection of North American press publications before 1900. Optical character recognition, while a reliable technology for later texts, is imperfectly adapted to the frequently broken and worn type fonts of colonial printers and not at all capable of interpreting the blackletter Gothic type (Fraktur) used in German-language newspapers. The *Virginia Gazette* for 1763, except for a handful of issues, no longer exists. Hence, the source of several stories printed in the colonies that indicated an origin in Williamsburg on a particular date could not be verified. The *South-Carolina Gazette*, though digitized, appears in an entirely different database, in which searchable transcriptions are often unreliable, while the *Maryland Gazette*, on the Maryland State Archives site, is not searchable at all. For this project, materials in America's Historical Newspapers were most frequently searched using keywords, those for South Carolina and Maryland visually scanned in their entirety for relevant items.

Of the twenty-one different newspapers published in British North America in 1763, seventeen contained in the Early American Newspapers / America's Historical Newspapers database give us some idea of the ways publishers and readers referred to the land newly acquired by Britain that year. Most striking perhaps, given our own habits of thought, the land in question was not "The West." The only "west," referring to a region or location that occurs with any degree of frequency in a database search, is "West Indies." The newly acquired region, in contrast, had no specific name. Instead, official treaties and documents, as well as newspaper articles and advertisements, referred to particular locations using specific geographical features. Thus, there was no "Ohio," but rather only land located relative to the Ohio River; no general "West," but only locations established relative to the Mississippi River, the far boundary of British possessions. The only geographic areas related to the acquisition with specific names in newspapers were "Louisiana"—that is, the portion of North America which extended from the west bank of the Mississippi River to the Rocky Mountains and which had been secretly ceded to the Spanish in 1762—and Florida, acquired from the Spanish in the treaty and split into two jurisdictions, Florida and West Florida.[10]

By far the most frequent term to appear in database searches that we might today associate with a geographic west is *frontier* (also known as *the back country*, inhabited by *back settlers* or *back inhabitants*). This frontier in 1763 did not yet extend west beyond the Appalachians. In Pennsylvania, the term generally referred to Berks, Cumberland, and Northampton Counties; in Virginia, to Augusta, Frederick, and Hampshire Counties. New Jersey's Sussex County was seen as a frontier region, as were (undesignated) parts of New York and Massachusetts. The portion of Britain's expanded North American empire inhabited by settler colonials lay on the Atlantic side of the mountains. Florida lay south of existing southern colonies and West Florida to their west along the Gulf Coast.

How much domestic news about the frontier, Indians, back-country settlers, and the prospects for the new western borderlands did the improved postal carrier and delivery routes bring to American readers in 1763? The glib answer is "a lot"—largely because of a brutal outbreak of violence on the frontier that we today know as Pontiac's War (or Rebellion). During the Seven Years' War, American news of intercolonial interest began to appear on the second or third pages. With the revival of hostilities between diverse Indian tribes and European settlers on the frontier in 1763, the numbers of newspaper items related to Indians and the frontier mushroomed, constituting the better portion of domestic news for the year. The first stories of plans for peace conferences with Indians and of Indian attacks at Fort Pitt appeared at the beginning of June. By the end of the year, at least 227 individual issues of American newspapers had published original items on the frontier and/or Indian–settler relations or had reused newsprint sources from elsewhere in the colonies.

What newspapers published about the conflict, the sources of that information, and its circulation through the colonies is more than a matter of mere curiosity. The types of information we receive, as the anthropologist Benedict Anderson claimed four decades ago, make a difference in the identities we claim and the virtual communities to which we think we belong. The historian Robert Parkinson has built on this insight to persuasively argue that an American identity was forged during the Revolutionary years, in large part through the circulation of newspapers with information received and consumed by the mainland provinces. Further, he maintains, for ordinary people, this nascent sense of nationhood rested in large part on news that positioned the British as fomenters of insurrection by Black and Native populations against white settlers. What the papers said in 1763 about the western frontier, and to whom, provides an additional dimension to this discussion because, as it turns out, the question of race was so thoroughly involved.[11]

Newspapers published three general types of stories, none of which was entirely new in 1763. Stories of attacks by Indians on forts on the Great Lakes or elsewhere in the Trans-Appalachian West often consisted of dispatches from the front focusing mainly on who was involved, the sequence of events that occurred, and the outcomes. Albany was often cited as a location of origin for these types of stories—in part because it had been a major military staging area for Canada and the Great Lakes during the recently completed war. Pennsylvania papers, especially the *Pennsylvania Gazette,* published news of attacks on Pennsylvania forts, with the *Maryland Gazette* doing the same for the Maryland and Virginia frontiers. Stories originating in Pennsylvania and New York papers were frequently reused elsewhere (Table 1.2).[12]

In contrast, news about the frontier in the deep southern Low Country (South Carolina and Georgia) generally came from the *South-Carolina Gazette.* Relatively isolated by land from other colonies—even from Savannah, Georgia, 110 miles away—news from Charles-Town was not often reprinted anywhere else. (It did make its way northward eventually, but the datelines of news reported about this region in more northerly papers seldom match the date of publication or the sequencing of words in the original Low Country newspaper stories.) Fear of Indian violence on the southern frontier was evident, but no stories were reported of Indian attacks on military targets. Far more frequent than in the north were stories—brief but telling—of violent disagreements among different Indian nations.[13] Stories from the northern frontier that reached this far south

Table 1.2: Origins of stories about frontiers and Natives, with later reuse elsewhere (in separate issues of newspapers)

	Place article originated	% of total articles originated*	# of times original articles were reported/reprinted/excerpted elsewhere	% of articles reused elsewhere
Portsmouth	0	0	0	0
Boston†	11	11.2	1	0.8
Providence	0	0	0	0
Newport	0	0	0	0
New London / New Haven	1	1.0	1	0.8
New York†	9	9.2	24	18.6
Philadelphia†	37	37.8	97	75.2
Annapolis	17	17.3	5	3.9
Charlestown	17	17.3	1	0.8
Savannah	6	6.1	0	0
Total issues with information on frontier	98	–	129	–

Notes: Whole numbers represent *approximate counts* of issues in which information or stories occurred. Use of both searchable and non-searchable databases have their own built-in sources of error, with searchable databases sometimes missing keywords and non-searchable databases relying solely on the eye of the researcher to catch references. Numbers should be understood as *minimum* representations of published issues with information on these topics.

* Percentages are rounded to nearest tenth.

† Multiple titles were published in these cities. Titles in the same city publishing the same news on the same date were counted separately.

were often shortened, published weeks after their first appearances, and concerned with whether the violence indicated that a general Indian alliance was afoot.[14] A large number of stories from the south concerned the upcoming congress of regional Indian leaders and southern governors to be held in the fall in Augusta, Georgia. The *South-Carolina Gazette* in particular focused on the actions of royal and provincial authorities and reflected a top-down view of colonial policy. Southern newspapers, connected more intimately with the British Caribbean and the two new Florida colonies than with British colonies further north, also provided a much stronger emphasis on troop movements, prospects for peace and lucrative trade—as well as the Crown's 1761 proclamation forbidding settlement on lands claimed by Indians or adjacent to them.[15]

The third category of stories issued mainly from Pennsylvania newspapers (principally the *Pennsylvania Gazette*) and concerned the revival of

Indian hostilities on the Virginia and Pennsylvania frontiers. Largely the work of local notables who served as the equivalent of stringers for newspapers circulated in their region, their correspondence with editors gave them significant sway in what appeared as news.[16] Extracts of their letters were widely circulated and provided a running narrative about Indian atrocities committed against ordinary settlers on the western frontiers of Pennsylvania and Virginia during the summer and fall of 1763. Between June, when the first stories of Indian attacks occurred, and the end of the calendar year, such correspondence-based stories appeared in newspapers published in every North American colony and in a total of eighty-three separate issues. The locales from which the first-person stories originated included Detroit, Fort Ontario, and Niagara on the Great Lakes; Forts Pitt, Ligonier, Bedford, and Augusta in Pennsylvania, as well as Carlisle, Lancaster, Reading, Bethlehem, Nazareth, Berks County, Paxton, Lancaster County, Shippensburg, and Tuscarawas; Albany and Fort Stanwix in New York; Cumberland and Frederick-Town in Maryland; and Winchester, Augusta County, Sta[u]nton, Roanoke, Fort Hope, and Green-Brier in Virginia. Though the stories of the mid-Atlantic western frontier by no means captured the experiences of the back inhabitants of every colony, the vivid depiction of Indian murders, scalpings, torture, and dismemberments made them vivid, fear-inducing—and reprintable. No colonial printer had yet declared "if it bleeds, it leads," but as commercial entrepreneurs, they all behaved as though they knew the principle.

Characters and a Narrative: Dividing the World into Native and White

Pontiac's War represented a furious warning to would-be settlers on the part of the half dozen or so tribal groups inhabiting the area north and west of the Ohio River. Western Native response to the peace settlement, though fierce, was not unwarranted. Colonial land companies and land speculators were indeed behaving as though the newly acquired land in the west was primarily for white settlement. Many excellent historical accounts exist of this short but brutal conflict, and I refer readers interested in the particulars to them. Most important to note here is that the numbers of identifiable groups involved in the hostilities, both European and Indian, was enormous. Indeed, it is difficult even now, with the benefit of over two and a half centuries of hindsight and historical scholarship, for the non-expert to keep all the players straight. Indian peoples caught up in one way or another included the Six Nations of the Haudenosaunee, or Iroquois, Confederation (the Mohawk, Onondaga, Oneida, Cayuga, Seneca, and Tuscarora peoples). These had supported the British against the French and their Algonquian allies during the Seven Years' War, although by the beginning of the 1763 attacks, the Seneca had withdrawn from the confederation. The Haudenosaunee claimed suzerainty over the tribes of the Ohio Country and the land controlled by them, a relationship the latter denied. Indians of the *pays d'en haut* (Ottawa, Ojibwe, and Pottawatomi, of the Ohio Country (Shawnee, Wyandot, Mingo, and Delaware), and of the Illinois Country (Miami, Kickapoo, Wea, Mascounten, and Piankashaw)—all peoples with their own complex histories, alliances, cultures, and problems—became part of a rebellion with many centers, in an effort to ensure that trade customs were respected and white settlement stopped. In the south and lower Mississippi Valley, the Creeks (divided into three branches) had fought both with and then against the British in the recently concluded war. The Cherokee, British allies, had long been at odds with Creeks over control over trade monopolies and hunting grounds. Likewise, the Chickasaw and Choctaw had long had a hostile relationship. Only the Catawba, by 1763 a people in sharp decline as a result of disease and continuing warfare, seemed to be a source of stability in the complex world of Indian relations.[17]

If the long list of Indian peoples involved in making sense of British–Native relations at the end of the Seven Years' War is confusing, that is the point. Only in retrospect is it possible to make sense of the racial marker *Indian:* all indigenous peoples were not the same. In the southernmost British colonies, in fact, the names of the particular nations continued to be used far more often in news stories than the single collective noun. Though most Americans know the conflict whose end preceded Pontiac's War as the French and Indian War, it is a misnomer. Indians peoples fought on both sides, and some remained neutral.[18]

Neither imperial officials nor provincials had any uniform system for dealing with Indians. In 1755, the Board of Trade established an Indian Department for North America as a wing of the British army. It had two principal officers, an Indian Superintendent for the Northern Department and one for the Southern Department. The Ohio River served as the dividing line between the two jurisdictions.[19] Moreover, the Crown and each of its North American provinces had relationships with nations and tribal alliances, and these were not always in agreement with one another. Virginia, Connecticut, Maryland, and Pennsylvania all claimed land also claimed by Native peoples and whose provenance was in dispute by both provincials and Indians. Further, relatively few of those who claimed ownership of frontier land were of English descent. The majority were Scots-Irish and German-speakers, the latter also of many European state origins. Many of these immigrants had been explicitly recruited by the prior generation to not only improve the land for the notables who leased it to them but also serve as buffers between the seaboard and the possibly hostile native populations. Back inhabitants were sometimes described by elites, even in print, as more nearly culturally akin to "savage" peoples than to their white European countrymen to the east. In other words, European settlers, particularly back inhabitants, evidenced nearly as much ethnic, status, and cultural diversity as did Indians.[20]

Perhaps, in retrospect, it should not surprise us how unsuccessfully those with differing interests and stakes in the outcome understood and negotiated the situation. Just as the pan-ethnic tribes of the Ohio Country had begun to adhere to the belief that whites and Natives were separate creations and belonged in separate places, so too had (some) colonial settlers begun to articulate the same viewpoint, with protagonists reversed. The result was violence. The back settlers of Pennsylvania, Maryland, and Virginia bore the brunt of brutal attacks from the Ohio Valley Indian coalition warning settlers out, and there is evidence that they gave nearly as good as they got.

Narratives of Indian violence were not new in British North America, but their widespread circulation among peoples of different colonies was.[21] How did newspapers come to develop a public narrative of racial conflict and racial distinctiveness? First, the new information network gave newspapers the opportunity to spread stories with American emphases that were popular with readers. More specifically, information networks—particularly newspapers—allowed the versions of the conflict that reached print in Pennsylvania, and to a much lesser extent in Maryland, to circulate widely. Table 1.3 summarizes the numbers of stories

Table 1.3: Newspapers originating materials about the frontier during 1763 (in issues) and where that material was reused (in issues)

Cities of origin	Cities where republished or excerpted										
	Annapolis	Boston (4 titles)	Charles-Town	New Haven / New London	New York (2 titles)	Newport	Philadelphia (3 titles)	Portsmouth	Providence	Savannah	Totals
Annapolis	–	2	1	–	–	1	–	1	–	–	5
Boston (4 titles)	–	–	–	–	–	–	–	1	–	–	1
Charles-Town	–	1	–	–	–	–	–	–	–	–	1
New Haven / New London	–	–	–	–	–	–	–	–	–	–	0
New York (2 titles)	2	8	2	2	–	4	3	2	2	–	25
Newport	–	–	–	–	–	–	–	–	–	–	0
Philadelphia (3 titles)	13	34	4	5	15	8	4	7	8	7	105
Portsmouth	–	–	–	–	–	–	–	–	–	–	0
Providence	–	–	–	–	–	–	–	–	–	–	0
Savannah	–	–	–	–	–	–	–	–	–	–	0
TOTALS	15	45	7	7	15	13	7	11	10	7	137

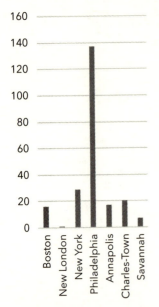

Chart 1.1: Originating print location of news items about the frontier, 1763

printed about frontier and Indian issues in American newspapers for the year 1763. Of the newspaper issues that printed in the colonies about Indians and frontier issues that year, about 60 percent of stories first saw print in a Philadelphia newspaper. Philadelphia and Annapolis together account as direct sources for about two-thirds of the colonial articles published. That is to say, most of the news concerning the frontier in British North American newspapers in 1763 came from or near the two colonies in which frontier violence was the fiercest. This version of frontier relations provided not only the most horrible and gruesome descriptions of what was happening on the frontier. It also was the most widely circulated domestic news. At some point during the year, frontier news from Philadelphia newspapers made its way into every newspaper in the colonies. Stories of frontier violence were most frequently reused, reprinted, or excerpted by newspapers along the northern postal route (Chart 1.1). Historian Robert Parkinson argues persuasively that the conflation of whiteness with Americanism was cemented in print descriptions of Indians and Blacks as both dangerous and inferior that were disseminated through the American newspaper network. The seeds of the notion of a racialized Other as antagonist to white America are clear in newspaper reportage of Pontiac's War.

Second, many of the stories printed consisted of extracts from letters, that is, firsthand accounts from frontier sites that relied on vivid description for their authority. At first, these stories centered on attacks on military posts and the civilian settlements that surrounded them. As the summer wore on, however, they homed in on stories of Indian attacks on civilians. The words most commonly used in the latter stories were *murder* and *massacre*. The correspondents who most often conveyed their impressions of frontier events did so by emphasizing ordinary frontier families as victims of sudden and senseless cruelty of the Indian foe. The immediacy of these narratives, juxtaposing as they did innocent frontier familial actors—mothers, fathers, small children, babes, lads, hired hands—with bloodthirsty and thieving savages, pitted unsuspecting white

Christian subjects of the King against an "Enemy" whose only characteristic was a satanic otherness. The murdered colonials often had names; Indians, with the exception of tribal chiefs, did not. Indigenes seemed to engage in aggression for no other identifiable reason than it was in their natures to do so.

Between the beginning of June, when such extracts from letters began to be seen in print, until the end of the calendar year, such accounts were published in nearly eighty different issues of newspapers, and in every colony. Without question, the design of the allied Indians on the northwestern borders was to spread terror among white settlers, and they succeeded in inciting fear, as the effects of their actions were amplified in circulating print. In contrast, perspectives of Natives were seldom directly available to the general public, except through the testimony of the bloody evidence. When they were, they came embedded in formal proceedings of congresses held by colonial officials and representatives of nearby tribes. Three such formal meetings were held: in Hartford, on May 28–30; in German Flats, near Albany, in late July; and in Augusta, Georgia, on November 5. Indian speeches could not compete in volume or length with stories of Indian atrocities. Sometimes they were dismissed as mere pretense designed to mislead.[22]

Third, in the absence of other explanations, speculation about who or what was behind frontier Indian attacks accumulated until the belief spread widely that Natives, either spurred by the defeated French or on their own, meant to eradicate British settlers. Prior to 1763, Indian attacks were nearly always coupled with links to French allies, who were sometimes described in the press as though they were puppet masters of groups called "French Indians" or the "scalping Indians." The French supplied scalping knives on French ships from Europe. They "not only delight in Cruelty and Bloodshed, but encourage their Indians to commit the most unheard of Barbarities." Scalping parties were said to consist of both French and their Indians.[23] Without the French as a formal enemy after the peace was concluded, accounts in the newspaper press continued to raise the question of whether the French were behind these latest attacks as well. An extract from a letter from Detroit, published in the August 25 *Maryland Gazette,* for example, captures the suspicion. After railing against "the most cruel and horrid Barbarities [committed] every Day" by the "Nations engaged in the War," the anonymous author, writing from Detroit on July 9, used the occasion to revive suspicions of the French as parties to the violence. They gave "their Parole d'Honeur" that British captain Robert Campbell, invited to a peace conference with Pontiac's army outside Fort Detroit's walls, would have safe passage—whereupon they immediately proved their bad faith by "delivering him into the Hands of the Enemy." A letter printed in the *Gazette* the week prior had described Captain Campbell's death, something the French presumably facilitated and condoned, in gory detail: "They killed him, taking his Heart, and eating it reeking from the Body, and then cut him to Pieces with their tomahawks.—Sir Robert Davies they boiled and eat; and an officer who was taken at Sandusky, but since escaped, saw the Skin of Lieutenant Robertson's Arm made into a Tobacco Pouch."[24]

An anonymous author in the July 25 *New-York Gazette*, after two months without respite from stories of frontier violence, wrote, "The Hostilities that are now carried on with such savage Cruelty, by most of the neighbouring Indian nations, against our Back Settlements, seem to have been meditated upon some Time past." French emissaries, he believed, were the likely culprits.

> It is evident that there must have been great Act and Application used, to infuse the same Spirit of Dislike and Mischief towards us, into so many different Indian Nations, remote from each other and unconnected in Interest. Probably some of our Traders have misbehaved toward them, and they might think themselves injured by some other particular Persons among us; but as they know we are always ready to hear and redress their Grievances, in a publick Manner, and as it has been solemnly stipulated by Treaty, that in Case of private Injury on either Side, there should be regular Complaints made, in order to obtain Redress, before any Acts of Hostilities were committed; which Terms we on our Part never violated. . . . [W]hatever be the Causes, their treacherous Violation of Treaty, and savage Cruelty, calls for the severest Chastisement.

In fact, however, Indian complaints spoke from the pages of newspapers rarely, if at all. As commercial printers amplified stories of frontier fear, Indian positions and grievances, chiefly about depredations on their land, were stated very clearly in summaries of congresses held between the representatives of regional Indian tribes and provincial authorities.

But dissemination of these complaints generally constituted onetime-only articulations in individual newspaper markets.

Combined, these factors ensured that emplotment and characterization now became widespread, a shared near-orthodoxy along northern paths of dissemination. By the end of the year, Cadwallader Colden, the royal governor of New York, claimed not to know the causes of Indian hostilities and feared "the Horrors and Desolation necessarily consequent to a general Defection of those Savages." A month later, Governor Francis Bernard of Massachusetts, whose province had not experienced the violence of the rebellion in any direct way, asked the colony's General Court to consider whether "if this flame is not soon extinguished, who can tell how far it will extend? . . . [I]f it is suffered to rage much longer, we may well expect that it will soon come to our own Homes."[25]

Notice of this racialized story about the frontier has become a commonplace in recent historical treatments of the pre-Revolutionary frontier period. Perhaps most skillfully told version comes from Peter Silver, who has labeled the pattern of description "the anti-Indian sublime." Linda Colley, a historian of Britain, has called it "a pornography of real or imagined Indian violence," and it colored journalism in England as well. These sensationalist and personal descriptions first saw print in newspapers during the Seven Years' War. They became widely disseminated during Pontiac's Rebellion, later spilling beyond the columns of newspapers into other forms of print. According to Silver, it was no coincidence that this story arose in an area newly peopled by Europeans of varied linguistic and cultural backgrounds—British, German, Scots-Irish, Quaker, Presbyterian, Moravian. These groups, initially inclined to be suspicious of all outsiders, became imaginatively transformed into a single people labeled "white." Natives with origins in a variety of peoples became "Indian." In a good number of the newspapers circulating in the British North American colonies, Scots-Irish and Germans, otherwise held in no high regard by the more well-off of English ethnicity, became transformed into the guardians of the frontier and the leading edge of civilization. Cultural pluralism on both parts led to a willingness to reduce the problem to a single issue: race.[26]

From a contemporary perspective, it is quite clear that this racialized scenario vastly oversimplified a very complex situation. But without any other overarching narrative to make the situation graspable—and without information that described accurately the various interacting groups and their histories, their claims, their differing stakes in the dispute, or their relationships with one another—the resulting narrative is not especially surprising. The tale, as transmitted by newspapers in the northern network, became a starkly racialized one of good and evil.

The limits of a study confined to one particular calendar year are many. Cultural attitudes do not generally take shape on a schedule bounded by the calendar. Moreover, the attitudes that dominated domestic news in 1763 neither began nor ended in that year. After a while, the war on the frontier abated, though it never ceased. Renegade Senecas made peace with their English adversaries in 1764. British troops reached an agreement with cornered Ohio Valley tribes in 1765 and with Indians in the Illinois Country in 1766.

These treaties and agreements did not accomplish any lasting reconciliation among British settlers and traders and the tribes of Britain's new northwest, however. The British generals Braddock, Amherst, and Bouquet all believed that the only solution to the region's Indian problem was eradication.[27] Like some of the frontier settlers, they seem to have come to the belief that the only good Indian was a dead Indian. No surprise then that by 1767, Shawnee leaders organized a conference of all western Indians would who attend in hopes that a larger confederacy might succeed in driving settlers back behind the mountains. Though they were unsuccessful in recruiting Indians of the southwest to join with them, a pan-Indian alliance remained alive for decades.[28]

Despite repeated urgings to do so, Indian peoples living on the newly ceded southwestern lands did not join with those of the Ohio and Illinois Country in an anti-British alliance at this time. The reasons, no doubt, were many. Nevertheless, the precarious peace reached in Augusta in November 1763 endured, nurtured by presents furnished by the British, a closer adherence to restrictions about white encroachment on Indian lands, a different vision by those in power about what a relationship with the Indians ought to look like, and a temporary emphasis on trade instead of settlement. Violence continued to be reported among the southwestern tribes, and sporadic murders of white settlers in the back country were duly noted. But anti-Indian fever did not inflame the colonies furthest south, at least not yet.

What attitudes and beliefs had the domestic news of 1763 established or reinforced? The last incident of Indian–settler violence of the year, experienced in December and reported in early 1764, provides some clues. On December 14, a number of residents of the Pennsylvania back country murdered six Christian Susquehannock Indians in Conestoga, near Lancaster. The provincial governor offered the remainder of the Conestoga group, about sixteen in all, protective custody in Lancaster. The vigilantes, who styled themselves the Paxton Boys, believed that all Indians posed a threat to their safety, even the so-called friendly ones. These presumably, whatever their protestations to the contrary, provided aid and information to enemy Indians. On December 27, frustrated frontiersmen broke into the enclosure at Lancaster and killed and scalped fourteen, including eight children. Following the murders, 250 people from the frontier marched on Philadelphia to present their grievances to the colony's Quaker elite.[29]

The Paxton Rebellion generated huge amounts of print in Philadelphia, mainly in the form of broadsides and pamphlets. Print debate in the city was fierce. Newspaper debate was not. Despite Philadelphia's key role as initial print disseminator of news about the frontier, the earliest stories about the Paxton Boys and the Indian murders appeared first in New York and Newport newspapers, not in Philadelphia. What became visible of the Paxton debate there tended to favor the province's establishment, with reference to frontier complaints omitted or foreshortened.[30] But as the controversy raged on in Philadelphia, newspapers there and elsewhere continued to publish stories of Indian murders, scalpings, and body mutilations. Anti-Indian reportage and sentiment endured. The Paxton incident finally became only a ripple in the print information network outside Pennsylvania.

Dehumanization begets violence, but what begets dehumanization? One answer is the development of shared cultural narratives that collapse complex motivation and multilayered histories into easily graspable stories: that is, morality tales about good and evil. Such stories often emerge in times of fear and uncertainty and make graspable situations and events that defy easy explanation. For many colonials in the mid-Atlantic region, the Indian uprisings were a source of confusion and terror—precisely the reactions their attackers intended to induce. Once in place, stories like the one that hardened into orthodoxy in the 1760s and circulated throughout the colonies in newspapers were called on again and again to explain conflicts and disagreements. One side was civilized; the other was not. When culturally distinct peoples come to see themselves as differing not only in behavior but in essence, the chances that they will reach any practical accommodation with one another is almost nil.

Could it have been otherwise? The story of information circulation in the Deep South, where accommodations and peacemaking were emphasized in news stories, suggests that the narrative need not have crystallized when it did and the way it did. If the newspapers had amplified the stories told by the representatives of the Indian nations who attended Congresses at Albany, Hartford, and Augusta, would people have read them? We cannot know. Hosts of advertisement for land in the new western regions, appearing immediately after the announcement of the preliminary peace in February, purported to offer farmers a way toward independence without providing any information at all about who believed they owned the land, or by what title, or what the advertisers stood to gain or lose if the frontier did not advance westward.[31] Though white frontier unrest and rebellion later made its way into newspapers, any deep discussion of its causes did not. Would more knowledge of what lay under the pressure for westward settlement have made for a different story? We can only speculate.

Once fear hardened attitudes into a widespread narrative in the north, once its structures of feeling coalesced into something tangible and transmissible, it was too late.

Expulsion or extirpation of the Native inhabitants of Trans-Appalachia could only be justified by a narrative in which Indians became all the same, constructed as congenitally incapable of anything but the most brutal and savage behavior. That belief was one newspapers supplied to the public.

It became codified little more than a decade later, in the declaration by which a people who now called themselves white declared their independence from an empire that gave them the West.

Notes

The author is grateful to Fred Anderson and John Brooke for sharing their knowledge and expertise. Any errors of fact or interpretation are my own. This essay is in memory of Andrew Cayton, a midwesterner and a scholar of the region.

1. Fred Anderson, "The Peace of Paris, 1763," in *The Making of Peace: Rulers, States, and the Aftermath of War*, ed. Williamson Murray and Jim Lacey (New York: Cambridge Univ. Press, 2009), 101–29.

2. Frederick J. Turner, "The Significance of the Frontier in American History (1893)," in *The Frontier in American History* (New York: Henry Holt, 1920), 1–38.

3. The anthropologist Benedict Anderson's *Imagined Communities: Reflections on the Origin and Spread of Nationalism*, rev. ed. (London, Verso: 2006) stimulated historical thinking about the ways that common experiences with printed texts can influence a group's sense of identity and structure and that group's mental image of its place in the world. Perhaps the best example of how the circulation of the printed and written word influenced group attitudes in this period is Robert G. Parkinson, *The Common Cause: Creating Race and Nation in the American Revolution* (Chapel Hill: Univ. of North Carolina Press, for the Omohundro Institute of Early American History and Culture, 2016). The body of literature on the causes of Pontiac's War, its progress, and its consequences is large. See especially Richard White, *The Middle Ground: Indians, Empires, and Republics in the Great Lakes Region, 1650–1815* (New York: Cambridge Univ. Press, 1991), 269–314; Fred Anderson, *Crucible of War: The Seven Years' War and the Fate of Empire in British North Americas, 1754–1766* (New York: Alfred A. Knopf, 2000), 535–71; Kevin Kenny, *Peaceable Kingdom Lost: The Paxton Boys and the Destruction of William Penn's Holy Experiment* (New York: Oxford Univ. Press, 2009); Gregory Evans Dowd, *War under Heaven: Pontiac, the Indian Nations and the British Empire* (Baltimore: Johns Hopkins Univ. Press, 2002); Greg Evans Dowd, *A Spirited Resistance: The North American Indian Struggle for Unity, 1745–1815* (Baltimore: Johns Hopkins Univ. Press, 1991), 23–46; Eric Hinderaker, *Elusive Empires: Constructing Colonialism in the Ohio Valley, 1673–1800* (Cambridge: Cambridge Univ. Press, 1997), 87–175; and Ned Blackhawk, *The Rediscovery of America: Native Peoples and the Unmaking of U.S. History* (New Haven: Yale Univ. Press, 2023), 152–72. On the importance of Pontiac's War in creating a racial imaginary for "whites" about "savages," see Peter Silver, *Our Savage Neighbors: How Indian War Transformed Early America* (New York: W. W. Norton, 2008).

4. On early American newspapers, see especially Charles E. Clark, *The Public Prints: The Newspaper in Anglo-American Culture, 1665–1740* (New York: Oxford Univ. Press, 1994); Charles E. Clark, "Early American Journalism: News and Opinion in the Popular Press," in *A History of the Book in America*: vol. 1 of 4, *The Colonial Book in the Atlantic World*, ed. Hugh Amory and David D. Hall (Cambridge: Cambridge Univ. Press and the American Antiquarian Society, 2000), 347–66; Parkinson, *Common Cause*, 26–77; Joseph M. Adelman, *Revolutionary Networks: The Business and Politics of Printing and News, 1763–1789* (Baltimore: Johns Hopkins Univ. Press, 2019), 19–50; and Ralph Frasca, *Benjamin Franklin's Printing Network: Disseminating Virtue in Early America* (Columbia: Univ. of Missouri Press, 2006).

5. Franklin's "syndicate" included his own *Pennsylvania Gazette* (1729) as well as the *South-Carolina Gazette* (1732), the *New-York Gazette, or Weekly Post-Boy* (1743), *Connecticut Gazette* (1755), and the *Wochentliche Philadelphische Staatsbote*

(1762). He underwrote his brother's *Newport Mercury* after the latter's death in 1735, training his nephew in the trade. The *New-York Mercury* (1752) began publication when one of Parker's printers for the *Gazette* broke with him. See Frasca, *Benjamin Franklin's Printing Network*, 33–154.

6. See Paul Douglas Newman, "Red Journalism: The Allegheny Indians, Benjamin Franklin's *Pennsylvania Gazette*, and the Ethnic Cleansing of Pennsylvania, 1747–1764," *Journalism History* 45, no. 33 (2019): 232.

7. Benjamin Franklin, *Autobiography* (New York: Henry Holt, 1916), 61. When a rival was Philadelphia's postmaster, Franklin could only send his paper through the mails by bribing the post riders. In *Colonial and Revolutionary Posts: A History of the American Postal Systems. Colonial and Revolutionary Period* (Richmond, VA: Dietz, 1931), Harry M. Konwiser argues that printers and postmasters were one and the same because the two enterprises were mutually dependent (22–25).

8. William Smith, "The Colonial Post Office," *American Historical Review* 21, no. 2 (1916): 265–68, 272; Fairfax Harrison, "The Colonial Post Office in Virginia," *William and Mary Quarterly* 4, no. 2 (1924): 173–92.

9. Smith, "Colonial Post Office," 272; *Journal kept by Hugh Findlay, Surveyor of the Post Roads on the Continent of North America* . . . (Brooklyn: Frank H. Norton, 1867), 58–70.

10. Printed maps existed, but they did not appear in newspapers. Much of the mapping in this era was associated with establishing titles to land. See Martin Brückner, *The Geographic Revolution in Early America: Maps, Literacy, and National Identity* (Chapel Hill: Univ. of North Carolina Press, for the Omohundro Institute of Early American History and Culture, 2006), 16–50.

11. Anderson, *Imagined Communities*, and Parkinson, *Common Cause*.

12. I refer to stories as "reused" because they took a variety of forms. Some were reprinted in toto, some were summarized, and some briefly alluded to.

13. *South-Carolina Gazette* (Charles-Town), July 16, Aug. 27, Oct. 22, 1763. (Hereafter, unless noted otherwise, all newspapers are from the year 1763.)

14. *South-Carolina Gazette*, June 30, July 2, 9, 20, Aug. 6, 30, Sept. 24, Oct. 1; *Georgia Gazette*, July 7, 28, Aug. 25, Sept. 8, 24, Nov. 10, 17.

15. *South-Carolina Gazette*, June 11, 18, 15, July 9, Sept. 10, 24, Oct. 8, 22, Nov. 5, 19; *Georgia Gazette*, Aug. 25, Nov. 17.

16. Silver, *Our Savage Neighbors*, 67–69. See also Newman, "Red Journalism," 227–49.

17. Many good treatments exist describing the situations of various Native peoples and groups during this period. See especially, in addition to works cited above, Daniel K. Richter, *Before the Revolution: America's Ancient Pasts* (Cambridge, MA: Belknap Press of Harvard Univ. Press, 2011); Susan Sleeper-Smith, *Indigenous Prosperity and American Conquest: Indian Women of the Ohio River Valley, 1690–1792* (Chapel Hill: Omohundro Institute for Early American History and Culture and the Univ. of North Carolina Press, 2018); Jane T. Merritt, *At the Crossroads: Indians and Em-*

pires on a Mid-Atlantic Frontier (Chapel Hill: Omohundro Institute for Early American History and Culture and the Univ. of North Carolina Press, 2003).

18. Richter, *Before the Revolution*, 388–89

19. John R. Alden, "The Albany Congress and the Creation of the Indian Superintendencies," *Mississippi Valley Historical Review* 27, no. 2 (1940): 193–210.

20. Patrick Griffin, *American Leviathan: Empire, Nation, and the Revolutionary Frontier* (New York: Hill & Wang, 2007), 19–94.

21. A number of important narratives had been published in New England in pamphlet form or as part of larger works, and the Indian captivity narrative was a recognizable genre there during the late seventeenth and early eighteenth centuries. Two of the most important included Mary Rowlandson, *The Sovereignty and Goodness of God, Together with the Faithfulness of His Promises Displayed; Being a Narrative of the Captivity and Restauration of Mrs. Mary Rowlandson* (Printed in British Colonial America: n.p., 1682); and John Williams, *The Redeemed Captive* (Boston: n.p., 1707), discussed at length in John Demos, *The Unredeemed Captive: A Family Story from Early America* (New York: Alfred A. Knopf, 1994). Most focused on the spiritual as well as temporal welfare of the captives, usually women.

22. On the Hartford Congress, consisting of Connecticut officials and representatives of the Six Nations, see *New York Gazette*, July 18; *New-York Mercury*, July 18; *Pennsylvania Gazette*, July 21; *Maryland Gazette*, July 21; *Providence Gazette*, July 30. On the Albany Congress, consisting of Sir William Johnson, Indian Superintendent for the Northern Department, and chiefs of Six Nations (except for the Seneca), see *New York Gazette*, Aug. 1; *Providence Gazette*, Aug. 6; *Newport Mercury*, Aug. 8; *Boston Post-Boy*, Aug. 8; *Boston News-Letter*, Aug. 12. On the Augusta (Georgia) Congress, consisting of the governors of Virginia, North Carolina, South Carolina, and Georgia; John Stuart, Indian superintendent of the Southern Department; and chiefs and warriors of the Cherokee, Creek, Choctaw, Chickasaw, and Catawba Peoples, see *South-Carolina Gazette*, June 18, July 2, 9, 16, Sept. 10, Oct. 8, 22, Nov. 5, 19; *Georgia Gazette*, Aug. 25, Nov. 17: *Pennsylvania Gazette*, Dec. 15; *Maryland Gazette*, Dec. 22.

23. *Boston Gazette*, Oct. 6, 1755; *Pennsylvania Gazette*, Nov. 18, 1756; *New-York Mercury*, Sept. 19, 1757.

24. *Maryland Gazette*, Aug. 18.

25. *New York Gazette*, Nov. 21; *Boston News-Letter*, Dec. 22.

26. Silver, *Our Savage Neighbors*, 73–143; Linda Colley, *Captives: The Story of Britain's Pursuit of Empire and How Its Soldiers and Civilians Were Held Captive by the Dream of Global Supremacy, 1600–1850* (New York: Pantheon, 2002), 177.

27. Richter, *Before the Revolution*, 388–414.

28. Dowd, *War under Heaven*, 264–71. See also Dowd, *Spirited Resistance*.

29. A thorough online account of the rebellion of the Paxton Boys with sources and documents, exists at *Digital Paxton: Digital Collection, Critical Edition, and Teaching Platform*, Historical Society of Pennsylvania and the Library Company

of Philadelphia, ed. Will Fenton, accessed Apr. 2, 2021. http://digitalpaxton.org/works/digital-paxton/index. The current definitive source on white anti-Native terrorism is Kenny, *Peaceable Kingdom Lost*.

30. *New-York Mercury,* Feb. 13, 1764; *Connecticut Gazette* (New Haven), Feb. 17, Mar. 2, 1764; *Providence Gazette,* Feb. 18, Mar. 3, 1764; *Boston Evening Post and Boston Gazette,* Feb. 20, 1764; *Newport Mercury,* Feb. 20, 27, 1764; *Boston Post-Boy,* Feb. 20, 1764; *Boston News-Letter,* Feb. 23, 1764; *New Hampshire Gazette,* Feb. 24, 1764; *Boston Evening Post,* Mar. 5, 1764; *New York Gazette,* Mar. 5, 1764; *Georgia Gazette,* Mar. 15, 1764.

31. Advertisements touting or related to new prospective settlements in the west appeared in *Pennsylvania Gazette,* Mar. 10, Apr. 7, Apr. 21, June 16, Sept. 29, Nov. 24; *Georgia Gazette,* Apr. 21, Aug. 25; *Newport Mercury,* Apr. 25, Nov. 21; *Boston News-Letter,* Apr. 28, Aug. 18; *New London Summary,* Apr. 29; *Providence Gazette,* Apr. 30, May 14, and Nov. 19; *Boston Evening Post,* May 2; *Boston Post-Boy,* May 2; *New York Gazette,* May 7; *South-Carolina Gazette,* May 28; *Maryland Gazette,* June 10, July 28, Aug. 4. The kinds of information that were public about these land schemes and what was not can be seen in Barbara Rasmussen's *Absentee Landowning and Exploitation in West Virginia, 1760–1920* (Lexington: Univ. Press of Kentucky, 1994). See also, as a starting place, Eugene M. Del Papa, "The Royal Proclamation of 1763: Its Effects upon Virginia Land Companies," *Virginia Magazine of History and Biography* 83, no. 4 (1975): 406–11.

Chapter 2

How the Western Antislavery Movement Redrafted American Freedom and Democracy

JEANNE GILLESPIE MCDONALD

Freedom and democracy in the United States were redrafted with a widening inclusion, grounded in revolutionary ideals and reforming the nation's understanding of the promise of the American experiment shepherded by a coalition of western antislavery leaders. A minority of free white and Black pioneers, transatlantic immigrants, men and women with varying degrees of personal and civic rights championed an inclusionary, egalitarian vision of national citizenship. In retrospect, given the primacy of sectionalism as a well-trod historical explanation for the Civil War, to focus on the Midwest seems banal in contextualizing present conflicts over racialized rights and policies situated in city and campus protest encampments. The tension between freedom (personal, human, and civic rights) and democracy (egalitarian, economic and social opportunity, and majoritarianism) is not new, nor is making places that align with ideals while disrupting established systems. After the founding of the United States, the most tenacious footholds of antislavery thought and activism in the nation were situated in the Old Northwest—the first territory intentionally set aside with slavery expressly prohibited and embodied many congressional disagreements and judicial tests over the expansion of liberty. As historian Michael A. Morrison posits,

> For more than a century, generations of historians working in shifts like coal miners have labored to unearth the real source and thus the true essence of sectional strife.... Territorial expansion and settlement promised literally enlarging freedom over space by the extension of American institutions into the Southwest and to the Pacific coast. They [Jacksonian expansionists] understood the political power of territorial aggrandizement ... and also promised to ensure personal freedom by meeting the territorial needs of a nation of autonomous, self-reliant, footloose yeomen ... to ameliorate class divisions and promote equality by providing the means of upward mobility through enhanced commercial opportunities and newly opened lands.

However, historian Jon K. Lauck has argued, as did Alexis de Tocqueville, that the Midwest in the nineteenth century "constituted the most advanced democratic society that the world had seen to date." In contrast, abolitionist Joshua Leavitt, an easterner and one of the founders of the 1840s Liberty Party, "felt that Illinois was 'the seat of war,' and that the antislavery leaders in the East were 'mere powder monkeys supplying ammunitions for the crucial battle being fought in the west.'" The clash between liberty and slavery manifested through a chronology of pressure points: uprisings, mobbing, massacres, legislation, court cases over freedom, transit, and return of free and enslaved African Americans, tariffs, trade, popular sovereignty, western expansion, and elections at all levels of government. The 1858 series of senatorial debates between Abraham Lincoln and Stephen Douglas in seven of nine congressional districts of Illinois laid bare the architecture of the House Divided. However, the western abolitionists had already inspected that House, identified what was salvageable, and sparked historical imagination in renovation.[1]

The argument over how to best fight slavery often led to fissures in abolitionist organizations and churches. Adopting additional causes like suffrage for women and African Americans, temperance, and more pernicious notions, such as anti-Masonic and anti-Catholic beliefs, tended to dilute energies, divide allegiances, and discriminate against German, Irish, and other immigrants. In the East, religious and emotionally charged rhetoric, moral suasion, was used to make converts to causes. Garrison's abolitionism—pacifist, perfectionist, and predicated on his persona—divided the American Anti-Slavery Society over women's leadership and church polity. When the New England Garrisonians and New York evangelical abolitionists fell out in 1840, the American and Foreign Anti-Slavery Society formed. Despite an enclave of Garrisonians on the Western Reserve in Ohio, the Western Antislavery Society, by 1840, a majority of western abolitionists no longer believed in the efficacy of non-resistance and moral suasion, so civil political processes were engaged, a clarification of goals ensued, and activism sprung from conviction justifying civil disobedience.

Petitioning and lobbying had been used from the early 1830s by Theodore Weld and Henry Stanton (husband of Elizabeth Cady Stanton) for lifting the gag rule on discussing slavery in Congress, the annexation of Texas, and the abolition of slavery in the District of Columbia. Along with other "rebels" at Lane Seminary in Cincinnati, Weld and Stanton debated slavery with other notable abolitionists—like James G. Birney, Gamaliel Bailey, Henry Ward Beecher, Harriet Beecher, John Rankin, and Hiram Wilson (who later ran the terminus of the Underground Railroad in Canada)—present. The "rebels" made their ways to Oberlin College, which became a bastion of antislavery activism in Ohio and beyond. The exercise of the right to petition enabled women and free African Americans to find their public, political voices even though they did not have suffrage. As abolitionists in new states attempted to protect and extend the freedom and rights granted them, generally, new residents saw themselves as egalitarian, fashioning a place untarnished by a powerful elite who owned everything. Even as the Constitution established a more egalitarian form of representative government than the British monarchy, it was contested through a secession of land acquisitions, before and after the 1820 Missouri Compromise, which saw tribes displaced by Jackson's Indian Removal Act of 1830 and war with Mexico from 1846 to 1848. The wrangling over freedom and democracy was distilled to the fight over slavery and its accompanying issues of political, economic, and cultural power. As territorial lands evolved into states, the competing interests of wealth, property, and labor manifested themselves philosophically and practically in legislatures and courts to protect, limit, and divest the rights of citizens at all governmental levels. Free African Americans steadily lost suffrage and emigration was hampered by Black laws. The fight for representation and democracy became increasingly tied to more material concerns over physical land and property rights. However, even proslavery politicians and Fire-Eaters recognized the powerful ideals of the Declaration and tried unsuccessfully to undercut its interpretation of inclusive rights.[2]

Early western abolitionists joined the biblical teaching that God created humanity with "all men are created equal" as a foundational principle to personal and civic rights. The appeal to natural rights in the Declaration was further supported by the exclusion of slavery in the 1787 Northwest Ordinance. These three intertwining "truths" revealed their understanding that the order of dominion was God—then humans—then the land. Slavery was incompatible with natural rights, natural law, and the order of the universe. However, proslavery forces also saw themselves as grounded in revolutionary traditions and particularly appealed to the Constitution for protection of minority diversity in social customs, religion, and property. The conflicting interpretations of the Declaration, the Northwest Ordinance of 1787, the Founders' Constitution, and the Bible justified stances over the morality and legality of slavery. These stances hardened into geographical boundaries, and soon both sides cried "sectionalism!" regarding judicial rulings, legislation, motives for land acquisitions, and the state of the union.

An antislavery interpretation of the Founders' Constitution was difficult because of the exclusionary rings run around freedom and democracy by a proslavery guaranty regardless of any "no property in men" intentions. The euphemistic status of "persons held to labor" and the insertion of a twenty-year expiration date of the transatlantic slave trade left plenty of legal room for states to make their own laws concerning free and enslaved African Americans (personal liberty laws) while establishing an enforced comity through fugitive slave laws. In historian William Wiecek's analysis, there were three strands of antislavery constitutionalism. Radical abolitionists (like William Goodell and Gerrit Smith) and Garrisonians saw the Constitution as proslavery, but the moderates of the Liberty Party worked out "a constitutional theory that complemented their political program." Rhode Island Quaker Arnold Buffum had traversed New England, New York, New Jersey, Pennsylvania, Ohio, and Indiana with an abolitionist message in Quaker meetinghouses primarily. "By the late 1830s, however, Buffum broke with Garrison to support political abolitionism by creating a third party dedicated to that goal. He accordingly assisted James G. Birney in founding the Liberty Party in 1840 and supported the Free-Soil campaign of 1848." Wiecek says,

Liberty politics until 1845 derived from their constitutional theory. Rarely in American history has a political party's platform been so integrally shaped by constitutional thought.... Arnold Buffam repulsed the charge that Libertymen meant to free slaves in the Southern states: "We intend no such thing.... In relation to slavery in the states, politically we claim no right to interfere." Salmon P. Chase [and Birney in Cincinnati] explained that the framers of the Constitution in 1787 "had no power to change the personal relations of the inhabitants of any State to each other, but were charged with the duty of framing a general system of government for the people of all the States, leaving those relations untouched.... [I]t was equally impossible for them to abolish slavery in the states where it existed."

Those teachings were retained in Free-Soil and Republican platforms, and it was those constraints that Lincoln acknowledged kept him from unconstitutionally abolishing slavery.[3] But interpreting the Constitution as either pro- or antislavery had left national abolitionist leaders at odds over whether scrapping the federal government was preferable to perfecting it. Western abolitionists agreed perfecting the union entailed resisting and reforming or repealing local, state, and federal laws supporting slavery and discrimination concerning rights while proslavery interpretations of the Bible fractured church affiliations and crippled any progressive reform of society.

Western abolitionists also understood inclusive democracy predicated on equality meant everyone, born or naturalized in the United States, had unalienable rights of freedom—life, liberty, and the pursuit of happiness. This was especially poignant in the new territories of the United States where white emigrants, free and enslaved African Americans, and transatlantic immigrants counted equally, whereas "Indians not taxed" were not counted because they were a nation within. The three-fifths rule was not applicable in census-taking for statehood when the bar of sixty thousand inhabitants was difficult to achieve in the hinterlands. Egalitarianism opened the coalition to immigrants who agreed with the western abolitionists and shut the door to Know-Nothings, or the American Party.

By the late 1830s, Northern abolitionists were all lumped together as "agitators," disunionists, and "radical" by most conservative Northern and Southern Whigs and Democrats. Everyone outside of Southern Democrats' circle of influence collectively pilloried them as "the slave power."

Northern Democrats who could be swayed by Southern Democrats' political patronage were pejoratively known as "doughfaces." Abolitionists began applying pressure on the Northern doughfaces to interrupt their Southern allegiances and disrupt partyism because there were not enough antislavery Whigs or Democrats to have influence. The way forward, in the minds of abolitionists, was to establish a third party, and nowhere was the Liberty Party stronger than in the Old Northwest. But, the founding of a new party needed a platform, and a return to first principles to repudiate slavery was the natural choice.

In the contest of ideals, both sides appealed to historical testimonies to bring "facts" revealing the intentions of the colonists and founders to assess the veracity of and disarm the opposing interpretations. Did the Declaration mean "all men," and did our Founders intend freedom for everyone? In a study of African American Revolutionary War pensioners, historian Judith L. Van Buskirk found that free African Americans often thought of liberation in a more social or civic sense while enslaved African Americans thought first of the personal liberty to be gained by military service. An old Revolutionary War soldier, quoted by associate editor Asa B. Brown in Chicago's *Western Citizen,* the leading northwestern antislavery newspaper west of Cincinnati's *Philanthropist,* addressed the equivocation by proslavery defenders that the "all men" in the Declaration of Independence was a "mere rhetorical flourish" applicable only to landed, white males: "Everybody there supposed that the contest was for rational liberty to be enjoyed by all, irrespective of the color of their skin. . . . [T]he soldier at his right hand in the company . . . was a black man, and as good a soldier as he ever saw; what no one ever dreamed that *that* black man or any other was fighting merely for the liberty of the white man. . . . [Everybody thought], except the tories, that the principle of that clause in the Declaration was to be universal in its application."[4] Even Stephen Douglas, the preeminent Illinois doughface, had a plausibility gap when trying to argue that the Declaration was exclusionary. Lincoln had an affinity with the inclusion of the Declaration, and other conservative Whigs and Democrats could find common ground with abolitionists.

To combat a proslavery usurpation of the Bible and the Constitution, the western antislavery movement demonstrated vigor and unity of purpose through a "practical abolitionism," which encompassed political activism and civil disobedience, with Black and white abolitionists in partnership, akin to what historian James Oakes has dubbed "the Antislavery Project." Historian Corey M. Brooks explains, "Scholars often stress the moral and religious impetuses for the formation of an abolitionist third party, but a false dichotomy between moral purity and pragmatic politics has obscured the strategic vision of the third-party movement. Third-party advocates construed their political program as both a moral protest *and* a practical tactical move.... Political abolitionists thus valued third-party politics as both a means to maintain their moral probity by providing nominees for whom abolitionists could conscionably vote *and* as a strategy for toppling the Slave Power." This was a deliberate agenda designed to advance freedom rather than a reaction to the Slave Power. Of course, proslavery forces thought this antislavery project was a conspiracy to rob them of their rights and property in slaves.[5]

In its wrangling over slavery, Illinois has often been described as a microcosm of the Union. However, the Old Northwestern states were more than just a derivative of the Northeast and Southern original states. Western expansion had ignited discourse over race and rights.[6] As historian John Craig Hammond says, "the weaknesses of the federal government in the West meant that the decision to permit or exclude slavery became, by default, a local question. Consequently, slavery entered local politics in western states and territories far more frequently and intensely than it did in national politics prior to 1819.... With the crisis of 1819, North–South sectionalism overtook East–West conflicts over slavery in the West. Southerners and northerners now tried to project their own irreconcilable visions of slavery and freedom onto the West."[7] Much of Illinois's early constitution and laws were sourced from other Old Northwestern and original southern states. Social status with a hierarchy of rights had been codified in Virginia law to divide free and enslaved African Americans from poor whites and white indentured servants to quell the strength of insurrections.[8] Early Kentucky and Virginia resolutions also factored into clashes between state and federal rights. Territorial laws had been designed to open lands for white inhabitants, yet the military had promised land as reward for Black soldiers serving in the Revolutionary War and the War of 1812. However, the derivative Illinois Black Laws barred free African Americans from emigrating to the region by charging enormous registration fees and demanding the filing of certificates of freedom. These competing interests and contradicting statutes contributed to tensions and rifts over civil rights in Illinois.[9]

The 1818 Illinois Constitution established a voluntary indenture system, a semantic workaround for slavery, which had been prohibited by the Northwest Ordinance.[10] Historian M. Scott Heerman says, "Notably, the [state] constitution protected the three major sources of bound labor: French Negroes born into bondage, servants held to lifelong contracts, and slaves annually trafficked into Illinois. Illinois masters exited the convention with their power over slaves largely intact."[11] The antislavery contingent in the US Congress voted against this constitution, seeing it as subverting the intentions of a slavery free territory, but the proslavery representatives conferred statehood.

Five years later, Illinois land speculators and industry leaders conspired with proslavery politicians to bring the question of a constitutional convention to voters to allow slavery. This begged the question of whether a state could decide for itself to be slave or free, echoed in Stephen Douglas's position of popular or "squatter" sovereignty some thirty years later.[12] Journalist David Ress points out that "the anti-slavery campaign [Governor Edward] Coles led was one of the first in the United States, and the very first to mobilize relatively large numbers of citizens to break with their leaders and oppose slavery."[13]

Coles's principles had dictated that he free his slaves regardless of financial loss. Coles was the son of a wealthy Virginian planter in Albemarle County and former secretary to Madison, a neighbor and correspondent of Jefferson, asking him for advice on slavery and receiving the usual equivocal answer. Jefferson believed the gradual abolition of slavery would be accomplished in the future by young men—not him. Coles was disillusioned but not dissuaded. Although he was elected governor in a four-way contest, he appealed to the general population's self-interests over the proslavery political and industrial elite. On August 2, 1824, the vote against the convention was 6,640 to 4,972, a 57 percent to 42 percent advantage, which translates to a decisive defeat.[14]

Coles unleashed the power of independent thought that made antislavery stakeholders out of pioneers. Voters were bombarded with propaganda, but the interests of the small farmer came to the fore.[15] And, as historian Suzanne Cooper Guasco puts it, "both pro- and anti-conventionists were forced to explain the advantages and disadvantages of introducing slavery for the average small, and southern-born, farmer. As a result, a comparison of free and slave labor and democratic and aristocratic society dominated the rhetoric of the convention campaign."[16]

Over the next decade, the furor regarding slavery receded. Conflicts with Indigenous tribes; land and water improvements; and economic issues like panics, depressions, and trade dominated the national stage. The antislavery leadership against the convention dispersed, but many pioneering abolitionists moved into northern counties like Putnam, Knox, Bureau, and LaSalle. A few local antislavery societies remained in southern Illinois counties, while new ones in Quincy and Putnam County were established and initially affiliated with the American Anti-Slavery Society.[17] But some anti-conventionists, like Rev. John Mason Peck, were also anti-abolitionist, thus preferring the American Colonization Society, missionary work, and/or other benevolent societies.

Newly manumitted slaves, formerly indentured servants, and more free African Americans settled onto farms and in villages, welding a safety net along waterways, across countryside, and into cities. These were the "first responders" to the kidnapped, self-emancipated, and freedom seekers to aid against slave catchers and racist violence. As partnerships sprang up between them and white allies, civil disobedience of fugitive slave and Black laws strengthened over time. By 1860, the Illinois Black population totaled 7,628. Nine towns with 100 or more African American residents included Chicago (955), Springfield (203), Shawneetown (201), Alton (187), Jacksonville (156), Galena (152), Quincy (152), Bloomington (145), and Peoria (109).[18] Additionally, free Black communities like New Philadelphia, Lakeview, Miller's Grove, Brushy Fork, Brooklyn, Rocky Fork, and Pinkstaff with Black neighborhoods in Belville, Springfield, Galesburg, and Aurora supported individuals like Priscilla "Mother" Baltimore, a Brooklyn, Illinois, founder, going into Missouri and helping the enslaved to escape, providing safer passages, and partnering with white abolitionists.[19]

A handful of original antislavery churches like Covenanter Presbyterians, Quakers, Baptist Friends of Humanity, and Methodist congregations remained firm in southern Illinois. Statewide, AME churches (some established by Bishop Paul Quinn) and Black Baptist churches quietly grew. Emigrants from the Burned Over District in New York state and Congregationalists were dependable abolitionists wherever they landed in northern Illinois, and there were a few integrated churches before the Civil War. In Ohio, the exodus from Lane Seminary to Oberlin College by Theodore Weld and his "rebels" (later the "seventy") pioneered antislavery preaching and petitioning. Illinois College, Knox College, Wheaton College, and Chicago Theological Seminary promoted antislavery stances that fractured denominations and Presbyterian congregations. Their college presidents—Rev. Dr. Edward Beecher, Elijah Lovejoy's friend and Harriet Beecher Stowe's brother; Rev. George W. Gale, from the Oneida Institute; and Rev. Jonathan Blanchard, a former American Anti-Slavery Society agent—were regarded suspiciously by public anti-intellectuals, received anti-Yankee and anti-missionary prejudice, and were editorialized against unmercifully by proslavery editors and clergy. Promoting black education, freedom, or rights was labelled as "agitating."[20]

Transplanted easterners who became western abolitionists concluded slavery had a political origin as well as originating in moral and ethical failures. Zebina Eastman, *Western Citizen* editor, explained, "But slavery in all its aspects was very largely a political institution. It was created by law; it must be abolished by law. There was no class of abolitionists that proposed the removal of slavery by the political power of the nation."[21] However, even antislavery Illinoisans opposed abolitionists as agitators and lawbreakers to be silenced.[22] In January 1837, the Illinois General Assembly passed an anti-abolitionism resolution, lobbied by Southern states, which stated: "We highly disapprove of the formation of abolition societies, and of the doctrines promulgated by them.... That the right of property in slaves, is sacred to the slave-holding States by the Federal Constitution, and that they cannot be deprived of that right without their consent.... That the General Government cannot abolish slavery in the District of Columbia, against the consent of the citizens of said District without a manifest breach of good faith." Abraham Lincoln was one of six dissenters and, along with Dan Stone, a fellow representative from Sangamon County, introduced into the record a protest that stated: "The undersigned hereby protest against the passage of the [Resolution]. They believe that the Institution of Slavery is founded both in Injustice and bad policy; but that the promulgation of Abolition Doctrines tends rather to Increase than to abate its evils." While they agreed with the rest of the original resolution, this is considered Lincoln's first official slavery stance.[23] The General Assembly's condemnation served to drive the antislavery opposition underground, that is, until an abolitionist editor was murdered in November of 1837.

When Elijah Parish Lovejoy, protecting his printing press, was killed by a proslavery mob, eastern abolitionists decried his use of defensive force. The Tappans in New York City, Garrison in Boston, Birney and Weld in Ohio, and southern abolitionists had already felt the mobocracy's chilling effect, yet a vast majority of eastern abolitionists felt that moral suasion and nonviolence (nonresistance) could soften proslavery stances. When Wendell Phillips made an impassioned defense of Lovejoy at Faneuil Hall in Boston, many eastern abolitionists finally recognized what western abolitionists already knew—those tools were not enough and took the tack that Lovejoy's violence was in self-defense.[24] Years later, in an 1859 speech to Brooklyn's Plymouth Church, Phillips justified John Brown's provocative violence: "I think you can make a better use of iron than forging it into chains. If you must have the metal, put it into Sharpe's rifles.... [M]en that still believe in violence, the five points of whose faith are the fist, the bowie knife, fire, poison, and the pistol, are ranged on the side of Liberty."[25]

At least a dozen or so of Weld's "Seventy" (about fifty lecturers trained by Weld at Lane Seminary in Cincinnati, at Oberlin College, or at various institutions in New York) and about a dozen American Home Missionaries, like the Yale Band who helped found Illinois College, were in positions as clergy and antislavery agents in Illinois.[26] The Rev. John Cross, a former American Anti-Slavery Society agent from the Northeast, and Dr. Richard Eels in Quincy (and others) recruited and organized Underground Railroad transportation. After Lovejoy's death, Illinois abolitionists also felt the need for an antislavery newspaper to keep them united, and William T. Allan, Weld's disciple, briefly an agent for the American Anti-Slavery Society, later for the antislavery *Western Citizen*, reported from Iroquois County, "There are a few decided antislavery men in that region ... but feel no personal responsibility—see nothing for them to do—favor gradual emancipation, colonization ... a good deal of East Tennessee antislavery in this part of the state. Some of it is genuine, and some theoretic. I like to see *practical, working* abolitionists."[27] Western abolitionists took Weld's mantra—"He works for humanity and not for fame"—to heart. The *Western Citizen* mail books are filled with lawyers, doctors, carpenters, merchants, ministers, bankers, coopers, shoemakers, laborers, teachers, stone masons, and farmers.[28] Some kept their politics under wraps, because Illinois voted viva voce (paper ballots were not used until 1848), which exposed men to ridicule or danger if voting against the majority.

Zebina Eastman's editorial work in Illinois, Indiana, Wisconsin, Iowa, and beyond melded the various factions, ensuring diversity of thought with no "tests of fellowship"—political or religious. Eastman, who emigrated from Vermont, had assisted Benjamin Lundy, an early Quaker abolitionist-editor who had also mentored Garrison, on the *Genius of Universal Emancipation* in Illinois as an interim paper to Lovejoy's *Alton Observer*. After Lundy's sudden death, he partnered with Hooper Warren, an editor who had supported Governor Coles with his paper, the *Edwardsville Spectator*, and produced the *Genius of Liberty* at Lowell.[29] Underfunding soon ended that paper, but abolitionists Dr. Charles V. Dyer, L. C. P. Freer, Philo Carpenter, Calvin DeWolf, and others proposed to bring Eastman to Chicago to inaugurate the *Western Citizen* as a Liberty Party organ as well as antislavery newspaper. Practical abolitionism was repeatedly emphasized, illustrated, and taught in the *Western Citizen* through reprinted speeches, court cases of freedom seekers and whites who aided them, minutes of antislavery societies, market prices for grain and commodities complete with shipping schedules (for transport of goods and the self-emancipated).

Eastman knew that the western antislavery impulse could not withstand the factionalism of eastern abolitionism and be effective in Illinois, so he continued Allan's call for a practical abolitionism. Ohio, fifteen years ahead in statehood, already was a well-organized two-party state, with the Whigs carrying the antislavery sentiment. Simplifying resolutions from abolitionist societies into the Liberty Party's "One Idea" helped keep western abolitionists from sidetracking into factions. Eastman said Lundy's "leading idea was armed with ten-fold more force than Garrison's immediatism or Gerrit Smith's unconstitutionality of slavery."[30] After a contentious Baptist church trial, the defense of Allan Pinkerton, an agnostic antislavery proponent and Lincoln's future bodyguard, was litigated through the *Western Citizen*'s editorial pages.[31] Readers understood that just because someone was religious did not mean they were antislavery. Eastman walked a fine line of garnering support from churches and ministers without making someone's denomination or lack of religion a test for party membership. A rival paper, the *Illinois Republican*, sent a note to the Communications page, "'Brother Eastman'.... None but a 'knave and a fool' would ever attempt to get up a cross between the 'Spirit Divine' and 'party spirit.'"[32] Eastman risked broadening the antislavery appeal across party and denominational divides. He supported candidates and encouraged his readers to follow what an incumbent or candidate did rather than how they answered questions.

Between 1842 and 1855, Eastman, with a succession of associate editors and contributors, while crediting Lundy, cemented the "One Idea," the abolishment of slavery that undergird abolitionists' political affiliations with the Liberty, Free Soil, Free Democrat, and Anti-Nebraska Parties through to becoming a plank in the nascent Republican Party.[33] He, with Ichabod Codding and Owen Lovejoy, spearheaded the transformation of antislavery societies in Illinois into political action groups thus changing the stigma of the "dirty abolitionist" into a vision of an active citizen even though promoting black education, freedom, or rights was labelled as "agitating."

Black Chicago abolitionists John Jones, Henry O. Wagoner, H. Ford Douglas, James D. Bonner, Henry Bradford, Barney L. Ford, Alexander Smith, Joseph H. Barquet(te), Rev. Abraham T. Hall, and their respective wives and families advised repeal of Black Laws, created vigilance committees, and were delegates to national and state black conventions. Free Black abolitionists statewide collaborated with white abolitionists, trusting them to provide resources to aid their cause and to speak truth to white voters and jurists who determined their fate.[34] Wiecek says the moderates inserted their views on "human brotherhood" in the Liberty Party platform of 1844, along with restoring equal rights. But he goes on to say that after 1844,

> Westerners dominated Liberty affairs, led by Chase. The Ohio Libertymen included Gamaliel Bailey, editor of the *Philanthropist* [and later, the *National Era* of Washington, DC], Samuel Lewis, Stanley Matthews (future justice of the Unites States Supreme Court), the brothers Edward and Benjamin F. Wade, James H. Paine, Edward S. Hamlin, and Leicester King. In Illinois, Zebina Eastman ... and Owen Lovejoy ... spoke for the party.... The emergence of western and moderate leadership within the Liberty party was signalized by the Southern and Western Liberty Convention, held in Cincinnati ... which had been called in an effort to broaden Liberty's appeal to Whigs and Democrats.

Eastman and other white Chicago abolitionists had already proved their support and partnership with the city's Black abolitionists on the underground railroad, literacy efforts, work toward repealing Illinois's Black Laws, and on local as well as national political issues. They lived their views of egalitarian and inclusive citizenship even as their party began being known as "expedients." As the national Liberty Party modulated its more radical stances, the core of the Illinois leadership stayed radical in relationship with their Black friends. Its leaders invited prominent Black speakers like H. Ford Douglas from Illinois, Sojourner Truth and Henry Bibb from Michigan, and Frederick Douglass from New York as stump speakers. Yet, they were moderate in constitutional views and political coalitions.[35]

Eastman's alliance with Ichabod Codding and Owen Lovejoy persuaded their staunch abolitionist and religious following to vote as a bloc to sway elections. Codding, under the tutelage of Weld, was a forceful speaker who melded antislavery appeal with the Gospel. In 1836 in Vermont, Eastman had been impressed by the content and delivery of his antislavery sermon, so when Codding visited Illinois in 1843, Eastman asked him to stay and work with agents Chauncey Cook, William T. Allan, John Cross, Edward Mathews, and Alanson St. Clair.[36] Owen Lovejoy, the brother of slain Elijah Lovejoy, also partnered with these agents, covering circuits for the Liberty Party as well as churches. His work as a farmer, minister, and political candidate gave him an appeal that confounded his detractors. As he avoided serious legal consequences for harboring the self-emancipated at his farm, his wit and wily escapes from deputies cemented his reputation as a fearless defender for freedom.[37]

As the Liberty Party waned nationally after 1848, Eastman kept political affiliations fluid, always advocating for the party carrying an antislavery plank. What became clear in Illinois was that it had one of the strongest Liberty Party constituencies and was well on its way to breaking the Jacksonian Democrats' power in the state by holding the balance of power in elections and getting antislavery candidates elected to local office and the General Assembly. As historian Reinhard O. Johnson summed up:

> no two states' parties conducted their Liberty affairs in exactly the same way, but certain regional nuances distinguished parties in the Old Northwest from those in many eastern states. . . . The distinctions had more to

do with intra-party relations within the states than any great policy disagreements. The ability and willingness of state party members in the Northwest to compromise on issues that caused problems in some eastern states clearly distinguished them from some areas in the East. Even though the overwhelming majority of Liberty men in the Old Northwest were transplanted New Englanders and New Yorkers, they did not bring moral absolutism in party affairs with them.... There was more internal bickering in the East.... [B]y the mid-1840s ... the Liberty Party devoted itself more exclusively to electoral matters ... accompanied by a less moralistic and more secular approach among many elements in the party ... [and] was part of the transition ... from political protest to the political involvement that led to the Free Soil merger ... [with] a larger constituency that encompassed disfranchised African Americans and women.[38]

While reverence for revolutionary ideals did not make abolitionism special, it did make it seem reasonable and not as radical as reputed as others saw the compatibility of beliefs in God's laws and natural rights. The strengthening of the federal fugitive slave laws in 1850 resulted in open defiance of the new regulations and Black laws in northern Illinois and other midwestern states. However, it was the repeal of the Missouri Compromise through the Kansas-Nebraska Act along with its popular or "squatter" sovereignty in May of 1854 proposed by Illinois politician Stephen Douglas that moved more white Illinoisans to oppose the spread of slavery in the territories. Moreover, the disaffected anti-Nebraskan factions of conscience Whigs, Democrat barnburners and Jeffersonians, and remaining Free-Soilers could find common ground with the formerly despised abolitionists on the strength of opposing the spread of slavery. The 1857 Dred Scott decision was further proof that the Slave Power had reached the judicial branch. The ineffectual Whigs and doughfaces accelerated the rise of third parties to contain the Slave Power before it spread. The Republican Party was founded in a conscious effort to keep liberty national and cordon off slavery in states where it existed. Lincoln and the new coalition refined their message, taught the fundamental founding principles, and instilled deep loyalty to a free Union.[39]

Duty to personal and public freedom and civic democracy in their most simple forms as representation, equal rights, and suffrage was also part of the antislavery plan, even though it came later for African Americans and still later for women. Suffrage in colonial America was a landed, white man's privilege. People believed deeply that a landed person was more invested and proved interest in the country. Westward expansion also changed that view as historian Allan Johnson explains: "The reaction of West upon East has too often been overlooked.... Yet there can be no doubt that it was the theory and practice of manhood suffrage in the new states which led the older Eastern States one by one to abandon their restrictions. This democratization of the East was a slow process. The nineteenth century was nearly spent before the conservatives abandoned their last stronghold."[40]

Historian Stanley Harrold says, "Carl F. Wieck argues weakly that in 1854 [Theodore] Parker influenced Lincoln through Herndon, and that Lincoln deliberately concealed Parker's impact on him. Whether or not this was the case, during the mid-1850s politically oriented Illinois abolitionists Codding, Eastman, and Lovejoy had more direct influence on Lincoln than any northeastern abolitionist leader, including Parker."[41] It could be argued that Lincoln did not need influencing, he just needed a constituency, and that antislavery men voting as a bloc could swing elections. And even though early on in his reentering politics Lincoln did not want to be associated with abolitionists (nor with the Know-Nothings), he began to admire their political savvy. His private agreement with their hatred of slavery was soon to become public. However, Eastman and other abolitionists had to be convinced that Lincoln was truly antislavery, because too many politicians had fooled them.

Eastman later wrote to William Herndon, Lincoln's law partner, that he traveled to Springfield in 1856 to see "what were Mr. Lincoln's particular feelings and scruples in regard to the [people of color] of the United States. I wanted to know if he was their friend—if he was their friend, we knew he was a politician that could be trusted.... You remember that after that, as long as I printed the *Western Citizen* or *Free West* it was sent to your office. I supposed Mr. Lincoln read it some times.... After that visit I told all my Liberty Party friends to stand by Abraham Lincoln."[42] Despising abolitionist, party, and religious factionalism, Eastman recollected,

> But there were anti-slavery people among all these sects, excepting the non-resistants, who believed in the saving power of the Declaration of In-

dependence. They believed in the necessity of continuing to administer the national government on the principles of the Declaration of Independence, and that failing to do so, all political parties had gone into a state of apostasy. The reform in Illinois, particularly, was propagated on this basis. Antislavery men here were trained to be so, on the truths of the Declaration of Independence. They were never divided or troubled with the divisions that characterized the east, under the stringent lead of Garrison, Gerrit Smith or Greeley. They fellowshiped all these, but followed the lead of none of them. They were working for a genuine liberty party to administer the government on the constitution as it is under the Declaration of Independence. It is necessary that this explanation and distinction be understood.[43]

Eastman's practical approach helped form a broad coalition of antislavery midwesterners. That seemingly irrefutable statement of the Declaration became the touchstone of agreement that the abolition of slavery—not the abolition of the union or abolition of the church—was the remedy for a sick nation and sick culture. This stance softened the public's perception that abolitionists propagated civil disorder with a judgmental, pious, divisive reform that westerners despised.

The Lincoln–Douglas debates honed Lincoln's arguments against slavery and for the preservation of the Union. The practical Illinois abolitionists gave Lincoln a ready example of hitching ideals to actions even as each kept one hand on their Bible and the other on their ballot. Historian William E. Dodd provides a closer differentiation by saying that the winds of antislavery shifted into a more conservative vein and that the

> policy of Lincoln in 1858 had been radical. The leaders of Illinois had taken the "bit in their teeth" in 1858 and defied Seward, Weed, Greeley, and Crittenden, all of whom favored a tacit support of Douglas and had held a conference in Chicago prior to the senatorial campaign in Illinois and had given Douglas assurance of their support. Lincoln's fight had been for principle, not simply for victory, while the great men in his party had held aloof and half wished for his failure.... The Republicans of the Northwest had built up a machine, an insurgent organization on the basis of human rights as against the rights and immunities of property. But the election of 1858 seemed to show that idealistic principles of the Declaration of Independence

do not win majorities in this country. The gains in Indiana, Illinois, and Iowa legislatures of that year were far from commensurate with the known growth of the anti-slavery counties.[44]

Meanwhile, Douglas was reaping chastisement from Buchanan and the Fire-Eaters for opposing the Kansas-Nebraska act in the senate thus enraging the administration and "slave power." It was no longer acceptable within the party to countenance dissension with the losses of Northern Democrat seats over the Kansas-Nebraska act. In not towing the Southern Democrat line by accepting the Lecompton constitution, Douglas was undermined in his reelection efforts in 1858 by party operatives in Chicago and elsewhere in Illinois. He was stripped of his chair of the Committee on Territories. One of Douglas's biographers observed, "The Republicans were relegated at times to the role of bystanders as the battle raged among Democrats."[45] His influence as a proslavery politician and consummate doughface never recovered on the national stage or in his home state, and any remaining question as to whether there was a Slave Power was answered by secession.[46]

The Republicans soon had to play defense after John Brown's raid on Harpers Ferry. Southerners were terrified the raid signaled that the abolitionist conspiracy was in play. Lincoln and his advisors read the tenor of the situation and strategized further messaging. Since neither Douglas's popular sovereignty nor Brown's violence satisfactorily answered the Constitution and territorial questions, Lincoln made the Republican antislavery constitutional answer at Cooper Union. He assured listeners that no one was going to abridge the rights of states where slavery already existed but that freedom was the preference and goal for new territorial acquisitions. At the Wigwam in Chicago, the delegates laid moderate antislavery constitutionalism, revolutionary ideals, and homesteading as planks in their platform, entrusting Lincoln to carry through. As the Democracy splintered, the Republican coalition remained solid enough to gain a plurality of votes. The proslavery Democrats were wounded as the newly minted Republicans elected Lincoln to the presidency, and the Slave Power declared war on the union to preempt, as they saw it, any move to abolish slavery in their states.

Some historians, among them Merton Dillon, say the antislavery movement failed because armies and coercion abolished slavery but not racism.

And while it was true racism was abundant in Illinois and throughout the Old Northwest, it is also true, for a moment in history, the battle for freedom and democracy overshadowed the exclusions. Another historian, Theodore Calvin Pease, sums up the development of Illinois thus:

> Society..., conventionalized and stiff, posing in every intellectual attitude, original in nothing had had a change worked in it. Men had come to think broadly in terms of general political principles; they had come to think more independently on the set forms of law, of slavery, and ... of the set dogmas and forms of church doctrine and discipline. The Illinois of 1818 like the nation it existed in was dreaming dreams and interpreting the future in terms of the past; in the Illinois of 1848, there were many men of vigorous mind who had visions of the future.[47]

The so-called antislavery project was only the beginning of a greater equality project, which saw the Constitution amended to rectify injustices, and it is still working today. However, it was the practical abolitionists of the West who led a renewed commitment to the American experiment, which was essential to making good on their promises to their Black partners and friends. Freedom and democracy were not given to African Americans, women, and immigrants by white men but were fought for and redrafted together in the antislavery movement of the western expansion. Indeed, the antislavery project could not have happened in any other place.

Notes

1. Michael A. Morrison, *Slavery and the American West: The Eclipse of Manifest Destiny and the Coming of the Civil War* (Chapel Hill: Univ. of North Carolina Press, 1997), 4, 5. See Jon K. Lauck, *The Good Country: A History of the American Midwest 1800–1900* (Univ. of Oklahoma Press, 2022), 20–50; James G. Birney to Joshua Leavitt, Oct. 30, 1837, in *Letters of James G. Birney,* ed. Dwight L. Drummond, 2 vols. (New York: D. Appleton-Century, 1938), 1:428–32; Robert Trendel, "Joshua Leavitt" (MA thesis, Southern Illinois Univ., 1969), 57. See also Reinhard O. Johnson, *The Liberty Party, 1840–1848: Antislavery Third-Party Politics in the United States* (Baton Rouge: Louisiana State Univ. Press, 2009), 164–221; Leonard L. Richards, *The Slave Power: The Free North and Southern Domination 1780–1860* (Baton Rouge: Louisiana State Univ. Press, 2000), 11–13.

2. J. Brent Morris, *Oberlin: Hotbed of Abolitionism—College, Community, and the Fight for Freedom and Equality in Antebellum American* (Chapel Hill: Univ. of North Carolina Press, 2014), 24–44; Stacey M. Robertson, *Hearts Beating for Liberty: Women Abolitionists in the Old Northwest* (Chapel Hill: Univ. of North Carolina Press, 2010), 32–36. See also Dana Elizabeth Weiner, *Race and Rights: Fighting Slavery and Prejudice in the Old Northwest, 1830–1870* (DeKalb: Northern Illinois Univ. Press, 2013); Julie Roy Jeffrey, *The Great Silent Army of Abolitionism: Ordinary Women in the Antislavery Movement* (Chapel Hill: Univ. of North Carolina Press, 1998), 86–93; Susan Zaeske, *Signatures of Citizenship: Petitioning, Antislavery, and Women's Political Identity* (Chapel Hill: Univ. of North Carolina Press, 2003); Kate Masur, *Until Justice Be Done: America's First Civil Rights Movement, From the Revolution to Reconstruction* (New York: W. W. Norton, 2021), 86, 87.

3. Sean Wilentz, *No Property in Man: Slavery and Antislavery at the Nation's Founding* (Cambridge, MA: Harvard Univ. Press, 2018); Paul Finkelman, "Slavery, the Constitution, and the Origins of the Civil War," *OAH Magazine of History* 25 (Apr. 2011): 14–18; James Oakes, *Freedom National: The Destruction of Slavery in the United States, 1861–1865* (New York: W. W. Norton, 2013), 26–48. See also Eric Foner, Introduction to *The Second Founding: How the Civil War and Reconstruction Remade the Constitution* (New York: W. W. Norton, 2019); William M. Wiecek, *The Sources of Antislavery Constitutionalism in America, 1760–1848* (Ithaca, NY: Cornell Univ. Press, 1977), 202–10; "Arnold Buffum," Rhode Island Heritage Hall of Fame website, https://riheritagehalloffame.com/arnold-buffum/; James Oakes, *Crooked Path to Abolition: Abraham Lincoln and the Antislavery Constitution* (New York: W. W. Norton, 2021), 54–98.

4. Judith L. Van Buskirk, "Claiming Their Due: African Americans in the Revolutionary War and Its Aftermath" in *War and Society in the American Revolution: Mobilization and Home Fronts*, ed. John Resch and Walter Sargent (DeKalb: Northern Illinois Univ. Press, 2007), 133–36; Asa B. Brown, "That Rhetorical Flourish!!!" *Western Citizen* (Chicago), Jan. 27, 1843.

5. Oakes, *Crooked Path to Abolition*, xiv; Corey M. Brooks, *Liberty Power: Antislavery Third Parties and the Transformation of American Politics* (Chicago: Univ. of Chicago Press, 2016), 40.

6. See Robert Michael Morrissey, *Empire by Collaboration: Indians, Colonists, and Governments in Colonial Illinois Country* (Philadelphia: Univ. of Pennsylvania Press, 2015); John Craig Hammond, *Slavery, Freedom, and Expansion in the Early American West* (Charlottesville: Univ. of Virginia Press, 2007); Nichole Etcheson, *The Emerging Midwest: Upland Southerners and the Political Culture of the Old Northwest, 1787–1861* (Bloomington: Indiana Univ. Press, 1996), 102.

7. Hammond, *Slavery, Freedom, and Expansion*, 6–7.

8. Ibram X. Kendi, *Stamped from the Beginning: The Definitive History of Racist Ideas in America* (New York: Bold Type, 2016), 53–54.

9. See Stephen Middleton, *The Black Laws in the Old Northwest: A Documentary History* (Westport, CT: Greenwood, 1993).

10. Frank Cicero Jr., *Creating the Land of Lincoln: The History and Constitutions of Illinois, 1778–1870* (Urbana: Univ. of Illinois Press, 2018), 44–68.

11. M. Scott Heerman, "In a State of Slavery: Black Servitude in Illinois, 1800–1830," *Early American Studies: An Interdisciplinary Journal* 14 (Winter 2016): 114–39.

12. James A. Rawley, "Stephen A. Douglas and the Kansas-Nebraska Act," in *The Nebraska-Kansas Act of 1854*, ed. John R. Wunder and Joann M. Ross (Lincoln: Univ. of Nebraska Press, 2008), 70–71.

13. David Ress, *Governor Edward Coles and the Vote to Forbid Slavery in Illinois, 1823–1824* (Jefferson, NC: McFarland, 2006), 3.

14. In *Democracy and Slavery in Frontier Illinois: The Bottomland Republic* (DeKalb: Northern Illinois Univ. Press), James Simeone characterizes the outcome as a "slim majority" of 1,668 votes (5–6). However, it was a 57-to-42 percent split in favor of no convention—a sizeable majority in any election. For a fuller discussion on how Thomas Jefferson was memorialized by antislavery rhetoric, see Michael F. Conlin, *One Nation Divided by Slavery: Remembering the American Revolution While Marching toward the Civil War* (Kent, OH: Kent State Univ. Press, 2015), 37–71. In Illinois, invoking Thomas Jefferson as a founding father and friend legitimized Coles's cause, but as the abolitionists continued their press for political power, using Jefferson's words undercut the Jacksonian Democrats who dominated the state from the 1830 to the 1850s and connected to them.

15. See pamphlet by the Society for the Mitigation and Gradual Abolition of Slavery throughout the British Dominions, *An Impartial Appeal to the Reason, Justice, and Patriotism of the People of Illinois on the Injurious Effects of Slave Labour* (Philadelphia: Ellerton & Henderson, Gogh Square, 1824).

16. Suzanne Cooper Guasco, "The Deadly Influence of Negro Capitalists: Southern Yeomen and Resistance to the Expansion of Slavery in Illinois," *Civil War History* 47 (Spring 2001): 7.

17. Hermann R. Muelder, *Fighters for Freedom: A History of Anti-Slavery Activities of Men and Women Associated with Knox College* (New York: Columbia Univ. Press, 1959), 121. For a fuller discussion, see Merton Lynn Dillon, "The Antislavery Movement in Illinois: 1824–1835," *Journal of the Illinois State Historical Society* 47 (Summer 1954): 149–66.

18. Sylvester C. Watkins Sr. "Some of Early Illinois' Free Negroes," *Journal of the Illinois State Historical Society* 56 (Autumn 1963): 495–507.

19. See Sundiata Keita Cha-Jua, *America's First Black Town: Brooklyn, Illinois, 1830–1915* (Urbana: Univ. of Illinois Press, 2000); Cheryl Janifer LaRoche, *Free Black Communities and the Underground Railroad: The Geography of Resistance* (Urbana: Univ. of Illinois Press, 2014); Anna-Lisa Cox, *The Bone and Sinew of the Land: American's Forgotten Black Pioneers and the Struggle for Equality* (New York: Public Affairs, 2018).

20. For discussions on antislavery churches, see John R. McKivigan, *The War against Proslavery Religion: Abolitionism and the Northern Churches, 1830–1865* (Ithaca, NY: Cornell Univ. Press, 1984); Linda Jeanne Evans, "Abolitionism in the

Illinois Churches, 1830–1965" (PhD diss., Northwestern Univ., 1981). See also Morris, *Oberlin*, a study on the impact of religion and the antislavery cause.

21. Zebina Eastman, "History of the Anti-Slavery Agitation, and the Growth of the Liberty and Republican Parties in the State of Illinois," in *Discovery and Conquests of the Northwest with the History of Chicago*, ed. Rufus Blanchard, 2 vols. (Chicago: R. Blanchard & Co., 1900), 1:135.

22. For a more complete picture of violence against abolitionists, see David Grimsted, *American Mobbing, 1828–1961: Toward Civil War* (New York: Oxford Univ. Press, 1998). Grimsted says there were seventy attacks on abolitionists, "about 6.6 percent of the nation's total and 18 percent of the mobs in all the free states east of the Mississippi. . . . [P]roperty damage was more extensive, with presses, churches, and meeting halls the favorite targets" (35).

23. Cicero, *Creating the Land of Lincoln*, 85, 86.

24. Wendell Phillips, "On the Murder of Lovejoy." *The World's Famous Orations. America: I (1761–1837)*, ed. William Jennings Bryan (New York: Funk & Wagnalls, 1906), reprinted at *Bartleby*, New York, 2003, www.bartleby.com/268/.

25. Wendell Phillips, "John Brown and the Spirit of Fifty-Nine," *Democratic Thinker* (blog), Nov. 20, 2013, https://democraticthinker.wordpress.com/2013/11/20/wendell-phillips-on-the-john-brown-affair/.

26. Charles Henry Rammelkamp, *Illinois College: A Centennial History 1829–1929* (New Haven: Yale Univ. Press, 1928), 1–39.

27. William T. Allan, "Report," *Western Citizen*, Jan. 4, 1844.

28. See Peter Willging's spreadsheet identifying the demographics of *Western Citizen* and *Free West* 1843–1855 mail books for DeKalb County: ser. 2, vols. 1842–80s, box 1, folder 1A, Zebina Eastman Research Collection at Chicago History Museum, Abakanowicz Research Center; also Edward Magdol, *The Antislavery Rank and File: A Social Profile of the Abolitionists' Constituency* (New York: Greenwood, 1986).

29. See Merton L. Dillon, *Benjamin Lundy and the Struggle for Negro Freedom* (Urbana: Univ. of Illinois Press, 1966).

30. Eastman, "History of the Anti-Slavery Agitation," 138.

31. In the spring of 1847, a series of articles and communications appeared in the *Western Citizen* detailing the trial, outcomes, and varying opinions from readers and participants.

32. Illinois Republican, "Brother Eastman," *Western Citizen*, June 15, 1847.

33. Reinhard O. Johnson, *The Liberty Party 1840–1848: Antislavery Third-Party Politics in the United States* (Baton Rouge: Louisiana State Univ. Press, 2009), 240–41.

34. See Hamilton Primary School website, Otter Creek Historical Society, 2019–24, hamiltonprimaryschool.com; Christopher Robert Reed, *Black Chicago's First Century* (Columbia: Univ. of Missouri Press, 2005), 98; Masur, *Until Justice Be Done*, 199.

35. See William F. Moore and Jane Ann Moore, *Collaborators for Emancipation: Abraham Lincoln and Owen Lovejoy* (Urbana: Univ. of Illinois Press, 2014). Wiecek, *Sources of Antislavery Constitutionalism*, 218.

36. Hannah Maria Preston Codding, "Ichabod Codding," *Proceedings of the State Historical Society of Wisconsin, 1897* (Madison: State Historical Society of Wisconsin, 1898), 7–9.

37. See Edward Magdol, *Owen Lovejoy: Abolitionist in Congress* (Rutgers, NJ: Rutgers Univ. Press, 1967), 52–148.

38. Reinhard O. Johnson, *The Liberty Party 1840–1848: Antislavery Third-Party Politics in the United States* (Baton Rouge: Louisiana State Univ. Press, 2009), 240–41.

39. For a fuller discussion of antislavery political coalitions, see Graham A. Peck, *Making an Antislavery Nation: Lincoln, Douglas, and the Battle Over Freedom* (Urbana: Univ. of Illinois Press, 2017).

40. Allan Johnson, "Illinois in the Democratic Movement of the Century: An Address Delivered at the Centennial Meeting of the Illinois State Historical Society, Apr. 17, 1918," *Journal of the Illinois State Historical Society* 11 (Apr. 1918): 8.

41. Harrold, Stanley, *Lincoln and the Abolitionists* (Carbondale: Southern Illinois Univ. Press, 2018).

42. Zebina Eastman to William Herndon, Jan. 2, 1866, in *Herdon's Informants: Letters, Interviews, and Statements about Abraham Lincoln*, ed. Douglas L. Wilson, Rodney O. Davis, and Terry Wilson (Urbana: Univ. of Illinois Press, 1998), 149, 150.

43. Eastman, "History of the Anti-Slavery Agitation," 137. See also Matthew Karp, "The People's Revolution of 1856: Antislavery Populism, National Politics, and the Emergence of the Republican Party," *Journal of the Civil War Era* 9 (Dec. 2019): 524–45.

44. William E. Dodd, "The Fight for the Northwest, 1860," *American Historical Review* 16, no. 4 (1911): 780, 781.

45. Robert W. Johannsen, *Stephen A. Douglas* (New York: Oxford Univ. Press, 1973), 722.

46. See Richards, *Slave Power*, 190–215; For a close discussion of the mechanizations of four Southern Democrats to control Congress in the 1850s, see Alice Elizabeth Malavasic, *The F Street Mess: How Southern Senators Rewrote the Kansas-Nebraska Act* (Chapel Hill: Univ. of North Carolina Press, 2017).

47. Theodore Calvin Pease, *The Frontier State: 1818–1848* (Urbana: Univ. of Illinois Press, 1987), 442.

Chapter 3

Ohio

At the Heart of History

KEVIN F. KERN AND GREGORY S. WILSON

In 1984, the Ohio Division of Travel and Tourism adopted "Ohio, the Heart of It All" as its official slogan to promote tourism. Although Ohio's vaguely heart-shaped borders played into its creation, the slogan also reflected a rejection of the state's Rust Belt image and then current disparaging references to Ohio as "flyover country" and an embrace of the idea of Ohio's centrality to American life and history. The state sought to combat the popular perception of the Midwest more generally: a region, as Andrew Cayton and Susan Gray argue "widely seen as the cutting edge of Western civilization in 1800" that had come "to be perceived as a cultural cul-de-sac" by the early twentieth century.[1] Similarly, we embrace the notion that, despite its sometimes bland public perception, Ohio, like the Midwest itself, has been at the center of major historical events and trends from prehistoric times to the present. Yet, at the same time, we argue that it has also paradoxically served to exemplify a place anywhere *but* the center in the popular imagination: the "Upper Country," the Frontier, the West, the Midwest, the Rust Belt. The US conquest, settling, and development of Ohio (and the Midwest more generally) may have been focused on "the West" perceived as distinctly different from the East, but it was also a central and transformative event for the country as a whole.

We examine here this paradox of how the physical and political place called Ohio has been concurrently both a distant, different dividing line between East and West and a space for various cultural exchanges and ideas and political and economic trends that have been central to—and defined so much of—US and North American history.

In his preface to the first edition of *Ohio and Its People,* George Knepper wrote: "States love to boast of their unique aspects, but Ohio's claim to fame is the antithesis of uniqueness. Indeed, Ohio's most important quality has been its representative character."[2] The state contained a "broad sampling" of people in the nineteenth and early twentieth centuries, whether native born from various states and regions or immigrants, Blacks or whites. No single group could dominate. Even later, Knepper wrote, "no single population center dominates the state as in Michigan or Illinois," and "no single crop dominates its agriculture" and no one industry its manufacturing. This proved challenging to Knepper as a historian: "One cannot generalize about the people of Ohio." The state possessed, and perhaps still does, a "balance" between northern and southern influences, industry and agriculture, urban and rural. It has been called the "westernmost of the eastern states and the easternmost of the western states." The state serves as a testing ground for various consumer products and political preferences. Stories and academic treatises alike use Ohio towns and cities as "typical" American places.

But we argue that instead of blandness or flyover country, Ohio's representativeness means its centrality to the major events of North American history, indeed global history, from prehistoric times to the recent past. Ohio was a critical part of the "conquest, settlement, and development of what we call the Midwest," one "of the most important events in the past quarter millennium of human history."[3] It has been a meeting ground for what historians acknowledge as important human events and transformations: prehistoric sites from the Adena and Hopewell, a Middle Ground among Native peoples, Euro-Americans, and African Americans, connections to the economic, transportation, and communication revolutions of the early to mid-nineteenth century, and the immigration, urbanization, and industrialization of the late nineteenth and early twentieth. Again, as Cayton and Gray have shown for the Midwest, unlike the South or New England, Ohio's story "was not about alienation from either the market or the nation. On the contrary, it was about near total identification with both."[4] It was home to eight US presidents and has been a political battleground in presidential elections. In short, our chapter explores via a general survey, moving chronologically, many of the key themes from this book: blurring the line between "east and west" and the transference of ideas and cultures. In *The Lost Region,* Jon Lauck reminds us of the Midwest's "influence on the course of American and global history."[5] Ohio's place in shaping the course of history is equally profound.

Yet, recent trends point to less optimistic ends. Since the 1970s, Ohio has led in more negative economic and social characteristics. Rather than being a place for leading innovation with a growing population, Ohio has fallen behind other states. Deindustrialization hammered Ohio and challenged its status as a central economic powerhouse. Recent economic development might alter this path, however. Additionally, it is also unclear whether Ohio will retain its status as a bellwether political battleground. It is no longer perceived as part of "the West," but in keeping with its paradoxical image, even its status as a midwestern state has come into question. While most Ohioans consider themselves midwesterners, in 2014, only a little more than half of self-identified midwesterners nationwide surveyed considered Ohio a midwestern state. Ohio is in danger of losing both its centrality to major events and its broader identity as a midwestern state. If it is part of the East, then it is an outlier at least politically, as the state may no longer be a battleground—emerging as a strong Republican state in a region that tends to favor Democrats in a polarized political environment.[6]

Prehistory: A Cultural Mecca

With the Appalachian foothills to the east, Lake Erie to the north, and the Ohio River to the south, Ohio occupies a geographically unique space on the North American continent. Straddling a continental divide that separates the Great Lakes and Mississippi watersheds, the state marks a transition both from the East Coast to the great central part of the continent stretching to the Rocky Mountains and from its northern to its southern river drainages. It also boasts several different landforms, including the Appalachian Plateau, Lake Plains, and Till Plains, each of which have their own unique resources. Quite apart from any human connections, what is now Ohio in an objective geographic sense represents part of North America's center, and these features loomed large in its subsequent prehistoric and historic development.[7]

Even in human cultural terms, the concept of Ohio's centrality is ancient. During the period of the Adena and Hopewell cultural traditions (circa twenty-eight hundred to fifteen hundred years ago), the area that is now Ohio was a cultural Mecca for the central North American continent. By the peak of the Hopewell era, the Hopewell Interaction Sphere—the reach of its cultural influence—extended throughout much of the eastern part of the continent, from Canada to Georgia in the east and along the Mississippi Valley from Minnesota to Texas in the west. The mounds and earthworks constructed during this period were among the most elaborate in all of North American prehistory. Recent archaeological research indicates the builders had standardized measurements and a relatively sophisticated understanding of geometry and astronomy. The area was also a major hub in the flow and exchange of exotic goods. Burial mounds contained marine shells from the Gulf and Atlantic coasts, silver from eastern Canada, native copper from the Upper Great Lakes, chalcedony from the Dakotas, and even obsidian from the Yellowstone area, nearly seventeen hundred miles away. As a hub of trade and a place of cultural exchange, the upper Ohio River valley—and especially the area between the Miami and Muskingum Rivers—was central to the Native peoples of central North America for hundreds of years.[8]

While the Ohio country's ceremonial centrality waned in the centuries after the Hopewell period, the region continued to be a place of cultural mingling and transference for much of the rest of prehistory. By the cusp of European contact, there were at least five different major cultural traditions in what is now Ohio: what archaeologists call the Fort Ancient, Monongahela Woodland, West Erie Basin, Sandusky, and Whittlesey complexes. Archeological investigations suggest that that this was a period of cultural diversity and probably conflict. Population levels rose during this period, as sedentary maize agriculture became the predominant lifeway and crops and villages demanded protection. Groups of people began moving in from the east and south into this fertile area and among these preexisting populations. Ohio was now a contested space among various groups who viewed its land and resources worth defending.[9]

1600-1800: A Middle Ground

The arrival of Europeans enlarged and exacerbated these contests. To the French, Ohio was part of the larger *pays d'en haut*, or upper country, comprising the Great Lakes region upstream from the major French settlements along the Saint Lawrence River Valley. This was the geographic center of the so-called French Crescent of North America, extending from the mouth of the Saint Lawrence River through the Great Lakes and down to the mouth of the Mississippi. To the British, it was "the West," the seemingly natural extension of its settler colonial empire on the East Coast. To its Native groups like the Shawnee, the Ohio Valley was literally the "Center of the Earth," which the Master of Life had created for them. What is now Ohio was a friction zone not just between the French and British empires but also among the various Native groups that called it home.[10]

Ohio's importance to North American and global power politics of the mid- to late 1600s was abundantly clear during the so-called Beaver Wars and their aftermath. These were a suite of conflicts that arose in response to European demand for furs and from preexisting competition among different Indian groups around the Great Lakes. Key players were the great Haudenosaunee (Iroquois) and Wendat (Huron) Confederacies, but the struggles also included other Indigenous peoples who surrounded the Great Lakes. A primary objective of these conflicts was control over the prolific Ohio Country hunting grounds. The Haudenosaunee emerged triumphant by the 1660s and then undertook a concerted effort to chase out all other people from what is now Ohio so that they alone could exploit its resources. The many conflicts—combined with the influx of more lethal weapons and pathogens from Europeans—proved disastrous to Native populations, including the erstwhile victors. In the wake of waning Haudenosaunee power in the early 1700s, the Ohio area became a haven and shatter zone to the refugees of the conflicts around the Great Lakes. They moved in along the major river drainages and formed multiethnic autonomous "republics" that resisted control by any group—European or Indigenous. The independence of these residents of such a key location vexed and challenged French, British, and Haudenosaunee alike.[11]

The relationships among the French, Indigenous peoples, and British in the Great Lakes region made the upper Ohio River valley part of what historian Richard White refers to as a Middle Ground—a place in which multiple cultures intermingled and vied with each other but which none could control completely. While Ohio Indigenous groups sought self-determination from Haudenosaunee and European control, the Ohio Country was becoming a linchpin of both French and British imperial designs. Its strategic importance prompted the French to dispatch military missions there to keep its Indian allies in line and to build a chain of forts to defend it. These actions led Great Britain and its colonies to counter these moves and secure the contested Ohio Country for themselves. By the mid-1700s, Ohio Seneca leader Tanaghrisson (known as "Half-King" by the British) said the Native peoples of the upper Ohio River valley lived in "a Country Between" the contending French, British, and colonial interests. It is no coincidence, then, that the spark starting the French and Indian, or Seven Years' War came from Virginia militia (under a young George Washington)—assisted by Tanaghrisson—attempting to secure the critical headwaters of the Ohio River against French control. This region—and, more importantly, the Native people living in it—proved crucial to the war's outcome. After Ohio Native groups and the Haudenosaunee declared their neutrality in the 1758 Treaty of Easton in exchange for guarantees that the Ohio Country would be safe from further colonial encroachment, the French position in North America became untenable. Without their Indigenous allies, the French were forced to abandon the Ohio Country, and less than a year later they met defeat at the Battle of Quebec. In the eighteenth-century global contest of empires, Ohio and its people played a key role even as those empires also perceived it as standing on the geographical periphery.[12]

The following fifty years witnessed a series of conflicts in and around Ohio as the British government, its colonies, the United States, and various Native American groups vied for control of the area. British violations of the Treaty of Easton—including the building of a new fort near what is now Sandusky—led to the Native American Resistance of 1763 (also known as Pontiac's War). The first fort to fall in this conflict was that very Fort Sandusky, and Ohio Natives were key players in the sieges of Forts Detroit and Pitt. Great Britain's response to the conflict was essentially a restoration of the Middle Ground through policies such as the Proclamation of 1763 and the Quebec Act of 1774, which sought to reserve the western lands for its Native groups and to regulate the profitable trade with them.[13]

Even as the British government tried to preserve Ohio as an Indian territory, its American colonies had other designs on the area. Historians commonly count the Proclamation of 1763 and the Quebec Act (the latter of which colonists labeled as one of the Intolerable Acts) as precipitating events of the American Revolution because they fostered colonial discontent by foiling intense interest in the fertile lands of the Ohio Country from both landless farmers and well-connected speculators in the east. In 1774, Governor Lord Dunmore of Virginia used an Indian raid as a pretext to launch a military expedition into Ohio designed to secure the colony's claim to the land. Lord Dunmore's War ushered in another phase of conflict in and around Ohio that lasted through the American Revolution and beyond. Some of the war's most infamous episodes took place on Ohio soil—the Pennsylvania militia's massacre of the Christian Lenape community at Gnadenhutten foremost among them—and the fighting there lasted long after the Battle of Yorktown. Some of the final shots of the Revolution were fired at Old Chillicothe (near present-day Oldtown, in Greene County), when George Rogers Clark attacked the Shawnee village on November 10, 1782.[14]

The end of the Revolution did not resolve the conflict over Ohio. Expanding settlement into the West became a key goal of the new United States, and the country's earliest concerted military actions under the Constitution were a series of campaigns against the Northwest Indian Confederacy in what is now western Ohio. In its attempt to halt further US encroachment into Middle Ground Ohio, the Confederacy dealt devastating defeats to expeditions led by Josiah Harmar and Arthur St. Clair in 1790 and 1791. Although these occurred on the periphery of US authority, they proved central to Washington's initiative to reorganize and reform the nation's armed forces. A country previously averse to standing armies now saw the formation of a larger, more effective US Army that not only defeated the Northwest Confederacy at the Battle of Fallen Timbers but also decisively put down the Whiskey Rebellion months later. The subsequent Treaty of Greenville cleared Indigenous claims to most of Ohio and made it a central focus of western settlement. Even so, Ohio would continue to be a focus of Indigenous resistance to the United States, with the rise of the Shawnee prophet Tenskwatawa and his brother Tecumseh in the early nineteenth century. Further, the state was a major front of the War of 1812, until Oliver Hazard Perry's victory at the Battle of Lake Erie ended centuries of Ohio being a contested space. These actions finally ended Ohio's Middle Ground status.[15]

1800-1860: From Periphery to Center

Although now part of "the West," Ohio was central to the nascent United States' imperial project. Thomas Jefferson predicated his vision of an Empire of Liberty—articulated even before the Revolution was over—on the westward expansion of the United States and its founding ideals to new territories. Ohio was the first testing ground of this idea, the guinea pig of US expansion. As the birthplace of the US public land system and the first territory officially settled by the new country, Ohio hosted the first implementation of the Land Ordinance of 1785 and the Northwest Ordinance—the documents that ultimately charted the course of US territorial assimilation. Virtually all of the other territories incorporated into the United States followed the lead established by the Ohio experiment. Paradoxically, through the conflicts and treaties of the 1790s-1810s, Ohio also proved to be a key testing ground for country's subsequent Indian removal and reservation policies, which were inextricably linked to its construction of an "Empire of Liberty."[16]

Yet even at the advent of United States—when Ohio was still firmly part of "the West" in the popular mind—the idea of the Ohio Country's potential as "the Heart of It All" had already taken hold among some of the most well-connected and influential individuals in American society. As early as the 1750s, Benjamin Franklin opined that the Ohio Country's "natural advantages" had fated it to become "a populous and powerful dominion; and a great accession of power" to the nation that would control it.[17] George Washington himself was an avid speculator in—and promoter of settlement to—the lands of the Ohio Country, extoling them as a rich source of minerals and farmland. Manasseh Cutler, a New England minister and tireless lobbyist for the Ohio Company of Associates, enthused that the region between Lake Erie and the Ohio River would become "the garden of the world, the seat of wealth, and the *center* of a great Empire."[18]

Ohio grew into these expectations with remarkable rapidity. Demographically, the state rose from having one of nation's smallest populations at the time of statehood to boasting the third largest in the Union by 1840, while Cincinnati became the first midwestern city to rank in the country's top ten. The state accepted migrants from all regions of the country: northeasterners primarily to the northern counties, southerners primarily to the southern counties, and mid-Atlantic settlers everywhere else. Adding to these the increasing numbers of European immigrants and African Americans seeking to escape slavery or to find opportunity, Ohio found itself one of the most diverse states in the Union by 1850: more than any other state at the time, its population represented that of the country as a whole.[19]

Ohio's resources and strategic location aided in its remarkable growth. The interdependent transportation and market revolutions intersected powerfully in Ohio. Ohio's canal system for the first time connected the Great Lakes and Ohio River watersheds, which made the state a crucial link in a transportation network stretching from the Gulf of Mexico to New York City and beyond. The subsequent railroad system turned Ohio into a major national transportation hub, with more railroad track mileage than any other state by 1860. The mines of its Appalachian Plateau, the factories of its burgeoning cities, and the productive farmland of its Lake and Till Plains provided Ohio with a naturally diverse economy that lifted it to be among the top three states in most measures of manufacturing and agriculture. Ohio typifies this blend of factories and farms that embodies midwestern identity. As the first state carved out of the public land system west of the Appalachians, Ohio had a head start in establishing the mercantile and industrial firms providing the raw materials and manufactured goods fueling westward expansion. Within a single generation, Ohio had shifted from being the frontline of US westward expansion to being one of the primary economic engines driving it further.[20]

Ohio's immense demographic and economic growth helped propel corresponding growth in political influence. With the third-largest congressional delegation and share of the Electoral College, the state quickly became a major force in national politics, producing its first president in 1840, with William Henry Harrison's election. Its diverse and representative population increasingly turned Ohio into a powerful swing state in national elections and one of the key players in the construction of the new party system in the years before the Civil War. Northern Ohio was a major base of the Free-Soil Party, which helped to split and destroy the Whigs as a national party. Some of those Free-Soilers—especially influential politicians like Salmon Chase—played a major role in the formation and rise to prominence of the new Republican Party of the 1850s. Ohio's strong association with the early GOP put it in a position to benefit from the party's dominance in the generation after the Civil War.[21]

Ohio's large and representative population also made it a central focus of the reform movements of the early nineteenth century. The diverse origins of its population meant that the state hosted an extremely diverse array of religious traditions and religious reform movements. The most radical of these reformers attempted to create utopian or religious-based communities, and Ohio became home to more of these than any other state, including five Shaker settlements, the German separatist community at Zoar, the Congregationalist-planned college and community at Oberlin, and the Latter-Day Saints community at Kirtland. Ohio was also a hotbed of the broader and more mainstream Second Great Awakening and its associated reform movements. Influential Presbyterian minister Lyman Beecher had cofounded the American Temperance Society and brought his zeal for the movement when he came to preside over Cincinnati's Lane Seminary in the 1830s. Charles Grandison Finney, often called the Father of Modern Revivalism, moved to Ohio to become a professor at Oberlin in 1835. Beyond religious reform, Oberlin also represented Ohio's central place in educational reforms of the era, such as admitting women and African Americans as official students. In addition, Joseph Ray's arithmetic texts and William Holmes McGuffey's readers—originally written and produced in Cincinnati—combined with Ohio's 1849 and 1853 influential school laws to model primary educational reforms for the entire country.[22]

Perhaps no reform movement was more famous or ultimately successful than the transatlantic abolition movement of the late 1700s and early 1800s. Although New England is usually associated with the rise of American abolitionism, Ohio was central to the movement. Its antislavery role began even before statehood. Under the provisions of the Northwest Ordinance, it was the first free territory brought into the United States. Other neighboring territories followed suit, helping to ensure that slavery would be a regional, rather than a national, institution. Ohio's diverse religious reformers—especially those among its growing Society of Friends (Quaker) community—were influential in the movement: Ohio produced the first abolitionist newspaper (Quaker Benjamin Lundy's *Genius of Universal Emancipation*), and Beecher's daughter Harriet

Beecher Stowe wrote perhaps the most influential piece of abolitionist literature—*Uncle Tom's Cabin*—based on her experiences with the movement in Cincinnati. Also from Cincinnati was Quaker businessman Levi Coffin, who became known as the president of the Underground Railroad for his tireless efforts in helping thousands of slaves escape to freedom. Oberlin College and its surrounding community played a disproportionate role in the abolitionist movement, drawing national attention through its outspoken promotion of emancipation and racial equality and its unapologetic and open violation of the Fugitive Slave Law. These culminated in the famed Oberlin-Wellington Rescue Cases of 1858–59, in which the campus and community banded together to rescue a captured enslaved person from the authorities and spirit him to Canada. This event and its participants' subsequent trials garnered headlines across the country and drew the ire of Southern proslavery and secessionist forces. The social activism of its resident abolitionists combined with its key geographic location between the slave states and Canada helped make Ohio the central trunk of the Underground Railroad.[23]

It was this atmosphere that fostered and radicalized the young John Brown. His stern abolitionist father had raised him in the northeast Ohio community of Hudson—where as a child he aided his father's Underground Railroad work and as a man in 1837 he publicly vowed in the local Congregationalist Church to destroy slavery. While Brown did not live to see the end of slavery, his actions in Kansas and Harpers Ferry (the latter of which also included participants of the Oberlin-Wellington Rescue) helped bring about the US Civil War; and when that war came, no state was more central to Union success than Ohio. Ohio, for example, produced more horses for the Union army and more wool for its uniforms and blankets than any other state and ranked among the top three for most other commodities. Beyond giving the Union the benefit of its immense agricultural and productive capacity, the state also gave more men per capita to the Union army—including such important figures as Generals Grant, Sherman, and Sheridan—than any other state. As the only state linking the eastern and western contiguous parts of the Union after Kentucky declared its neutrality, Ohio was literally central to the country, and it remained a crucial transportation hub for the Union for the duration of the war.

Ohio emerged as a social, economic, and political center in the immediate postwar years. Ohioans were front and center in the battle over Reconstruction. Two of the most prominent leaders of the Radical Republicans were Senator Benjamin Wade and Representative John Bingham, the latter the primary author of the Fourteenth Amendment. Congressman James Garfield also rose to prominence as a Civil War hero and Radical Republican and used that to win the presidency in 1880.[24] Senator John Sherman of Ohio, brother to William Tecumseh, authored the first Reconstruction Act in 1867. And when the feud between Congress and President Andrew Johnson reached a boiling point, Representative James Ashley of Toledo introduced the impeachment resolution. Bingham led the House committee that presented the charges against Johnson. Presiding over Johnson's trial in the Senate was Ohioan Salmon Chase, the chief justice of the US Supreme Court. Impeachment failed, but Johnson was finished as a political force.

On the other side of the debate, Ohio's Democrats were national figures during the Civil War era as well, befitting the state's battleground reputation. Perhaps the most prominent among them was Clement Vallandigham. A lawyer from Dayton, he was recognized as the foremost opponent of Lincoln and leader of the Peace Democrats, or Copperheads, as their enemies called them. While other Democrats joined Republicans in a Unionist Party for the Civil War, Vallandigham stuck to his guns and lashed out against Lincoln and all who would support him. Exiled to the South by Lincoln in 1863, he eventually made his way to Canada where he ran, and lost, in absentia for Ohio governor that year.[25]

1870-1970: A Century at the Center

For a period of about a hundred years, Ohio continued its place at the center of the major transformations and movements of American history, and in some cases global history. Ohioans were among those who defined the era, or set the tempo for innovation, whether in technology, politics, or culture. Those in Ohio and many outside the state saw it as a place of importance, a state that attracted commerce and capital, people, and movements. Rather than representative of something bland and backward, the state and its sons and daughters were among those driving change. In this era, Ohio mirrored the Midwest as "great meeting ground of ethnicity and culture" that "helps explain the American character or at least creates the perception of Midwesterners as the archetypical Americans."[26] As Wilbur Wright stated in 1910, "Ohio stands at the gateway between East and West" whose "sons" "possess the boundless energy and enthusiasm of the West, and combine it with the salt of conservatism of the East."[27] In this period, geographic perceptions of Ohio shifted from being part of "the West" to part of a new region, the Middle West, or *Midwest,* a term that came into use in the 1910s.

It is fair to say that after the Civil War, the Midwest embodied the massive transformations brought about by the Second Industrial Revolution in the United States. Ohio was central to many of these. Industries centered on resources such as coal, oil, and natural gas helped with the rise of other industries, such as railroads, glass, machine tools, and steel. Dayton was home to the Wright Brothers, James Patterson's National Cash Register Company, and Delco, founded by Charles Kettering. Akron became the Rubber Capital of the World, with four major tire manufacturing firms centered there: Goodyear, Goodrich, Firestone, and General Tire. Youngstown and Cleveland became leaders in steel production. The state's impressive list of innovators includes Thomas Edison of Milan, and Granville Woods of Columbus, popularly known as the Black Edison.[28]

Industrialization went hand in hand with population growth, and Ohio became a major destination point for migrants. This encouraged a further mixing of cultures, as native-born Ohioans mixed with whites and Blacks from the South and immigrants from southern and eastern Europe. Some 75 percent of Cleveland's residents were nonnative born, and around the turn of the twentieth century one could hear some forty different languages as these immigrants worked and lived amid the warrens of factories and neighborhoods of the sprawling city. Additionally, countless other folks traveled through Ohio, as the railroads moved people and products across the nation as they had done before the Civil War.[29]

Not only industries and cities made Ohio the heart of this era, so did the many protests, reform movements, and labor clashes. The revival of the temperance and prohibitionist movements began in Ohio with what would become nationally important organizations, the Women's Christian Temperance Union and the Anti-Saloon League. Ohio was at the heart of the progressive movement that followed. Prominent leaders included mayors Tom Johnson of Cleveland and Sam "Golden Rule" Jones of Toledo, and governor and 1920 Democratic presidential nominee James M. Cox. Author and activist Harriet Taylor Upton led the charge for women's rights and became the first woman to serve on the Republican National Executive Committee. Hallie Quinn Brown was a national leader for African American education, temperance, and women's rights. Massillon's Jacob Coxey led "Coxey's Army," the first major protest march on Washington, DC, during the depression of 1893–97. Major unions got their start in Ohio, among them the United Mine Workers and the American Federation of Labor in the 1880s; later in the 1930s and 1940s, Ohio's workers were critical to the formation of the United Auto Workers, United Rubber Workers, and the United Steel Workers.[30]

Ohio's centrality and diversity meant the state retained its status as a battleground for major political parties. Ohio was among a handful of states in this period that were up for grabs for either major party. Elections were decided by razor-thin margins; only 1.4 percent separated the Republican and Democratic candidates in presidential contests between 1876 and 1892. Ohio was particularly important for the GOP. The state sent native sons Grant, Hayes, Garfield, Harrison, McKinley, Taft, and Harding to the White House. For a time in the industrial era, Ohio was home to more radical ideas as well. Although not an Ohioan, Eugene Debs was a midwesterner—a Hoosier—and was arrested in Canton, Ohio, in 1918, for giving an antiwar speech. He was there because Ohio witnessed a significant number of local officials embracing socialism, among them Max Hayes and Charles Ruthenberg of Cleveland. Ruthenberg went on to become one of the founders of the Communist Party USA, in Chicago, in 1919.[31]

Ohioans have been at the forefront in the arts and entertainment. The state boasts a long list of notables. Among the many nationally known writers through the first half of the twentieth century are Sherwood Anderson, Louis Bromfield (who would later create Malabar Farm), Charles Chesnutt, Hart Crane, Paul Laurence Dunbar, Zane Grey, William Dean Howells, Robert McCloskey, and James Thurber. Those who have earned national renown since the 1940s include Thomas Berger, Erma Bombeck, Lois McMaster Bujold, Jane Curry, Rita Dove, Harlan Ellison, Virginia Hamilton, Jerome Lawrence and his playwright partner Robert E. Lee, Lois Lenski, Toni Morrison, Andre (Alice) Norton, R. L. Stine, Mel Watkins, and James Wright. Ohioans contributed to the visual art world as well, with such notables as George Bellows, Charles Burchfield, Howard Chandler Christy, Robert Henri, Karl Kappes, Maya Lin, John Ruthven, Alice Schille, Viktor Schreckengost, Clyde Singer, and John Henry Twatchman.

Ohioans have also made their marks in sports. The Red Legs of Cincinnati was the first professional baseball team, and the formation of professional football started in Canton. Notable athletes include Larry Csonka, Ken Griffey Jr., Archie Griffin, Scott Hamilton, John Havlicek, LeBron James, Madeline Manning, Thurman Munson, Jesse Owens, Alan Page, Pete Rose, and Cy Young.

In popular music, disc jockey Alan "Moondog" Freed is credited with popularizing the phrase *rock 'n' roll* during his radio program on Cleveland's WJW. Largely for this, the city is home to the Rock & Roll Hall of Fame.[32] Ohio's many notable musical artists and groups include, to name just a few, The Black Keys, Doris Day, Devo, Chrissy Hynde, The Isley Brothers, John Legend, Art Tatum, Twenty One Pilots, and Bobby Womack. Among those in film and television are Halle Berry, Drew Carey, Dorothy Dandridge, Phyllis Diller, Clark Gable, Teri Garr, Patricia Heaton, Hal Holbrook, Paul Newman, Martin Sheen, Steven Spielberg, and Fred Willard.

This Second Industrial Revolution defined so much of the United States, as these major industries formed the backbone of the nation's economic might. Of course, the downside of this tremendous growth in manufacturing and technology was that the Great Depression of the 1930s fell hard on Ohioans. Unemployment rates were among the highest the nation in the state's major cities, especially in Akron, Cleveland, and Youngstown. When World War II came, these same places witnessed rapid growth, attracting male workers and female "Rosies" to provide war materiel. Akron contributed significantly to the synthetic rubber program, while Dayton played an important role in the Manhattan Project. The pilot of the *Enola Gay*, which dropped the first atomic weapon on Japan, was Columbus native Col. Paul Tibbets.[33]

Ohio's population grew in the post–World War II boom, from 6.9 million in 1940 to 10.65 million in 1970. Its factories and workers produced core manufacturing products, and its per capita income was above the national average. Cities remained strong, suburbs expanded, and even small towns saw more and more of the consumer age reach their doorsteps and living rooms.

Optimism surrounded Ohio sports. Teams were regular national contenders, including the Browns, Reds, Indians, and Ohio State football. Columbus native Jack Nicklaus dominated men's golf. It seemed Ohioans were indeed at the heart of the American experience, able to do anything—even orbit the Earth as John Glenn did or walk on the moon like Neil Armstrong.[34]

The World War II experience and massive expansion in consumer goods, wealth, and employment brought into sharper relief the inequalities of the boom's benefits. The veneer of consensus and normalcy masked a series of difficult issues. Southern Blacks organized some of the most famous events in the civil rights movement, including the Montgomery bus boycott and the integration of schools in Little Rock. Freedom Summer came about in 1964 as a mass voter registration drive in the South. It attracted hundreds of white college students from the North, and experienced civil rights workers like Robert Moses trained these students in nonviolence in Oxford, on the campus of what was then Western College for Women, now part of Miami University. While much attention went to the southern civil rights movement, Ohio and the Midwest experienced deep segregation and racial discrimination as well. Blacks were often denied access to suburban developments, education, and employment. Central cities witnessed more white flight and loss of businesses and their tax dollars. Ohioans helped drive the northern civil rights movement as they organized and demonstrated against these inequities. National leaders like Martin Luther King Jr. and Malcolm X came to Cleveland in support of local efforts. The city made history for electing Carl Stokes as the first African American mayor of a major city.[35]

Ohioans also contributed to second-wave feminism—famously through Ohio native Gloria Steinem, but grassroots organizations sprang up across the state. Women led marches, wrote letters, and pressured the mostly male legislators in Ohio to promote women's rights. One success was Ohio's approval of the Equal Rights Amendment in 1974, although momentum stalled nationally, and the amendment failed to gain the approval of thirty states. Ohio also drew national attention for two other iconic moments. The first was the 1969 fire on the Cuyahoga River. On the one hand, a burning river that oozed but didn't flow highlighted the negative effects of industrialization across the state and the nation. On the other hand, it galvanized the growing environmental movement. The second was at Kent State University in 1970, when members of the Ohio National Guard fired on protestors, killing four students and wounding nine others. The event captured the great divide over the Vietnam War but also the various political and cultural changes coursing through Ohio and American society.

Since 1970: Falling Behind?

If Ohio was central to so much of what we might consider national or even global history, how has the state fared since the 1970s? How representative has Ohio been, and what significant national and global trends and issues has the state either followed or led? For all the many positive things the post–World War II boom generated, there were clearly signs of trouble for Ohio. Once a major destination, the heart of it all, Ohio became a place that symbolized all that was wrong. It was the Rust Belt to America's Sun Belt, a state remembered for what it once was, no longer a place of excitement, hope, and innovation. Flyover country.

Deindustrialization is the flip side of the new economy based on services; as the steel industry declined in the 1970s and early 1980s, Ohio became infamous for shutdowns and demonstrations in Youngstown. But these stories of economic decline hit other Ohio cities hard as well, including Akron, Canton, Dayton, and Toledo. Major cities began a wrenching process of functional transformation—from manufacturing to services and entertainment, as well as a demographic transformation, with smaller, often poorer, populations. Some fared better than others; Columbus, for example, avoided the more devastating effects as its economy had the buffer of other industries besides manufacturing. Manufacturing still plays an important role in Ohio's economy but employs fewer workers. Its wages for production workers lag behind inflation rates. Ohio ranks third behind California and Texas in manufacturing employment, but it has still lost some 396,000 higher-paying manufacturing jobs since 1990. Ohioans have worked to reorient the state's economy, and innovative organizations and companies continue to compete, including a new Intel facility to produce computer chips scheduled to open near New Albany in 2027. Intel is calling this the new Silicon Heartland, and perhaps Ohio and the Midwest can capture more of these new developments, but the state ranks below average on research and development. It had represented the mainstream economy of the Second Industrial Revolution, but it is finding it hard to stay ahead in the twenty-first century.

Since 1970, Ohio's population has remained relatively stagnant while the United States as a whole and other states have grown. The state's population is also less diverse than the nation's. In 2020, just over 80 percent of Ohioans were white, compared to 64 percent of the United States. Other data points show Ohio either in the middle or at the bottom for good things and the top for bad ones. As of 2022, Ohio's median household income was $65,720, about $9,000 less than the national average. The state ranks twenty-sixth among states for income inequality, twenty-second in per pupil spending on K–12 education ($15,583), but only forty-first in per capita higher education spending ($692). Ohio spent $6,741 per full time enrolled student, which is 61 percent of the national average and down 17.4 percent since 1980. Its overall educational attainment level ranks thirty-fourth. The health and income issues go hand in hand with the recent opioid crisis, as Ohio was in the top five states in opioid death rates in the 2010s. As of 2023, Ohio was the third highest in overdose deaths. These data points reveal a state falling behind.[36]

In the arena of national politics, Ohio's status as a bellwether state remains uncertain. The Republicans have had a lock on state offices and representation in Congress since the 1990s. Ted Strickland was the lone Democratic governor (2007–11) in Ohio since the 1990s. Republicans have controlled the state Supreme Court since 1986, and the state legislature almost completely since 1995; only in 2009–10 did Democrats control the Ohio house. And the state is losing representation in Congress as its population declines, going from twenty-four congressional seats in the 1960s to fifteen in 2022. From the 1990s through 2012, Ohio was among a handful of states where presidential elections were decided by single digits. The 2016 election and Donald Trump upended the usual battleground map. Trump won Ohio by roughly 8 percentage points in both 2016 and 2020, although he lost the national popular vote in 2016 and both the popular and electoral vote in 2020. In both elections, Ohio voted over ten points further to the right than the nation as a whole. It remains to be seen whether Ohio becomes a state no longer of interest to Democrats hoping to capture the White House.[37] In this sense, Ohio might resemble other Republican strongholds in the Midwest, such as Indiana. Throughout the region, partisanship has grown, with urban areas more reliably Democratic and rural areas more reliably Republican.[38] As of mid-2024, Ohioans voted to enshrine abortion rights in the state constitution; whether this portends a shift back to the middle or not remains unknown.

Conclusion

In the minds of many, Ohioans and others included, the state has become synonymous with American normalcy, "bland and predictable" as Andrew Cayton has noted.[39] Jeffrey Hammond has celebrated Ohio's lack of distinctiveness as distinctive. Ohio, "one of those placeless places," is the necessary foil to more exciting identities. Ohio, Hammond says, "really *is* the whole country," a microcosm of America.[40] But despite being lumped in with the derogatory notion of the Midwest as flyover country, Ohio has been at the center of major historical events and trends from prehistoric times to roughly the middle of the twentieth century. The political place called Ohio has been a space for various cultural exchanges and ideas, for political and economic trends that defined so much of US and North American history. Yet it has also served as place outside the center, a distinctive place within names like the West, the Midwest, and the Rust Belt. Even as it was defined in such ways, Ohio served as a political bellwether, a blend of America that meant close elections among both major parties. Yet here, too, that might be changing as the state becomes more Republican and polarized, losing its battleground status. Demographically, the state looks less like America—older, whiter, less educated than average. Coming full circle, the state recently readopted the motto "Ohio, the Heart of It All." It remains to be seen if this recycled slogan is merely aspirational or if Ohio yet again serves as place between East and West, a microcosm of America.

Notes

1. Andrew R. L. Cayton and Susan E. Gray, "The Story of the Midwest," in *The Identity of the American Midwest: Essays on Regional History*, ed. Andrew R. L. Cayton and Susan E. Gray (Bloomington: Indiana Univ. Press, 2007), 3.
2. George Knepper, *Ohio and Its People*, 2nd ed. (Kent: Kent State Univ. Press, 1997), xi–xii.
3. Andrew Cayton, "General Overview," in *The American Midwest: An Interpretive Encyclopedia*, ed. Richard Sisson, Chistian Zacher, and Andrew Cayton (Bloomington: Indiana Univ. Press, 2007), xix.
4. Cayton and Gray, "Story of the Midwest," 10.
5. Jon K. Lauck, *The Lost Region: Toward a Revival of Midwestern History* (Iowa City: Univ. of Iowa Press, 2013), 14.
6. Walt Hickey, "Which States Are in the Midwest?," *FiveThirtyEight*, last modified Apr. 29, 2014, https://fivethirtyeight.com/features/what-states-are-in-the-midwest/.
7. Leonard Peacefull, *A Geography of Ohio* (Kent: Kent State Univ. Press, 1996), 1–15.
8. The literature on Hopewell archaeology is extensive. For some comprehensive analyses, see David S. Brose and N'omi Greber, eds., *Hopewell Archaeology: The Chillicothe Conference* (Kent: Kent State Univ. Press, 1979); Paul J. Pacheco, ed., *A View from the Core: A Synthesis of Ohio Hopewell Archaeology* (Columbus: Ohio Archaeological Council, 1996); and Brian G. Redmond, Bret J. Ruby, and Jarrod Burks, eds., *Encountering Hopewell in the Twenty-first Century, Ohio and Beyond*, vols. 1 and 2 (Akron: Univ. of Akron Press, 2019).
9. Bradley T. Lepper, *Ohio Archaeology: An Illustrated Chronicle of Ohio's Ancient American Indian Cultures* (Wilmington: Orange Frazer Press, 2005), 170–236.
10. Richard White, *The Middle Ground: Indians, Empires, and Republics in the Great Lakes Region, 1650–1815* (Cambridge: Cambridge Univ. Press, 1991); R. David Edmunds, "A German Chocolate Cake, with White Coconut Icing: Ohio and the Native American World," *Ohio and the World, 1753–2053: Essays Toward a New History of Ohio*, ed. Geoffrey Parker, Richard Sisson, and William Russell Coil (Columbus: Ohio State Univ. Press, 2005), 23.
11. White, *Middle Ground*, 1–222; Fred Anderson, *The War that Made America* (New York: Penguin, 2006).
12. White, *Middle Ground*, 223–68; Michael N. McConnell, *A Country Between: The Upper Ohio Valley and its Peoples, 1724–1774* (Lincoln: Univ. of Nebraska Press, 1992).
13. Kevin F. Kern and Gregory S. Wilson, *Ohio: A History of the Buckeye State*, 2nd ed. (Hoboken, NJ: Wiley-Blackwell, 2024), 67–98.
14. Kern and Wilson, *Ohio*, 67–98; David Skaggs and Larry Nelson, eds. *The Sixty Years' War for the Great Lakes, 1754–1815* (East Lansing: Michigan State Univ. Press, 2010).

15. Colin G. Calloway. *The Victory with No Name: The Native American Defeat of the First American Army* (New York: Oxford Univ. Press, 2016); Skaggs and Nelson, *Sixty Years' War.*

16. Kern and Wilson, *Ohio*, 100–123.

17. Andrew R. L. Cayton, "While We Are in the World, We Must Converse with the World: The Significance of Ohio in World History," in Parker, Sisson, and Coil, *Ohio and the World*, 6.

18. Andrew R. L. Cayton, "The Significance of Ohio in the Early American Republic," in *The Center of a Great Empire: The Ohio Country in the Early Republic*, ed. Andrew R. L. Cayton and Stuart D. Hobbs, (Athens: Ohio Univ. Press, 2005), 1–10.

19. Hubert G. H. Wilhelm and Allen G. Noble, "Ohio's Settlement Landscape," in Peaceful, *Geography of Ohio*, 80–108.

20. Kern and Wilson, *Ohio*, 160–212.

21. Kern and Wilson, *Ohio*, 185–244.

22. Kern and Wilson, *Ohio*, 125–59.

23. Kern and Wilson, *Ohio*, 125–59; J. Brent Morris, *Oberlin, Hotbed of Abolitionism: College, Community, and the Fight for Freedom and Equality in Antebellum America* (Chapel Hill: Univ. of North Carolina Press, 2014).

24. John B. Shaw, "James A. Garfield," in *Buckeye Presidents: Ohioans in the White House*, ed. Philip Weeks (Kent: Kent State Univ. Press, 2003), 115–40.

25. Kern and Wilson, *Ohio*, 226–29.

26. R. Douglas Hurt, "Midwest Distinctiveness," in Cayton and Gray, *American Midwest*, 160–79, 178.

27. "Wilbur Wright before the Ohio Society of New York," Jan. 10, 1910, in *The Papers of Wilbur and Orville Wright*, ed. Marvin W. McFarland, 2 vols. (New York: McGraw-Hill, 1953), 2:978.

28. See Neil Baldwin, *Edison: Inventing the Century* (New York: Hyperion, 1995); Mark Bernstein, *Grand Eccentrics: Turning the Century: Dayton and the Inventing of America* (Wilmington: Orange Frazer Press, 1996); Rayvon Fouche, *Black Inventors in the Age of Segregation: Granville T. Woods, Lewis H. Latimer, and Shelby J. Davidson* (Baltimore: Johns Hopkins Univ. Press, 2003); Fred Howard, *Wilbur and Orville: A Biography of the Wright Brothers* (New York: Knopf, 1987).

29. Andrew R. L. Cayton, *Ohio: The History of a People* (Columbus: Ohio State Univ. Press, 2002), 165.

30. Florence Allen, *The Ohio Woman Suffrage Movement* (Cleveland: Committee for the Preservation of Ohio Woman Suffrage Records, 1952); Jack S. Blocker Jr., *"Give to the Winds Thy Fears": The Women's Temperance Crusade, 1873–1874* (New York: Praeger, 1985); Stephanie Elise Booth, *Buckeye Women: The History of Ohio's Daughters* (Athens: Ohio Univ. Press, 2001); Tom Johnson, *My Story*, ed. Elizabeth J. Hauer (Kent: Kent State Univ. Press, 1993); Marnie Jones, *Holy Toledo: Religion and Politics in the Life of "Golden Rule" Jones* (Lexington: Univ. Press of Kentucky, 1998); Richard Judd, *Socialist Cities: Municipal Politics and the Grassroots of American Socialism* (Albany: State Univ. of New York Press, 1989); K. Austin Kerr,

Organized for Prohibition: A New History of the Anti-Saloon League (New Haven: Yale Univ. Press, 1985); Carlos A. Schwantes, *Coxey's Army: An American Odyssey* (Lincoln: Univ. of Nebraska Press, 1985).

31. R. Hal Williams, *Realigning America: McKinley, Bryan, and the Remarkable Election of 1896* (Lawrence: Univ. Press of Kansas, 2010).

32. See Kern and Wilson, *Ohio*, 399.

33. Mark Bowles, *Chains of Opportunity: The University of Akron and the Emergence of the Polymer Age, 1909–2007* (Akron: Univ. of Akron Press, 2008); Linda Carrick Thomas, *Polonium in the Playhouse: The Manhattan Project's Secret Chemistry Work in Dayton, Ohio* (Columbus: Ohio State Univ. Press, 2017).

34. See Kern and Wilson, *Ohio*, 428–30.

35. Jacqueline Johnson, *Finding Freedom: Memorializing the Voices of Freedom Summer* (Oxford, OH: Miami Univ. Press, 2013); Leonard Moore, *Carl B. Stokes and the Rise of Black Political Power* (Urbana: Univ. of Illinois Press, 2003).

36. "Drug Overdose by Mortality by State," Centers for Disease Control and Prevention website, accessed July 27, 2024, https://www.cdc.gov/nchs/pressroom/sosmap/drug_poisoning_mortality/drug_poisoning.htm; "State Health Facts," Kaiser Family Foundation website, accessed June 1, 2020, https://www.kff.org/statedata/; David A. Tandberg and Sophia A. Laderman, *Evaluating State Funding Effort for Higher Education*, MHEC Policy Brief, Midwestern Higher Education Compact, June 2018, https://www.mhec.org/sites/default/files/resources/mhec_affordability_series6.pdf; "State Profile: Ohio," State Higher Education Finance website, accessed May 14, 2024, https://shef.sheeo.org/state-profile/ohio/; "2022 Public Elementary-Secondary Education Finance Data," US Census Bureau website, page last revised Apr. 23, 2024, https://www.census.gov/data/tables/2022/econ/school-finances/secondary-education-finance.html; "American Community Survey," US Census Bureau website, page last revised June 18, 2024, https://www.census.gov/programs-surveys/acs/data.html; "Quick Facts: Ohio," US Census Bureau website, accessed June 15, 2020, https://www.census.gov/quickfacts/OH.

37. Charlie Mahtesian, "How Trump Rewired the Electoral Map," *Politico*, Feb. 7, 2020, https://www.politico.com/news/magazine/2020/02/07/election-2020-new-electoral-map-110496.

38. See Kevin Fahey, "What Happened? The 2020 Election Confirmed That Ohio Is No Longer a Swing State," *LSE Blogs*, London School of Economics and Political Science, https://blogs.lse.ac.uk/usappblog/2021/09/02/what-happened-the-2020-election-confirmed-that-ohio-is-no-longer-a-swing-state/.

39. Cayton, *Ohio*, 399.

40. Jeffrey Hammond, "Ohio States," *American Scholar* 70 (Summer 2001): 42–43.

Chapter 4

A Conversation of Conspiracy

Regionalism and the Unstable Politics of the Early Republic, 1787–1807

TIMOTHY C. HEMMIS

In a quiet neighborhood in Canonsburg, Pennsylvania, stands a moss-covered stone monument dedicated to the memory of Col. George Morgan and his estate, Morganza. Erected in 1928, the stone cenotaph commemorates Morgan as an "Ardent Patriot during the Revolution" and mentions how in 1806 he denounced Aaron Burr's treasonous plot and immediately notified President Thomas Jefferson. It also cites Morgan's work as a trader, explorer, and "progressive farmer and a friend of the Indians." During the Revolutionary War, the merchant Morgan became a commissioned officer and diplomat at Fort Pitt to Native Americans. A political squabble with Gen. Lachlan McIntosh left Morgan disgraced and disgruntled.

After the war, Morgan became involved in various land speculation plots, including the Spanish New Madrid scheme. Conveniently, the monument leaves out his virulent land speculations schemes and his work with the Spanish. In the late 1780s, Morgan openly recruited Americans to join the Spanish colony of New Madrid in present-day Missouri. The "Ardent Patriot during the Revolution" was willing to shed his new nation for financial stability. Morgan's honeymoon with the Spanish did not last long, as he abandoned New Madrid and returned home. Still, his efforts highlight the fluid nature of American loyalty. Forgotten by many, the Morgan monument stands as a testament to a conversation of conspiracy that took place in his home in the summer of 1806, which highlights the East–West regionalism and the unstable politics of the Early Republic.

Colonel George Morgan Monument, Canonsburg, Pennsylvania. (Photo by Timothy C. Hemmis.)

The most prominent part of the monument is Morgan's effort to foil Aaron Burr's plot, as Morgan and his sons were key witnesses against him in 1807. The Burr conspiracy illuminates the East–West divide in the Early Republic. Traditionally, the historical narrative focuses on the North–South sectionalism of Antebellum America; however, before the clear divide between the Mason-Dixon line there was also a geographic rift between East and West (today the Midwest). The East–West divide has been buried in the history of the America frontier. Frederick Jackson Turner's famous thesis often portrayed the American frontier as a region where the East tried to regulate and control the West; Turner rightfully recognized that there were independent regions in the United States.[1] However, he did not explore the events that helped shape this East–West regionalism—especially the seemingly anti-American episodes like the Burr conspiracy or George Morgan's New Madrid. Often in reaction to Turner, many twentieth-century historians became more interested in these questions: what was the real American West, and was there really a frontier?[2] These historiographic subjects often gloss over the East–West rivalry of the Early Republic. However, more recent scholars, such as Andrew Cayton and Peter Onuf, have also explored the East–West regionalism of the young republic. Both demonstrate that settling the American West, especially the Old Northwest in the 1780s, was critical to national interest and security.[3] Even President George Washington worried about the British and Spanish influence on the westerners. In a letter to Henry Knox, Washington wrote: "They will become a distinct people from us—have different views—different interests & instead of adding strength to the union, may in case of a rupture with either of those powers [British and Spanish] be a formidable and dangerous neighbor."[4] The East–West divide was a legitimate threat to the young republic, and national leaders understood what was at stake.

Morgan and Burr's 1806 conversation exemplifies the regionalism of the Early Republic as the country was still trying to figure out whether it was seventeen separate republics or one nation. After the late war, Morgan returned to the civilian world as a land speculator and merchant. In 1788, he briefly joined the Spanish to form a colony along the western side Mississippi River in present-day Missouri. The Spanish wanted to create a buffer colony in the interior of the continent, similar to what they did with Texas several decades later with Stephen F. Austin's colony. Because of Morgan's work at New Madrid, Burr sought out his old friend. Morgan seemed a favorable ally in his plot, but that notion proved to be a mistake. Ultimately, both Morgan's New Madrid adventure and Burr's conspiracy highlight the unstable nature of the Early Republic and how regionalism developed and evolved in a short period of time.

During the summer of 1806, George Morgan received a note from his old colleague and friend the former vice president of the United States, Aaron Burr, who insisted on having dinner with him. Their conversation centered on the country's East–West split, and Burr wanted to entice Morgan and his family to join his cause. Burr believed he could create a western empire, because there was an East–West political and cultural rift in the United States. However, he grossly miscalculated the situation.

Burr sought Morgan's help for many reasons, but chiefly for his experience and connections with the Spanish. In 1787, Morgan had worked with the New Jersey Land Society and attempted to get land on the east side of the Mississippi River settled; however, Congress stymied their plans. Morgan then approached Spanish minister to the United States Don Diego De Gardoqui, who resided in New York, about a new project. Gardoqui secretly wanted to recruit American farmers to populate the Spanish lands that bordered the young republic, to protect Spanish interests in Louisiana and Texas. Morgan's familiarity with the region made him a prime candidate for this mission. In the 1760s, as a young man, Morgan lived in the Illinois Country, where he had connections with the area's French, Spanish, and Anglo families.[5] Additionally, Morgan's unhappiness with the unstable national government under the Articles of Confederation led to his involvement with Gardoqui.

Economically, the American republic struggled, and many looked to the borderlands to solve their fiscal problems. One such group was the New Jersey Land Society, which had hired Morgan, the merchant, land speculator, Indian diplomat, and colonel in the Continental Army as its chief agent. The society wanted to purchase land in the Illinois Country containing the settlements of Kaskaskia and Prairie du Rocher. With this area, Morgan and the company proposed to create a new state, named Louisiana, in present-day Illinois. They offered Congress to pay "one third of a dollar per Acre" and dispose of any Indian claim that existed on the land.[6] It was a good deal for the company. Congress accepted the proposal with one small change: it increased the price to two thirds of a dollar per acre, which caused Morgan and the New Jersey Land Society to rethink the deal.

Not satisfied with Congress's counteroffer, Morgan abruptly ended the society's attempt to purchase the land. In addition to the price increase, Congress did not want to include the lowlands near the river in the purchase, which was exactly the land that Morgan and the New Jersey Land Society wanted for livestock. More importantly, those lowlands were crucial to free Mississippi River access. Morgan and his colleagues suggested, "The extreme unhealthiness of this Country arises from Lands being unimproved: the richest parts of them being Swamps, & Ponds; which being stagnant, corrupt the Air & produce malignant Distempers . . . having it in their power to drain these Lakes & Marshes [was necessary] for their own advantage." Additionally, they also opposed Congress's proposed land reserved for the French inhabitants.[7] Morgan believed Congress had given the French inhabitants some of the region's best lands. Because of these congressional stipulations, the New Jersey Land Society suddenly stopped its pursuit of the land. Despite congressional approval, Morgan left the New Jersey Land Society and moved onto his next project: Spanish New Madrid.

At the same time he schemed in Illinois; Morgan had also been in conversation with the Spanish minister Don Diego Gardoqui. It is unclear who initiated the connection, but Gardoqui met with several open-minded American adventurers—including George Morgan, John Brown (from the failed state of Franklin), and infamous Brig. Gen. James Wilkinson—to help the Spanish in their quest to control the Mississippi River Valley. Many Americans, especially those in the west, became enamored with the Spanish. Gardoqui's plan was to get several highly respected Americans to join the Spanish to create a buffer zone between the Spanish colonies and the Republic.

Morgan was no stranger to the Spanish. During the American War for Independence, he wrote to Governor Bernardo Galvez in 1777 encouraging an American raid on the British in West Florida.[8] His contact in New Orleans was merchant Oliver Pollock, an American agent, who, lived in New Orleans for several years following the Revolution. Morgan knew Pollock for many years as he traded with him and used his associates in New Orleans. Morgan's friendship with Pollock aided him in his bid for Spanish New Madrid.

Morgan's conversation with Gardoqui rejuvenated his personal desire for financial and political stability. The Early Republic before the Constitution was an uncertain environment that witnessed events such as Shay's Rebellion (1786–87). Morgan saw the Spanish New Madrid colony as an opportunity for a fresh start. In September 1787, Morgan proposed the colony. He was anxious to get out west, but before he left in 1788, he issued various demands for his personal security including a commission in the Spanish Army for him and his son, land, and sending his daughters to the finest Catholic schools in New Orleans. The New Madrid venture would set up the Morgan family for generations.

A patriot from the American Revolution, Morgan demanded the right to self-government and other republican ideals for the new colony. He argued that it was the only way to entice Americans west. Ambitiously, Morgan promised the Spanish that he could bring one hundred thousand people to settle in New Madrid. A difficult undertaking, but Morgan confidently believed he could guarantee such a large number.

Even without an approval in hand, Morgan steamed ahead in his plan for the Spanish colony on the western side of the Mississippi River. One of the first things he did was to name the colony, New Madrid, and he required the land be recorded with surveyors and geographers. He even asked his close friend Thomas Hutchins, the Geographer of the United States, to join him in his adventure. In early 1789, Hutchins planned to resign his position and join the Spanish colony.[9] However, he died before acting. Morgan also brought with him experience from his adventures in Illinois and lessons he learned from others. He applied this to his work in New Madrid. The Pennsylvanian demanded a variety of concessions, but unlike with his experience in the Illinois Country, Morgan wanted full authority over the new Spanish colony.

One of the greatest draws about moving to New Madrid was free access to the Mississippi. Morgan's proposal was a few years before Pinckney's Treaty (1795's Treaty of San Lorenzo) that granted Americans the free navigation of the Mississippi River and the right to trade in New Orleans without duties. Besides, Morgan promised the Spanish, "like many men of some wealth who are in the United States, become the vassals of the Spanish Majesty. If these proposals are accepted, [you] will convenient[ly] authorize me to grant passports for their purposes, or the proceeds of them in flour, Wheat, Flax, Hemp, Iron, Tobacco, Indigo, or other merchandise that will be able to carry New Orleans, the via of Ohio River."[10] Morgan believed that free trade on the Mississippi would be the most important incentive for emigrants.

Additionally, Morgan promised land grants to new settlers, but he reserved the mineral rights of gold and silver for the Spanish monarchy. Morgan believed that the economic pull of land would entice Americans to migrate to the new Spanish colony. He stated, "We have heard that Spain's policy does not grant his subjects in America the use of their property and [the freedom of] moving from one place to another without the permission of the Government, if it is wise to do so it will be an exception in favor of the establishment" of New Madrid.[11] Morgan wanted free movement of property including slaves in New Madrid. Ultimately, he wanted to eliminate any polices that would hinder the colony's commercial achievement.

Morgan wanted as many enticements as possible to increase movement to the new settlement. He believed economic success and stability was stronger than political and national loyalty (as it was with him) and the list of incentives he proposed bore that idea. In October 1788, Morgan began to publish handbills to advertise the new Spanish settlement.[12] The handbills proclaimed: "All Persons who settle with me at New Madrid and their posterity, will have the free Navigation of the Mississippi, and a Market at New Orleans, free from Duties, for all the Produce of their Lands."[13] Morgan played to the international and domestic problems that plagued the American farmers on the western frontier. He appealed to the economic significance of the Mississippi River, which was a major issue before the ratification of Pinckney's Treaty in 1795.

Hastily, Morgan began his expedition in winter of 1788–89, leaving Fort Pitt sailing down the Ohio River. Gardoqui believed in Morgan, stating, "I am nevertheless persuaded that what appears a serious forestalling proceeds from a desire to avail himself of the present state of this country and form his natural efficiency and perhaps from some little ill-will against this government from which he parted in disgust."[14] Still, Morgan was upset with the US government, because he had little faith in Congress under the Articles of Confederation, especially since it never recognized his previous land grants. So he went ahead with his Spanish plans, at huge personal risk, as he did not have final royal approval.

Morgan and his team set out from Pittsburgh in 1788 to survey New Madrid and to scout out the best lands for themselves. New Madrid was an open secret to both frontierspeople and American leaders. Reports from Morgan's adventure found their way to Gen. Henry Knox, Brig. Gen. Josiah Harmar, and other American leaders.[15] For example, Knox was well aware of Morgan's plan, as he mentioned "the artifices of Mr. Gardoqui and George Morgan" in the same letter as comments on the loyalist and British instigator Dr. John Connelly.[16] Furthermore, Gardoqui and Morgan also ran into competition from James Wilkinson's plan for Kentucky. Wilkinson, an American army officer and secret Spanish informant, worked with Governor Esteban Miro to foil Morgan's New Madrid, because he lobbied for Kentucky's monopoly on the Mississippi River if it became an independent state under the protection of the Spanish. Wilkinson believed that Kentuckians shared more in common with the Spanish than with the eastern states; therefore, he planned to separate Kentucky from the United States. Additionally, New Madrid threatened Wilkinson's Kentucky plan, because it would break his monopoly with the Spanish. An independent Kentucky provided the Spanish with leverage against the American Republic. Still, Morgan and Gardoqui's New Madrid colony also could wreck Wilkinson's scheme, as he secretly swore loyalty to the Spanish majesty. In 1789, with the governor's ear, Wilkinson effectively derailed Morgan's effort. Once Miro received Morgan's requests and conditions, Miro hesitated in giving his blessing. The governor cited that "the letter of Don Diego Gardoqui ... will show Your Lordship the ambiguity and the lack of clearness with which he writes me, keeping from me the conditions of the project of Colonel Morgan."[17] Unknown to Morgan, Wilkinson's persuasion forced Miro to balk at Morgan's plan for New Madrid.

Involved in many schemes on the American frontier, Gardoqui wanted to dislodge it from the United States and to construct barriers of protection between New Spain and the Americans. The Spanish planned to use the unstable political conditions in the United States to their advantage, drawing new subjects to their settlements. Gardoqui eagerly believed in Morgan's plans to build New Madrid because he saw it as an opportunity to draw Americans to the Spanish side of the Mississippi. He supported Morgan's early work to set up New Madrid, writing, "I believe that if H. M. [His Majesty] should be pleased to agree not a moment should be lost in giving orders to the Governor at New Orleans not to impede nor disconcert him and so cause the chance to fail." The mercantile and agricultural prospects of New Madrid were promoted as the major attractions for American immigrants. Gardoqui suggested, "No doubt Your Excellency will detect the allusions to my efforts to get these people [Americans] to place themselves under the protection of the King, impressing upon them the mercantile advantages that must result." Gardoqui believed he persuaded one of the most important Americans to his side to create a new colony in the interior of North America. Morgan's popularity would be an essential draw to entice new American settlers to New Madrid. Gardoqui reported, "I understand that the prudent people begin to fear the results of Morgan's project and the good that will accrue to those who settle among us." He bragged, "Many are those who have told me in confidence I have known how to avail myself of the occasion to secure one of the most important and best liked men of the country; so that, without vanity, I may be the acquisition of this person I am permitted the honor of serving H. M. with many thousands of vassals who by God's help will serve as a barrier to defend his just rights."[18] Gardoqui did his best to persuade the King to see the value of Morgan's New Madrid.

The Spanish favored western sectionalism and disquiet on the American frontier, because it created a barrier to protect their own interests. Gardoqui secretly wanted Morgan and other entrepreneurial Americans to give up their citizenship to create a new colony on the frontier, which would bolster Spanish claims in North America. Gardoqui also had dealings with the proposed frontier state of Franklin, an independence movement of the eastern area of Tennessee.[19] The people of Franklin even attempted to become the fourteenth state of the United States of America. However, that new state never materialized.

The American West in the 1780s was turbulent, filled with competing empires vying for control. The people of the frontier had to determine their own identities and loyalties. The western people often saw themselves differently than the eastern Americans, and because of the new American national government's failures some men looked for other options.[20] One of those frontier visionaries was George Morgan, who believed in Gardoqui's promises of American-like civil liberties coupled with the economic potential of the Spanish to continue on his mission for wealth.

The idea of economic freedom and opportunity was the principle one that enticed many of Morgan's followers to New Madrid. Morgan was willing to move himself and his family there for the promise of economic stability and the chance to make a profit on the frontier. In a letter to Governor Miro, Morgan laid out the reasons he chose to join the Spanish. He clearly stated: "Amongst other Inducements for leaving my Native Country, are the desire of improving my Fortune and the wish to establish my Family in Peace under a certain and secure Government." Additionally, Morgan also mentioned the Indiana land grant and how it was "unjustly deprived by the State of Virginia" and wrote, "It has been out of the Power of Congress to protect Us."[21] These motives pushed Morgan to work with the Spanish, and he was anxious to start New Madrid.

On February 14, 1789, Morgan and his party arrived at the mouth of the Ohio near present-day Cairo, Illinois. Under the pretense of approval, he commenced with the building of the colony. He launched his own agenda that ran contrary to the Spanish instructions. For example, Morgan offered 320-acre tracts of land, much larger than the Spanish recommended.[22] Additionally, he offered free lots to the first hundred settlers in the city of New Madrid. Miro did not approve these incentives. Furthermore, rumors swirled that Morgan had promised his clients a republican-style civilian government. These reports troubled the Spanish administration in New Orleans so much it they reprimanded Morgan. The Anglo-American apologized to Governor Miro for his actions, stating, "I beg of you to rest assured that I shall avoid the like mistakes in the future."[23]

Morgan's dream of his own colony did not last long. He quickly had a falling out with the Spanish, possibly about his salary and or more likely his political authority in New Madrid. By July 1789, Morgan traveled to New Orleans to meet with Miro to discuss his political position in New Madrid. With advice from Wilkinson, Miro bypassed Morgan and he appointed a new military commandant there: Pedro Foucher. Morgan did not approve of the young officer, and he saw his position as a personal slight. By the end of the month, Morgan set sail for Philadelphia and never returned to New Madrid. Additionally, when he arrived in Philadelphia, the new US Constitution had been ratified, which gave Morgan new hope for the Indiana Land Company and his other schemes. The nation's new government, coupled with the falling out with the Spanish, put Morgan on a familiar path. By the end of 1789 Morgan had abandoned the Spanish and the new colony at New Madrid to return to his estate in Prospect, New Jersey.

Morgan did not write directly about why he left the Spanish service, but he did leave a clue in a letter to Gardoqui, the Spanish minster in Philadelphia. He stated: "Our love of Liberty Civil and religious is our ruling Passion: Give us these & all Princes or Rulers & all Countries are alike to US: but they must be given as our Right & not as an Indulgence which we may be deprived of at Pleasure by any man or Sett of Men whatever. If Spain does not adopt this Idea in regard to forming her Settlements on the Mississippi She will have no Settlements there six Months after the first Dispute between her and the U.S."[24]

George Morgan had realized that without the political ideals and rights guaranteed by the American Revolution, the Spanish American colony of New Madrid could not last, because no American would want to move to a tyrannical Spanish colony. Economic incentives led to political actions. One could speculate that Morgan's business interests now aligned with his new political ideals of the American Revolution. Morgan wanted to reap the profits of western movement into the Spanish lands, but not without being exercising the new American political rights.

Morgan returned to the United States and eventually became a gentleman farmer just outside of Pittsburgh. He still remained hopeful of the getting a return on his Ohio land speculation schemes, but the federal government denied him and his companies. In 1796, western Pennsylvania became Morgan's home, when his brother left him his frontier estate, Morganza. The area had been the hotbed of resistance and defiance toward the new federal government during the 1794 Whiskey Rebellion. Although Morgan had not been involved in that rebellion, the frontier settlers saw themselves as a distinct people within the East–West divide in the young republic.

Beginning in 1791, the federal government imposed an excise tax on whiskey. Westerners in Pennsylvania and Virginia rebelled against the tax, and protests turned violent in 1794. In September, President Washington sent in a delegation to meet with the westerners to broker a peace. The federal delegation recommended that the army be sent to western Pennsylvania to ensure the amity.[25] With the prodding of Alexander Hamilton, Washington agreed and federalized a nearly thirteen thousand–man militia from Pennsylvania, Virginia, New Jersey, and Maryland. By October, the federal militia arrived in western Pennsylvania, and its mere presence ended the destruction of property and violence.

In the summer of 1806, seeking to use the East–West hostilities left over from the Whiskey Rebellion, the estranged Vice President Burr toured western Pennsylvania to recruit people to his side. He sought out his old friend Morgan, because he knew of his flirtation with the Spanish in 1788–89 and his assumed hatred of the federal government. Morgan lived in the heart of Whiskey Rebellion country, and while visiting the region Burr anticipated to persuade his old friend to join him.

On August 24, 1806, Burr sent word to Morgan that he was in the area and wanted to visit his homestead. Delighted to have an old friend visit, Morgan sent his sons to greet the former vice president and opened their home to him. Later that evening, after dinner, Burr revealed his vision for the future and his plot against the US government, based on the East–West regionalism and western expansion. At one point, Burr suggested that there would be more people west of the Alleghany Mountains than on the eastern coast. He believed those western lands would eventually break away from the eastern states. However, he wanted to speed that process up and mentioned that within five years he could raise a small army of westerners and easily take Washington, DC. He boasted that "with five hundred men, New York could be taken; and that with two hundred, congress could be driven into the Potomac River." During the dinner conversation, George Morgan responded to Burr, boldly claiming, "By God, sir with that force you cannot take our little town of Canonsburg."[26]

Burr also tried to persuade George's eldest son, John Morgan, an adjutant general in the New Jersey State Militia, to join him. Burr was curious as to whether the younger Morgan "could raise a regiment in Washington County; or whether I could raise one with more facticity in New Jersey." The conversation continued throughout the evening, Burr attempted to convince young George Morgan Jr. to join him on his military expedition. Burr suggested that "he should like to see George at the head of a corps of grenadiers; he was a fine, stout-looking fellow."[27] He openly talked about his plans, because he completely misread the Morgans and their political morality. The Morgans were extremely suspicious of Burr's motives against the fledgling republic. Although their political affiliation is unclear, because of George Morgan's friendship with Thomas Jefferson, one can surmise that they were republicans, and they acted in the nation's best interest by turning on Burr.

Burr recognized the significant differences between the western people and citizens in the eastern half of the United States. And he hoped that the westerners who were part of the Whiskey Rebellion would join in his plot to destroy the republic. He wanted to capitalize on the rebellion's leader David Bradford's popularity to bring westerners to his cause. Burr insisted that the Morgan boys take him to Washington, Pennsylvania. His request to meet Bradford was suspicious at best. Fortunately, John Morgan informed Burr that Bradford had escaped federal prosecution by running away to Spanish-held Baton Rouge. The former vice president also was curious about the Morgans' feelings toward the federal government. John Morgan stated, "Colonel Burr mentioned to me, that he had met with several, who had been concerned in the western insurrection: and particularly a major in the North-Western Territory (whose name I do not recollect) who had told him, that if he were ever engaged in another business of the kind, he pledged himself it should not end without bloodshed."[28] Burr wanted to exploit the East–West regionalism for his own gain.

So, after Burr left Morganza, George Morgan penned a frantic letter to his friend President Jefferson to alert him about the former vice president's intentions. Morgan's communication with Jefferson was one of the first accounts of Burr's treachery. In October 1806, Gen. James Wilkinson turned on his coconspirator Burr, when he sent Jefferson a ciphered letter from Jefferson as proof of his treason.[29] Burr's conspiracy was not just a rumor but a reality. In January 1807, Jefferson revealed to Congress his schemes against the nation. He reported, "I received intimations that designs were in agitation in the Western country, unlawful, & unfriendly to the peace of the Union; and that the prime mover in these was Aaron Burr."[30] Burr became public enemy number one, and he escaped to the southwest in an attempt to avoid capture.

On February 19, 1807, Lt. Edmund P. Gaines captured Burr in present-day McIntosh, Alabama, and the latter went to trial for treason against the United States of America in 1807.[31] He was sent to Richmond to stand trial. The trial began during the summer, and George Morgan and his sons were named as key witnesses. On August 19, 1807, the Morgans were called to testify. First, Gen. John Morgan took the witness stand; then his father,

George Morgan; and last, Thomas Morgan. The witnesses were questioned by both the prosecution and defense attorneys. Unprecedently, Burr, himself a lawyer, examined the Morgans. He brought up George Morgan's brief involvement with the Spanish along the Mississippi River. When he asked Morgan if he lived on the Mississippi, he responded "I did, with the approbation of my country, in order to take up and distribute lands to all my countrymen to the west of the Mississippi."[32] Burr showed Morgan's character as questionable at best, because of his past. Surprisingly, the trial ended in Burr's acquittal.

Despite Burr's exoneration, the case highlights the East–West regionalism that existed in the American Republic. Although both had unfortunate timing, men like Burr and Morgan were opportunists, whether in politics or business. Morgan's failure with the Spanish in 1789 forced him to return to the republic. Morgan's past with Spanish made him an attractive ally to Burr in 1806, which led to the conversation of conspiracy at George Morgan's homestead, which, in turn, led to one of the most infamous trials in American history and to the 1807 passing of the Insurrection Act. Burr's plot to dislodge the west from the eastern states was a legitimate threat to the young republic. George Morgan, now a firmly a Jeffersonian Republican, was well aware of the consequences of a civil war as he fought in the American War for Independence. He knew that Burr's schemes that manipulated the East–West regionalism would have been disastrous for the nation. Fortunately, the extreme East–West regionalism Burr counted on had already begun to wane with the republican Jefferson as president. Ultimately, Burr's plans to dislodge the West from the East failed.

The stone monument to George Morgan and his patriotic accolades now stands as a reminder of the complicated history of the American republic. It does not mention Morgan's own anti-American New Madrid scheme with the Spanish. The East–West regionalism that existed in the Early Republic would be eclipsed by the North–South sectionalism in the 1820s, but the stark cultural divide between the people west of the Appalachian Mountains and the East Coast remains to this day.

Notes

1. Frederick Jackson Turner, *The Frontier in American History* (New York: Henry Holt, 1921), 159.
2. There is a larger historiography that grapples with these two questions and the following is a selected list of scholarship in that debate: Henry Nash Smith, *Virgin Land: The American West as Symbol and Myth* (Cambridge, MA: Harvard Univ. Press, 1950; Donald Worster, *An Unsettled Country: Changing Landscapes of the American West* (Albuquerque: New Mexico Univ. Press, 1994; Richard Slotkin, *The Fatal Environment: The Myth of the Frontier in the Age of Industrialization, 1800–1890* (Norman: Univ. of Oklahoma Press, 1998); William Cronon, *Nature's Metropolis: Chicago and the Great West* (New York: W. W. Norton, 1991); Patricia Nelson Limerick, *The Legacy of Conquest: The Unbroken Past of the American West* (New York: W. W. Norton, 1987); and Jeremy Adelman, and Stephen Aron. "From Borderlands to Borders: Empires, Nation-States, and the Peoples in between in North American History," *American Historical Review* 104, no. 3 (1999): 814–41.
3. Andrew R. L. Cayton. ""Separate Interests" and the Nation-State: The Washington Administration and the Origins of Regionalism in the Trans-Appalachian West," *Journal of American History* 79, no. 1 (1992): 39–67; Peter S. Onuf, "Liberty, Development, and Union: Visions of the West in the 1780s," *William and Mary Quarterly* 43, no. 2 (1986): 179–213.
4. George Washington to Henry Knox, Dec. 5, 1784, *Founders Online*, National Archives, https://founders.archives.gov/documents/Washington/04-02-02-0137.
5. George Morgan was a junior partner with the Baynton, Wharton, & Morgan Company in Philadelphia, which wanted to create a trading monopoly in the Illinois Country when trading was limited by the British Crown.
6. George Morgan, "Memorial to Congress for the New Jersey Land Society," *Papers of the Continental Congress, 1774–1789*, item 41, 6: 510, Microfilm Publication M247, roll 51, Memorials Addressed to Congress, Record Group 360, National Archives, Washington, DC.
7. George Morgan, "Reasons Why It Will Not Suit the New Jersey Land Society to Make the Proposed Purchase," and *Papers of the Continental Congress, 1774–1789*, both from vol. 6, p. 514 of item 41.
8. George Morgan, "Morgan to Governor Bernardo Galvez, Apr. 22, 1777," box 2, folder 2b George Morgan Papers, Illinois History and Lincoln Collection, Univ. of Illinois Urbana-Champaign.
9. Thomas Hutchins to Daniel Clarke, Dec. 2, 1788, legajo 2370 Archivo General de Indias, Seville, Spain, via Historic New Orleans Collection..
10. George Morgan, "Translation of Colonel Morgan's Plan for the Establishment of a Colony of population on the Mississippi," in *Ĉonspiración española? 1787–1789*, ed. José Navarro Latorre, José and Fernando Solano Costa (Zaragoza: Institución Fernando el Católico, 1949), 244.

11. George Morgan, "Translation of Colonel Morgan's Plan," 244, 246.

12. George Morgan, "Handbill of the Settlement, October 3, 1788," in Max Savelle, *George Morgan; Colony Builder* (1932; repr., New York: AMS Press, 1967), 206a.

13. Morgan, "Handbill, October 3, 1788," 206a.

14. Don Diego de Gardoqui to José Moñino y Redondo, 1st Count of Floridablanca, Dec. 24, 1788, Don Diego De Gardoqui Papers, Special Collections, Tulane Univ.

15. George McCully et al. to Dr. Nathaniel Bedford and William Turnbull, from New Madrid, Apr. 14, 1789, vol. 10, Josiah Harmar Papers, William L. Clements Library, Univ. of Michigan.

16. Henry Knox, Note on Troops in North Carolina and Georgia, available through: Adam Matthew Digital Archives, American History, 1493–1945, Gilder Lehrman Institute of American History, New York.

17. Louis Houck, *The Spanish Regime in Missouri* (New York: Arno, 1971), 278.

18. Gardoqui to Floridablanca, Dec. 24, 1788.

19. Kevin T. Barksdale, *The Lost State of Franklin: America's First Secession* (Lexington: Univ. Press of Kentucky, 2008), 146.

20. Leland D. Baldwin, *Whiskey Rebels: The Story of a Frontier Uprising* (Pittsburgh: Univ. of Pittsburgh Press, 1967), 13; Thomas P. Slaughter, *The Whiskey Rebellion: Frontier Epilogue to the American Revolution* (Oxford: Oxford Univ. Press, 1986), 60.

21. Morgan to Miro, May 24, 1789, Cuban Papers Legajo 2361, Archivo Nacional de Cuba (Cuban Papers), via the Historic New Orleans Collection.

22. "New Madrid Handbill," legajo 2361.

23. Morgan to Miro, May 24, 1789, legajo 2361.

24. George Morgan to Don Diego de Gardoqui, Feb. 24, 1791, quoted in Savelle, *George Morgan Colony Builder*, 228.

25. Slaughter, *Whiskey Rebellion*, 198.

26. Robertson, *Trial of Aaron Burr for Treason*, 570.

27. Robertson, *Trial of Aaron Burr for Treason*, 562.

28. Robertson, *Trial of Aaron Burr for Treason*, 563.

29. Aaron Burr to James Wilkinson, July 22–29, 1806, *Political Correspondence and Public Papers of Aaron Burr*, ed. Mary-Jo Kline, and Joanne Wood Ryan (Princeton, NJ: Princeton Univ. Press, 1983), 986–87.

30. Thomas Jefferson to Congress, Message on Aaron Burr. Jan. 22, 1807, Thomas Jefferson Papers at the Library of Congress: ser. 1, General Correspondence, 1651 to 1827, Library of Congress, https://www.loc.gov/item/mtjbib016838/.

31. Edmund Gaines, "Gaines to James Wilkinson and Governor Robert Williams, Feb. 19, 1807," in *The American Historical Magazine and Tennessee Historical Society Quarterly* 1 (Apr. 1896): 146–47.

32. Robertson, *Trial of Aaron Burr for Treason*, 568.

Chapter 5

Tippecanoe

An American Epic

MARY STOCKWELL

East Looks West toward "Tippecanoe"

In the summer of 1840, Ralph Waldo Emerson was working on a collection of writings that would make him famous. Known collectively as *Essays*, the volume would include such classic pieces as "Self-Reliance" and "The Over-Soul." But on the Fourth of July, he was called away from his work by a commotion in the street in front of his house, which stood on the main stagecoach line through Concord, Massachusetts. The location gave him a front-row seat at the parade that local Whigs had staged in honor of their presidential candidate, William Henry Harrison.[1]

Emerson left no detailed description of the parade, but the next day he wrote in his diary: "The simplest things are always better than curiosities. The most imposing part of the Harrison celebration of the Fourth of July in Concord, as in Baltimore, was the ball, twelve or thirteen feet in diameter, which, as it mounts the little heights and descends the little slopes of the road, draws all eyes with a certain sublime movement, especially as the imagination is incessantly addressed with its political significancy. So the Log Cabin is a lively watchword."[2]

The giant ball rolling through Concord symbolized the Whigs' contempt for Thomas Hart Benton, Missouri's Democratic senator and a staunch ally of Andrew Jackson, who had demanded that the censure of the former president, recorded in the *Congressional Record* be circled and struck out.[3] Whigs across the country competed to see which town could build the biggest ball, both in opposition to the Democrats and in support of "Tippecanoe," their nickname for Harrison, who had defeated the Indians along the Tippecanoe Creek in 1811. Log cabins and barrels of hard cider had also become important symbols of Harrison's campaign after the Democratic editor of the *Baltimore Republican* wrote: "Give him a barrel of hard cider, and settle a pension of two thousand a year on him, and my word for it, he will sit the remainder of his days in his log cabin by the side of a 'sea coal' fire, and study moral philosophy."[4]

A hundred years later, and fifteen miles down the road from Concord, in Cambridge, another New Englander tried to explain Harrison's campaign. He was the historian Arthur Schlesinger Jr. A Harvard graduate with a BA in history and a Junior Fellow at the college, Schlesinger presented a series of lectures on his thesis that Jacksonian politics was primarily a movement of laboring men, especially in eastern cities, rather than a distinctly western phenomenon. His lectures were later collected into *The Age of Jackson,* which won the 1946 Pulitzer Prize for history. The work was so universally praised that on its merits Schlesinger was appointed associate professor of history at Harvard.[5]

His analysis of Harrison's campaign in *The Age of Jackson* remains the standard interpretation of the event for historians. He argued that 1840 Whig leaders were determined to find a candidate who was a military hero, like Andrew Jackson, but who held no opinions of his own on any major issue. The Whigs could thus easily contrast their candidate, a blank slate, against their opponent President Martin Van Buren, Jackson's handpicked successor, whom they would paint as a corrupt aristocrat. With the bar set so low, Harrison perfectly fit the bill. As Schlesinger put it, "a Westerner, a military hero, and a plain man of the people, innocent of the Jacksonian controversies, who could be a better nominee than William Henry Harrison?"[6]

Schlesinger saw little remarkable about Harrison's campaign beyond its silliness. With their unfortunate quote about Harrison retiring to his log cabin with a barrel of cider, he argued, the Democrats played right into the hands of Whig mythmakers. Whig bankers, journalists, and politicians embraced the snide remark and made it the foundation of Harrison's campaign. "Yes," they shouted back at the opposition, "the Whig Party *is* the party of hard cider and log cabins, and it will defend them to the end against the sneers of the Democrats."[7]

With their log cabin and hard cider symbols in place, the Whigs transformed Harrison, a "Virginia aristocrat," into a "plain man of the people." Now the unwitting tool of eastern political operatives, most especially New York's Horace Greeley, editor of the *Log Cabin,* Harrison embraced the image that his campaign had concocted for him as he took to the stump on his own behalf. "The weatherbeaten old soldier," as Schlesinger described him, stood before thousands of people, "exchanging his silk hat for a broad-brimmed rustic model, speaking with great earnestness to little effect" to the "delighted crowd," which was already "exhilarated with Whig hard cider." In the end, Harrison's campaign was the "most conclusive evidence of the triumph of Jackson," not Harrison. The Whig Party, pro-banking and anti-labor, won the election, "but it had to assume the manner of the popular party in order to do it."[8]

Fifty years after *The Age of Jackson* was published, and two hundred miles down the Atlantic Coast from Boston, in New York City, Schlesinger, now a professor at the City University of New York, became the editor of a new series of biographies on the American presidents. The task of writing a biography of William Henry Harrison fell to Gail Collins, a *New York Times* op-ed columnist. Collins, a Cincinnati native, comically defended her assignment in the prologue of *William Henry Harrison* by explaining that her father had helped to tear down Harrison's home in North Bend on the Ohio River during the 1960s. He had worked for Cincinnati Gas & Electric, and the company demolished the building to make way for a new power station. As Collins confessed, she had to write Harrison's story because she "owed him."[9]

While she credited Harrison with inventing the modern presidential campaign, Collins had little respect for him as a person or a leader. She described the Log Cabin campaign as a joke, since the man at its center was a phony. Harrison was not born in a log cabin but was instead a member of one of the wealthiest families in Virginia. He was not an important politician but a petty officeholder who, as Indiana's governor, had purchased millions of acres of Indian land for pennies on the dollar. Finally, Harrison was no military hero. In fact, his nickname, "Tippecanoe," came from a skirmish he fought against Indians in November 1811, which Collins dismissed: "He didn't win a big military victory at Tippecanoe—it was a minor fight against an outnumbered village of Indians, and because Harrison screwed up the defense of the camp the white Americans suffered most of the casualties."[10]

For all their differences, Emerson, Schlesinger, and Collins found Harrison's 1840 campaign baffling. Emerson remained completely mystified, while Schlesinger when looking at Harrison saw only Jackson. Schlesinger's interpretation has been so influential that later specialized studies of Harrison's campaign, including Robert Grey Gunderson's *The Log Cabin Campaign* and Ronald G. Shafer's *The Carnival Campaign,* for all their added detail, follow his lead. Still more historians, writing in the decade before Shafer published his work, likewise dismissed Harrison as a problematic character. Alfred Cave's *Prophets of the Great Spirit,* Robert Owens's *Jefferson's Hammer,* and Adam Jortner's *The Gods of Prophetstown* all portray Harrison, in varying degrees, as a greedy landgrabber, a second-rate general, and a fanatic who harassed peaceful Indians. Finally, for Collins, if something truly significant once happened to Harrison, west of Harvard Square and beyond the Hudson River, then it was better left forgotten.[11]

A Midwestern Story

Most of these works—written from a distinctly eastern perspective, even the ones published by academic presses west of the Mississippi—ignored the dramatic story being told about Harrison in the 1840 campaign. This powerful tale described Harrison's heroic struggle against the Shawnee chief Tecumseh for control of the vast country that lay across the Appalachians, north of the Ohio, and west to the Mississippi, the fabled Ohio Country, which today we call the Midwest. If we imagine that we are hearing this tale for the first time, we can better understand why millions of Americans were so excited about Harrison's run for the White House in 1840.

The youngest child of Benjamin Harrison V, a signer of the Declaration of Independence, William Henry Harrison was born on the Berkeley

Plantation in Charles City, Virginia in 1773. When he was eighteen, he joined the army and, in August 1794, fought alongside Gen. Anthony Wayne at the Battle of Fallen Timbers. A year later, he was at Wayne's side during the negotiations for the Treaty of Greeneville. Elected Ohio's first representative to the US Congress, he proposed a law allowing people to buy western land on credit. In 1800, he became the governor of the Indiana Territory. His main responsibility was purchasing land from the Indians and opening the surrendered territory for sale and settlement.

The core story of Harrison's life began in 1806 when he encountered Tenskwatawa, the Shawnee Prophet who preached a return to tradition among the tribes, and welcomed Indians to Prophet's Town on the Tippecanoe Creek. After meeting the Prophet, Harrison doubted whether he was the true leader of revivalist movement in his territory. He soon discovered that the man behind the movement was the Prophet's older brother, Tecumseh, a renowned warrior and gifted orator. To stop the advance of the Americans across the Ohio, the Shawnee leader was piecing together the largest Indian confederation in history from tribes living near the Great Lakes and beyond.

Harrison confronted Tecumseh at two dramatic meetings in Vincennes, in 1810 and 1811. The charismatic chief told Harrison that the Indians would never sell land to the Americans again. Instead, he would win a homeland for them north of Ohio River. While the Shawnee claimed his goals were peaceful, Harrison suspected that Tecumseh was planning a massacre across the frontier. In November 1811, after Tecumseh had gone south to win more allies, Harrison headed to the Tippecanoe Creek where, on the morning of November 7, 1811, his army defeated Tecumseh's warriors under the Prophet's command.

Although Harrison had prevented a massacre, his conflict with Tecumseh was far from over. When the War of 1812 broke out, Tecumseh joined the British, who promised him an Indian state in the old Ohio Country, while Harrison commanded his nation's Army of the Northwest. He built Fort Meigs on the Maumee River and defended the post against two sieges led by Tecumseh and Gen. Henry Proctor. After the defeat of the British navy on Lake Erie in September 1813, Harrison chased the Indians and British into Canada. On the afternoon of October 5, 1813, along the Thames River, he faced Tecumseh in battle for the final time. Tecumseh died in

The print for Harrison's 1840 campaign clearly identifies the three great battles he fought and won for his nation. The names are written within the laurel leaf crown beneath his portrait: Tippecanoe, Fort Meigs, and the Thames. (Peter S. Duval, *Gen. William H. Harrison of Tippecanoe, Fort Meigs and the Thames.* [Philadelphia: Published at the Office of the US Military magazine, circa 1840], available at the Library of Congress, https://www.loc.gov/pictures/item/2003677557/.)

the fight, a musket ball shot through his heart. Harrison claimed victory at last in the long battle to secure the Midwest for the United States.[12]

Quest for an American Epic

In 1840, few Americans, in a total population of 17 million, had ever heard the story of Harrison's life. Its main outlines had been told in three biographies: the first, written by Moses Dawson in Cincinnati in 1824; an anonymous volume published in New York in 1835; and a memoir written by Judge James Hall in Philadelphia in 1836. However, by 1840, these works were out of print. Accounts of Tippecanoe, Fort Meigs, and the Thames had been covered in newspapers like *Niles' National Register* and in journals like Philadelphia's *Portfolio*. However, most Americans alive in 1840 would not have read these accounts, since the majority had been born since the War of 1812. A state-by-state comparison of the total population from the 1840 US Census shows that at least 60 percent of the population was thirty years or younger. They had no living memory of William Henry Harrison or his struggle against Tecumseh. As the campaign unfolded in 1840, they were hearing the story of this dramatic contest for the first time, a story which had all the earmarks of an ancient epic.[13]

Leaders in the founding generation, most notably John Adams and his son John Quincy Adams, had long called for the writing of an America epic. As the senior Adams explained to the poet John Trumbull, "I should hope to live to see our young American in Possession of an Heroic Poem equal to those the most esteemed in any Country." Thirty years later, the younger Adams, in his *Lectures on Rhetoric*, urged Americans to study Homer's epics, especially the speeches of his main characters, to learn the best rhetorical methods for republican orators.[14]

Father and son both expected a national epic to be written according to Aristotle's definition of an epic in his *Poetics*: a long narrative poem in dactylic hexameter, or heroic hexameter, which focused on a main story within a wider, more complex, and even fantastical tale. Epics written in this style include Homer's *Iliad* and *Odyssey*, along with Virgil's *Aeneid*. There had been several attempts at writing such a poem, including Trumbull's own 1872 *M'Fingal*, followed by Timothy Dwight's 1785 *The Conquest of Canaan* and Joel Barlow's 1807 *The Columbiad*, but none of these had captured the public's imagination.[15]

More recently, scholars have defined an epic as a dramatic narrative, which can take many forms, that expresses the "living history" of a people. Though rooted in a specific place and time, an epic transcends its point in history and speaks to people across the ages. An epic accomplishes this by exploring the mysteries of human experience: life and death; love and hate; men and women; passion and grief; honor and shame; and finally the trauma of war, specifically "what it achieves, what it costs, and what it serves."[16]

Parson Weems's *A History of the Life and Death, Virtues and Exploits of General George Washington* was the closest thing to the modern definition of an epic that Americans were reading in 1840. The book, which told the famous story of a young George Washington confessing to his father that he had chopped down the cherry tree, took hold of the popular imagination. Americans were also reading epic tales in the novels of James Fenimore Cooper, whose five-volume *Leatherstocking Tales,* published between 1823 and 1841, described the adventures of Natty Bumppo, a backwoodsman who lived along the Hudson River. Natty was brave, loyal, and always ready to defend the weak and innocent, like Cora and Alice Munro, whom he guided to Fort William Henry during the French and Indian War in Cooper's most famous novel, *The Last of the Mohicans.*[17]

Harrison's Epic Goes National

In the 1840 campaign, a third great epic, which told the story of Harrison's battle against Tecumseh for control of the heart of the nation, unfolded before Americans. Like Achilles, who fought Hector before the walls of Troy, Harrison fought Tecumseh and his followers at Tippecanoe, Fort Meigs, and the Thames. Like Aeneas, who carried his father out of burning Troy, sailing west into an unknown country, and founding the city of Rome, Harrison left Virginia and headed into the wilderness, carrying the dreams of his father's revolutionary generation. Like Washington in Weems's biography, Harrison was always honorable. Like Natty Bumppo, he shepherded his people through the wilderness, protecting women and children especially, from Tecumseh's plans for their massacre.

The source for this epic was Harrison himself, especially his letters to the War Department during his tenure as Indiana's governor. Harrison was an excellent writer who could describe events occurring around him in accurate detail and then lay out possible contingencies for future actions. He could also explain the historical significance of events happening around him. His love of ancient Greek and Roman history shaped his perception of Tecumseh, whom he described as "one of those uncommon geniuses" who might have built an empire like the Incans or Aztecs, if not for the United States.[18]

Harrison's correspondence, including the detailed records he kept on Tecumseh and Tenskwatawa, was the basis for Dawson's 1824 biography, a fact clear in its subtitle: *With a Detail of His Negotiations and Wars with the Indians, Until the Final Overthrow of the Celebrated Chief Tecumseh and His Brother the Prophet.* Dawson's work was the starting point for campaign biographies written in 1840 by Whig journalists, politicians, and historians. Local Whig committees interested in finding out more about their candidate than the snippets that were provided in Whig newspapers commissioned still more biographies. Under pressure from readers, William Ogden Niles, editor of *Niles' National Register,* collected stories about Harrison from his family's weekly newspaper in *The Tippecanoe Textbook.* All of these works concentrated primarily on the dramatic story of Harrison's confrontation with Tecumseh, which culminated in his victories at Tippecanoe, Fort Meigs, and the Thames.[19]

The specific ways Harrison's story passed from his many biographies to the American people would require a book-length analysis. But a good place to start is taking a closer look at the symbol of the log cabin and then examining the speeches, rallies, and songs at the heart of his campaign.

The log cabins that Harrison's supporters built in 1840 were more than just a humorous response to a Democratic editor's quip. A Whig journalist noted that the snide remark "vibrates from the rivers to the ends of the land," bringing back memories of what life had been like in the log cabins that settlers first built upon arriving in the western country and the bloody attacks of Indians on their settlements.[20] Harrison had finally ended the slaughter by defeating the "savage Tecumseh." If he had failed, the frontier would still be a battleground marked by "havoc and death." Instead, his victory had opened the West, or better the Midwest, not just to a handful of log cabins but to hundreds of thousands of his fellow citizens.[21]

Harrison's life story, from his youth in Virginia to his final triumph over Tecumseh, was likewise told in speeches by his supporters on the campaign trail. Daniel Webster spoke of Harrison as a brave hero born with the "blood of the Revolution" in his veins. John Bear, the Buckeye Blacksmith, praised Harrison for leaving his wealthy family in Virginia and settling in the free land north of the Ohio. Bear identified with Harrison because he had left Maryland to escape the grip of slaveholders who controlled everything in the South, including the votes of poor whites like himself. Soldiers who had served with Harrison at Fallen Timbers and Tippecanoe and during the War of 1812 recalled his courage under fire, with some of the best speeches given by Richard Mentor Johnson, the Democratic vice presidential candidate. Johnson traveled the country, telling the story of Harrison's fight against Tecumseh at the Battle of the Thames, before taking credit for being the man who actually killed him.[22]

On May 29, 1840, James Brooks, *New York Express* editor, gave one of the most memorable speeches of the campaign to a crowd of a hundred thousand gathered at the Tippecanoe Battlefield. After veterans of the fight presented him with their tattered battle flag, Brooks thrilled the crowd by comparing Harrison to the heroes of ancient Rome. "And why should it not be so?" Brooks asked, "For if the winning of provinces for Rome won ovations for the conquerors, what triumphs should your Harrison not have who saved whole empires for his country; avenging all the cruelties of the savage upon you, by the success of his arms." The crowd's excitement grew even greater at twilight, when fireworks lit up the northern edge of the battlefield while a rainbow appeared across the southern horizon.[23]

The story of Harrison's fight against Tecumseh was an important part of rallies held in his honor, including three major gatherings in Ohio, the candidate's current home state. At each one, the story of Harrison's epic struggle was highlighted, starting with a celebration on Washington's birthday in Columbus. Tens of thousands of people stood for hours in icy rain on High Street, the main thoroughfare through the town, to cheer for their candidate. The most wonderful sight that passed before them was a massive replica of Fort Meigs, twenty-eight feet long and pulled by a team of six horses. The miniature fort was surrounded by wooden pickets with seven blockhouses and twelve brass cannons, all manned by forty toy soldiers. A banner waving above the float on a thirty-foot pole proclaimed the words Harrison spoke when General Procter ordered him to surrender: "Tell Procter when he gets possession of the Fort, he will gain more honor, in the estimation of his King and country, than he would acquire by a thousand capitulations."[24]

Four months later, forty thousand people gathered near the ruins of Fort Meigs. On the evening of June 10, the day before Harrison was to arrive to speak, his supporters recreated Tecumseh's attack on the post just as it had happened in the summer of 1813. Precisely at midnight, the whole camp was roused by gunfire echoing from the woods to the east of the fort. Soon soldiers emerged from the ruins, racing through the imaginary main gate that once stood there. After an hour of mock fighting, Tecumseh and his warriors were again defeated.[25]

Still one more huge crowd, estimated at a hundred thousand, gathered in Dayton on September 10, 1840, the twenty-seventh anniversary of the Battle of Lake Erie. Harrison arrived in a carriage from North Bend and mounted a white horse. Everyone who knew the story of Tippecanoe remembered that the Prophet had ordered his warriors to kill Harrison, who would be riding a white horse. Harrison survived because, in the confusion of the battle, he could not find his usual horse and rode a dark one instead. Now, high on another white horse, he made his way through the crowd. Riding at his side was old Col. John Johnston, the Indian agent who had warned Harrison that Tecumseh, and not the Prophet, was the true leader of the Indians massing on the Tippecanoe Creek.[26]

Even more Americans learned about Harrison's epic struggle against Tecumseh through songs. Many pundits commented that Harrison would be the first candidate "sung" into the White House. Sheets of easy-to-play music, marches, ballads, and quicksteps, were snapped up by amateur musicians, who played the tunes for their families, and local bands, who performed the songs at Whig rallies. Harrison's less well-off supporters, who owned no musical instruments, purchased "songsters," pocket-sized collections of lyrics, for just pennies. The songs printed in these small books, without notes or musical scales, were meant to be sung along with popular tunes of the day, the titles of which appeared below the lyrics.

Printed as sheet music or in songsters, every song told some part of Harrison's life, including his long struggle against Tecumseh. The three places where he wrested control of the Midwest from the Shawnee chief—the "Wabash banks, Fort Meigs, the Thames"—were mentioned again and again, reminding Americans of the bloody fighting that had once engulfed their land, along with Harrison's brave deeds that saved them.

The cover of the sheet music for "Old Tippecanoe" shows nine images of William Henry Harrison's military and political career, placed in a circle around the central engraving of his farm in North Bend, Ohio. (James Fuller Queen, *Baltimore Convention, Old Tippecanoe, a Patriotic Song* [Philadelphia: Leopold. Meignen & Co. Publishers & Importers of Music, 1840], available at the Library of Congress, https://www.loc.gov/item/2008661355/.)

Everywhere Harrison went on his long campaign for the White House, he heard Americans singing his praises—and remembering his bravery—most especially against Tecumseh.[27]

The best songs put people right in the center of the struggle. The "Soldier of Tippecanoe" imagined waiting with Harrison's army "in the deep green grass" with the bright stars above on the night before the Battle of Tippecanoe. "Old Tippecanoe" captured the fear of Tecumseh, "who was rallying his forces, in innocents blood his hands to imbrue." One of the most beautiful, "Song of an Old Soldier," recounted Harrison's life in a classical form, with metered rhythms and compound adjectives, reminiscent of Homer's epics:

> When the Indian's loud yell and his tomahawk flashing,
> Spread terror around us, and hope was with few,
> Oh, then, through the ranks of the enemy dashing,
> Sprang forth to the rescue old Tippecanoe.
> The iron-armed soldier, the true-hearted soldier,
> The gallant old soldier of Tippecanoe.[28]

Harrison's followers learned even more about his life by looking at the many images that usually decorated the borders of sheet music and sometimes a few pages in the songsters. Often drawn in a series of circles, the vignettes told the story of Harrison's life in one striking picture after another. Looking at them, Americans could see Harrison dashing with Wayne's orders at Fallen Timbers, fighting Tecumseh at Fort Meigs and the Thames, and welcoming guests from near and far to his humble home in the woods. The same technique was used in broadsides that summarized the major events of Harrison's life, all in service to his country, on just one page. The most prominent image, usually placed at the top of the broadside, showed Harrison and Tecumseh meeting for the first time on the lawn before the Governor's Mansion in Vincennes in 1810—with their weapons drawn.[29]

The story of Harrison's battle against Tecumseh helped him win the White House, but only one month after his inauguration he was dead and laid to rest near his farm in North Bend. As if awakening from a dream, many Americans wondered what it meant that, for the first time in their history, a president had died in office. Eulogists worried that their countrymen had forgotten that earthly glory was fleeting, and so God, who watched over the nation with fatherly care, struck Harrison down as a lesson to them. Still, even in death, they could not forget the story that had launched Harrison into office. Their many discourses remain an untapped resource for understanding how the story of Harrison's fight against Tecumseh—whose confederation "infused terror into every cabin and hamlet on the frontier"—had touched Americans. They were still grateful to Harrison, even in death, for his defeat of the Shawnee chief at the "deadly Battle of Tippecanoe," the "blazing lines of Fort Meigs," and the "victory of the Thames."[30]

The panorama of the contest between Harrison and Tecumseh for control of the Midwest had been wonderful to behold. But now there could be no retreating into a vanished time to avoid questions about what would become of the country west of the Mississippi. Should Texas be brought into the Union? Should the southwest be acquired from Mexico? Should Free-Soilers or slaveholders settle the Great Plains from the Mississippi to the Rockies? Answering these questions, especially the latter one, would lead to a bloody civil war that would make the fight between Harrison and Tecumseh seem a dream.

The End of an Epic

As time passed, Harrison faded into the background, while Tecumseh came to the forefront. Like a hero in a classic tragedy, as Aristotle defined the form in his *Poetics*, Tecumseh fought a hopeless fight, doomed to failure and his eventual death. But his story, like all tragedies, remains strangely compelling, for it provides a catharsis of feelings that Harrison's epic tale never can. Ironically, Harrison had prepared the way for Tecumseh's transformation by helping Benjamin Drake write the first biography of the Shawnee leader in 1840. Future authors would use this book as the starting point for their ever more glowing accounts of Tecumseh.[31]

That Tecumseh had planned a massacre across the western frontier, only to be stopped by Harrison at Tippecanoe, Fort Meigs, and the Thames, has been forgotten. Once called the "Patriot Chief" in campaign songs, Harrison has been replaced by a new "Patriot Chief," Tecumseh, or as the historian Alvin Josephy described him in his book of the same name, the "greatest of all American Indian leaders, a majestic human who might have given all the Indians a nation of their own." Josephy forgot to add that the price to be paid for this nation would have been the Midwest, where today over 65 million Americans live, a price that Harrison, or "Tippecanoe," had refused to pay.[32]

Notes

1. Ralph Waldo Emerson, *Essays* (Boston: James Munroe & Company, 1841).
2. 1840 entry, *Journals of Ralph Waldo Emerson: with Annotations*, vol. 5, ed. Edward Waldo Emerson and Waldo Emerson Forbes (Boston: Houghton Mifflin, 1909), 425–26.
3. "Senate Reverses a Presidential Censure," US Senate website, accessed June 28, 2024, https://www.senate.gov/about/origins-foundations/parties-leadership/senate-reverses-a-presidential-censure.htm.
4. Robert Grey Gunderson, *The Log-Cabin Campaign* (Lexington: Univ. Press of Kentucky, 1957), 30.
5. Donald B. Cole, "The Age of Jackson after Forty Years," *Reviews in American History*, 14 (Mar. 1986): 149–51; Samuel P. Jacobs, "Schlesinger, Revered Intellectual, Is Dead at 89," *Harvard Crimson*, Mar. 2, 2007.
6. Arthur Schlesinger Jr., *The Age of Jackson* (Boston: Little, Brown, 1945), 289–90.
7. Schlesinger, *Age of Jackson*, 290–91.
8. Schlesinger, *Age of Jackson*, 290–91, 305.
9. Gail Collins, *William Henry Harrison* (New York: Times Books, Henry Holt, 2012), 1–3.
10. Collins, *William Henry Harrison*, 4, 9–47.
11. Ronald G. Shafer, *The Carnival Campaign: How the Rollicking 1840 Campaign of "Tippecanoe and Tyler, Too" Changed Presidential Elections Forever* (Chicago: Chicago Review Press, 2016); Alfred Cave, *Prophets of the Great Spirit: Native American Revitalization Movements in Eastern North America* (Lincoln: Univ. of Nebraska Press, 2006); Robert Owens, *Jefferson's Hammer: William Henry Harrison and the Origins of American Indian Policy* (Norman: Univ. of Oklahoma Press, 2007); Adam Jortner, *The Gods of Prophetstown: The Battle of Tippecanoe and the Holy War for the American Frontier* (New York: Oxford Univ. Press, 2011). Of these contemporary works, only Shafer's *Carnival Campaign* describes Harrison as a significant military figure on the western frontier.
12. The best source on Harrison's confrontation with Tecumseh and the Prophet remains Logan Esarey's edition of Harrison's letters, *Governors Messages and Letters: Messages and Letters of William Henry Harrison*, 2 vols. (Indianapolis: Indiana Historical Commission, 1922).

13. Moses A. Dawson, *A Historical Narrative of the Civil and Military Services of Major-General William H. Harrison* (Cincinnati: Printed by M. Dawson, at the Advertiser Office, 1824); *A Brief Sketch of the Life and Public Services of William Henry Harrison* (New York: T. & C. Wood, Stationers, 1835); James Hall, *A Memoir of the Public Services of William Henry Harrison, of Ohio* (Philadelphia: Key & Biddle, 1836), 102–3; 6th US Census, 1840, in *Compendium of the Enumeration of the Inhabitants and Statistics of the United States* (Washington, DC: T. Allen, 1841).

14. John P. McWilliams, *The American Epic: Transforming a Genre 1770–1860* (Cambridge: Cambridge Univ. Press, 1989), 15, 17, 21–24.

15. Aristotle, *Poetics*, trans S. H. Butcher (Mineola, NY: Dover, 1997), 47–52.

16. Katherine Callen King, *Ancient Epic* (New York: Wiley-Blackwell, 2012), 2–3; Hélène A. Guerber, *The Book of the Epics: The World's Great Epics Told in Story* (New York: Biblo & Tannen, 1966), 5.

17. McWilliams, *American Epic*, 37–41, 136–44; Mason Locke Weems, *A History of the Life and Death, Virtues and Exploits of General George Washington*, 3rd ed. (Philadelphia: Printed by John Bioren, 1800); James Fenimore Cooper, *The Leatherstocking Tales*, vols. 1 and 2 (1823, 1841; repr. New York: Library of America, 1985).

18. William Henry Harrison to Secretary Eustis, Aug. 7, 1811, *Governors' Messages and Letters*, ed. Logan Esarey, 2 vols. (Indianapolis: Indiana Historical Society, 1922), 1:549.

19. William Henry Harrison to Moses A. Dawson, Apr. 15, 1823, box 3, folder 3, William Henry Papers and Documents, Indiana Historical Society, Bloomington; Harrison's campaign biographies include Isaac Rand Jackson, *A Sketch of the Life And Public Services of General William Henry Harrison, of Ohio* (St. Louis: Churchill & Harris, Printers, 1840); Richard Hildreth, *The People's Presidential Candidate; Or, the Life of William Henry Harrison of Ohio* (Boston: Weeks, Jordan & Company, 1840); Samuel J. Burr, *The Life and Times of William Henry Harrison* (New York: L. W. Ransom, 1840; Philadelphia: R. W. Pomeroy, 1840); Benjamin Drake and Charles Todd, *Sketches of the Civil and Military Services of William Henry Harrison* (Cincinnati: U. P. James, 1840); William Ogden Niles, *The Tippecanoe Textbook, Compiled from Niles' Register and Other Sources, by William Ogden Niles, and Respectfully Dedicated to the Young Men of the United States* (Baltimore: Duff Green & Cushing & Brother; Philadelphia: Hogan & Thompson and T. K. & P. J Collins, 1840).

20. Preface to *The Great Convention of 1840: Description of the Convention of the People, Held at Columbus, on the 21st and 22nd February, 1840* (Columbus: Cutler & Wright, 1840), 7.

21. "Harrison Song," "The Hero of Ohio," and "Old Tippecanoe," all in *Tippecanoe Songs of the Log Cabin Boys and Girls of 1840*, Anthony Banning Norton, ed. (Mount Vernon, OH: A. B. Norton & Co., 1888), 31, 64, 89.

22. *Niles' National Register*, June 27, 1840; *The Life and Travels of John W. Bear* (Baltimore: D. Binswanger & Co., Printers, 1873), 8–11; *A Biographical Sketch of Col. Richard M. Johnson, of Kentucky. By a Kentuckian* (New York: Saxton & Miles, 1843).

23. *Niles' National Register*, June 27, 1840.

24. Miller, *Great Convention of 1840*, 14–16.

25. M. A. Leeson, comp., *Commemorative Historical and Biographical Record of Wood County, Ohio* (Chicago: J. H. Beers & Company, 1897), 86.

26. *Log Cabin* (Dayton, OH), Nov. 18, 1840, 1–4.

27. Leslie L Hunter, "The Role of Music in the 1840 Campaign of William Henry Harrison," *Bulletin of Historical Research in Music Education* 10, no. 2 (1989): 107–10; Derek B. Scott, "The U.S. Presidential Songster, 1840–1900," *Cheap Print and Popular Song in the Nineteenth Century: A Cultural History of the Songster*, ed. Paul Watt, Derek Scott, and Patrick Spedding (New York: Oxford Univ. Press, 2017), 73–90; "Should Brave Soldiers Be Forgot," *Tippecanoe Songs of the Log Cabin Boys and Girls of 1840*, ed. A. B. Norton (Mount Vernon, OH: A. B. Norton & Co., 1888), 7.

28. "Soldier of Tippecanoe," "Old Tippecanoe," and "Song of an Old Soldier," *Tippecanoe Songs*, 9–12.

29. "*Log Cabin Anecdotes: Illustrated Incidents in the Life of General William Henry Harrison*" (New York: J. P. Guffing, 1840) is an excellent example of a broadside from Harrison's 1840 campaign, with copies now housed in the Prints and Photographs Division of the Library of Congress, https://www.loc.gov/resource/cph.3g02103/, and the Smithsonian's National Portrait Gallery, https://npg.si.edu/object/npg_NPG.82.12.

30. An excellent representative sample is John Payne Cleaveland, *A Eulogy on William Henry Harrison, Late President of the United States: Delivered at Ann Arbor, Michigan, April 22, 1841* (Ann Arbor: T. M. Ladd & Co., 1841).

31. Benjamin Drake, *Life of Tecumseh, and of His Brother the Prophet, with a Historical Sketch of the Shawanoe Indians* (Cincinnati: E. Morgan & Co., 1841).

32. "The Patriot Chief," *The Harrison Medal Minstrel* (Philadelphia: Grigg & Elliott, 1840), 138–39; Alvin Josephy, *The Patriot Chiefs: A Chronicle of American Indian Resistance*, rev. ed. (New York: Penguin, 1993), 173.

Chapter 6

Between Northeastern Stockholders and Southern Slaveowners

The 1856 Presidential Election and the Formation of the Midwest

ANDREW W. WILEY

In recent years, historians have taken a renewed interest in the formation of the American Midwest. This chapter seeks to further this scholarship by examining the 1856 presidential campaign. That year, the expansion of slavery threatened the bonds between Americans living west of the Appalachian Mountains to the Mississippi River Valley. Those living in free states opposed it, while their slave-state neighbors supported it: the West was seemingly divided. Or was it? On Election Day, enough free-state westerners voted against an antislavery Republican that they handed the presidency to a Democrat. Despite the victory, the results obscured changing regional sentiments. Antislavery concerns among their constituents had forced Democrats north of the Ohio River to craft a unique campaign that promoted anti-northeastern prejudices while downplaying fears of slavery's expansion. Four years before the Civil War, free-state westerners had drawn new distinctions between themselves and their slaveowning neighbors—they were becoming midwesterners.[1]

When did Americans north of the Ohio River between the Appalachian Mountains and the Mississippi River valley, what most Americans called the Old Northwest, become midwesterners? Familial ties, commercial links, suspicions of eastern Americans, and racism against African

Americans had linked western Americans. According to some historians, the Civil War, rather than early debates over slavery, permanently severed these connections. Examining the 1856 Democratic presidential campaign, however, reveals that concerns about slavery's expansion were already straining western ties and forced Democrats in the Midwest to adapt their message for a region that was neither southern nor eastern. Their efforts were partially successful, as their candidate won two midwestern states in the presidential election along with numerous state and local races. Though some in the region had eschewed the overtly antislavery Republican Party, the unique 1856 Democratic campaign in the Old Northwest, which downplayed slavery's expansion, indicated that the Midwest was taking shape prior to the Civil War.[2]

Senator Stephen A. Douglas of Illinois seemed to have divided westerners in 1854 when he pushed a bill through Congress organizing Kansas and Nebraska into territories. Douglas had kicked a hornet's nest. The legislation repealed the 1820 Missouri Compromise, which gave settlers in both territories the right to legalize slavery. Slaveowners loved the legislation, whereas residents of the free states hated it for opening once forbidden lands to the South's peculiar institution. The act raised another concern for many white free laborers hoping to move to Kansas—living near African Americans. Though these potential migrants hated slavery, anti-Black attitudes ran high north of the Ohio River and culminated in a wave of exclusion laws in the mid-1850s. Indiana and Illinois voters banned African American settlement via their state constitutions while residents in other states considered similar measures. When Congress passed the Kansas-Nebraska Act, midwesterners feared it would end any chance at keeping slavery out of the West.[3]

Outrage over the Kansas-Nebraska Act in the free states finished off the old political order and broke a crucial tie between westerners. The Whig Party, which had been declining since 1852, collapsed as antislavery voters looked for more effective means of containing slavery. In 1854, former Whigs had two new political options, the Know-Nothing and Republican Parties. While Know-Nothings waffled on containing slavery, Republicans had a hook for voters in the Old Northwest: repealing the Kansas-Nebraska Act. Already wounded, free-state Democrats faced their new opponents with another serious problem, dissension in the ranks. One irate Democrat even considered challenging Congressman William

Hayden English, of southern Indiana, for his seat in the US House of Representatives. Though party leaders forced the challenger to relent, any threat from within to the party stalwart was a serious problem. While Democrats survived the turmoil, the Whig Party's destruction ended a political tie between free-and slave-state westerners.[4]

Voters signaled their displeasure with Democrats in the 1854 elections. Despite warning that Republican victories meant emancipation, racial miscegenation, and disunion, twenty-five Democrats from the Old Northwest lost their seats in the US House; a mix of Republicans and Know-Nothings replaced them. Worse for Democrats, Kansas exploded into violence the following year when numerous Missourians hoping to ensure a proslavery Kansas raided the territory and illegally voted in territorial elections. Proslavery Kansans later won a majority in the territorial legislature through the illegal voting. In response, antislavery settlers began arming themselves and retaliating against their slaveowning neighbors. The 1854 elections coupled with reactions to the violence in Kansas indicated that free-state westerners were growing increasingly wary of westerners south of the Ohio River. Since the Old Northwest carried a hefty number of electoral votes, a rising antislavery movement there might produce a Republican victory in the 1856 presidential election.[5]

Ironically, one organization offered Democrats a chance to awaken latent anti–New England hatred in the Old Northwest and minimize concerns about Southern meddling in Kansas. Wanting to ensure a free Kansas, northeasterners had formed emigrant aid societies. The organizations assisted free-state settlers moving west with money and sometimes arms. In 1854, Eli Thayer formed the most well-known such group, the Massachusetts Emigrant Aid Company. Renamed the New England Emigrant Aid Company after a merger, Thayer's creation had offices throughout the Northeast while abolitionist ministers gave passionate sermons to drum up support among their congregations. Though popular in New England, the company won many enemies in the South. Thayer became a marked man, with some Southerners offering a cash reward for his capture. Slave-state westerners offered their contempt for the organization as well, calling it dangerous. Despite these objections, the society was powerful and motivated.[6]

Thanks to the fertile breeding ground of anti-northeastern prejudice in the Old Northwest, Democrats sought to brand the aid societies as barbaric organizations committed to a free Kansas or violence. When celebrated minister Henry Ward Beecher published a circular celebrating the New England Emigrant Aid Society, he helped make the organization a target for Democratic fearmongering. One Ohio Democrat published a letter from former provisional territorial governor William Walker in which he singled out the organization. Walker alleged that free-state settlers who were members of the society, or, as he termed them, "New England ruffians," were the worst kind of settlers in Kansas and had committed numerous crimes. He related a story that a mob had removed a proslavery settler who had claimed land close to the society's headquarters in Lawrence, Kansas. Hoping to show that the violence was entirely the fault of New England settlers and not Southerners, Ohio Democrats eagerly publicized the letter.[7]

Democrats in the Old Northwest blamed any setback for antislavery Kansans on the emigrant societies. After proslavery men won majorities in the territorial legislature, Democrats condemned the aid societies for losing Kansas, saying that if they had left the territory alone antislavery settlers would have won instead. A Cincinnati, Ohio, newspaper editor concluded, "Now it seems to us that if the eastern people had not manifested such a feverous fury to forestall the question of slavery in Kansas . . . this Missourian invasion would not have happened." The editor of Indiana's largest Democratic newspaper likewise published the accusations and, despite the defeat of antislavery candidates in the Kansas elections, confidently predicted, "We believe that Kansas will come into the Union a free State." Stoking anti-northeastern prejudices while minimizing Southern efforts to expand slavery would become a running theme for Democrats in the Old Northwest in the coming years.[8]

Douglas, a former New Englander himself, warred against the societies on the floor of the US Senate. Referring to the organizations as "lawful and laudable," some free-state senators had called the emigrants a necessary counter against the proslavery Missourians who had fraudulently voted in the territorial elections. Douglas chided his colleagues. He blamed the organizations saying, "violence is the natural, and perhaps unavoidable, result of 'the experiment' attempted by the Emigrant Aid Societies to control the political destinies of the Territory by foreign interference." Proslavery later senators joined him in his accusations. Several defended the Missourians and laid the blame for the crisis in

Kansas squarely on the aid societies. From newspapers at home to the halls of Congress, Democrats from the Old Northwest singled out New Englanders as the primary culprits for the mini civil war in Kansas and the possibility that it might become a slave state.[9]

Ohio Democrats were especially eager to blame New Englanders and the aid societies for the violence in Kansas. The party had suffered numerous losses in 1854 and seemed vulnerable in 1856. One party member turned the accusations that Republicans had leveled against Missourians onto the emigrant societies. Beginning in November 1854, the Democrat charged New Englanders in the society with a series of crimes in the territory alleging that members had traveled to Kansas, cast votes, and returned home without putting down roots, a crime Missourians had commonly committed. Among the more serious offenses the Ohio Democrat levelled against the society were sacking proslavery cities, killing proslavery settlers, and ignoring the territorial government. Most of the charges were dubious at best and proslavery men had committed many of the same crimes against free state settlers. Accuracy however did not matter to most Democrats. In their minds the New England societies had provoked the entire controversy.[10]

Democrats in the Old Northwest continued to pitch conspiracy theories about the aid societies well into the presidential canvass. The editor of Indiana's main Democratic newspaper published an alleged exposé of the New England Emigrant Aid Company in September 1856. He first implied that the enterprise was "formed in the East to operate in the West." He continued: "They intend not only to settle up the Territories with Abolitionists, but also to colonize . . . Southern States." Further depicting the scheme as evidence of a northeastern conspiracy, the editor yawped, "These colonies are to be controlled by the Societies located in Massachusetts." Following the diatribe, he printed a supposed speech Thayer had given in which the abolitionist allegedly said that antislavery men might form new organizations and colonize slave states like Virginia. Just as they had done during the two previous years, Democrats continued stoking anti–New England prejudices.[11]

Some Democrats brought up older animosities to link the societies with past northeastern misdeeds. Former US senator Edward Allen Hannegan promoted one conspiracy theory in a letter. Claiming land speculators had created the aid societies, he charged, "The first cause of trouble was the unjustifiable attempt of Eastern capitalists through what is termed the Emigrant Aid Society to engross the most valuable lands in the Territory, solely for the purpose of private speculation." Hannegan further insinuated that few of the New Englanders intended to settle down in the territory. His words were meant to evoke bitter memories in western minds. Policies of the Second Bank of the United States, headquartered in the East, had led to land speculation and contributed to the Panic of 1819. The term *capitalists* reminded readers of the eastern institution that had played a role in the great economic turmoil decades earlier.[12]

Party members in the Old Northwest found more fuel for their antinortheastern campaign when Republicans in Norwich, Connecticut, called for a New England wide convention to raise money for the aid societies. Democrats found news of the meeting irresistible. Though the planners did not announce the location of the meeting, critics brought up an older meeting that had happened in Hartford, Connecticut, in 1814 when they labeled the proposed meeting of New England abolitionists a "new Hartford Convention." Most Americans were quite familiar with the term. Almost every reader remembered the 1814 meeting where New England delegates denounced the War of 1812 and supposedly talked of New England secession. The pledge of secrecy that the delegates took before the meeting further contributed to suspicions that the delegates were planning disunion. Drawing on fears of treacherous New Englanders working against the country once again, Democrats shrewdly utilized news of the proposed 1856 convention.[13]

One event in late May showed the extent of anti-northeastern sentiments in the West. On May 22, 1856, Congressman Preston Brooks of South Carolina beat Senator Charles Sumner of Massachusetts on the floor of the US Senate with his cane. The attack was retaliation after Sumner insulted Brooks's cousin Senator Andrew P. Butler of South Carolina. Democrats in the Old Northwest excused the bloody act. One Democrat printed Sumner's speech and defended Butler, calling him an "esteemed Senator, whose character is as pure as that of any other man." Another Democrat noted that Douglas and Lewis Cass, two famous western Democrats, had condemned Sumner's speech as ungentlemanly, while a party convention in Van Buren County, Michigan, accused Republicans of "endeavouring to raise an act of personal violence to the dignity of a principle, involving freedom of speech." Despite the attack, the northeastern senator's plight garnered little sympathy outside Republican circles in the Old Northwest.[14]

Anti-northeastern rhetoric was so palpable that some non-Democrats coopted it. Though he hated Democrats and the Kansas-Nebraska Act, newly converted Know-Nothing Richard Wigginton Thompson saw an advantage for his party. Thompson argued that western and southern states had been united against northeastern interests. The Hartford Convention and the sectional crises of 1820 and 1850 were instances when northeastern business interests had tried to break up the southern and western states—according to Thompson, Kansas was just the latest example. Though Democrats had caused the crisis, northeasterners were exacerbating it to put "a stop to the growth of the West, and make her great agricultural interests dependent upon and subsidiary to commercial interests of the East." Thompson then censured the aid societies for delaying Kansas's admission to the Union and keeping the crisis going for political gain. In his speech, he sounded like his Democratic foes.[15]

Though they scapegoated northeasterners for the Kansas violence, Democrats in the Old Northwest still needed to calm fears about slavery's expansion. The Kansas-Nebraska Act, fraudulent voting, and violence in the territory seemed to guarantee a new slave state. At a meeting in southern Indiana, party leaders laid out a strategy to peel off some antislavery voters in the region. They first denied that the Kansas-Nebraska Act forced slavery on the Kansans. One delegate dutifully taking notes recorded a speaker who encouraged Democrats to say that the "Nebraska Bill," as he called it, only allowed the possibility of bringing slaves into the territory; rather than forcing slavery on Kansas, the law left Kansans to decide on slavery for themselves. By mid-1856, however, these were hollow words. Every day brought more news hinting that Kansas was on the verge of adopting a slave-state constitution.[16]

While confident about Kansas's free-state future, Democrats regularly published reassuring letters from visitors to the territory. William Phillips wrote to a friend in Ottawa, Illinois, that most Kansans were antislavery: "With all their laws establishing slavery and protecting the owner in his property, they cannot induce men to emigrate here with their slaves." Additional letters seemed to confirm the account. In March 1856, a correspondent of the *St. Louis Democrat* reported little violence in the territory. Another correspondent assured readers, "As to the civil war in

Kansas, there has been some trouble and probably will be so . . . but as yet I know of no hostilities like those reported in at the East." As if wishing it to happen, a Michigan Democrat published the two accounts, adding, "The lattest news from Kansas reports all quiet in that Territory." Each editor was an optimist as it turned out.[17]

The antislavery settlers filling Kansas gave Democrats another tool to beat back fears of a Southern slave power conspiracy. The New England Aid Company frequently published lists of Kansas emigrants and Democrats seized on the information as proof the antislavery settlers were winning the race to settle the territory. One Democrat assured his Indiana readers: "The National Kansas Committee says, there are today thirty thousand 'free state' settlers in Kansas, and only about five thousand 'proslavery.'" Another editor published a dubious story about the societies, arguing they were sending so many emigrants that some were left without provisions: "I saw many—very many poor families, landed at Leavenworth—sent out by the New England Aid Societies who had not the means to bury the dead of their company." Democrats were confident. Although their fellows south of the Ohio River promised voters a new slave state, those on the north side jubilantly predicted a free Kansas.[18]

When they sacked the antislavery settlement of Lawrence on May 21, 1856, proslavery forces in Kansas made it harder for Democrats in the Old Northwest to win antislavery voters. Though Republicans were outraged, Democrats reacted differently. Party leaders dissected many firsthand accounts of the attack to discredit them. When one eyewitness spoke at an Ohio Republican meeting, a local Democratic newspaper editor published the account. This was the second time the speaker had given his report, and he had changed some details. Pointing them out, the editor charged, "Can anyone take that which he states for truth, when he states one day that he was in Lawrence at the time . . . and the next avows he was not?" Despite their efforts, Democrats in the region needed something dramatic to allay fears of a slave power intent on spreading slavery.[19]

The party first played up a united West with blasts from the past. Westerners revered national figures from their region, and Democrats rushed to claim them. Of course they lionized Andrew Jackson. Democrats published stories about the seventh president well into the 1850s, reminding voters that he was a leading light in their party for decades. For the 1856 election, Democrats turned to another famous man from west of the

Appalachians: Henry Clay. Though popular, Clay was more problematic for the party. The deceased Kentuckian had been the most celebrated member of the Whig Party, the Democrats' main rival before 1854. Though many Whigs honored Clay, Democrats, especially Jackson, had hated him. One western Democrat had denounced Clay as a coward in 1844, calling him the "black leg of Ashland"—Ashland was Clay's home in Lexington, Kentucky. The past campaigns left Democrats with some work to do if they wanted to coopt the fallen Whig's memory.[20]

Democratic efforts to adopt Clay's legacy began when he died in 1852. When newspapers carried news of his death, Americans from all parties mourned, draping entire towns in black. By 1855, knowing they needed former Whig voters, Democrats were claiming Clay as one of their own, elevating his memory beyond the party battles of the past. They praised the man for his many compromises and wished he were alive to save the Union again. One Michigan Democrat lumped him in with Thomas Jefferson and other leading statesmen from American history. Others directly addressed former Whigs to win them over, some holding joint conventions with Clay's old followers; the meetings had been impossible only four years earlier. If Democrats could claim Clay, it would go a long way toward winning his former supporters. Unfortunately, Clay had died four years earlier, ruling out a direct endorsement from the political legend.[21]

Clay's former enemies did have one living link to the famed politician—a surviving son. James B. Clay had followed his father's political beliefs most of his life and was a solid Whig until the party collapsed in 1854. Once that party fell apart, the younger Clay looked over his options. He first rejected the Know-Nothings, for their hatred of immigrants, before doing the unthinkable: he, the son of the most famous Whig, joined the Democratic Party. A zealous convert, the younger Clay traveled through Kentucky making speeches and saying he wanted to "strike a blow for the Union." Democrats throughout the West joyfully printed his words while the news angered former Whigs who had become Know-Nothings or Republicans. They condemned the younger Clay for his audacity in joining their fallen leader's old enemies. Though the younger Clay was not his father, his endorsement was close enough for most Democrats.[22]

Democrats had also nominated a national ticket that offered them a chance to allay the fears among free state westerners. After rejecting the Illinoisan Douglas, the party chose Pennsylvanian James Buchanan for president. Though Buchanan was popular among most Democrats despite his northeastern origins, most former Whigs in the Old Northwest and elsewhere despised him for an old scandal. After John Quincy Adams won the 1824 presidential election, Jackson charged Clay with using his power to influence the election after it was thrown into the US House. Adams later appointed the Kentuckian to the office of US secretary of state, a plum position for someone with presidential aspirations Many blamed Buchanan for originating the story, including several Know-Nothings who condemned the Pennsylvanian for the years of political acrimony. A northeasterner and a personal enemy of one western icon, Buchanan was on shaky ground in a region critical to his presidential hopes.[23]

To balance the ticket, Democrats needed a western-born vice presidential candidate; Kentuckian John C. Breckinridge fit the bill. He was born west of the Appalachians, had owned several enslaved workers, and was a rising star in the party. Since Breckinridge was a friend of Douglas, his elevation would also be an olive branch to the Illinoisan and his disappointed supporters. Convention delegates from the slave states quickly backed him. Winning over Democrats from the Old Northwest, however, proved a harder task. On the first ballot, only the Ohio and Iowa delegations voted for him. On subsequent ballots, delegates from the other western free states slowly got behind Breckinridge, and he swept to victory. The young man accepted the nomination with a speech evoking the Union and condemning sectionalism. By the convention's end, the party was elated. Democrats had one eastern candidate and one western candidate—in their eyes, a well-balanced ticket.[24]

Democrats in the Old Northwest welcomed the national ticket with gusto, and one committee from Indiana thought they could use the newly minted vice presidential candidate to alleviate free state fears about slavery. Hoping to hold the largest political rally in the region's history, the Democratic committee sent a representative who personally invited Breckinridge to the rally. Although political candidates generally stayed home during the nineteenth century, the Kentuckian bucked this tradition with a tour through the Northwest. He accepted the committee's invitation without hesitation. For the meeting's location, the members chose the Tippecanoe battlefield—Kentucky militiamen had assisted in the battle, making the symbolism of a united American West more explicit for attendees. With excited Democrats from all over the West and a national candidate on the guest list, the meeting was sure to go a long way in delivering the Old Northwest to Buchanan.[25]

The Tippecanoe meeting gained greater prestige later that month. In an appeal to former Whigs, the younger Clay agreed to join Breckinridge. The sight of Clay and Breckinridge on one stage was sure to impress the politically homeless former Whigs. The committee then added another name to the guest list: Douglas. Despite losing the nomination, the Illinois senator campaigned for Buchanan, and his presence was likely to command even more listeners, despite his role in passing the Kansas-Nebraska Act two years earlier. The meeting's timing was also crucial. Wanting to maximize its punch, planners scheduled it for September, a few months before the presidential election. The most well-known Democrats from north and south of the Ohio River meeting at the Tippecanoe battlefield would send a message that the entire West was united behind Buchanan. Breckinridge readied his group then set off. Starting in Kentucky, the young politician delivered speeches admonishing listeners to vote Democratic.[26]

Breckinridge and his guests crossed the Ohio River speaking in every town where they stopped. Enthusiastic audiences, unfamiliar with seeing national candidates, flocked to see the young man. When the party finally reached Tippecanoe, hundreds turned out. Breckinridge was the featured speaker, and he chose his words carefully. Though he supported slavery and the rights of slaveowners, he assured listeners that his party only supported self-determination in Kansas. He ardently denied any Southern conspiracy to push slavery on the Kansans saying that "he was connected with no political organization which desired to extend slavery." Flanked by Clay and Douglas, Breckinridge finished his speech talking of a united West: "The beautiful Ohio, then, instead of being a barrier between us, will continue to only be an imaginary boundary between a community of brothers." The message was a simple one. Slaveowners were not forcing slavery on the Kansans, and there was no slave power conspiracy.[27]

Breckinridge inadvertently opened himself and his party to critics with his carefully tailored speech; his words were a little too antislavery for more than a few Southern political enemies. One Louisiana Know-Nothing pointed to another speech in Ohio where Breckinridge had likewise said that "he was connected with no political organization which desired to extend slavery." The Southerner asked "whether the Buchanan Democracy of Louisiana endorse the declaration of their candidate for the Vice Presidency!" An Indiana Know-Nothing spoke in the same vein. Charging Democrats with running a dual campaign, he asserted, "It may probably astonish the Democracy of our neighboring state across the river to learn... some little leaders among their brethren, are boldly taking a free-soil position." Though the allegations were laughable at best—Breckinridge later served in the Confederate army and as the Confederate secretary of war—his attempts to win western free state voters made him vulnerable to charges of duplicity.[28]

The fall elections brought welcome news for Democrats. Party members in Illinois held their seats in the US House while those in Indiana and Ohio regained a combined thirteen seats. Indiana Democrats also recaptured majorities in the General Assembly, won the governor's mansion, and later regained a US Senate seat. The news, however, was not all rosy. Democrats lost a combined three congressional seats from Michigan, Wisconsin, and Iowa, along with the governor's race in Illinois, a sign of weakness in those states. Despite these setbacks, the presidential election brought more success when Buchanan won Indiana and Illinois. Combined with his wins elsewhere, the Pennsylvanian captured the presidency. Republican John C. Frémont won Iowa, Ohio, Michigan, and Wisconsin in the Old Northwest, but his power was concentrated in the Northeast; he took every state in the region except Pennsylvania. Two years after Democrats in the Old Northwest were at a nadir, their midwestern-style political campaign had helped them eke out crucial victories.[29]

Democrats north of the Ohio River continued their anti-northeastern rhetoric after the election had ended. One published an insulting poem that recounted some of New England's alleged crimes against the country. The "New England of the Revolution," the author lamented, was gone. What replaced it was "that New England which arms her 'paupers' to go to Kansas to incite civil and servile war, and murder citizens of the United States." Calling the region lost, he continued, "New England has been overrun by the Goths and Vandals of Black Republicanism." Of course, the author ignored the four Old Northwestern states where majorities had backed Frémont and the monumental efforts Democrats had taken to reassure antislavery voters in the region concerned about the institution's expansion. Though on the surface, enough voters in the Old Northwest had rejected the Republican Party, Democrats had run a campaign assuring them that slavery was contained.[30]

As Buchanan packed his bags for the White House, there were ominous signs for the victorious politician. An Indiana Democrat warned, "If [Buchanan] follows the footsteps of [President Franklin Pierce] and slavery be introduced into Kansas... his election is to be deplored by every friend of humanity." The new president should have heeded these words. Wanting to end the Kansas controversy, Buchanan endorsed a proslavery state constitution in late 1857. In 1860, angry voters in the Old Northwest, including majorities in Indiana and Illinois, voted for Lincoln as the party swept to victory. Ironically, northern Democrats who had nominated Douglas that year campaigned on restoring order in Kansas and holding new elections while preserving the Union. Four years after they had first run a midwestern-style campaign, Democrats in the Old Northwest repeated some of the same rhetoric. In 1860, however, they were unsuccessful.[31]

Though they were still suspicious of northeasterners and enough voters had supported Buchanan in 1856, the Democratic campaign in what Americans called the Old Northwest showed that debates over slavery were already drawing a new border down the Ohio River to go along with the one down the Appalachian Mountains. Alarmed at the possibility of slavery in the territories, voters in the Old Northwest demanded guarantees that slavery would be confined to the South. In response, Democrats in the region crafted a unique campaign that reminded voters of their suspicions of northeasterners and allayed fears of slavery's expansion. Due to the sectional strife, party members had created a midwestern campaign for midwestern voters. While successful, the campaign indicated that the days of a united West were numbered. Decades before the term entered the American lexicon, westerners living north of the Ohio River from the Appalachian Mountains to the Mississippi River Valley were becoming midwesterners.

Notes

1. Part of this research was included in Andrew W. Wiley, "'A Steady Opposition to Every Evolution of Radicalism': Western Conservatism in Civil War Era Indiana" (PhD diss., Univ. of Calgary, 2019), and "Commemorating the old battleground: the celebrations of the Battle of Tippecanoe and 1850s politics," *American Nineteenth-Century History* 25 (Nov. 2024), https://www.tandfonline.com/doi/full/10.1080/14664658.2024.2357446?src=exp-la.

2. For additional scholarship on the nineteenth century West or Midwest, see Nicole Etcheson, *The Emerging Midwest: Upland Southerners and the Political Culture of the Old Northwest, 1787–1861* (Bloomington: Indiana Univ. Press, 1996), xi–xiii; Susan E. Gray, *The Yankee West: Community Life on the Michigan Frontier* (Chapel Hill: Univ. of North Carolina Press, 1996), 1–14; Adam Arenson, *The Great Heart of the Republic: St. Louis and the Cultural Civil War* (Columbia: Univ. of Missouri Press, 2011), 1–8; Stephen I. Rockenbach, *War upon our Border: Two Ohio Valley Communities Navigate the Civil War* (Charlottesville: Univ. of Virginia Press, 2016), 1–10; Richard F. Nation, *At Home in the Hoosier Hills: Agriculture, Politics, and Religion in Southern Indiana, 1810–1870* (Bloomington: Indiana Univ. Press, 2005), 1–5; Aaron Astor, *Rebels on the Border: Civil War, Emancipation, and the Reconstruction of Kentucky and Missouri* (Baton Rouge: Louisiana State Univ. Press, 2012), 1–9. Examples of historians who argue the Civil War split the West include Christopher Phillips, *The Rivers Ran Backward: The Civil War and the Remaking of the American Middle Border* (New York: Oxford Univ. Press, 2016), 5–14; and Matthew E. Stanley, *The Loyal West: Civil War and Reunion in Middle America* (Urbana: Univ. Press of Illinois, 2016), 62–65. One historian who argued the division took place before the war is Stanley Harrold, in *Border War: Fighting over Slavery before the Civil War* (Chapel Hill: Univ. of North Carolina Press, 2010), xi–xv. For additional information on some of the origins of the term *middle west* or *Midwest*, see James R. Shortridge, *The Middle West: Its Meaning in American Culture* (Lawrence: Univ. Press of Kansas, 1989), 16–17.

3. Nichole Etcheson, *Bleeding Kansas: Contested Liberty in the Civil War Era* (Lawrence: Univ. Press of Kansas, 2004), 9–27; Eugene H. Berwanger, *The Frontier against Slavery: Western Anti-Negro Prejudice and the Slavery Extension Controversy* (Urbana: Univ. of Illinois Press, 2002), 3–6, 22–23, 25, 32–33, 37–38, 49, 122.

4. E. D. Logan to William Hayden English, June 1, 1854, box 1, folder 15, William Hayden English Papers Box 1 Folder 15, Indiana Historical Society (hereafter cited as IHS), Indianapolis; Etcheson, *Bleeding Kansas*, 23; Phillips, *Rivers Ran Backward*, 25–26. The scholarship on the fall of the Whig Party and rise of the Know-Nothings and Republicans is vast; one example is Tyler Anbinder, *Nativism and Slavery: The Northern Know-Nothings and the Politics of the 1850s* (New York: Oxford Univ. Press, 1992).

5. *Crawfordsville (IN) Review*, Oct. 7, 1854; *Daily State Sentinel* (Indianapolis), Dec. 7, 1855; William E. Gienapp, *The Origins of the Republican Party, 1852–1856* (New York: Oxford Univ. Press, 1988), 113–27; Etcheson, *Bleeding Kansas*, 50–60, 103–7.

6. *Union and Eastern Journal* (Biddeford, ME), Feb. 9, 1855; *Glasgow (MO) Weekly Times*, Nov. 1, 1855; "Letters of Louisa Lovejoy, 1856–1864, Part III," *Kansas Historical Quarterly* 14, no. 4 (1947): 368–70; Etcheson, *Bleeding Kansas*, 35–37.

7. Lyman Beecher et al., "Circular New England Emigrant Aid Company, 1855," available at the Kansas Historical Society website, Accessed Oct. 10, 2020, https://www.kshs.org/index.php?url=km/items/view/90690. *Cadiz (OH) Democratic Sentinel*, Dec. 19, 1855.

8. *Daily State Sentinel* (Indianapolis), Apr. 25, 1855; Etcheson, *Bleeding Kansas*, 54–60.

9. *Ottawa (IL) Free Trader*, Apr. 19, 1856. For Douglas's background including his settlement in Illinois, see Martin H. Quitt, *Stephen A. Douglas and Antebellum Democracy* (New York: Cambridge Univ. Press, 2012), 13–64.

10. *Eaton (OH) Democrat*, Aug. 7, 1856. Ohio Democrats suffered numerous losses in the 1854 elections. See Gienapp, *Origins of the Republican Party*, 113–21.

11. *Weekly Indiana State Sentinel* (Indianapolis), Sept. 11, 1856.

12. *Daily State Sentinel* (Indianapolis), July 7, 1856. Thomas H. Greer, "Economic and Social Effects of the Depression of 1819 on the Old Northwest," *Indiana Magazine of History* 44 (Sept. 1948): 227–43.

13. *Daily State Sentinel* (Indianapolis), July 4, 1856. Donald R. Hickey, *The War of 1812: A Forgotten Conflict* (Urbana: Univ. of Illinois Press, 1989), 275–77.

14. *M'Arthur (OH) Democrat*, June 19, 1856; *Paw Paw (MI) Free Press*, June 2, July 28, 1856; Etcheson, *Bleeding Kansas*, 98–102, 104–5.

15. *Speech of R. W. Thompson, Upon the Political Aspects of the Slavery Question Made at a Public Meeting of the People. Terre-Haute, Indiana, the 11th Day of August, 1855* (Terre Haute: Express Power-Press Print, 1855), 21, 25–37, 39–41, 54–55, 70–71.

16. Michael C. Kerr Political Scrapbook, box 2, folder 178, Walter Q. Gresham Papers, IHS.

17. *Ottawa Free Trader*, July 28, 1855; *Grand River Times* (Grand Haven, MI), Mar. 5, 1856.

18. *Daily State Sentinel* (Indianapolis), Aug. 9, 1856; *M'Arthur (OH) Democrat*, Aug. 7, 1856. James Stirling, *Letters from the Slave States* (London: John W. Parker & Son, West Strand, 1857), vii–viii, 93.

19. *Cadiz Democratic Sentinel*, July 23, 1856; Etcheson, *Bleeding Kansas*, 98–107.

20. *Paw Paw (MI) Free Press*, Mar. 24, 1856; *Spirit of Democracy* (Woodsfield, OH), Oct. 8, 1856; *Indiana State Sentinel* (Indianapolis), Oct. 10, 1844. For more on the origins of the animosity between Jackson and Clay, see Donald Ratcliffe, *The One-Party Presidential Contest: Adams, Jackson, and 1824's Five-Horse Race* (Lawrence: Univ. Press of Kansas, 2015), 253–57.

21. *Paw Paw (MI) Free Press*, Aug. 27, 1855; William J. Blakes to John G. Davis, June 18, 1855, box 2, folder 2, John G. Davis Papers, IHS. Sarah Bischoff Paulus, "America's Long Eulogy for Compromise: Henry Clay and American Politics, 1854–58," *Journal of the Civil War Era* 4 (Mar. 2014): 29–30.

22. *Democrat and Sentinel* (Edensburg, OH), Aug. 13, 1856; Lindsey Apple, *The Family Legacy of Henry Clay: In the Shadow of a Kentucky Patriarch* (Lexington: Univ. Press of Kentucky, 2011), 105–8.

23. *Official Proceedings of the Democratic National Convention Held in Cincinnati* (Cincinnati: Enquirer Company Steam Printing Establishment, 1856), 39–42; *Daily Journal* (Evansville, IN), June 11, 1856. Ratcliffe, *One-Party Presidential Contest*, 237–44, 253–55.

24. *Official Proceedings of the Democratic National Convention Held in Cincinnati*, 63–69; William C. Davis, *Breckinridge: Statesman, Soldier, Symbol* (Lexington: Univ. Press of Kentucky, 2010), 27–28, 57, 140–44, 172; Quitt, *Stephen A. Douglas and Antebellum Democracy*, 126–27.

25. B. W. Engle to Joseph A. Wright, Aug. 6, 1856, box 1, folder 12, Joseph A. Wright Papers, Indiana State Library (hereafter cited as ISL), Indianapolis. Adam Jortner, *The Gods of Prophetstown: The Battle of Tippecanoe and the Holy War for the American Frontier* (New York: Oxford Univ. Press, 2012), 190–200.

26. *Daily State Sentinel* (Indianapolis), Aug. 23, 1856; Davis, *Breckinridge*, 154.

27. *Weekly Indiana State Sentinel*, Sept. 11, 1856; Davis, *Breckinridge*, 147, 150–56.

28. *Southern Sentinel* (Iberville Parish, LA), Sept. 27, 1856; *Daily Journal* (Evansville), Aug. 5 1856; Davis, *Breckinridge*, 150, 154–64, 293.

29. *Weekly Indiana State Sentinel* (Indianapolis), Nov. 22, 1856; Gienapp, *Origins of the Republican Party*, 414–17; *Daily State Sentinel* (Indianapolis), Dec. 3, 1857.

30. *Ashland (OH) Union*, Nov. 19, 1856.

31. A. Johnston to Allen, Hamilton, Nov. 12, 1856, box 20, folder 11, Hamilton Family Papers, ISL; Etcheson, *Bleeding Kansas*, 159; Michael F. Holt, *The Election of 1860: "A Campaign Fraught with Consequences"* (Lawrence: Univ. Press of Kansas, 2017), 134–66, 194–95.

Chapter 7

German or Yankee?

Defining Ohio Identity on the Pennsylvania Border

RANDALL S. GOODEN

In April 1998, a group of township and village officials from Mahoning County, Ohio, met at the offices of Eastgate Regional Development and Transportation Agency—the local regional development council—in Youngstown. The meeting took place in response to a proposal by trustees of Poland Township and the mayor of the Village of Poland to reroute State Route 170, which ran south from the City of Struthers through Poland and Springfield Townships and Columbiana County. The highway carried heavy truck traffic between area landfills and limestone quarries and Interstate 680, the expressway that joined Interstate 80, north of Youngstown, with the Ohio Turnpike, south of the city. During the replacement of a bridge in Poland Village, the state route had been temporarily redirected along Western Reserve Road, a county road that skirted the border between Poland and Springfield Townships, and Poland wanted to make the change permanent.[1]

Mayor Ruth Wilkes of Poland cited the risks the heavily traveled highway posed to children, as it passed by schools in her village. State Route 170—whether its path was altered or not—also passed by two schools in Springfield Township and New Middletown Village, which lay within Springfield. The argument about school safety paled, and the contrasting cultures and economies of Poland and Springfield loomed large—not just in the spoken conversation but in the unspoken differences among the officials gathered in the room.

"I'd like you to try driving a corn planter down Kushner's Hill like I'm going to be doing this afternoon," Trustee Lee Kohler of Springfield Township challenged. Kohler's statement came as he explained that Western Reserve Road was not capable of consistently handling the heavy truck traffic of a state route. At a deeper level, the challenge defined the differences between Poland and Springfield.

Kohler had become a trustee in large part because of his prominence as a farmer in Springfield Township. Agriculture remained economically, socially, and politically important in the township in the late twentieth century as it had since the earliest days of settlement. Kohler exemplified that importance as a leader in local government and as head of the board of the Canfield Fair—the largest county fair in Ohio. His community role drew from deep family roots in the township's early Pennsylvania German—or Pennsylvania Dutch—culture.

Fellow trustee Reed Metzka accompanied Kohler to the meeting, and Metzka's background added to the contrasts of Springfield with Poland. Metzka, a leader in local Democratic politics (Kohler was a Republican), was a truck driver. His family had been part of an early-twentieth-century migration into Springfield Township of families of eastern European and Italian heritage. That migration swelled in the years following World War II. In Springfield, the farming and industrial experiences of its people melded into a tension of coexistence that exasperated internal community rivalries but gave the people a common working-class front in interacting with those outside the township.

Mayor Wilkes and Trustee Franklin Bennett of Poland Township, who joined her at the meeting, represented a different kind of community. Wilkes, Bennett, and their colleagues were from professional backgrounds—attorneys and architects. Poland Township had a history of agriculture and mining and residual industries, but the core of Poland rested in its white-collar, suburban identity.

The differences at that regional development council meeting did not occur in a vacuum. They took place because of the heterogeneous formation of society along Ohio's border with Pennsylvania that began with the first white settlement. At the turn of the eighteenth into the nineteenth century, two distinct areas of settlement butted against each other along the border between the Northwest Territory and Pennsylvania. The Connecticut Western Reserve, carved out of the area running south from Lake Erie to the 41º latitude north, consisted of the remnants of that New England state's claims to the Ohio Country—based on Connecticut's colonial charter. The federal government had extended the Seven Ranges north from the Ohio River along the Pennsylvania line to the Western Reserve. While settlement occurred in these two areas during the same period, the patterns of settlement were quite different. Part of this had to do with the difference in surveys—townships in the Western Reserve were twenty-five square miles. Those in the Seven Ranges were thirty-six square miles. This resulted in a sparser, less cohesive population to the south.

The Western Reserve consisted of Connecticut's western lands held back from its cession to the national government in 1786. The Connecticut Legislature vested the Connecticut Land Company with the lands and allowed its stockholders to claim tracts of land. The company surveyed the area. The southeastern corner of the reserve—next to the Pennsylvania line—was labeled Township 1 in Range 1 for land grant purposes. That move established the future confines of Poland Township.[2]

Lands south of the Western Reserve belonged to the federal government and had been placed in the expansive jurisdiction of Washington County, with its seat in Marietta, in 1788. As the population grew along the Ohio River, Jefferson County was formed in 1797, and Steubenville became the county seat. The new county included the area of Springfield Township, but no part of the county north of the Ohio River at present-day East Liverpool, Ohio, had been surveyed. The federal government remedied that with a survey in 1798–99.[3] During the survey, Springfield Township received its geographic designation as Range 1, Township 9, and its name because the surveyors camped in a field with a "fine spring."[4]

The histories of the respective land claims, surveys, and modes of land sales influenced the patterns of settlement in the Western Reserve and the extension of the Seven Ranges. These factors determined the origins of the settlers and resulted in cultural distinctions between the two areas.

New England stamped the Western Reserve with its character. Stockholders in the Connecticut Land Company had received large tracts of land and sold smaller parcels to settlers. Most of the marketing of the land took place in Connecticut, but many of the stockholders actively worked in the

Western Reserve to develop it and attract people. Many of those people came from contiguous areas of Pennsylvania. In addition, some squatters from Pennsylvania had taken up residence in the reserve before the land company was organized, and the company legitimized their claims. The route for migration into the northern portion of the Western Reserve passed from New England through New York and along the southern shore of Lake Erie, but the path of settlement in the southern portion reached up from the Ohio Valley through the Beaver Valley to the Mahoning Valley—having been fed by the Forbes Road and Cumberland Road. Many New Englanders traveled southward and took these roads west, but the southern route also encouraged settlement from Pennsylvania. Regardless of the origins of the early residents of the Western Reserve, however, Connecticut's political and social culture became important.[5]

"Even at this writing a large part of the Western Reserve, particularly the eastern section, is quite as much like New England as Connecticut itself," historian Harriet Taylor Upton wrote in 1910. An early resident of Poland, Hannah Smith recalled, "Poland was at the time [1803] the largest settlement on the Reserve, there being about forty families. She noted, "Three of these were Yankees, the rest Scotch-Irish from Pennsylvania." Smith explained that the Pennsylvanians "were a pretty rough, hard lot, so far as customs and manners were concerned" but "our three Yankee families had some education and in time gave a character to the settlement that it held for a long time."[6]

The settlement of Poland came about through the work of Turhand Kirtland, an agent for the Connecticut Land Company. In 1798, Kirtland chose a mill site on Yellow Creek and convinced his brother-in-law Jonathan Fowler to leave Connecticut to locate at the mill site and establish a tavern nearby. Settlement grew, and with it, Connecticut surrendered its jurisdiction over the Western Reserve to the Northwest Territory in 1800, and the territorial government organized a county in the reserve. Trumbull County encompassed the entire area, and Poland was situated at the county's extreme southeastern corner.[7]

From the start, the settlement patterns of Springfield differed from those of the Western Reserve. With the survey of the extension of the Seven Ranges taking place later than that of the Western Reserve, settlement in Springfield lagged somewhat. Whereas New Englanders generally focused on village life in their township centers, settlers in the Seven Ranges built towns to serve the farms but centered their lives on their families and their farms. Springfield's first white settlers followed the Forbes Road and Ohio and Beaver Rivers into the area from Pennsylvania and Maryland. They were not as well off as the people of the Western Reserve, and they paid less for their land, purchased at the federal land office in Steubenville. These people descended from German settlers on the eastern edge of the Appalachians and kept the solitary and insular habits of the mountain fringes. Known as Pennsylvania Dutch, they brought their culture to the Ohio frontier. Later waves of German American migrants and immigrants from Germany came to Springfield and added to that culture.[8]

Springfield Township historian Harry P. Davis wrote that these German Americans "were noted for their solid prosperity, and in the early days offered stubborn resistance to the new surroundings, and the tendency with which they clung to their language, customs and traditions of their forefathers." Davis continued, "As compared to some other groups, these people showed less inclination to education and had a greater desire to live together in separate communities than any other pioneer population." He added that the "contrast between their content and solitude, their devotion to labor, their economy, and introspective tendency of their minds with that of other peoples were remarkable."[9]

The family of Peter and Margaret Musser of York County, Pennsylvania, led the first settlers to Springfield. They purchased land in late 1800 and early 1801 in the extreme southeastern section of the township at the federal land office in Steubenville. Within a year, seventeen other families bought land in the township from the federal government. Six others bought land from Musser.[10]

With Ohio statehood in 1803, Columbiana County was created and took in the extension of the Seven Ranges. Springfield Township was organized as a unit of local government at the same time and included not just the township's surveyed bounds but areas to the south and west as well. While Trumbull County and Poland became part of the state of Ohio, too, the creation of a new county and a formal township government south of the Western Reserve solidified the distinctions between Poland and Springfield.

As settlement increased, geography further accentuated the differences between the people of the extended Seven Ranges and the Western Reserve. Along the Pennsylvania line, the Ohio–Beaver–Mahoning River

In 1812, Ohio still identified with its pioneer history, as expressed in the designation of the Connecticut Western Reserve and the original federal lands in the Steubenville District to the south on this map. Trumbull and Columbiana Counties butted against the Pennsylvania border. (John Melish and J. Vallance. *Ohio*. [Columbus {?}: John Melish, 1812], available via the Library of Congress, https://www.loc.gov/item/2011585887/.)

transportation corridor not only provided ingress for settlers from New England and Pennsylvania, but it evolved into a land and water route, and a road passed from the Beaver Valley into the Seven Ranges extension and the Western Reserve. It passed through the Musser settlement—which became known as Petersburg—and northward to Poland Village. By 1805, after Ohio statehood, this route became a state road.[11]

This road brought the people of Poland and Springfield into closer contact, but that close contact emphasized their differences. Yankees who passed back and forth through the Seven Ranges into Pennsylvania during the period described the Dutch or German American farmland as poor and underutilized and the towns as inconsequential.[12] For their part, the German American settlers of Ohio saw the New Englanders as cheap, prideful, and sanctimonious and often made light of them in their writings.[13]

In both cases, tendencies toward exclusivism characterized the New England settlers of the Western Reserve and the Dutch of the Seven Ranges. They brought with them the experiences of their places of origin, but those experiences merged with new ones in Ohio, and part of these included interactions with new groups. In turn, these interactions took place as each group strived for new identities as Ohioans and midwesterners. While jealously guarding their heritages, both the Dutch and the Yankees crossed in the early 1800s from whom their parents were to whom they and their children would be, and those new identities developed because of their contacts with other ethnic groups.

Much of the friction that took place between Poland's Yankees and the Springfield Dutch in the first years of settlement occurred because of religious differences and moral interpretations. Youngstown industrialist and amateur historian Joseph G. Butler Jr. stressed the early influence of religion on the Western Reserve pioneers. "In religion, they were Congregational, or Presbyterian, for in their home state of Connecticut the Congregational church was almost akin to the state church until the political revolution of 1818," he wrote.[14] While the people of the Western Reserve were not as homogeneous in religion as Butler suggested, his impression comes from the influence of those two churches on the region's society. The Plan of Union, the 1801 agreement between Congregational and Presbyterian Churches for cooperative missionary efforts on frontier, was responsible for the standing of those churches in the Western Reserve.[15] Even before that, however, a Presbyterian church was established in Poland—principally because of the ties of the Scots-Irish settlers of the township to the church.[16] Congregational missionaries arrived under the direction of the Connecticut Missionary Society and served as ambassadors—even enforcers—of New England culture.[17]

Amy DeRogatis notes in *Moral Geography: Maps, Missionaries, and the American Frontier*, "The most vulnerable places, according to the society were located on the periphery of the Western Reserve." Missionary letters described the settlements on the boundaries of the Western Reserve as spatially disorganized and generally immoral. As Congregational minister Abraham Scott attempted to spread his work south into Columbiana County, he found the people in a deplorable religious state in his view and blamed it on their rejection of Plan of Union missionaries.[18]

"It was practically assumed by the first-comers to Northern Ohio that the population was to be composed of Yankees wholly and always, and as such would of course be only Congregationally inclined," reflected an Ohio Congregational minister at the end of the nineteenth century. "Such bliss was not in store for the Buckeyes." The minister complained, "Almost at once the Pennsylvania Dutch and the Scotch-Irish began to profane the sacred soil with their presence."[19]

In truth, the people of Springfield Township were no less religious than those of Poland. The Dunkards, German Reformists, and Lutherans who settled there simply preferred their own religious heritages. Historian Glenn Weaver noted an "aversion to New England theology, and thus the interdenominational agencies, many of them strongly Congregational in their membership, were eyed with suspicion."[20] Nineteenth-century Lutheran Church historian Joel Swartz elaborated: "The truth is, the German people are both a conservative and convivial people." He characterized them as "averse to great and sudden changes" and explained that they "move slowly, but when they take an advanced position, it is with an intention to hold it."[21]

Swartz's description aptly fit the people of Springfield Township. The development of church life there was more sedate and understated but nonetheless active early in the township's history. Members of the German Reformed and Lutheran Churches built a small meetinghouse in 1802 at a settlement known as Old Springfield, on the state road between Petersburg and New Middletown. The two churches commonly shared meetinghouses and ministers in isolated areas during the 1800s and overlooked differences in ceremony and the use of music. As the century progressed, other Lutheran congregations sprung up in other settlements in the township.[22] Besides adherents of the German Reformed and Lutheran Churches, members of the Church of the Brethren—Dunkards or German Baptists—practiced their religion in Springfield Township. They worshipped at members' homes as early as 1808 and formed a center for the religion in the northwestern part of the township, near the Poland boundary.[23]

The contrasting religious environments in Poland and Springfield became especially evident as the religious revivalism of the early nineteenth century, the Second Great Awakening, profoundly affected Poland but not Springfield. Springfield's use of the German language in church services—and in everyday life—insulated its religious and social institutions. "As indicative of this it may be said that the Second Great Revival almost passed unnoticed by the German Reformed Church, not only because of the language barrier but also because the catechectical system which this denomination cherished almost precluded emotional revivalism on an extended scale," explained Weaver.[24]

The barriers extended to the social and political movements that spun off the Second Great Awakening and accentuated the differing views of Poland and Springfield toward reform efforts. Temperance activity, transplanted from New England, appeared in Poland as early as 1805, and the antialcohol crusade centered on the churches.[25] The Yankees gained part of their reputation for sanctimony from their zeal for the movement. Temperance houses, or dry taverns, popped up in the Western Reserve. This rubbed against the people of Springfield, where a significant farm-based distilling industry grew by 1820 and a notorious drinking establishment on the southern edge of New Middletown earned the place the name "Hell's Corners."

Swartz suggested that rough-and-tumble taverns were not common. "The German does not, as a rule, prefer solitary drinking," he admitted, but he contended that German American men preferred drinking at home among family members. "At once cheered and restrained by the presence of his family, he drinks his beer, but abhors the idea that he could disgrace himself before his loved ones by beastly excess," he insisted.[26] A historian of the Reformed Church elaborated, "Many of the fathers of the Reformed Church now living [in 1885], remember when intoxicating drinks were freely used upon all churchly occasions, and considered as one of the *spiritual influences* required to stimulate church work." The writer recalled that German American families of the early nineteenth century kept beer, wine, and liquor available for guests "and especially the pastor at the time of spiritual visitation."[27]

Reformers and their resistors often associated the temperance movement with the antislavery movement, and differences separated the people of Poland and Springfield on this subject as well. The Yankees viewed slavery, like alcohol, as a moral issue. As early as 1803, a debating society in Poland pondered the question "Is slaveholding proper or improper?"[28] The issue fermented until a new wave of migration from New England—precipitated by the year without a summer, 1816—coincided with a growing national division over the issue. The newcomers brought more zealous attitudes toward both temperance and slavery and influenced not only the area's religious and social thought but its political thought as well. As a result, in the 1820s the Western Reserve connected Jacksonian democracy to moral and economic irresponsibility and to proslavery and slavery-neutral politics. These views eventually transformed the region into a center of Whig and then Republican activity. Poland residents heartily participated in abolitionism, and an Underground Railroad station in the township fed stations farther north, in Youngstown and Ashtabula.[29]

The Underground Railroad route into Poland passed along the state road through Springfield Township, but Springfield—while not proslavery—followed the slavery-neutral politics that the Yankees increasingly abhorred. The Springfield Dutch, like many Americans of German heritage, favored Jacksonian democracy, and Springfield became strongly Democrat and remained so far into the twentieth century. Abolitionists made efforts to bring out antislavery sentiment among the Springfield Dutch, but that never gelled. Henry Kurtz, editor of the Church of the Brethren's *Gospel Visitor* and a Springfield resident, mirrored his township's views. In the aftermath of the Compromise of 1850, Kurtz tempered an antislavery essay in the periodical with editorial commentary decrying the politicization of moral issues. He argued that moral problems could only be cured by religion—not politics.[30]

Following a speaking junket through Springfield, the editor of the *New Lisbon Anti-Slavery Bugle* expressed the frustration of reformers toward this attitude and the growing misunderstanding and mistrust between the two townships. He called the village of New Springfield, his first stop, "a very unattractive place with an attractive name" and questioned the intelligence of the German-speaking population. "Though the town may not be blessed with a scriptural flowing of milk and honey, it is unquestionably flooded with Lager Beer and Whiskey, possessing no less than four permanent doggeries, and one locomotive ditto," he told his readers. "Rum barrels you know, are rather an unstable foundation on which to build anti-slavery reform." The editor appreciated the challenge for antislavery activism in New Springfield but expected little success. Two days later, he arrived at Petersburg, six miles east—along the Pennsylvania line. The journalist remarked, "The people of Petersburg and vicinity, though good honest neighbors, and excellent farmers, are not particularly given to the investigation of moral reform, nor do they consider intellectual activity a cardinal virtue," and they possessed "a strong infusion of that phlegmatic trait of character, which is the delight of the Dutchman." He concluded, "*If* they ever become converted to the right they will stand until eternity is half gone; but that little *if* promises to bar their progress for some time to come."[31]

The issues of temperance and abolition pointed to the cultural and political divide between the German Americans—the Dutch—and the Yankees. The creation of a new county in the 1840s exasperated this divide by erasing political boundaries between the Seven Ranges and the Western Reserve. In 1846, The Ohio Legislature approved the creation of Mahoning County. It took Poland and nine other townships from southern Trumbull County and Springfield and the four other counties in the northern tier of Columbiana County and put them together. The legislature did this without seeking a referendum, and petitions from the new county pushed back against its creation. Ohio Democrats saw Mahoning County as a Whig scheme. Indeed, in the 1840s a trend existed for the Democrat-leaning German Americans in Columbiana County to consolidate their power by running slates of candidates in county elections, and a split in Columbiana County diluted German American influence.[32]

The new county had an artificial feel, and it pushed contrasting cultures together. This push became harder as social issues like temperance and slavery—particularly slavery—became more and more rancorous across the nation and intensified political and social polarization down to the local level. Both Poland and Springfield Townships overwhelmingly supported the Union when the Civil War broke out and sent large numbers of men into the US Army. Still, different opinions on the issues and conduct of the war existed. A September 1861 county Union convention nominated Youngstown Democratic politician and industrialist David Tod for governor, and Republican and Democrat support for the war seemed to coalesce, but rifts could be seen. "The most radical anti-slavery Republicans are *all* for Tod," reported a correspondent for the *Cleveland*

Morning Leader. "Nobody is opposed, but a very few Democrats [who] are beyond all hope of redemption, and who are in sentiment and feeling secessionists of the most dangerous kind."[33]

Little real secessionist sentiment existed among Democrats; however, a segment of the Democratic Party desired negotiation with the South. As the war progressed, and President Lincoln issued the Emancipation Proclamation, these Democrats complained that the war's purpose had turned

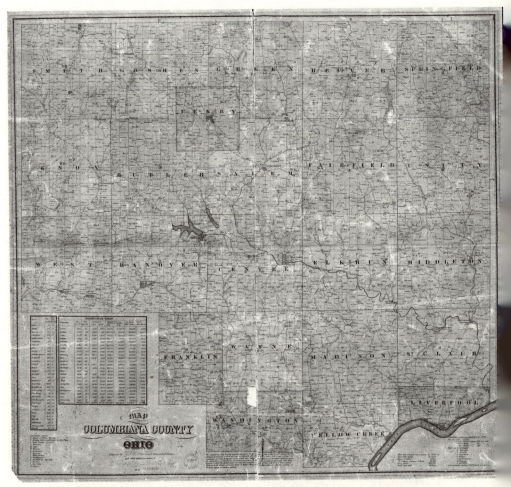

This 1841 map shows Columbiana County before it lost Springfield Township–in the northeast corner–in the creation of Mahoning County. (J. P. Willard, *Map of Columbiana County, Ohio* [Salem, OH{?}: Lewis Vail Esq., 1841], available via the Library of Congress, https://www.loc.gov/item/2012586252/.)

from preserving the Union to ending slavery. The introduction of the draft exasperated the situation, and opposition to war policy became more pointed. Such opposition rooted itself among Springfield Democrats.

Kenneth H. Wheeler explains similar opposition in Holmes County, another heavily German American area of Ohio. "Instead of seeing themselves as part of a grand social structure, these people thought about their existence in terms of the local area they inhabited, rarely considering the world beyond," he writes. He adds that "when the Civil War caused the national government to exert unprecedented influence in the lives of American citizens," it was viewed "as a threat to their local autonomy, the bedrock of their liberties."[34]

Still, a New Springfield correspondent to the *Mahoning Register*, the Republican newspaper in Youngstown, assured readers early in 1863: "The Union sentiment still holds sway."[35] Nevertheless, three months later reassurances seemed hollow. The raising of a Confederate flag at New Springfield revealed resentment against the federal government. Springfield struggled to find draft officials, and a federal marshal was fired upon when he hunted deserters in the township. Meanwhile, Poland boasted that it had exceeded its quota of army volunteers.[36]

"Ethnic ties provided an additional security to group settlements but sharpened the divides between strangers and friends," Robert M. Sandow further explains in his book *Deserter Country*. "During the war, ethnic loyalties offered the potential to undermine national allegiance."[37] In a flamboyant instance, Solomon and Susanna Heaver tried to express their opposition to the war in the safety and security of their German church. They presented their new son as Jefferson Davis Heaver at his christening at Old Springfield Reformed Church. Church leaders apparently chose their American identity over their German ethnicity. They refused to record the child's name as such.[38]

The Civil War experience marked Springfield Township as a rebel place, or at least emphasized its place on the periphery of Mahoning County and Ohio. It held onto its German American traditions and resisted challenges. This resembled the experiences of people of Pennsylvania as they moved from the nineteenth century into the twentieth. "As time went on, Pennsylvania German culture was shaped and tested by political and market forces, the arrival of new German-speaking immigrants, a civil war and two world wars, rising mass culture, and dramatic changes in transportation and technology," explains Dianna Wenger and Simon J. Bronner. "Rather than totally assimilate into the dominant culture, however, Pennsylvania Germans used the rhetoric of liberty to defend their right to remain culturally and ethnically distinct while also being good American citizens."[39]

Nonconformity perhaps served the Springfield Dutch better than rhetoric in their cultural defense. Their neighbors to the north viewed this as laziness and ignorance. One visitor from Poland inquired if the "loungers" on Springfield's corners and in its stores were "strikers," and the reply came that "they didn't strike enough—that some were living on the dignity of what they might have gained, and the others on the means of their expectations." He described the innkeeper at a "Dutch hotel" as jumping "spiritedly about talking simultaneously a half dozen languages," and concluded that "in the country as well as in the villages no very great pride is displayed or manifested."[40]

Poland, meanwhile, prided itself as a center of culture and education. "In education particularly, the Yankee background is easily discernible," observes Kenneth Lottick, a, historian of education. "In fact, the very development of education in the Reserve was quite contingent upon the precedents established on the Charles and the Connecticut." He adds that an "ingredient of moral fervor, a quality much present in the 'Connecticut Spirit' of the first comers," enhanced the educational culture of the area.[41] In a recent study, Bluford Adams has suggested this development of culture and education in the Western Reserve was a manifestation of combined New England and midwestern influences and not the transplanting of raw New England values.[42] Nevertheless, in antebellum times Poland became the home of an academy, a women's college, a law college, and a medical college. The women's college evolved into the coed Poland Union Seminary and claimed William McKinley as a student and, later in the century, Ida M. Tarbell as headmistress. Poland assumed an increasingly sedate, prim, and proper status, not only as it continued to face the less than temperate Springfield Township to the south but as industrial Youngstown and other communities along the Mahoning River grew to the north.[43] Adams points to a late-nineteenth-century trend in which New England "preservationists" resisted the erosion of their parent culture in the face of outside influences and viewed villages in the Western Reserve, such as Poland, as places where "one could still find the republican simplicity, strict morality, deep piety, and racial purity of old New England."[44]

Poland's image as a quiet, yet influential cultural and educational center contrasted with that of Springfield Township during the late nineteenth century, and attitudes toward alcohol continued to distinguish the two places. The antebellum temperance movement had grown into the prohibition movement, and in the midst of that crusade, alcohol had become Springfield's "predominant feature of business," according to one detractor. Singling out the community of New Springfield, he lamented, "this nefarious business stigmatizes the moral portion of that beautiful village and engenders its bad reputation abroad."[45] To be fair, the whiskey produced in Springfield Township was not consumed in the township alone but in nearby communities that enjoyed more pious reputations. As a result, liquor production grew beyond home or farm-based industry into corporate concerns. By the end of the nineteenth century, three substantial distilleries operated in Springfield Township—including Wire, Welsh & Company, which was known internationally.

Springfield Township farms fed the distilleries with their corn and rye, but the importance of the township's grain production went beyond its use in liquor production. As Youngstown flourished as a US iron and steel center, and its population exploded, Springfield provided more grain for the city's people and livestock than any other township in Mahoning County.[46] This economic standing gave Springfield added political importance, and the township became a key ally—partly because of the economic relationship but also because of distance—as Youngstown successfully competed to replace the traditional Western Reserve town, Canfield, as the county seat. Springfield's rising political status elevated local justice of the peace Jonathan Schillinger to county treasurer and then to county commissioner, and Poland diminished in political influence.

According to Adams, struggles such as those mounted by Springfield in its alliance with Youngstown "forced the Yankee Westerners to alter or even abandon their attempts to install New England–style institutions and cultural practices." Adams argues that "the Old Northwest took shape as the nation's most culturally hybridized and politically contested region" through these struggles, and in the process, antagonists picked away at "what they saw as the paternalism, moral superciliousness, and cultural imperialism of the Yankees."[47]

Springfield chided Poland through local newspaper columns. For example, a New Middletown writer referred to Poland as the "has-been hamlet on Yellow Creek." The Yankees did not give ground easily. A Poland resident reciprocated by calling New Middletown a "graveyard town."[48] Rivalry between Poland and Springfield intensified in the 1890s when the townships competed for railroad routes and as parts of Springfield favored Columbiana over Poland as the hub for their telephone service.

In the twentieth century, Youngstown's growth turned Poland into a suburb. In the midcentury, New Middletown in Springfield Township became a bedroom community for Youngstown steelworkers as housing development took place, Poland became more splintered as its northern communities of Struthers and Lowellville—with their industrial cultures and heavy immigrant populations—increasingly contrasted with the Yankee setting of Poland Village, which attracted those who wanted a slow-to-change community. In contrast, the influx of steelworkers into Springfield did not markedly change its setting; many of the move-ins were people of southern and eastern European heritage who sought a rural setting because their families had left farm life for a strange, new industrial culture in Youngstown.

The proximity of Poland and Springfield made it impossible for the two communities not to intermingle. Economic interaction took place. Young people from Springfield attended the schools in Poland—particularly in the nineteenth century before Springfield had its own high school. The towns' athletic teams competed against each other—in expressions of their intense rivalry. Yet, the proximity made the differences even more distinctive.

Through the twentieth century, the hybridization that Adams discusses, took place, with Poland struggling to maintain its Yankee aspects while the Springfield Dutch just as doggedly tried to preserve their culture. In the end, New England culture remained an important part of the identity of Poland and other scattered communities through the Western Reserve. Likewise, German American culture remained important in Springfield and localities across what George W. Knepper has called Ohio's "backbone"—historic Columbiana, Stark, Wayne, Holmes, and Knox Counties.[49] In a study of German American interaction with other groups, historian Kathleen Neils Conzen has commented, "There were significant conflicts with other Americans over regions that both worlds touched, in which neither emerged really victorious and both were fundamentally changed."[50] Her words apply to the conflict between Poland in the Yankee Western Reserve and Springfield in the Dutch—the German American—northern extension of the Seven Ranges.

In the twenty-first century, State Route 170 still follows the course it had when Poland and Springfield officials debated changing it—that path which had carried a state highway since the first decade of the nineteenth century. To the astute observer, the drive along the highway from Poland to Petersburg shows the effects of the contrasting and conflicting histories of Poland and Springfield in architecture and land use. Influenced by religion and the cultural and political attitudes and even language of the Western Reserve and the Seven Ranges, distinctive characteristics formed and reformed as the townships acted and reacted to local occurrences and to state and national trends and events. The Second Great Awakening, the great debates over slavery and temperance, the formation of Mahoning County, the Civil War, industrialization, and outmigration from the cities all affected the two townships. Both townships—situated on the Pennsylvania border—were gateways to the Midwest. Yet, both lent very different impressions of the identity of Ohio and the Midwest. The progression of history, however, shows that the relationship of these opposing places resulted in a newer culture that suffered and at the same time thrived from competition. The distinctive sectionalism between the Western Reserve and the Seven Ranges on the border between East and Midwest became part of the region's identity.

Notes

1. "Route Move Opposed," *Youngstown (OH) Vindicator*, May 19, 1998.
2. Harriet Taylor Upton, *History of the Western Reserve*, ed. H. G. Cutler (New York: Lewis, 1910), 9–11.
3. "Origins of Springfield Township Lie in Northwest Territory," *New Middletown (OH) Postmark*, Jan. 10, 2003.
4. Harry P. Davis, *Historical Collections of Springfield Township, Mahoning County, Ohio* (New Middletown: By the author, 1939), 7.
5. Upton, *History of the Western Reserve*, 21, 28.
6. Upton, *History of the Western Reserve*, 11, 630, 632.
7. Mahoning Valley Historical Society, *Historical Collections of the Mahoning Valley*, (Youngstown, OH: Mahoning Valley Historical Society), 10–11, 20, 473.
8. "The Pioneers of Springfield Township," *New Middletown Postmark*, Jan. 17, 2003; David T. Stephens and Alexander T. Bobersky, "The Origins of Land Buyers, Steubenville Land Office, 1800–1820," *Material Culture* 22 (Summer 1990): 39.
9. Davis, *Historical Collections of Springfield Township, Ohio*, 2.
10. "The Pioneers of Springfield Township," *New Middletown Postmark*.

11. "Notes from an Early Surveyor of the Township," *New Middletown Postmark*, Jan. 31, 2003.

12. Martha Pallante, "The Trek West: Early Travel Narratives and Perceptions of the Frontier," *Michigan Historical Review* 21 (Spring 1995): 93–96.

13. "The Fraternity of German Baptists," *Gospel Visitor*, June 1851, 37; *Der Vatersland Freund* (Canton, OH), 1834–41.

14. Jos. G. Butler Jr., *History of Youngstown and the Mahoning Valley Ohio*, 3 vols. (New York: American Historical Society, 1921), 1:123.

15. Amy DeRogatis. "Models of Piety: Plan of Union Missionaries on the Western Reserve, 1800–1806," *Journal of Presbyterian History* 79 (Winter 2001): 258.

16. Mahoning Valley Historical Society, *Historical Collections of the Mahoning Valley*, 473–74.

17. DeRogatis. "Models of Piety," 268.

18. Amy DeRogatis, *Moral Geography: Maps, Missionaries, and the American Frontier* (New York: Columbia Univ. Press, 2003), 56.

19. Rev. Delavan L. Leonard, "The Necrology of our Churches, 1800–1899," in *1796–1896 Centennial of Ohio Congregationalism Papers of the Ohio Church History Society*, 7 vols. (Oberlin: Ohio Church History Society, 1896), 7:21–22.

20. Glenn Weaver, "The German Reformed Church and the Home Missionary Movement before 1863: A Study in Cultural and Religious Isolation," *Church History* 22 (Dec. 1953): 299.

21. Joel Swartz, "The Lutheran Church," in *One Hundred Years of Temperance: A Memorial Volume of the Centennial Temperance Conference Held in Philadelphia, Pa., September, 1885* (New York: National Temperance Society and Publication House, 1886), 334.

22. Randall S. Gooden, "Old Springfield Was First Church," *New Middletown Postmark*, Feb. 14, 2003.

23. "Early History of the Church of the Brethren," *New Middletown Postmark*, Apr. 18, 2003.

24. Weaver, "The German Reformed Church and the Home Missionary Movement before 1863," 298–99.

25. Upton, *History of the Western Reserve*, 54.

26. Swartz, "Lutheran Church," 334.

27. Rev. W. C. Hendrickson, "The German Reformed Church," in *One Hundred Years of Temperance*, 384.

28. Mahoning Valley Historical Society, *Historical Collections of the Mahoning Valley*, 34–35.

29. Butler, *History of Youngstown and the Mahoning Valley Ohio*, 148–53, 430.

30. *Gospel Visitor*, Jan. 1851, 158–59.

31. "Field Notes," *New Lisbon (OH) Anti-Slavery Bugle*, Dec. 19, 1857.

32. *Der Vatersland Freund* (Canton, OH), Feb. 4, 1846; *Portage Sentinel* (Ravenna, OH), Feb. 4, Mar. 11, Apr. 8, 1846; *Cadiz (OH) Sentinel*, Feb. 18, 1846.

33. "Union Convention in Mahoning County," *Cleveland Morning Leader*, Sept. 4, 1861.

34. Kenneth H. Wheeler, "Local Autonomy and Civil War Draft Resistance: Holmes County, Ohio. *Civil War History* 45 (June 1999): 147, 157.

35. "New Springfield Correspondence," *Mahoning Register* (Youngstown, OH), Mar. 5, 1863.

36. *Mahoning Register*, Aug. 21, 1862, June 25, 1863; *Highland Weekly News* (Hillsboro, OH), July 16, 1863.

37. Robert M. Sandow, *Deserter Country: Civil War Opposition in the Pennsylvania Appalachians* (New York: Fordham Univ. Press, 2011), 18.

38. *Highland Weekly News*, July 16, 1863.

39. Diana Wenger and Simon J. Bronner, "Communities and Identities: Nineteenth to the Twenty-First Centuries," in *Pennsylvania Germans: An Interpretive Encyclopedia*, ed. Simon J. Bronner, and Joshua R. Brown (Baltimore: Johns Hopkins Univ. Press, 2017), 53.

40. "Springfield Township Observations," *Mahoning Vindicator* (Youngstown, OH), Oct. 31, 1873.

41. Kenneth V. Lottick, "The Connecticut Reserve and the Civil War," *History of Education Journal* 8 (Spring 1957): 92–95.

42. Bluford Adams, *Old and New New Englanders: Immigration and Regional Identity in the Gilded Age* (Ann Arbor: Univ. of Michigan Press, 2014), 172–74, 192–93.

43. Butler, *History of Youngstown and the Mahoning Valley Ohio*, 550–51.

44. Adams, *Old and New New Englanders*, 180–87.

45. *Columbiana (OH) Independent Register*, Feb. 15, 1872.

46. *New Middletown Postmark*, Mar. 20, 1998.

47. Adams, *Old and New New Englanders*, 173.

48. *Mahoning Dispatch* (Canfield, OH), Feb. 1898.

49. George W. Knepper, *Ohio and Its People* (Kent: Kent State Univ. Press, 1989), 173.

50. Kathleen Neils Conzen, "Phantom Landscapes of Colonization," in *The German-American Encounter: Conflict and Cooperation Between Two Cultures, 1800–2000*, ed. Frank Trommler and Elliott Shore (New York: Berghahn, 2001), 13.

Chapter 8

Where Does the Eastern Edge of the Midwest Fall in Ohio?

GREGORY S. ROSE

In 1784, Thomas Jefferson sketched a map of ten future states he envisioned arising within the newly acquired "Territory Northwest of the River Ohio," basically outlined by three prominent natural features: the Ohio River on the south, the Mississippi River on the west, and the Great Lakes on the north. His conceptual states, except as they touched those natural features, were bordered by straight lines based on latitude and longitude.[1] In time, five states and a portion of a sixth emerged from the Northwest Territory as guided by the Northwest Ordinance of 1787 and divided by surveyed lines differently located than Jefferson's, markers far more difficult to establish on the ground than on paper.[2] What became Ohio encompassed the entire state that Jefferson proposed to call "Washington" and parts of "Saratoga" and "Metropotamia."[3]

Although the somewhat amorphous "Midwest" region has expanded to include states beyond those originally within the Northwest Territory, Ohio still typically marks the Midwest's eastern edge. However, is assigning an entire state to one or another region—an area having certain shared internal characteristics differing from those found beyond it—the best approach to understanding a region's true extent? From a geographer's perspective, a border—the sharp demarcation between political entities—

is not necessarily a boundary—the transition zone marking a region's edge.[4] True regional boundaries typically ignore state borders unless states are employed as convenient divisions for data collection. As definitive as Ohio's border with Pennsylvania appears on the map, nothing in the environment or on the ground, apart from occasional markers or road signs, makes apparent that one has entered a different state or region. While the obvious natural feature of the Ohio River separates Ohio from West Virginia and Kentucky, multiple shared economic and cultural similarities on either side exceed differences, making the riverine physical border not necessarily a regional boundary. Abraham Lincoln described the ineffectiveness of borders during the Civil War: rivers are easily crossed and surveyor's lines are markers "over which people may walk back and forth without any consciousness of their presence."[5]

The establishment of Ohio's eastern border predated by many decades the development or presence of any economic or cultural characteristics that could form the basis for identifying the Midwest as a region or Ohio as part of it. Before Jefferson's map and statehood in 1803, what became Ohio's eastern border was already defined by Pennsylvania's western border and the Ohio River, which, south of the Pennsylvania line, marked Virginia's contact with Ohio. Establishing the western and southern borders of Pennsylvania and Virginia required years of negotiations, starting with resolution of competing territorial claims in colonial-era charters of New York, Connecticut, Pennsylvania, and Virginia, the latter receiving a grant of five hundred thousand acres of "Pennsylvania" territory in 1749.[6] According to its charter, Pennsylvania's southeastern corner touched Delaware's northern arc and its eastern border continued northward along the Delaware River; Pennsylvania's southwestern corner was located 5° longitude west of its southeastern corner, and the western border extended northward by that same value: always 5° longitude west of its riverine eastern border.[7] Mirroring the meandering Delaware River between Pennsylvania and New Jersey yielded a sinuous and difficult-to-define western border for Pennsylvania.

A joint commission labored from 1779 to 1786 to determine whether Pennsylvania or Virginia would retain disputed territory and where Pennsylvania's borders would be drawn.[8] The solution carried an extension of the Mason-Dixon line to a point 5° longitude west of the Delaware River, "and from thence a line to be produced due north as far as the states extended," forming, as declared in 1784, "'the boundary forever.'" "Forever" lasted barely a century. Remaining uncertainty over portions of the north–south line separating Ohio and Pennsylvania required appointment of a bistate boundary commission in 1878 to again identify and mark the border, firmly establishing it according to the latest surveying technology. The eighteenth-century surveyors accompanied by axmen spent two years, as seasons and weather permitted, hacking through forests and slogging through swamps to clear a twenty-to-thirty-foot swath and dragging measurement chains, with "monuments of such stones as were at hand were erected at irregular distances," to mark the border.[9] A century later, similar effort often was required to locate the line, as trees had regrown in many places and stone monuments had fallen or been commandeered for other purposes. This newly confirmed straight-line border between Ohio and Pennsylvania, combined with the natural barrier of the Ohio River on the southeast, established the eastern limits of the political entity of Ohio but said nothing about the state's regional affiliation: was Ohio in the Midwest?

Because state borders represent convenient markers for data collection and statistical analyses, combinations of states often are gathered into regions for comparative purposes. The 1850 census was the first to place states within regional groupings to present information collected by the national government.[10] Although some 1850 and 1860 statistics on land area, population, and density grouped Ohio with the Middle Atlantic region of Pennsylvania and its neighbors, state-based analyses typically included Ohio on the eastern edge of a region carrying labels such as the *Middle West, Midwest, West, Old Northwest, Northwest, Interior, Great Lakes,* or *Northcentral States* (often divided into East North Central, including Ohio, and West North Central subregions).[11] This variety of terms reflects historically evolving conceptions of this stretch of the nation's interior. Many studies of midwestern economic, socioeconomic, social, political, and cultural phenomena place Ohio fully within a state-based Midwest region, and similar conceptions of a Midwest that includes Ohio continue appearing in response to a narrowly focused recurring question, now typically posed on the internet: "Where is the Midwest, and what states belong in it?"[12] As the political region of the Northwest Territory matured economically and culturally, and as the nation expanded westward to incorporate subsequent Northwests, Ohio, as the original state, was left, however uncomfortably or debatably so, encompassed within but clearly on the eastern edge of an expanded Midwest.[13]

Other researchers have produced maps freeing regional conceptions from the political borders of Ohio by extending the Midwest eastward beyond Ohio, dividing the state between or among regions, or creating new states or regions. A 1955 geography of the North American Midwest distributed Ohio among four regions.[14] Two regions encompassing eastern and southern Ohio appeared on the Midwest's periphery: the Upper Ohio Valley and the Lower Ohio Valley, both including parts Pennsylvania, West Virginia, Kentucky, and Tennessee, which are not typically considered midwestern. Central and western Ohio fell within two other regions—the East-Central Lowland and the Lower Great Lakes, both elements of the "Inner Midwest." Another author's map of economic provinces placed the eastern portion of Ohio within the "Great Lakes and Northeastern Province," the western areas in the "Midwestern Province," and the southernmost part along the Ohio River in the "Southern Province."[15] Some researchers examining the nation's evolution have proposed new formations and names for current states or new regional combinations replacing the more traditional but variously defined Midwest. In these, Ohio becomes the center of larger entities encompassing parts of neighboring states and called "The Foundry" or "Industry" or "Rust Belt" or, in a concept using the population of metropolitan areas, transportation networks, and physical geography as the basis for reducing the states from fifty to thirty-eight, is split among the new states of Erie, Allegheny, Appalachia, and Mackinac.[16] Another approach created fifty states with equal populations to yield equal federal political representation, with Ohio divided among four reconceived states: Maumee, Firelands, Scioto, and Allegheny.[17] A reformatting of states into "megaregions" based on commuter traffic flow again apportioned Ohio into four zones tied to and named after the major metropolitan areas within or on the periphery of the state; later versions of this proposal included some quite creative names for the new national regions.[18]

During the last half century or so, researchers examining how people perceive vernacular or cultural regions have used that information to draw the eastern edge of the Midwest through central or eastern Ohio[19] (Fig. 8.1). A 1960 survey of postmasters asked if they thought their communities fell within or outside of the Midwest. The results revealed a core of the Midwest

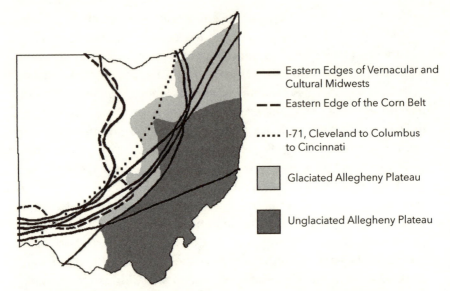

Fig. 8.1. Multiple elements can be considered in identifying the eastern edge of the Midwest. The dashed line approximates the eastern edge of the Corn Belt and the dotted line is the path of I-71 across the state from Cleveland through Columbus to Cincinnati. The solid lines represent generalized edges of vernacular or cultural Midwests mapped by the various studies referenced in this chapter. Most significant are the edges they have roughly in common, rather than the precise location of each delineation, and their similarities to the other edges on the map. This includes the Glaciated and Unglaciated Allegheny Plateaus.

reaching eastward to the northern end of the Ohio–Pennsylvania border with the rest of that line, southeast Ohio, and a range of counties inland from the Ohio River in the Midwest's periphery.[20] A map of vernacular regions based on the distribution of geographical terms in business names found common use of *Middle West, Midwest,* and *Mid-American* extending into eastern Ohio but not to the Pennsylvania or Ohio River borders, although those names appeared in southwestern Pennsylvania as secondary or tertiary monikers.[21] A national summary map of regional terms excluded eastern and southeastern Ohio from the Midwest, yet the same researcher's map of US cultural regions included far western Pennsylvania within the Middle West.[22] Another author's map of the appearance of *Midwest(ern)* or *Middle West(ern)* in business names placed Ohio in the lowest usage category but extended the terms into extreme western Pennsylvania.[23] A study of regional identities selected on warranty cards submitted by purchasers of a cultural relic—Cobra CB radios—mapped the eastern margin of the Midwest cutting through central Ohio.[24] And a researcher studying "state-level popular literature" discovered that only in west-central Ohio was midwestern affiliation strong; in the eastern half of the state, "middle-western self-identity in 1980 fell below one-third of the respondents."[25]

Direct surveys of Ohioans produced similar uncertainties regarding the regional affiliation of the state's eastern part. In one study, about half of Ohio college students agreed their state fell within the Midwest's core while just 10 percent of surveyed university students in various states included eastern Ohio in the Midwest; in a different study, Ohio college students excluded the state's eastern and southeastern border areas from the Midwest.[26] Some internet responses to the ongoing "Where is the Midwest?" question produce maps that draw regional boundaries within states, and those exclude southeastern and east central Ohio from the Midwest.[27] A recent two-part approach confirmed the eastern Ohio dilemma.[28] The first step in October 2023 asked twenty-two thousand people across twenty-two potential midwestern states if they considered themselves living in the region. Among Ohioans surveyed, 78.2 percent identified as midwesterners. Recognizing the state's edge location, a January 2024 survey of two thousand Ohio residents offered three regional possible locations: Midwest (selected by 87.2 percent), South (3.9 percent) and Appalachia (8.9 percent). Most significantly, a map generated from the data showed the highest Appalachia concentration in southeastern Ohio, along the Ohio River and inland by three counties or so from the northern tip of West Virginia through Ohio's southernmost curve. Perhaps the most straightforward description of eastern Ohio's uncertain regional attachment appears on a map of popular regions of North America in which the area falls into a "No Regional Affiliation" category, while central and western Ohio are firmly in the Midwest.[29]

The geographic, cultural, and perceptual studies reviewed above suggest that while the east and southeast are the least midwestern parts of Ohio, they best represent the "borderland place" where East Meets (Mid)west.[30] Evidence supporting a cultural region's boundaries also arises from the characteristics of the population establishing the enduring cultural elements defining that region. This is especially the case for what one geographer described as an area's "First Effective Settlers," Euro-American immigrants who filled what may have been or was perceived as unoccupied territory or displaced indigenous or previous inhabitants to form a new "self-perpetuating society" and established the area's "later social and cultural geography."[31] The Mormon culture region of Utah and surrounding states provides the signal example of the impact of First Effective Settlers on a locale's initial or existing and subsequent culture. Following arrival of Mormon immigrants in 1847, largely originating in northern states, Mormon religious communities enlarged and expanded over subsequent decades, displacing indigenous peoples and societies, ultimately creating a distinctive Euro-American cultural region within the western United States.[32]

Can the Midwest's eastern edge in Ohio be defined according to the birthplaces, as recorded in the 1850 census, of its Euro-American First Effective Settlers? For millennia, the Indigenous peoples formed Ohio's First Effective Settlers, only to be dispossessed, beginning at the cusp of the nineteenth century, through warfare, treaties ceding land, forced departures, and westward migrating Euro-Americans. From directly east of Ohio, Pennsylvanians represented the largest group of nineteenth-century settlers; other immigrants arrived from southeast, notably Virginia, and northeast, particularly New York and New England (with Connecticut contributing the most).[33] Yankees from New England and New York collected in northeast Ohio and along the Lake Erie shore; Pennsylvanians filled the center of the state from east to west, roughly along and north of the old National Road; and Southerners most heavily concentrated south of the National Road and closer to the Ohio River. The flow and distribution of Ohio's early-to-mid-nineteenth-century immigrants spread different nativity and cultural groups largely into an east–west alignment, basically perpendicular to the north–south alignment of the cultural Midwest, meaning that population origins cannot be used to define the eastern edge of the Midwest in Ohio.[34]

Do other types of evidence support the notion of an eastern and southeastern Ohio meeting place between the Midwest and the East? And might that, in combination with geographic, cultural, and perceptual factors, provide a definitive eastern boundary of the Midwest in Ohio? Five categories of physical evidence are proposed as possibilities: the eastern extent of the Corn Belt, general climate conditions for corn production, the pattern of forest associations, the location of different soil types, and the physiographic or landform regions occurring in eastern Ohio.

The Corn Belt and the Midwest appear essentially coterminous if the outlines used to define both regions ignore state borders.[35] Traditional Corn Belt environmental characteristics include relatively flat or gently rolling topography, deep and good to excellent soils developed on glacial material originally covered with grasslands or deciduous forests, and temperature ranges, length of frost free period, and sufficient precipitation necessary to support high levels of corn production.[36] North, west, south, and east of the Corn Belt core, growing conditions are less ideal, as topography, soils, temperature, and/or precipitation became limitations, which are today partially overcome by hybridization and specialization. From its early-nineteenth-century midwestern footprint in the Scioto and Miami river valleys of southcentral and southwestern Ohio, the incipient Corn Belt expanded as populations migrated westward and northward into new territories and states to generally encompass the western half of Ohio; most of Indiana, except the southern quarter; a limited zone in Michigan's southcentral Lower Peninsula; nearly all of Illinois and Iowa; a small section of southcentral and southwestern Wisconsin; and slices of southwestern Minnesota, southeastern North Dakota, eastern South Dakota, eastern Nebraska, northeastern Kansas, and northern Missouri.[37] Tallgrass prairie formed the natural or original vegetation in the most productive core of the Corn Belt, although many areas within the Corn Belt had been forested or included small, isolated grasslands within forested areas.

While the term *Corn Belt* appeared in the early 1880s, not until four decades later did the agricultural economist and geographer O. E. Baker become "the first to draw and spatially define" it, using data from 1919 agricultural census.[38] Baker's "east central United States" Corn Belt, based on where maize "is produced in great quantities and is more important than any other crop" (an assessment prior to largescale introduction of soybeans), encompassed "western Ohio, central and northern Indiana and Illinois"; most of Iowa; and adjacent parts of Minnesota, South Dakota, Nebraska, Kansas, and Missouri.[39] Nearly a century of agricultural activity and production data collected by the Census Bureau prior to Baker's cartographic analysis also revealed a midwestern zone where the growing of maize concentrated.[40] The 1820 census canvassers were the first to ask whether inhabitants were engaged in agriculture, but true data gathering did not begin until the 1840 census, for which separate schedules collected actual agricultural production statistics.[41] Maps built on information from 1840 and 1850 show "Corn Belt counties" extending from the southwestern quarter of Ohio through southeastern Iowa to include scattered counties in northern Missouri, while also noting the early trans-Appalachian Corn Belt zones in northern Kentucky and central Tennessee.[42]

By 1880, three additional decades of population expansion and agricultural maturation had moved the western margin of the Corn Belt fully across southern Iowa, with tendrils reaching into northern Iowa, eastern Nebraska, and eastern Kansas.[43] The only adjustment in Ohio incorporated the newly drained Black Swamp region in the northwest: the state's eastern half remained excluded.[44] The *Report on the Productions of Agriculture,* published with the 1880 Census, presented maps of various measures of corn production—bushels per acre, per acre of improved land, or per person—with the highest values in each category typically extending no farther eastward than central Ohio.[45] Maps of data from the nineteenth century through Baker's outline in the 1920s to the most recent USDA maps provide a generally consistent shape for the Corn Belt region, with central Ohio representing its eastern edge.[46]

Southeastern Ohio's exclusion from the Corn Belt is not due to climate conditions unsatisfactory for maize production.[47] Existing across the state are all the characteristics of temperature, frost-free season, growing degree days, and precipitation typically found within the Corn Belt. During the growing season, optimal daytime temperatures for corn are 77 to 91° F, nighttime temperatures are 62 to 74° F, mean temperatures range from 68 to 73° F, and a minimum frost free season of 150 days is required for full maturity. Only in the very northeastern-most tip of Ohio are the growing season temperature characteristics less that what is needed for the "average mid-season corn hybrid" to be harvested as grain. Where corn production is greatest in the United States, at least twenty-five inches of natural precipitation (excluding irrigation) fall annually. All of Ohio receives well over thirty inches; only the shoreline counties closest to Lake Erie receive less than thirty-five inches.

The naturally occurring vegetation predominant in southeastern Ohio also was not dramatically different than that found in other originally forested areas of the Corn Belt. Not all of what became the Corn Belt was forested: before the plow, much of this agricultural region in Iowa, Illinois, and western Indiana was covered in tallgrass prairie, an eastward extension of the Great Plains described as the Prairie Peninsula.[48] East of the peninsula in northwest, southwest, and central Ohio, small and scattered remnants of grasslands appeared amid the eastern hardwoods.[49] Consisting primarily of beech-maple mixed mesophytic forests augmented locally with oaks, hickories, tulip trees, walnuts, and swamp forests in low areas, these deciduous woodlands were cleared to create the western and central Ohio parts of the Corn Belt.[50] Beech-maple forests also extended into northeastern Ohio. In southeastern Ohio, the original vegetation was a variant of the mixed mesophytic forest where similar species to those of central and western Ohio—beech, maple, oaks, hickories—were joined by chestnuts (before the blight), sweetgums, hemlocks, and white pines.[51]

While the climate and vegetation of eastern and southeastern Ohio are not sufficiently distinctive to explain why the Corn Belt fails to reach these areas, the soils differ from those typically found within the Corn Belt. Developing from the inorganic material derived from bedrock or deposited material underlying the surface, the vegetative cover, and climate conditions, the resulting soils have varying potentials for agriculture, some more naturally fertile than others, although today all are typically amended by chemical fertilizers and supplements.[52] For most of the Corn Belt in Ohio and limited sections of the eastern part of the state, the base material at the surface was deposited by glaciers and predominantly consists of glacial till, while most soils in southeastern Ohio originated atop weathered bedrock.[53] Mollisols, "the major soils of the corn belt," developed on predominantly glacial materials underneath the prairies covering much of Illinois and Iowa and parts of Indiana. The secondary Corn Belt soil is Udalfs, a principal suborder of the Alfasols, also developed mostly on glacial materials but underneath deciduous forests and typically underlying the remainder of the Corn Belt in Indiana and western, central, and northeastern Ohio. However, in most of eastern Ohio beyond the Corn Belt, soils differ. Here is found the Dystrochreptsa soils group, part of the principal suborder of the Ochrepts, formed directly from weathered sandstone and shale bedrock on moderate or steep slopes covered by mixed deciduous hardwoods and coniferous (hemlocks and pines) vegetation.[54] These bedrock-derived soils generally exhibit low fertility.

The hillier topography of eastern and southeastern Ohio, coupled with the less productive soils, represents a significant limiting factor keeping the area from matching the high-yielding, highly mechanized maize production found westward on flatter ground with better original soils in the Iowa, Illinois, and Indiana core and in other parts of Ohio within the Corn Belt.[55] Topographic variation is one factor geologists employ to define landform zones, natural regions, and geomorphological or physiographic provinces in the United States.[56] Comparable geologic structures and evolutionary histories join areas together, permitting delineation of regions with shared geologic features into provinces or subunits displaying similarities within and, in most cases, sharp boundaries between. The corners of the Corn Belt triangle—central Ohio to southeastern North Dakota to northeastern Kansas—place that agricultural region comfortably within the Central Lowlands physiographic province. The Central Lowlands, a "vast plain" and "the agricultural heartland of the continent," displays key features such as "low altitude" and a "mantle of glacial deposits that largely conceal the underlying rock formations." While the Central Lowlands narrowly stretches into central New York State along the lake plain south of lakes Erie and Ontario, most of the eastern edge of the province in Ohio trends slightly southwest to northeast through the state's center. This eastern edge abuts the western margin of the Appalachian Plateaus, a province with higher elevation described as "deeply incised by winding stream valleys; considerable local relief; hillsides steep."[57] Within the Appalachian Plateaus are two sections: the Glaciated Allegheny Plateau, which in Ohio cuts from the northeast southward toward the Ohio River, and the unglaciated Allegany Plateau section, including southeastern Ohio.[58] The contact zone between the Central Lowlands and the Appalachian Plateaus in Ohio is not a sharp escarpment but a "knob belt," or "line of hills lacking a straight and imposing front," obscured in part due to glacial deposits.[59]

The southeastern and eastern Ohio meeting places of flatter topography in the Central Lowlands and hillier topography of the Appalachian Plateaus physiographic regions fall relatively close to the eastern edge of the Corn Belt. Of course, corn is grown east of this margin. Fields on gentle slopes and valleys within the hilly topography of the Appalachian Plateaus in eastern Ohio produce corn, and leading scientific research on maize is conducted at the Ohio Agricultural Research and Development Center at Wooster, within the Glaciated Allegheny Plateau section. But the stereotypical midwestern Corn Belt farm scape—flat land with crops extending to the horizon—is not a feature of eastern Ohio.

The geographic, cultural, and perceptual eastern boundaries of the Midwest generally align with the boundaries of the Central Lowlands and Appalachian Plateaus and the Corn Belt. While the contact points between the two physiographic regions may be found on the landscape, the eastern edges of the geographic, cultural, and perceptual Midwests are not sharply defined, nor do they conform to political borders. Rather, boundaries between different vernacular or cultural regions, such as the Midwest and East, are best viewed as transition zones where characteristics most associated with one geographic region begin to merge almost imperceptibly with those of another. Geographers recognize that regional boundaries are transitional. A comprehensive examination of the Midwest described the Upper Ohio Valley, including eastern and southeastern Ohio, as being "in a peripheral position with reference to the Midwest," not at the "very heart of the Midwest" but in "an outer zone or periphery."[60] Similarly, a classic study of cultural regions by geographer D. W. Meinig introduced the concept of core, domain, and sphere as an effective approach to considering the territorial extent and social expression of a cultural region. In this model, the core is "a centralized zone of concentration" best representing "the particular features characteristic of the culture under study." Areas where "the particular culture under study is *dominant*" but less pervasive than in the core comprise the domain, and "the zone of outer influence" is the sphere, where the "culture is represented only by certain of its elements."[61]

Southeastern Ohio does not fit within the core of the Midwest, as defined by cultural, perceptual, vernacular, and environmental regions, nor within the Corn Belt. However, these parts of Ohio are not without regional affiliation as noted above: for many, they typically fall within Appalachia, albeit also on that region's margin.[62] Southeastern Ohio's position on the Midwest's periphery or "Eastern Fringe" does not exclude it from being at least somewhat midwestern and the rest of the state from being within the Midwest's domain. Ohio was the first state created through the Northwest Ordinance, which outlined the political structure for the Northwest Territory, "codified and implemented rules for a rural egalitarian society," and formed the basis for midwesterners' self-perception. As the "eldest child," Ohio's economic and sociocultural development established the basic characteristics of midwestern-ness, despite arguments that as the Midwest expanded westward and matured, the state's eastern geographical position should have excluded it from the region.⁶³ While for many the Midwest is represented by family farmsteads dotted among fields of elephant's-eye-high corn, the reality is different. While maintaining its vitally important agricultural base, over the last two centuries Ohio has become more industrial, urban, and diverse, yielding other economic and ethnic characteristics that also can mark the state's Midwest-to-East transition zone.⁶⁴ Ohio's juxtaposition of agricultural and industrial, urban and rural, and multiple ethnicities may be more visible than in other Midwest states, but the entire region has undergone these transformations to some degree.

One of the ten new states on Thomas Jefferson's back-of-the-envelope concept for the Northwest Territory was named Washington.⁶⁵ Washington's eastern border was Pennsylvania, and the Ohio River but its western border—where that proposed state met two others, Metropotamia and Saratoga—sliced north–south through the center of what is now Ohio, appearing, perhaps presciently, roughly aligned with much of the eastern edge of the Midwest's core. Today, a readily recognized feature serves as an approximate surrogate for the generally coterminous cultural, perceptual, agricultural, environmental, and physiographic boundaries of the eastern edge of the core Midwest in eastern and southeastern Ohio: the I-71 corridor from Cleveland to Columbus to Cincinnati. This rough marker reveals not only where the Midwest merges into the East but also, at its southern end, where the Midwest merges into the South. Eastern Ohio clearly falls east of the core and domain but is best placed on the periphery of or within the sphere of the Midwest, still carrying some midwestern traits while serving as the transition zone "where East meets (Mid)West."

Notes

1. Frank Jacobs, "Jefferson's 'Absurd' Plan for New Northwestern States," *Big Think,* July 23, 2010, https://bigthink.com/strange-maps/248-friends-polypotamians-countrymen; David Hartley, [A Map of the United States East of the Mississippi River], 1784, available at the William L. Clements Library Image Bank, University of Michigan, Ann Arbor, https://quod.lib.umich.edu/w/wc11ic/x-813/wc1000907.

2. Robert M. Taylor Jr., ed., *The Northwest Ordinance, 1787: A Bicentennial Handbook* (Indianapolis: Indiana Historical Society, 1987).

3. Jacobs, "Jefferson's 'Absurd' Plan for New Northwestern States"; Hartley, [Map of the United States].

4. Matthew Salafia, "Borders and Boundaries and Barriers, Oh My!" *Reviews in American History* 38, no. 4 (2010): 651–52.

5. H. W. Brands, *The Zealot and the Emancipator: John Brown, Abraham Lincoln, and the Struggle for American Freedom* (New York: Doubleday, 2020), 345.

6. Donald W. Meinig, *The Shaping of America: A Geographical Perspective on 500 Years of History:* vol. 1 of 4: *Atlantic America, 1492–1800* (New Haven: Yale Univ. Press, 1986), 7–10, 232–35, 349–51; Charlie Grymes, "Virginia-Pennsylvania Boundary," *Virginia Places*, accessed May 3, 2024. http://www.virginiaplaces.org/boundaries/paboundary.html.

7. Grymes, "Virginia-Pennsylvania Boundary."

8. Grymes, "Virginia-Pennsylvania Boundary."

9. *Report of the Joint Commission Appointed by the States of Pennsylvania and Ohio, to Ascertain and Re-Mark the Boundary Line between Said States* (Columbus: G. J. Brand & Co., State Printers, 1883), 5–6.

10. Geography Division, "Statistical Groupings of States and Counties," *Geographic Areas Reference Manual*, US Department of Commerce, Economics and Statistics Administration, Bureau of the Census, Nov. 1994, 6-1–6-8, https://www2.census.gov/geo/pdfs/reference/GARM/Ch6GARM.pdf.

11. Carl Ubbelohde, "History and the Midwest as a Region," *Wisconsin Magazine of History* 78, no. 1 (1994): 35–47; Geography Division, "Statistical Groupings of States and Counties," 6-4–6-11.

12. Raymond D. Gastil, *Cultural Regions of the United States* (Seattle: Univ. of Washington Press, 1975), 16–40; John Fraser Hart, "The Middle West," *Annals of the Association of American Geographers* 62, no. 2 (1972): 258–82; Dean R. Louder et al., *This Remarkable Continent: An Atlas of United States and Canadian Society and Cultures* (College Station: Texas A&M Univ. Press, 1982); Walt Hickey, "Which States Are in the Midwest?" *FiveThirtyEight*, Apr. 29, 2014, https://fivethirtyeight.com/features/what-states-are-in-the-midwest; Spencer Quain, "As a Geography undergrad, I just had to have a go at it." Twitter, Jan. 29, 2020, 6:11 P.M., https://mobile.twitter.com/SpencerQuain/status/1222658437084930050; Soo Oh, "We Asked Readers to Define the Midwest. Here's What We Learned," *Vox*, Feb. 16, 2016, https://www.vox.com/2016/2/16/10889440/midwest-analysis; David Montgomery, "Let's Settle It: This Is What Makes up the Midwest," *St. Paul Pioneer Press*, Jan. 29, 2016; Ricky Swanson, "Why Are Ohio and Michigan Considered Part of the Midwest When Geographically They Are Fairly Far East?," Quora, 2018, https://www.quora.com/Why-are-Ohio-and-Michigan-considered-part-of-the-Midwest-when-geographically-they-are-fairly-far-east.

13. Roscoe Carlyle Buley, *The Old Northwest: Pioneer Period, 1815–1840*, 2 vols. (Bloomington: Indiana Univ. Press, 1951), 1:vii; James R. Shortridge, "The Emergence of 'Middle West' as an American Regional Label," *Annals of the Association of American Geographers* 74, no. 2 (1984): 210–13; James R. Shortridge, *The Middle West: Its Meaning in American Culture* (Lawrence: Univ. Press of Kansas, 1989), 14–26, 92.

14. John H. Garland, "The Heart of a Continent," in *The North American Midwest: A Regional Geography*, ed. John H. Garland (New York: Wiley, 1955), 15–16.

15. Gastil, *Cultural Regions of the United States*, 19.

16. Joel Garreau, *The Nine Nations of North America* (New York: Avon, 1982), 49–97; Louder et al., *This Remarkable Continent*, 223.

17. Reid Wilson, "The 50 States, Redrawn with Equal Population," *Washington Post* (blog), Nov. 25, 2013, https://www.washingtonpost.com/blogs/govbeat/wp/2013/11/25/the-50-states-redrawn-with-equal-population/.

18. Laura Bliss, "Get Lost in this New-and-Improved Map of America's Megaregions," *Bloomberg*, Feb. 7, 2017, https://www.bloomberg.com/news/articles/2017-02-07/america-s-commutes-mapped-into-megaregions; Garrett Dash Nelson and Alasdair Rae, "An Economic Geography of the United States: From Commutes to Megaregions," *PLoS ONE* 11, Nov. 30, 2017, e0166083, https://doi.org/10.1371/journal.pone.0166083.

19. The solid lines on Fig. 8.1 represent generalized edges of vernacular or cultural Midwests mapped by the studies referred to in this chapter. Most significant are the edges they have roughly in common rather than the precise location of each delineation.

20. Joseph W. Brownell, "The Cultural Midwest," *Journal of Geography* 59, no. 2 (1960): 81–85.

21. Wilbur Zelinsky, "North America's Vernacular Regions," *Annals of the Association of American Geographers* 70, no. 1 (1980): 8, 14.

22. Wilbur Zelinsky, *The Cultural Geography of the United States* (Englewood Cliffs, NJ: Prentice-Hall, 1973), 118–19.

23. Shortridge, *Middle West*, 92–94.

24. James R. Shortridge, "Changing Use of Four American Regional Labels," *Annals of the Association of American Geographers* 77, no. 3 (1987): 326–28; James R. Shortridge, "The Vernacular Middle West," *Annals of the Association of American Geographers* 75, no. 1 (1985): 48–57.

25. Shortridge, *Middle West*, 98, 84–90.

26. Shortridge, *Middle West*, 84–90.

27. David Montgomery, "We Mapped 'the Midwest' for You, So Stop Arguing," *Bloomberg*, Aug. 29, 2019, https://www.bloomberg.com/news/articles/2019-08-29/where-is-the-midwest-here-s-what-you-told-us.

28. Jon R. Lauck, "Introduction: Finding the Boundaries of the American Midwest," *Middle West Review* 10, no. 2 (2024): xi–xx.

29. Zelinsky, "North America's Vernacular Regions," 12–16.

30. Shortridge, *Middle West*, 105.

31. Zelinsky, *Cultural Geography of the United States*, 13.

32. D. W. Meinig, "The Mormon Culture Region: Strategies and Patterns in the Geography of the American West, 1847–1964," *Annals of the Association of American Geographers* 55, no. 2 (1965): 192–97, 213–16; Donald W. Meinig, *The Shaping of America: A Geographical Perspective on 500 Years of History*: vol. 2, *Continental America, 1800–1867* (New Haven: Yale Univ. Press, 1993), 231.

33. Hubert G. H. Wilhelm, *The Origin and Distribution of Settlement Groups, Ohio, 1850* (Athens, OH: Hubert G. H. Wilhelm, 1982), 38, 43, 51, 55, 60.

34. Shortridge, *Middle West*, 105–6; Meinig, *Shaping of America*, 1:226; Zelinsky, *Cultural Geography of the United States*, 118–19, 81.

35. John C. Hudson, *Making the Corn Belt: A Geographical History of Middle-Western Agriculture* (Bloomington: Indiana Univ. Press, 1994), 1–14; Christopher R. Laingen, "The Agrarian Midwest: A Geographical Analysis," in *Finding a New Midwestern History*, ed. Jon K. Lauck, Gleaves Whitney, and Joseph Hogan (Lincoln: Univ. of Nebraska Press, 2018), 143–60.

36. Hart, "Middle West," 263, 269–72; R. E. Neild and J. E. Newman, "Growing Season Characteristics and Requirements in the Corn Belt." *National Corn Handbook-40*, Purdue Univ., Cooperative Extension Service, Apr. 1990, https://www.extension.purdue.edu/extmedia/NCH/NCH-40.html; Oliver E. Baker, "Agricultural Regions of North America: Part IV—The Corn Belt," *Economic Geography* 3, no. 4 (1927): 448–54; Laingen, "Agrarian Midwest," 147–48; Jon K. Lauck, ed., *The Interior Borderlands: Regional Identity in the Midwest and the Great Plains* (Sioux Falls, SD: Center for Western Studies, 2019); E. Cotton Mather, "The American Great Plains," *Annals of the Association of American Geographers* 62, no. 2 (1972): 237–57; John H. Paterson, *North America: A Geography of the United States and Canada* (New York: Oxford Univ. Press, 1994), 273; Howard G. Roepke, "Changes in Corn Production on the Northern Margin of the Corn Belt," *Agricultural History* 33, no. 3 (1959): 126–32; Gregory S. Rose, "The Northern Borderland as an Environmentally, Agriculturally, and Culturally Distinctive Subregion of the Midwest in the late 1800s," in *North Country: Essays on the Upper Midwest and Regional Identity*, ed. Jon K. Lauck and Gleaves Whitney (Norman: Univ. of Oklahoma Press, 2023), 66–89; Brad Tennant, "Where the Midwest Ends and the Great Plains Begin," *Studies in Midwestern History* 1, no. 6 (2015): 39, 46–48.

37. Cynthia Clampitt, *Midwest Maize: How Corn Shaped the U.S. Heartland* (Urbana: Univ. of Illinois Press, 2015), 26–34; Hudson, *Making the Corn Belt*, 3, 8–9, 42, 65–69; John C. Hudson and Christopher R. Laingen, *American Farms, American Food: A Geography of Agriculture and Food Production in the United States* (Lanham, MD: Lexington, 2016), 23; Laingen, "Agrarian Midwest," 143–60.

38. William Warntz, "An Historical Consideration of the Terms 'Corn' and 'Corn Belt' in the United States," *Agricultural History* 31, no. 2 (1957): 43; Baker, "Agricultural Regions of North America," 447–48; Hudson, *Making the Corn Belt*, 1–2; Laingen, "The Agrarian Midwest," 147.

39. Baker, "Agricultural Regions of North America," 447–48; Hudson, *Making the Corn Belt*, 1–14; Hudson and Laingen, *American Farms*, 25–31; Laingen, "Agrarian Midwest," 145–48; Warntz, "Historical Consideration," 40–45.

40. Hudson, *Making the Corn Belt*, 1–14; Hudson and Laingen, *American Farms*, 25–31; Laingen, "Agrarian Midwest," 145–48; Warntz, "Historical Consideration," 40–45.

41. "Census of Agriculture," US Census Bureau, last revised, Dec. 14, 2023, https://www.census.gov/history/www/programs/agriculture/census_of_agriculture.html.

42. Hudson, *Making the Corn Belt*, 9, 88–109.

43. Hudson, *Making the Corn Belt*, 11.

44. Martin R. Kaatz, "The Black Swamp: A Study in Historical Geography," *Annals of the Association of American Geographers* 45, no. 1 (1955): 1–35.

45. Department of the Interior, Census Office, *Report of the Productions of Agriculture as Returned at the Tenth Census, 1880* (Washington, DC: GPO, 1883), maps 6–9.

46. "Corn for Grain 2022: Production by County for Selected States," US Department of Agriculture, National Agricultural Statistics Service, accessed May 3, 2024, https://www.nass.usda.gov/Charts_and_Maps/Crops_County/cr-pr.php; "Major Types of Farming in the United States," 1959, USDA Census of Agriculture Historical Archive, Albert R. Mann Library at Cornell University and USDA's National Agricultural Statistics Service, https://agcensus.library.cornell.edu/wp-content/uploads/1959-A_Graphic_Summary_of_Land_Utilization-CHARTS_AND_MAPS-971-Table-26.pdf; Hudson, *Making the Corn Belt*, 205; Hudson and Laingen, *American Farms*, 25; Laingen, "Agrarian Midwest," 146–48.

47. Neild and Newman, "Growing Season Characteristics"; "US Climate Data, Ohio," US Climate Data, 2024, https://www.usclimatedata.com/climate/ohio/united-states/3205.

48. E. Lucy Braun, *Deciduous Forests of Eastern North America* (New York: Free Press, 1950), 185–91; Henry Allan Gleason, "The Vegetational History of the Middle West," *Annals of the Association of American Geographers* 12, no. 1 (1922): 39–85; Hart, "Middle West," 259; Edgar Nelson Transeau, "The Prairie Peninsula," *Ecology* 16, no. 3 (1935): 423–37.

49. Clyde H. Jones, "Studies in Ohio Floristics-III. Vegetation of Ohio Prairies," *Bulletin of the Torrey Botanical Club* 71, no. 5 (1944): 537.

50. Braun, *Deciduous Forests of Eastern North America*, 305–18, 324–26, 179–91; Transeau, "Prairie Peninsula," 424–27, 429, 430.

51. Braun, *Deciduous Forests of Eastern North America*, 87–121; Transeau, "Prairie Peninsula," 429, 430, 433.

52. "Soil," US Department of Agriculture, National Resources Conservation Service, accessed July 3, 2024, https://www.nrcs.usda.gov/wps/portal/nrcs/detail/soils/edu/?cid=nrcs142p2_054280.

53. William D. Thornbury, *Regional Geomorphology of the United States* (New York: John Wiley & Sons, 1965), 221, 132.

54. Henry D. Foth and John W. Schafer, *Soil Geography and Land Use* (New York: John Wiley, 1980), 38–40, 111–13, 116–17, 38–40, 143, 149–51, 72–74.

55. Hart, "Middle West," 262, 263.

56. Charles B. Hunt, *Natural Regions of the United States and Canada* (San Francisco: W. H. Freeman and Company, 1974); 3–4; Thornbury, *Regional Geomorphology of the United States*, vii.

57. Hunt, *Natural Regions of the United States and Canada*, 3–4, 12–15, 326–28, 6, 330, 5.

58. Thornbury, *Regional Geomorphology of the United States*, 221, 132.

59. Hunt, *Natural Regions of the United States and Canada*, 3; Thornbury, *Regional Geomorphology of the United States*, 212.

60. H. F. Raup, "The Upper Ohio Valley," in *The North American Midwest: A Regional Geography*, ed. John H. Garland (New York: Wiley, 1955), 172; Garland, "Heart of a Continent," 16, 15.

61. Meinig, "Mormon Culture Region," 213–16.

62. Phillip J. Obermiller, "From the Mountains to the Midwest: Observations on Appalachia, Regionalism, and Regional Studies," *Middle West Review* 4, no. 1 (2017): 55–61; Deanna L. Tribe, "Appalachia or the Midwest? Appalachian Cultural Awareness in Southern Ohio," ED307089, Mar. 1989, https://eric.ed.gov/?id=ED307089; Deanna L. Tribe, "Contemporary Images of Appalachian Ohio: The View from Within," *Journal of the Appalachian Studies Association* 5 (1993): 26–33.

63. Shortridge, *Middle West*, 106–9; Hart, "Middle West," 61–69.

64. In this volume, See Jon K. Lauck's preface, vii–xxvi; Donna M. DeBlasio and Martha I. Pallante, "Italian Americans in Ohio's Mahoning Valley: Creating Identity in the Industrial Midwest," 176–92; Randall S. Gooden, "German or Yankee? Defining Ohio Identity on the Pennsylvania Border," 139–57; Kenneth J. Heineman, "Political Cultures in Conflict: Locating Ohio into a Region during and after the Era of the New Deal," 257–73; and Greg Wilson and Kevin Kern, "Ohio: At the Heart of History," 68–89.

65. Jacobs, "Jefferson's 'Absurd' Plan for New Northwestern States"; Hartley, [Map of the United States].

Chapter 9

Italian Americans in Ohio's Mahoning Valley

Creating Identity in the Industrial Midwest

DONNA M. DEBLASIO AND MARTHA I. PALLANTE

Ohio's Mahoning Valley is at the eastern edge of the region called the Connecticut Western Reserve. Its original settlers were from New England, mainly Anglo-Saxon Protestants. As the nation industrialized throughout the nineteenth century and into the twentieth, the valley saw a dramatic increase in iron and steel production. Jobs provided by these industries drew diverse peoples—initially German and Irish immigrants, and later people from southern and eastern Europe. African Americans, Latinos, and others followed. Each brought their distinctive cultures and traditions, adding richness and diversity to the valley. Italians and Italian Americans formed one of the largest ethnic communities in the valley. Their experiences provide distinctive lenses with which to examine the creation of a uniquely midwestern identity.

Living at the eastern perimeter of the region defined as the *Midwest*, the residents of the valley find themselves grasping for identity. They have little in common with western parts of Ohio and relate better to Pittsburgh or Buffalo. Easterners, however, envision them living among cornfields and dairy cows. With their identities rooted in the industrial revolution and its corresponding immigration, the inhabitants of the Mahoning Valley perceive themselves as part of a region stretching from

Chicago to western Pennsylvania, New York, and West Virginia. The region, externally labeled the Rust Belt, shares more with places such as Scranton and Bethlehem, Pennsylvania, than with rural Ohio. Scholars have also generally failed to identify the regionalism of areas such as the Mahoning Valley within the larger Midwest.

Daniel Nelson defines the *Midwest* as the states of Ohio, Indiana, Illinois, Michigan, Wisconsin, Minnesota, and Iowa. He contends that this region is diverse, what binds it is a "commonality of experience which overshadows geographic and other distinctions."[1] Jon Teaford conceives it "as a region whose cities possessed certain social, political, economic, cultural, and ethnic characteristics that distinguished them as a class apart from the other metropolises."[2]

This leaves us with two questions about midwestern identity and the Mahoning Valley specifically: who defines the Midwest, and what makes it unique? Where the Midwest begins may be in the eye of the beholder. From the East Coast, it is Pittsburgh. From Harrisburg or Ithaca, Cleveland is the Midwest. From Youngstown or Warren, the definitions are blurred. The answers to the second question are also matters of perception. Previous works suggest several regional models. The most common focus is on large metropolitan areas, such as Chicago. A second large body of scholarship looks at rural regions. Hal Barron suggests that smaller rural communities across America's heartland modernized at different paces than larger cities. The changes were slower, allowing residents to exert greater control.[3] The same is true of scholarship examining Italian immigration. Canonical works by Humbert Nelli and Thomas Kessner examine the experiences of Italians in large cities with diverse economies. More recent scholarship, such as that of Matthew Frye Jacobson and Thomas Guglielmo, focuses on the issues of "whiteness" and race in nineteenth- and twentieth-century American metropolises.[4] Others, like Nelson, examine the settlement and modernization of rural regions left untouched by demographic shifts in the late nineteenth and early twentieth centuries. Like Barron, Gunther Peck studies small communities in the rural plains of mid-America, labor markets, and recruiting practices in company towns. This leaves a dearth of scholarship on small to medium-sized cities with diverse populations. These communities offer a different perspective on what it means to be midwestern. This gap in the scholarship creates space for new appraisals of the immigrant experience.

The Mahoning Valley's reliance on steel and its auxiliaries makes this area exceptional compared to larger industrial communities. These industries are unique in many ways, especially in that the majority of their employees were, by necessity, adult males. The physical strength required to perform the various tasks related to steel and its associated processes meant that few children and women could work on the shop floor. Prior to World War II, women in the steel industry were confined to office work, food service, or medical support. These positions rarely went to southern and eastern Europe immigrants. Boys could do few things in heavy industry—they intermittently carried water and ran errands.

In the valley, steel and related industries paid enough that most families did not require women and children to seek outside employment. Instead, they supplemented family income in a variety of ways: taking in boarders, running small groceries out of their homes, or selling pizza from their back porches. Boys did odd jobs, while girls helped at home. While supplemental incomes were important, this money could provide savings for a down payment on a house and other kinds of discretionary spending—occasional trips to the movies or the local amusement park. Children generally stayed in school, since they were unable to work in the mill, thus producing a better educated population than is normally associated with working-class communities.

The conditions of the industrial Midwest and the ways industrial communities developed in the late 1800s allowed immigrant groups to forge distinct identities and communities. Scholars have neglected the study of work conditions in the region's midsized and smaller cities. Similarly, the traditional narratives about second-wave immigrants focus on their experiences in large urban areas, leaving smaller metropolises understudied. The examination of the valley's Italians shows that this ethnic group's experiences do not fit the traditional narrative. In this region, Italians and Italian Americans were better educated and acquired property faster than their large-city counterparts. Does this make them uniquely midwestern?

Three concomitant factors in the Midwest enabled Italian immigrants and their offspring to forge unique communities and experiences: the rapid conversion to heavy industry, demographic shifts that resulted in burgeoning urban growth, and immigration from southern and eastern Europe causing previously unseen heterogeneity. Two areas—Smoky

Hollow, northeast of downtown Youngstown, and the smaller community of Niles, eight miles northwest of Youngstown—constitute the focus of this chapter, providing a snapshot of the larger region with a high density of Italians and Italian Americans.

Beginning in the 1790s, the Mahoning Valley was an iron manufacturing region. The first blast furnace west of the Alleghenies opened in 1803, on the banks of Yellow Creek in what is now Struthers. James and Daniel Heaton, who built it, later established two more furnaces, one in Niles and the other in Youngstown. The iron industry flourished by 1840, after the discovery of coal, iron ore, and limestone, necessary for iron smelting. After depleting those resources, the valley continued to manufacture iron, thanks to the demands of the railroads and government needs during the Civil War. Mass production of steel began in the 1850s, with the invention of the Bessemer process. The valley poured its first Bessemer steel in 1895. From humble beginnings, the valley became one of the largest steel manufacturing regions in the nation; mills lined the Mahoning River from Lowellville to Warren. By 1923, three major firms: the Youngstown Sheet & Tube Company, Republic Iron & Steel, and Carnegie-Illinois Steel (US Steel) dominated the valley. Support industries, including Niles Fire Brick, which made refractory brick, also thrived.[5]

Between 1880 and 1930, with the advent of steel production, the valley underwent a demographic transformation. The region's industrial growth and the shift from small foundries to full-scale factories fueled rapid and diverse population growth. Youngstown, the largest city in Mahoning County, went from a population of 15,435 in 1880 to more than 170,000 in 1930. While some of this growth stemmed from migration, most resulted from southern and eastern European immigration. By 1920, the foreign-born represented 25.6 percent of the city's total population. In Smoky Hollow, the proportion was higher, at 34 percent.[6] Dominic Ciarniello, who arrived in Youngstown in 1920, described the hollow as a place where the residents shared a common sense of heritage: "So, it was more or less a *paisano* community."[7] In Niles, the change was equally dramatic. The Italian-born population of Trumbull County, where Niles sits, was zero in 1880 and 253 in 1890. By 1900, that number had reached 999 out of a population of 46,591.[8] Many were part of a chain migration that passed through Niles Fire Brick. Michael Patrone recounted his father's recruitment by fellow Bagnolese Lorenzo Pallante: "He brought the message back [to Bagnoli] that he had the job with the Niles Fire Brick and that they needed more men . . . and my dad got word of it, and he said, 'Well I'll go over there and see if I could get a job with them.'"[9] By 1930, Italians and their American-born children represented a significant portion of the population of Youngstown and Niles.

The 1924 passage of the National Origins Act dried up the source of Italian immigration; Youngstown's foreign-born population declined to 19.4 percent. Italians and Italian Americans represented 17,988 of the city's 170,002 residents. Niles, which had a population of 16,314, listed 3,295 as foreign-born; of those 1,888, or 11.6 percent, claimed Italy as their place of origin, and 2,218 had one Italian-born parent. Slightly more than a quarter of the population claimed Italian descent.[10] Italian Americans still constitute the second-largest ethnic group in the valley and are arguably the most visible.

This large presence gave Italian Americans an unusual advantage. For example, in workplaces where some entered the lower ranks of management, it meant more reliable employment. The Niles Fire Brick payroll records reveal that on shifts where Italians were foremen, the percentage of Italians among the regular workers was higher and they worked more frequently.[11] The payroll ledgers show a pattern of wage equity with the company's "more American" employees of old New England or Welsh descent.

While many of Smoky Hollow's residents worked in steel mills, a large number worked for smaller ancillary companies. Truscon Steel, later a subsidiary of Republic Iron & Steel, was located near the hollow. Dominic Mastropietro noted that his brothers worked at Truscon, "Quite a few people from the neighborhood" worked there. The Donofrio brothers, according to their sons Rudy and Vito, worked at Truscon, "all [their] life." During World War II, Truscon employed many women, including several from the hollow. Clotilda DiLullo DeBlasio described her job as a weld inspector: "They put you on the tank as soon as you got there. They . . . show you how to chip the weld . . . clean it and look for cracks . . . if you found a crack, you marked it with a crayon, C."[12] These smaller companies required a more skilled and better educated workforce than the integrated steel mills, which employed hundreds of unskilled workers. They also offered more security and regular employment.

Despite stereotypes, not all Italian immigrants were agricultural workers. A significant proportion of the men were skilled workers—commonly bricklayers and stonemasons. Brothers Gaetano and Pasquale DiLullo, who left San Pietro Avellana for greater opportunities in the United States, were skilled stonemasons. They settled in Smoky Hollow, where they married and raised their families. When not working as masons, they found employment lining furnaces with refractory brick.[13] As at Niles Fire Brick, Smoky Hollow's workers were often in a good position to earn more money and improve their living conditions.

The Fire Brick proprietor, John R. Thomas, recruited immigrant Italian workers for their ceramic skills. While the factory was in the "workshop" stage, these immigrants (1893–95) represented 13 percent of the work force, earning more than 15 percent of the wages. By 1915, they constituted just over 40 percent of the workforce and earned just under 40 percent of the wages; transient labor recently arrived from Italy accounted for the difference.[14] Michael Patrone offered that while the jobs at Fire Brick were dirty and not always "desirable," they were steady, and "most of the people that worked there had big families and the income was sufficient."[15] He added that families such as his supplemented their incomes by having adolescent boys hawk newspapers, and selling homemade bread or pizza or braided garlic from their gardens. This marks a substantial divergence from earning patterns in larger metropolitan areas and accounts for these immigrants' rapid progress toward home ownership and educational advancement.

The valley's Italians and Italian Americans exhibited a high degree of home ownership early on, unlike their counterparts in eastern communities such as Buffalo, where "the Italian quarter had the city's highest densities . . . [and] contained the highest percentage of buildings controlled by agents or lessees who rented from an owner and then in turn to as many families as they could." Virginia Yans-McGlaughlin notes that Italians and Italian Americans purchased property, but not in great numbers until the 1920s. To do so meant "sacrificing their children's education and career prospects."[16] In the Mahoning Valley, immigrants purchased homes much earlier than their counterparts elsewhere; the area mirrored the midwestern model of heartland cities, which Teaford describes as "a region of owner-occupied homes." He adds, "Apartment living and rent paying remained less common in heartland cities than in the metropolises of the Atlantic coast.... [W]orking class Midwesterners were less likely than their southern counterparts to lease their modest dwellings."[17]

Smoky Hollow, just below and to the east of a major north south artery, was not platted until the 1890s. Until it then, the hollow was a picnic grounds for the city's elite. Some of the city's most important families—among them the Wicks, and the Bonnels—were the original owners. With the hollow's proximity to the mills, working class men and women quickly settled in. Most of the residences were single-family dwellings although there were a few multiple units, but nothing resembling the tenement houses in larger cities.[18]

Most of the houses were wood-framed, although some were brick. The single-family dwellings were two stories tall and two or three rooms deep. They had steeply pitched gabled roofs and two bay facades, with full-width front porches. Indoor plumbing, if there was any, consisted of a toilet and shower in the basement. Coal furnaces provided central heating. The properties were typical of working-class neighborhoods, with lots about 30 feet wide by 125 feet long, abutting paved sidewalks.[19]

Descriptions of these domiciles abound in the oral histories. Rudy Donofrio summed up the form of the majority of the dwellings: "They were small, like thirty-foot lots. The houses were just one room after the other. The only bathroom ... was in the cellar. We had a commode, and we had a shower there."[20] Other interviewees' descriptions jibe with his.[21] Donofrio points out something that many Smoky Hollow homeowners shared: they took in boarders. This meant tight living quarters, since the boarders shared space with the family. Boarding was common in industrial America, especially in the Midwest. As Gwendolyn Wright notes in *Building the Dream: A Social History of Housing in America*, "economic pressures meant that between one quarter and one half of all working-class households ... included boarders or lodgers."[22] Most of these were related to the homeowners or hailed from the same town in the Old Country. Donofrio describes space use: "Where the front was, that was usually supposed to be the living room. That was my mom and dad's bedroom. Then the next room was a fairly good size, which would be a like a dining room, but we used that as our combined dining room and living room. When we had big meals, we used that room for our big meals."[23] Carmella Gaetano echoed Donofrio:

"They had five boarders in a three-bedroom house.... Five children, mother and father all slept in one bedroom.... in the living room and the boarders had a single cot in each room."[24] The census records support these memories. For example, in 1910 the Porfirio family consisted of Clorinda and Alphonso Porfirio, daughter Venturina, and several boarders.[25]

To augment their diets, most Smoky Hollow and Niles residents cultivated gardens. Although their lots were small, they made good use of them. As one interviewee noted, everyone had a garden.[26] Grace Sheehan and Anna Marie Macali also recounted the importance of gardens in Niles. Sheehan recalled that her parents planted a garden in their backyard, stretching "all the way to the railroad tracks," and they canned "thousands and thousands of quarts of vegetables."[27] Macali said her father planted "a big garden... my mother canned everything." Much of their food came from that family plot. Her mother "could revolve a meal between the garden and an egg."[28]

Many had wood-fired ovens in the backyard, used during warm weather to keep houses cool. Rudy Donofrio recalled, "You could be going up the street and you could smell the bread because the ovens were outside."[29] Annette Lefoer seconded him: "I had a large oven outside. And I'd put maybe a hundred pounds or more, and I'd mix flour.... And the whole neighborhood would be there eating pizza, because they could smell it for a mile long."[30] Michael Patrone recalled a similar situation in Niles. His mother, feeding a family of ten, baked in an outdoor oven. He stated, "Twelve of them would be enough to take care of the member[s] of the family for dinner."[31]

The hollow, with its neat rows of houses, uniform lots, and ubiquitous gardens fits Teaford's description of midwestern cities, dotted with "single family homes surrounded by neat yards," which after 1945 continued "to characterize the metropolitan landscape of the Midwest."[32] Italians put their indelible mark on their neighborhoods, creating communities that were products of midwestern, rather than East Coast, sensibilities. The same was true on Niles's east side, which extended from the Fire Brick, stretching through an area eleven blocks to the east, encompassing several blocks on each side. The oldest houses were like those in Smoky Hallow, with two rooms up and two rooms downstairs. Patrone recalled that in his family home, the upstairs rooms provided sleeping space for nine children, while his parents used a converted front room:

"They made what was supposed to be the kitchen the living room. The kitchen was down in the basement."[33] Marie Fredricka recounted that her parents' house was similar. Her mother "had two bedrooms, a kitchen, bathroom, a cellar."[34] As families moved east, the homes became larger and more elaborate. Anna Marie Macali described her family home, built in 1927, as having three rooms on the ground floor and three bedrooms upstairs with a bath, affirming, "We always lived with indoor plumbing."[35]

The prosperity that allowed the valley's Italians to move quickly to home ownership encouraged them to keep their children in school and consider college. This runs counter to most Italian and Italian American communities during the first half of the twentieth century. Italian enclaves elsewhere harbored deep-seated distrust of education and "did not make their children better than themselves."[36] They perceived their children as economic assets and were suspicious of any education beyond the minimum. Many Italians saw education as "effeminate," and useless, associating it with Italy's exploitive upper classes.[37] In Niles and Smoky Hollow, parents viewed schooling their children as desirable. By the 1920s, it was the norm. Michael Patrone's family is a good example of upwardly mobility. Although his parents were illiterate, he and his siblings attended high school. His mother inspected each report card, and "when we finished high school, that was a great day." Although some of the children "had to go to work and get a job right away," five attended college. He stated, "She was on us all the time: 'you have got to get an education.... You will be better in your life. You will be able to compete in the world.'"[38] His father's employer at Niles Fire Brick, T. E. Thomas, fostered this sentiment. Thomas wrote to the school board suggesting employment at his firm was limited to primarily adults and that "young men" would be better served by remaining in school. If needed, he would provide limited employment in the evenings or weekends.[39] From 1918 forward, children born to Italian parents in this community understood that education was important and school attendance was the norm.[40] Marie Fredricka, a 1932 Niles graduate, noted the importance of education in her family. Of her five siblings, four finished high school, and her only brother went to Western Reserve, in Cleveland.[41]

In Smoky Hollow, adolescents attended The Rayen School or East High, believing education was key to a better life. Domenic Ciarniello credits his job at General Fireproofing with his training: "When I was going to East

High School, I had a little machine shop practice and I did learn decimals and learned how to read a micrometer, and a little blueprint reading experience, which helped a lot and it made my work much easier. I could meet the production standards, and I enjoyed my work."[42] Dominic Conti noted that although it was during the Depression, "We went to East High School and we graduated in 1933. The boys from the hollow, most of them—Dom Rosselli, Ed Finamore—they went to Rayen School."[43] Clotilda DeBlasio, Dominic Mastropietro, and Nicholas Nazzarini recalled similar circumstances.[44] Donetta Clemente Vechiarelli's experiences bridged the two communities. She related that before she married and moved to Smoky Hollow, she "went to Jefferson, Lincoln and then McKinley High School."[45] The high percentage of women in this first generation that attended and finished high school mimics patterns in the native-born population.

The massive immigration between 1880 and 1924 contributed to the nation's growing industrial economy but also triggered a backlash, in the form of a revitalized Ku Klux Klan. As Nelson notes, this version of the Klan was not related to the post–Civil War South's incarnation. Revived in Georgia in 1915, this Klan targeted a perceived new threat: foreigners from southern and eastern Europe, who were largely Catholic or Jewish. The new KKK base was the Midwest. The Mahoning Valley, with its increasing immigrant population became a center of Klan activity in the 1920s.[46] Italians and Italian Americans were aware of the growing tensions in their communities. Donald Pallante recalled neighborhood children taunting his older brother: "Honkee, dago, sheene, wop. Eat spaghetti with snakes on top." Similarly, Carmella Gaetano was embarrassed by her pierced ears as a representation of her ethnicity, "The kids used to say, 'Oh look at that little wop with the earrings on.'"[47] Low-level discrimination and harassment permeated the region but was generally ignored or tolerated.

While this childish behavior existed, the Italian residents of the ethnically diverse Smoky Hollow fondly recall it as a welcoming place where everyone was treated like family. Several interviewees mentioned neighbors who were Slovak, Croatian, German, or members of other white ethnic groups and contend that everyone got along. Michael Lariccia, echoing many of his neighbors, stated, "There were Jewish, Italian, and German people ... they were all nice people. They were all working people and tried do the best they could. If anybody needed help, they surely got it. They were all hard workers. We never had any trouble down Smoky Hollow."[48] Indeed, the hollow became a place where ethnic and regional differences melted away as they all became "ethnic Americans," finding solidarity as strangers in a strange land. There were few Black people in the hollow until after World War II; indeed, in 1920, Blacks made up only 6 percent of Youngstown's population; by 1940, this increased to 8.5 percent. The 1920 census reported only a scattering of Smoky Hollow residents who were Black; their numbers increased by 1930, reflecting the Great Migration from the South. Then, during and after World War II, the Black population in the Mahoning Valley grew exponentially, thanks to the prosperous steel industry.[49]

Niles was less ethnically diverse than Smoky Hollow. Italians dominated the community; the Irish were the next-largest ethnic group. In 1920, there were 1,165 foreign born Italians and 128 Irish. There was one Black person in Niles in 1920 and only 214 ten years later, out of a total population of 16,314.[50] The second coming of the Ku Klux Klan, which now added southern and eastern Europeans and Catholics and Jews to its hate list, eventually drew the ethnic groups together. Klan activity in the valley peaked between 1923 and 1924. Youngstown and Niles elected mayors with open ties to the Klan. Elected officials saw ethnic communities with connections to bootlegging as popular targets. They did not expect a united response among their marks.

Instead of exploiting local ethnic rivalries, the foreign-language press noted their cooperation. Youngstown's *Il Cittadino Italo-Americano* published editorials and letters from other ethnic groups. Editions in the late summer of 1924 contained a message from a local rabbi proposing that despite their differences, Catholics and Jews had a common enemy: the Ku Klux Klan. The message to the community was that it is not we who are un-American—it is the Klan, which seeks to deprive citizens of their rights. The editorial staff pointed out that many Italian Americans had patriotically served in World War I. The August 9, 1924, edition contained an editorial, "*La Riposta*," which reminded readers of their duties as good citizens: "Italians, our moment has arrived.... We dry our tears with the vote of thousands ... who without work leave our homeland anxious to come to the land of Columbus in search of daily bread.... [W]e vote for those men of Christ who preach for brotherhood and against hatred and slavery.... [W]e respond to the abuses of power not with violence but by crushing it with the vote."[51] Italians and Italian Americans had a new identity and explicitly identified the threat to that newborn sense of belonging.[52]

In Niles, with its Klan mayor, Harvey Kistler, tensions were particularly acute. Pasquale Ruberto, who arrived from Italy in 1914, recounted the Klan's boldness: "They wanted to get Catholic people out of the country." He continued, "They put masks on, and they were marching [down] the street.... They were burning the cross down."[53] Mainstream newspapers suggested that local Irish and Italian Catholics instigated the tension and violence. Events culminated in a confrontation on November 1, 1924.[54] Although local entrepreneurs and bootleggers organized the initial resistance, the November 1 events took on a new dimension in response to a rumor sweeping through town. Whether the rumor had validity is unknown, but the response was noteworthy. The message circulated that the Klan planned to desecrate the sanctuaries of the two Catholic churches, St. Stephen and Our Lady of Mount Carmel, and violate the Humility of Mary nuns housed at St Stephen. The response was electric; men and women, adolescents and elderly folks, turned out in response. Chappy Ross recalled a human barricade circling the convent. Joe Jennings and Marie Fredericka, too young to participate, recalled women and teenage girls "smuggling guns" in their aprons to people mounting the defense.[55] Louise Liste, eight years old, stated that her parents joined the crowd: "My father and all our neighbors . . . went to face them. . . . My mother went with my father. . . . [S]he raised one of the hoods, and it was the grocer." She remembered, "When my mother and father came back home they was crying; they said that everything was over and that all the neighbors got together and they scared them."[56] Their response was the grassroots activity of a group pushed to the limit. Seventy years later, Don Pallante still struggled with the prejudice that inspired the movement: "Fear of competition, fear of unknown, fear of... I think they resented the fact that we were a stranger in their midst."[57] Italians and Italian Americans obviously resented the Klan's characterizations of them being less than true Americans. Nelson sees that midwestern industrial workers who opposed the Klan gained agency.[58]

Although the Mahoning Valley sits on the border between the traditional designations of the East and the Midwest, it exhibits many uniquely midwestern characteristics. The valley was dominated by one industry and was at the nexus of what Nelson and Teaford call the industrial Midwest. Heavy industry dominated this region, which is not unique to the Midwest but is one of the major reasons for its economic success. Nelson notes that the "classic transfer of labor from farm to factory, common to New England

... and the South, did not occur in the Midwest until the post–World War II years," resulting in midwestern industrialists seeking labor in places like Europe and the American South.[59] This is certainly true of the Mahoning Valley between 1900 and 1924.

For the valley's Italians and Italian Americans, the reliance on a single heavy industry meant fewer women and children were employed. Families relied on men to earn a living wage; women and children provided supplemental income that gave savings and discretionary spending. In this setting, children stayed in school, many completed high school, and some went to college. The nature of work in the Midwest allowed for more social mobility and opportunity, even for immigrants.

The higher incomes allowed Italian Americans to purchase homes quickly. Their neighborhoods resembled Teaford's description of the plan of midwestern industrial communities: neat plots of small houses, gardens, paved streets and sidewalks. Unlike in larger cities, towns in the Mahoning Valley did not have high-rise tenements often associated with the working class. Multiple family units were duplexes or quads. Since the valley's urban areas did not have the population density of eastern metropolises, smaller, affordable houses became the norm. The ability to own property, educate one's children, engage in leisure activities, and do honest work all aided Italians in adapting to their new home and becoming Americans.

Notes

A version of this chapter appeared in *Italian Americana* 40 (Summer 2022): 99–125.

1. Daniel Nelson, *Farm and Factory: Workers in the Midwest 1880–1990* (Bloomington: Indiana Univ. Press, 1995), vii.

2. Jon C. Teaford. *Cities of the Heartland: Rise and Fall of the Industrial Midwest* (Bloomington: Indiana Univ. Press, 1994), vi.

3. Hal Barron, *Mixed Harvests: The Second Great Transformation in the Rural North, 1870–1930* (Chapel Hill: Univ. of North Carolina Press, 1997).

4. The historiographic context of this study has both greater breadth and depth. James S. Olson, *The Ethnic Dimension in America History* (New York: St. Martin's, 1999); Lance Liebman and Norman Yetman, *Ethnic Relations in America* (Edgewood Cliffs, NJ: Prentice-Hall, 1982); and Norman Yetman, *Majority and Minority: The Dynamics of Race and Ethnicity in American Life* (Boston: Allyn & Bacon, 1991) did much to establish the foundations. Milton Gordon, *Assimilation in American Life: The Role of Race, Religion, and Natural Origins* (New York: Oxford Univ. Press, 1964)

and Will Herberg, *Protestant, Catholic and Jew: An Essay in American Religious Sociology* (Garden City, NY: Anchor, 1955) offer context. The consensus historians of the 1950s and early 1960s yielded to works which view immigrants from multiple perspectives and provide agency to their subjects. The powerlessness Oscar Handlin described in *The Uprooted: The Epic Story of the Great Migration that Made the American People* (New York: Grosset & Dunlap, 1951) yielded to revisionists such as Humbert Nelli, *Italians in Chicago, 1880–1930* (New York: Oxford Univ. Press, 1970) and Thomas Kessner, *The Golden Door: Italian and Jewish Immigrant Mobility in New York City, 1880–1915* (New York: Oxford Univ. Press, !977). The next generation of scholars, such as Dino Cinel, *From Italy to San Francisco:* The *Immigrant Experience* (Stanford, CA: Stanford Univ. Press, 1982), and Donna Gabaccia, *From Sicily to Elizabeth Street: Housing and Social Change among Italian Immigrants, 1880–1930* (Albany: State Univ. of New York Press, 1984) suggest that while Italian immigrants faced prejudice and hardship, they gained agency. Michael LaSorte, *La Merica: Images of Italian Greenhorn Experience* (Philadelphia: Temple Univ. Press, 1985) and Robert A. Orsi, *The Madonna of 115th Street: Faith and Community in Italian Harlem, 1880–1950* (New Haven: Yale Univ. Press, 1985) perceived experiences from the immigrants' points of view. More recent scholarship examines the issues of power, agency, discrimination and perceptions of ethnicity and race. See Thomas A. Guglielmo, *White on Arrival: Italians, Race, Color, and Power in Chicago, 1890–1945* (New York: Oxford Univ. Press, 2003); Matthew Frye Jacobson, *Whiteness of a Different Color* (Cambridge: Harvard Univ. Press, 1998); *Barbarian Virtues: The United States Encounters Foreign Peoples at Home and Abroad, 1876–1917* (New York: Hill & Wang, 2000); and David R. Roediger, *Working toward Whiteness: How America's Immigrants Became White: The Strange Journey from Ellis Island to the Suburbs,* rev. ed. (New York: Basic Books, 2018).

5. Joseph G. Butler Jr., *History of Youngstown and the Mahoning Valley, Ohio,* 3 vols. (Chicago: American Historical Society, 1921), 1:651–751; Frederick J. Blue et. al. *Mahoning Memories: A History of Youngstown and Mahoning County* (Virginia Beach, VA: Donning, 1995), 63–146.

6. 1930 US Census, "Population, Table 13, Composition of the Population, by Counties," "Composition and Characteristics, Table 15, Composition of the Population, for Cities and Villages of 10,000 or more," "Composition and Characteristics, Table 18, Foreign-Born White, by country of Birth, for Counties and for Cities and Villages of 10,000 or more," and "Composition and Characteristics, Table 19, Native White of Foreign or Mixed Parentage, by country of Birth, for Counties and for Cities and Villages of 10,000 or more," 483–84, 493–94, 500–503, 504–7.

7. Dominic Ciarniello, interviewed by Annette D. Mills, Apr. 25, 1976, transcript, 1, Youngstown State Univ. Oral History Program (hereafter cited as YSUOHP).

8. "Ohio-County level Results, 1880, 1890, 1900," *Historical Census Browser,* Univ. of Virginia, accessed Aug. 7, 2012; page discontinued as of July 4, 2024, http://mapserver.lib.virginia.edu/php/county.php.

9. Michael Patrone, interviewed by Matthew Butts, Feb. 6, 1990, transcript, 4–5, YSUOHP.

10. 1930 US Census, "Population, Table 13," "Composition and Characteristics, Table 15," "Composition and Characteristics, Table 18," and "Composition and Characteristics, Table 19," 483–84, 493–94, 500–503, 504–7.

11. Martha Pallante, "To Work and Live: Brickyard Laborers, Immigration and Assimilation in an Ohio Town, 1890–1925," *Northeast Ohio Journal of History* 2 (Sept. 2003), https://blogs.uakron.edu/nojh/2003/09/20/to-work-and-live/.

12. Domenic Mastropietro, interviewed by Joseph E. Mancini, Nov. 8, 1990, transcript, 6, Rudy Donofrio, interviewed by Joseph Mancini, Nov. 8, 1990, transcript. 4–5, Vito Donofrio, interviewed by Joseph Mancini, Dec. 4. 1990, transcript, 4, and Clotilda DeBlasio, interviewed by Joseph Lambert, Oct. 30, 1990, transcript, 11, all in YSUOHP.

13. DeBlasio interview, 4–5. US Bureau of the Census, Sixteenth Annual Census of the United States, 1940.

14. Pallante, "To Work and Live"; Niles Fire Brick Payrolls, vols. 1–3, Niles Fire Brick Collection, Youngstown Historical Society of Industry and Labor / Ohio History Connection.

15. Michael Patrone, interviewed by James Allgren, Nov. 5, 1994, transcript, 4, YSUOHP.

16. Virginia Yans-McLaughlin, *Family and Community: Italian Immigrants in Buffalo, 1880–1930* (Urbana: Univ. of Illinois Press, 1982), 117, 48.

17. Teaford, *Cities of the Heartland*, 240.

18. *Sanborn Fire Insurance Map, Youngstown, Ohio* (New York: Sanborn Map Company, 1897); *Sanborn Fire Insurance Map, Youngstown, Ohio* (New York: Sanborn Map Company, 1907).

19. Mahoning County (Ohio) Auditor's Office, Registry of Deeds, accessed June 20, 2020, http://oh-mahoning-auditor.publicaccessnow.com/.

20. Rudy Donofrio interview, 13.

21. For more descriptions, see Vito Donofrio interview, 9–10; Carmella Gaetano, interviewed by Joseph Mancini, Dec. 3, 1990, transcript, 26, Michael Lariccia interviewed by Annette D. Mills, Apr. 24, 1976, transcript, 12, Catherine Mascardine interviewed by Joseph Mancini, Nov. 25, 1990, transcript, 13–15, Mastropietro interview, 4–5, Lucy Nazzarini interview, 4, 8–9, Sue Quatro interviewed by Annette Mills, Apr. 14, 1976, transcript, 1, 10, Donetta Vecchiarelli interviewed by Joseph E. Mancini, Oct. 23, 1990, Transcript, 2, 12, all in YSUOHP.

22. Gwendolyn Wright, *Building the Dream: A Social History of American Housing* (Cambridge, MA, MIT Press, 1981), 186.

23. Rudy Donofrio interview, 14.

24. Gaetano interview, 4.

25. US Bureau of the Census, Thirteenth Annual Census of the United States, 1910.

26. Stella Ann Zone, interviewed by Joseph E. Mancini, Oct. 30, 1990, transcript, 15, YSUOHP.

27. Grace Ross Sheehan, interviewed by James Allgren, Feb. 22, 1994, transcript, 5, YSUOHP.

28. Anna Marie Macali, interviewed by Marcelle Wilson, Oct. 25, 1994, transcript, 4, YSUOHP.

29. Rudy Donofrio interview, 32.

30. Annette Lefoer, interviewed by Annette Mills, Apr. 6, 1976, transcript, 7, YSUOHP.

31. Michael Patrone, interviewed by June Ladd, Dec. 14, 1993, transcript, 33, YSUOHP.

32. Teaford, *Cities of the Heartland*, 240.

33. Patrone, interviewed by Ladd, 23-24.

34. Marie Fredricka, interviewed by Marcelle Wilson, Oct. 19, 1994, transcript, 3, YSUOHP.

35. Macali interview, 11.

36. Leonard Dinnerstein and David Reimers, *Ethnic Americans: A History of Immigration* (New York: Harper & Row, 1988), 55.

37. Charles H. Mindel, Thanh Van Tranh, and Roosevelt Wright Jr., *Ethnic Families in America: Patterns and Variations*, 3rd ed. (New York: Elseview Press, 1988), 119.

38. Patrone, interviewed by Ladd, 14

39. T. E. Thomas to Niles City Schools, n.d., correspondence book 26, May 24, 1912, to Feb. 15, 1913, Niles Fire Brick Collection.

40. See Niles High School yearbooks, 1918-28, Niles Historical Society Collections, Niles, OH.

41. Fredericka interview, 3-4.

42. Ciarniello interview, 13

43. Dominic Conti, interviewed by Annette Mills, May 8, 1976, transcript, 2, YSUOHP.

44. DeBlasio interview; Domenic A. Mastropietro, interviewed by Joseph E. Mancini, Nov. 8, 1990, transcript, 3, and Nicholas Nazzarini, interviewed by Annette D. Mills, Apr. 12, 1976, transcript, 1, both in YSUOHP

45. Donetta C. Vecchiarelli, interviewed by Joseph Mancini, Oct. 23, 1990, transcript, 1, YSUOHP.

46. The literature on the 1920s KKK is vast. See Linda Gordon, *The Second Coming of the KKK: The Ku Klux Klan of the 1920s and the American Political Tradition* (New York: Liveright, 2017); Felix Harcourt: *Ku Klux Kulture: America and the Klan in the 1920s* (Chicago: Univ. of Chicago Press, 2017); William D. Jenkins, *Steel Valley Klan: The Ku Klux Klan in Ohio's Mahoning Valley* (Kent: Kent State Univ. Press, 1991): Thomas R. Pegram, *One Hundred Percent Americanism: The Rebirth and Decline of the Ku Klux Klan in the 1920s* (Chicago: Univ. of Chicago Press, 2011); Richard K. Tucker, *The Rise and Fall of the Ku Klux Klan in Middle America* (Hamden, CT: Archon, 1991); M. William Lutholtz: *Grand Dragon: D. C. Stephenson and the Ku Klux Klan in Indiana* (West Lafayette, IN: Purdue Univ. Press, 1991); and Kathleen Blee: *Women of the Ku Klux Klan: Racism and Gender in the 1920s* (Berkeley,: Univ. of California Press, 1991).

47. Donald Pallante, interview by James Allgren, Nov. 5, 1993, transcript, 16 YSUOHP; Gaetano interview, 9. This language, while explicit, represents the period.

48. Michael Lariccia, interviewed by Annette D. Mills, Apr. 24, 1976, transcript, 7, YSUOHP.

49. Although it is outside the period of study, by the late 1950s, Blacks became a major presence in the Hollow (as well as the city of Youngstown), making this neighborhood ethnically and racially diverse. Indeed, many Black residents made their mark on the city, including the Youngstown City Schools first Black superintendent, Dr. Robert Pegues in 1972. US Census 1930, "Population, Table 13," "Composition and Characteristics, Table 15," "Composition and Characteristics, Table 18," and "Composition and Characteristics, Table 19," 483–84, 493–94, 500–503, 504–7.

50. US Census, 1930, "Population, Table 13, " "Composition and Characteristics, Table 15," "Composition and Characteristics, Table 18," "Composition and Characteristics, Table 19," 483–84; 493–94, 500–503, 504–7.

51. Ashley Zampogna, "America May Not Perish: The Italian American Fight against the Ku Klux Klan in the Mahoning Valley" (MA thesis, Youngstown State Univ., 2008), 79 (excerpt translated by Zampogna).

52. Donna M. DeBlasio and Martha I. Pallante, "Memories of Work and the Definition of Community: The Making of Italian Americans in the Mahoning Valley," *Ohio History* 121 (2014): 89–118.

53. Pasquale Ruberto, interviewed by William Jenkins, Jan. 9, 1985, transcript, 3, YSUOHP.

54. William Jenkins, *Steel Valley Klan: The Ku Klux Klan in Ohio's Mahoning Valley* (Kent: Kent State Univ. Press, 1990), 117–20.

55. Joseph Jennings, interviewed by Stephen Papalas, Aug. 20, 1982, transcript, 5, and Rita Jennings Gregory, interviewed by Stephen Papalas, Aug. 19, 1982, transcript, 6, both in YSUOHP.

56. Louise Liste, interviewed by Joseph Lambert, Oct. 27, 1990, transcript, 4, YSUOHP

57. Pallante interview, 16

58. Nelson, *Farm and Factory*, 111.

59. Nelson, *Farm and Factory*, vii.

Chapter 10

"Opera Was Not Written for New York Alone"

The Middling Promotion of Operas in English on the Redpath Chautauqua Circuits

CODY A. NORLING

In September 1924, Chicago music critic Glenn Dillard Gunn wrote in the *Herald-Examiner* of a significant moment for the dissemination of opera to the American public: "While the managements of the Chicago Civic and the New York Metropolitan operas solemnly debate the artistic and commercial possibility and advisability of opera in English, the people of 110 American . . . cities have been listening to it with enthusiasm . . . in the chautauqua tent."[1] For Gunn, the presentation of operas in English by the Redpath Chautauqua Bureau's Chicago office "greatly increased [opera's] influence in the cultural life of the country," and the use of any other language "would forever kill the appeal of opera with the masses." The once-ubiquitous national taste for operas in English was, however, on the wane by the time of commercial chautauqua's rise in the 1910s, as were independently touring opera troupes in general. Nevertheless, while audiences increasingly took to popular musical comedy and untranslated operatic repertoires continued their retreat into the gilded halls of urban centers, Redpath touted its predominantly rural presentation of English-language operas as a meaningful contribution to the cultural identity of small-town America.[2] If, as Katherine Preston has noted, "the benefits of management offered" by the nineteenth century's Redpath Lyceum Bureau represented "a major impact on the production of English-language opera," then the centralized promotional efforts of its early-twentieth-century chautauqua circuits represented the culmination of that impact.[3]

This chapter highlights the operatic programing of the Redpath Chautauqua Bureau in order to further illuminate the ways cultural institutions and their associated ideologies straddled tangible and intangible regional divides. To do so, it traces chautauqua's transition from a nineteenth-century Methodist education center on the shores of New York's Lake Chautauqua to a dominant social force in early-twentieth-century midwestern communities, attracting millions of attendees annually with promises of education and uplifting enculturation.[4] Given opera's place within period debates about American artistic progress and shifting notions of cultural hierarchies, commercial circuit bureaus such as Redpath billed their operatic fare as an exemplar of chautauqua's aspirational appeal on weeklong community programs.[5] As Redpath's promotional materials and business correspondence indicate, however, circuit managers were also careful to assuage their audience's distrust of opera's urban and theatrical associations by promoting English-language productions with democratizing, nationalistic rhetoric. Thus, rather than solely the domain of northeastern elites, operas on the chautauqua circuits were deemed culturally significant for Middle-American mass audiences, and chautauqua opera troupes routinely advertised their roles in the genre's nationwide, egalitarian diffusion. This tactic was especially apparent in Redpath's promotion of German-born contralto Ernestine Schumann-Heink and Indiana-born conductor May Valentine, whose careers greatly benefited from an "all-American," egalitarian distinction that marked them as opera presenters for a wider public. Positioned between both regions and social strata, Redpath maintained a middling sensibility with its operatic promotional efforts, promising its audiences access to a genre becoming increasingly recognized as inaccessible. Operas in English under chautauqua tents ultimately offered allusions to northeastern musical aspirations within assurances of midwestern communal values and, as such, served as noticeable points of intersection amid public constructions of the region's cultural boundaries.

From Chautauqua, New York, to Cedar Rapids, Iowa, and Beyond

The eventual nationwide popularity of circuit chautauquas in the early part of the twentieth century began with a single institution in Chautauqua, New York. Later known affectionately as the "Mother Chautauqua," the Chautauqua Assembly opened in August 1874 as a summer training program for Christian educators and sought to provide education and enlightenment through lectures, sermons, and hymns.[6] The concept was successful, and the multi-week, Sunday-school assembly expanded into an annual destination for public education. For founders John Heyl Vincent, a Methodist minister, and Lewis Miller, a philanthropic investor, the original Chautauqua Institution's programming was intended to be, in a word, inspirational. It "was founded... as a consecrating offering for magnifying God's word and work," wrote Miller, who further added that attendees could "stop and find their best place for reveries" and "when thus strengthened,... weave into the fibre of their home-work the newly gathered inspiration and strength."[7] By 1878, the regional popularity of the summer sessions at Lake Chautauqua opened possibilities for far-reaching adult education in rural areas otherwise lacking an educational infrastructure for instruction beyond childhood.

In the spirit of the "Mother Chautauqua," communities and civic organizations began organizing independent, local chautauqua programs throughout the Northeast and well into the Midwest. Funded by civic-minded community leaders and held in large canvas tents during the summer months, local chautauqua assemblies annually presented chautauqua's educational programming to their communities. Vincent stressed the importance of his growing chautauqua ideal's egalitarian aims: "Education, once the peculiar privilege of the few, must on our earthly estate become the valued possession of the many.... Chautauqua pleads for universal education."[8] Thus, the movement's Methodist values gave way to an adaptable, nondenominational model of civic and educational engagement that found eager audiences in midwestern towns stretching from Ohio to Kansas and Missouri to Minnesota.[9] The resulting demand for readily available lecturers and educational presentations was largely filled by lyceum agencies, whose production of semi-regular "lecture-demonstrations" throughout the former Union states equipped them to contend with the new geographical requirements of chautauqua's exponential westward growth. As the largest and most well-respected supplier of lyceum talent, the Redpath Lyceum Bureau of Boston began to expand its chautauqua offerings in 1880.[10]

Nevertheless, sporadic summer schedules and lengthy travel times made these independent chautauquas expensive undertakings.[11] For the 1904 season, Iowa-born Redpath manager Keith Vawter (1872–1937) organized a series of fifteen independent midwestern chautauquas in an attempt to reduce what he described as the impracticalities "manifest in long railroad jumps and the many open dates resulting therefrom."[12] The resulting circuit of consecutive, participating towns streamlined the supply of chautauqua talent through the wholesale presentation of programming to each location in turn—from supplying talent and tents to handling all scheduling and advance advertisement. The organization of towns into circuits and the steady supply of full-time talent created a standardized system of deployment that reduced travel expenses and otherwise lost revenue from unscheduled dates. Moreover, with local committees selling tickets and underwriting financial risks, talent bureaus such as Redpath all but guaranteed themselves sizeable annual profits. By 1907, thirty-three previously independent midwestern chautauquas joined Vawter's centralized circuit system.[13]

The national prevalence of tent chautauqua increased throughout the 1910s and into the 1920s, and circuit bureaus concentrated their efforts in the rural Midwest, where chautauqua's Protestant underpinnings and stated community values were well received (Fig. 10.1). With the financial success of his circuit model, Vawter established a regional office in Cedar Rapids, Iowa (the Redpath-Vawter circuit) where he managed a string of more than one hundred participating towns in Iowa, Minnesota, South Dakota, Missouri, and Nebraska. At this time, the Redpath Chautauqua Bureau significantly increased its operations to include several regional branches throughout the United States. No doubt bolstered by a turn-of-the-century outpouring of midwestern regionalist activities that historians of the Midwest have come to call the "Midwestern Moment," communities around the region began to sign up in droves for progressive chautauqua programing.[14] Indeed, its overwhelming popularity in the Midwest necessitated additional circuits within the region, including those managed by Wisconsin-born Nebraskan Charles F. Horner (1878–1967) in Kansas City (the Redpath-Horner circuit) and Iowan Harry P. Harrison (1878–1968) in

Fig. 10.1. *Vawter Chautauqua.* (Shelby, Iowa, August 24–28, 1910s, Redpath Chautauqua Collection, University of Iowa Libraries, Iowa City.)

Chicago (the Redpath-Harrison circuit), and others in Columbus, Ohio, and Lincoln, Nebraska.[15] In 1915, preseason estimates showed that some 5 million spectators were to attend roughly three thousand chautauquas across the United States and, in 1920, the Redpath-Horner circuit reported that, of the five thousand scheduled chautauquas nationwide, half took place in midwestern states.[16] During the circuit's peak years in the early 1920s, upward of 20 million Americans attended nine thousand chautauquas each summer, the majority of which were delivered via Vawter's midwestern circuit model.[17]

The concentration of chautauquas in the Midwest was certainly not lost on contemporaneous observers, and by the second decade of the century, what was once a northeastern institution became a recognizable fixture of midwestern cultural identity. "When the 'Chautauqua belt' is spoken of," noted one period journalist, "the Middle West is meant."[18] As early in the circuit period as 1912, the New York–based magazine *World's Work* claimed that "the heart of the chautauqua movement is in Iowa, the home of progress and reform."[19] Manager Harry P. Harrison likewise remembered circuit chautauqua in a specifically regional context: "The America that watched the first tent rise in an Iowa meadow in 1904 ... saw the last tent come down, twenty-nine years later in a little Illinois village."[20] For Harrison, whose circuit bestrode regional lines between midwestern and southeastern states, "it had been an accepted axiom that good crops meant good Chautauqua."[21] Even the metropolitan-minded Carol Kennicott of Sinclair Lewis's *Main Street* experienced "a week of culture under canvas" in the fictitious town of Gopher Prairie, Minnesota.[22]

Operatic Fare as Middling Cultural Commodity on the Circuits

More than organizational and operational changes, the westward spread and commercialization of chautauquas during the first decade of the twentieth century induced changes in programing as well. Though lectures and sermons remained prominent on circuit programs, the increased dependence on annual ticket sales created an equally increased dependence on diversified attractions (Fig. 10.2). As such, musical acts, initially a secondary feature of chautauqua's lecture-dominated programs, began to proliferate among bureau talent rosters. Harrison himself noted that

THE PROGRAM DAY BY DAY

SHELBY, IOWA, AUG. 24-28

Programs Begin Promptly. Be on Time.

1st DAY

2:30 P.M.	Appropriate Opening	GEO. B. TACK & COMPANY
3:00 P.M.	Lecture	"Taste the Apples"
		JAS. HARDIN SMITH
	Admission 36c, War Tax 4c, Total 40c	
4:00 P.M.	Vesper Service	
8:00 P.M.	Quartet Music	GEO. B. TACK & COMPANY
	Admission 45c, War Tax 5c, Total 50c	

2nd DAY

9:00 A.M.	Organization of Juniors for the Dramatic Play, "The Magic Piper"	
2:30 P.M.	Prelude by	THE OXFORD COMPANY
	Half Hour of Great Vocal Classics	
3:00 P.M.	Recital Entertainment	"Mister Antonio"
	M. BERYL BUCKLEY	
	Admission 36c, War Tax 4c, Total 40c	
8:00 P.M.	Music by	THE OXFORD COMPANY
	Chautauqua's Premier Vocal Artists	
	Admission 54c, War Tax 6c, Total 60c	

3rd DAY

9:00 A.M.	Rehearsal of the "Magic Piper" by Juniors	
2:30 P.M.	Music by	THE WEBERS
	An Afternoon of Delightful Music	
	Admission 36c, War Tax 4c, Total 40c	
8:00 P.M.	Prelude by	THE WEBERS
	Music of Excellence and Charm	
8:30 P.M.	Lecture	OPIE READ
	Unique, Scholarly, Humorous, Penetrating	
	Admission 45c, War Tax 5c, Total 50c	

4th DAY

9:00 A.M.	Rehearsal of the "Magic Piper" by Juniors	
2:30 P.M.	Prelude by	THE HUSSARS
	A Little Touch of Jazz	
3:00 P.M.	Lecture	"The Testing of a Nation"
	W. E. WENNER	
	Admission 36c, War Tax 4c, Total 40c	
8:00 P.M.	Joy Night Supreme—Music and Fun	THE HUSSARS
	Admission 54c, War Tax 6c, Total 60c	

5th DAY

9:00 A.M.	Dress Rehearsal of "Magic Piper" by Juniors	
2:30 P.M.	Prelude by	THE PUGH COMPANY
	A Half Hour of Smiles	
3:00 P.M.	Lecture	"Americanism versus Bolshevism"
	HON. HARRY N. ROUTZOHN	
	Admission 36c, War Tax 4c, Total 40c	
7:30 P.M.	Prelude to the Evening Program	"THE MAGIC PIPER"
	Produced by the Juniors	
8:00 P.M.	Entertainment	JESS PUGH
	Platform's Greatest Laugh-maker	
	Admission 45c, War Tax 5c, **Total 50c**	

NOTE—Each Musical Company has an appropriate Sunday Program. Season Tickets, $1.50, War Tax 15c, which will be collected when ticket is delivered.

E

Fig. 10.2. Five-day schedule for *Vawter Chautauqua*. (Shelby, Iowa, August 24–28, 1910s, Redpath Chautauqua Collection, University of Iowa Libraries, Iowa City.)

"it took all kinds of music to build a Chautauqua program.... There were brass bands and soprano soloists, sober-faced choirs and male quartets. They sang everything from Richard Wagner to Carrie Jacobs Bond, played everything from the harp to the xylophone."[23] As musicologist Paige Lush has more recently asserted, "music helped to define chautauqua," and its programming was "a deliberate—and often formulaic—endeavor."[24] To meet the demands of their predominantly small-town audiences that sought to separate themselves from the perceived moral failings of urban popular culture, bureaus used the enculturating principles and wholesome promotional rhetoric of the "Mother Chautauqua" to meticulously curate their rosters. In 1920, talent manager Louis Runner proclaimed that chautauqua's "musical numbers are presented, not in the depraved surrounding of a cabaret, not the noisy disregard of the cafe dining room, not in the free and easy abandon of the vaudeville stage.... [but in] an atmosphere in which standards of living must be maintained."[25] Indeed, aspirational culture was a lucrative commodity for circuit bureaus, and a two-dollar ticket promised audiences exposure to content promoted as edification, a recognizable—if perhaps merely rhetorical—departure from the popular entertainments offered by touring vaudeville.[26] As one period journalist reported, chautauqua sold itself as "the stage improved and purified," "classical music popularized, popular music dignified," and, above all, "entertainment having educational value."[27]

From operatic quartets and concert prima donnas to costumed opera scenes and staged productions, operas and operatic selections were standard fare on Redpath's circuit programs. The variety of chautauqua's musical acts also made for widespread exposure to operatic repertoires via such otherwise disparate mediums as transcriptions for military bands and dramatic spoken-word readings accompanied by musical excerpts.[28] Staged operas, either "grand" or "light," also maintained a certain amount of variety when performed by stock companies that toured with mixed repertoires and ambiguous generic distinctions. Harry Leiter's so-called Light Opera Company, for example, produced such seemingly disparate works as W. S. Gilbert and Arthur Sullivan's *The Mikado*, Giacomo Puccini's *La bohème*, Giuseppe Verdi's *Il trovatore*, and Reginald De Koven's *Robin Hood*.[29] Though such companies invariably toured with reduced personnel and equipment as necessitated by the streamlined circuit system, many retained some of the scenery and costuming common to larger productions.

Redpath's productions ran the gamut from costumed scenes by the five-member English Opera Singers to the use of "full costume with scenic and lighting effects" for Ralph Dunbar's production of *The Mikado*, which featured a cast of twenty and an orchestra of eight.[30] Regarding the latter, one journalist reported that "the tent at night [took] on the appearance of an oriental garden with Japanese lanterns hanging everywhere."[31]

Nevertheless, despite the prevalence of operatic programming on Redpath circuits, opera was not universally exempt from mistrust among rural audiences, and as a result, promoters were deliberately middling in their public characterization. In the Midwest, opera's changing position within cultural hierarchies and its troubling associations with staged theater created a shifting public perception for the genre that vacillated between elitist art and indecent theatrical amusement, neither of which was socially acceptable under chautauqua tents. As Lawrence Levine charted in his study of American cultural "sacralization," operas experienced a drastic transition from expressions of nineteenth-century popular entertainment to examples of rarefied art at the outset of the twentieth century, when "more and more, opera in America meant foreign-language opera performed in opera houses like [New York's] Academy of Music and the Metropolitan Opera House, which were deeply influenced if not controlled by wealthy patrons."[32] The resulting bipartite perception of opera as a manifestation of urban excess and popular immorality—a sentiment reflected in 1923 by Iowa radio pioneer Henry Field's promises of "good music, free from either Jazz or Grand Opera"—was clearly a concern for Redpath's circuit bureaus, which took continued action to downplay such boorish connotations in their promotional efforts.[33] Engendered by the impulse to separate chautauqua from elitist operatic stereotypes, Harrison later recalled, "In contrast to grand opera, chautauqua had no high-minded patrons in diamond chokers ready to make up annual deficits. It must pay its own way."[34] Furthermore, much like Redpath's known efforts to assuage its audience's antitheatrical prejudices through assurances of the medium's cultural redemption, many chautauqua operas were similarly redeemed through both a perceived air of respectability and their presentation as significant contributions to the operagoing capacity of the nation's audiences more broadly.[35]

To do so, Redpath capitalized on the longstanding egalitarian rhetoric surrounding the presentation of operas in English. As an undeniably lucrative enterprise produced by itinerate troupes for sometimes socially mixed audiences, English-language opera was ubiquitous among nineteenth-century popular entertainments across the United States. Companies produced a nationally and stylistically mixed repertoire containing both "light" and "grand" operas either written in or translated to English. The troupes of Clara Louise Kellogg, Emma Abbott (the "People's Pima Donna"), Emma Juch, and, later, Henry Savage toured extensively with elaborate, staged productions of a translated repertory offered at popular prices for audiences accustomed to opera as a form of variety entertainment.[36] With the Gilded Age growth of foreign-language repertoires that increasingly traded on perceptions of social exclusivity, English-language operas were promoted as nationalistic alternatives to imported, European productions. Thus viewed as socially equalizing purveyors of opera for the entire nation, late-century English-language companies were often received as ostensibly democratic cultural institutions, and the advertised use of English became a recognizable signifier of public-spirited programming for middle-class audiences.[37] "It is because the pleasure, the refinement, and the educational force of the operas are being 'democratized'—taken from the few and given to the many—that the progress of the opera in English is worth recounting," wrote Henry Savage in 1900.[38] Rather than characterizing opera as an "indulgence peculiar to the wealthy inhabitants of the metropolis," Savage predicted that "even the provincial city in America will ... have its regular season of opera in English."

With the outbreak of war in Europe, these connotations became enveloped in the anti-foreign sentiments that stretched across regions. The widespread mistrust of so-called hyphenated Americans and its effects on the cosmopolitan world of classical music have been well-studied, and as E. Douglas Bomberger has recently written of the wartime experiences of musicians in the United States, "in a time of national crisis, no one [was] immune from the influence of politics."[39] Conspicuous incidents occurred in both the Northeast and the Midwest alike. The arrest and deportation of the Boston Symphony conductor Karl Muck provides a telling example, as does a report of a public assault on a German-born member of the Chicago Civic Opera's orchestra.[40] The postwar years offered little in the way of respite. In 1919, violent riots surrounding the Star Opera Company's German-language season in New York confirmed ongoing tensions, and in 1921, Chicago's Opera in Our Language Foundation began its efforts to ensure that "foreign works and artists [were] heard only in English."[41] The subsequent Emergency Quota Act of 1921 and Immigration Act of 1924 placed annual limits on immigration, echoing President Calvin Coolidge's proclamation that "America must be kept American."[42]

All the while, Chautauqua bureaus touted the longstanding nationalistic implications of their musical—and specifically operatic—programing as essential to American community values. "By the time the United States entered the war," writes Charlotte Canning, "the Chautauqua movement had been striving for more than forty years to make the United States 'safe for democracy,'" and the combination of this legacy and wartime fervor made for a potent marketing opportunity.[43] The resulting promotional rhetoric, when mobilized behind chautauqua's operatic offerings, reassured its audiences of the genre's democratizing value beyond coastal urban centers. More specifically, associations between English-language operas and flagrant Americanism were important selling points for Redpath's chautauqua circuits and ultimately helped to create a socially acceptable cultural middle ground in which their operas could thrive in a liminal space between urban cosmopolitanism and immodest stage entertainment.

That multiple performers and companies sold their English-language productions on promises of nationwide accessibility suggests the tactic's commercial viability. "One seldom hears anything in a foreign tongue," wrote veteran circuit-chautauqua performer Clay Smith in 1922, noting, "Even the biggest artists get down to earth and sing in English."[44] Redpath's promotional material for Howard Tooley's company, for example, claimed that he aimed to "give every community a chance to have an 'Opera Season'" by presenting "an all American company with the standard repertoire in English," adding, "This is the day of Americanization of Opera."[45] A brochure for William Hinshaw's company similarly asserted that "Opera was not written for New York alone" and operas in English belonged to "the great mass of common people," while another flyer for the People's Grand Opera Association sought to put "America First in Music as in all else" by offering Redpath audiences "Grand Opera in the English language with all American artists, citizens of the United States ... making it possible for Americans to sing in Grand Opera in America for the American People in our mother tongue."[46] For impresario Milton Aborn, such efforts looked "to give to singers of this country the same opportunity for such preparation here as formerly made a European trip necessary."[47] Simply put, Redpath's staged operas were made acceptable for its discerning audiences by virtue of the vernacular and the recognizable connotations with which it came. This proved significant in Redpath's careful promotion of its headlining operatic acts, including both Ernestine Schumann-Heink, a German-born star of the Metropolitan Opera Company, and May Valentine, a homegrown midwestern conductor.

The Cases of Ernestine Schumann-Heink and May Valentine

Perhaps the highest profile case of Redpath's efforts to position its operatic offerings as middling, nationalistic endeavors is that of famed contralto Ernestine Schumann-Heink (1861–1936). As a German citizen touring in a time of widespread anti-German sentiment and a perennial favorite on the Redpath circuits, Schumann-Heink did much to cultivate a democratic, America-loving persona in her promotion and performative mythos, both on and off the Redpath circuits. This careful attention to the expectations of American audiences who mistrusted displays of foreignness allowed Schumann-Heink the professional freedom and public favorability denied to some of her Germanic colleagues.[48] A 1931 film short, "Schumann-Heink Says Hear America First," echoes both her history of American patriotism and the democratizing rhetoric of chautauqua's opera companies when Schumann-Heink proclaims to Americans, "You will not be forced to go over to Europe to get all the great [opera] stars, but you will have your own stars in your own country."[49]

For Redpath-Harrison, Schumann-Heink's carefully considered public image made for an opportune business relationship that balanced cosmopolitan prestige with folksy Americanism. Schumann-Heink largely worked as a concert soloist for sporadic, conspicuous engagements on Harrison's circuit; yet her continued use of operatic repertoires and previous career as an onstage operatic prima donna with such well-known companies as New York's Metropolitan Opera ensured a marked link to staged, foreign operas. Thus, the need to hedge potential audience uncertainties was nevertheless apparent. In addition to continued emphases on motherhood and philanthropic generosity that were common in the promotion of female opera singers, it is clear that while on contract with Redpath, Schumann-Heink's public image was routinely predicated on a sense of egalitarian obligation to her chautauqua audiences.[50] Despite a multilingual concert program, Redpath showcased the foreign-born performer's use of English texts and repertoires, noting in one brochure that she "delights to sing in English" for her "great American audiences."[51] As a result, "HER AUDIENCE FEELS LIKE ONE BIG FAMILY," it claimed, making Schumann-Heink the de facto matriarch "in her wholehearted way." Schumann-Heink was pitched as a people's performer, and Harrison described her as one of the "folk of simple tastes" with a "simple, warmhearted modest manner," who "shared her knowledge ... with any youngster at hand to listen," an image far from that of the stereotypically aloof foreign diva. Furthermore, Harrison later recalled that, during a tour in Ohio, Schumann-Heink graciously gave a purportedly pro-bono performance for a local organizer who could not pay her usual fee.[52]

This public-spirited narrative was a veritable marketing boon for Redpath's management, which was increasingly willing to pay top dollar for Schumann-Heink's noted voice. Despite her reported acts of altruism, Schumann-Heink's 1914 contract clearly listed her fee as $1,000.[53] In 1919, Harrison claimed that she "would not take any dates for less than $1,500" and in 1922, her chautauqua fee ranged from $2,000 to $2,500 per engagement.[54] Redpath's investment in the conflation of opera and nationalism afforded by an association with Schumann-Heink did not go unnoticed by the US Department of the Treasury when it described her wartime chautauqua work as "a fine example of the spirit of America."[55]

Operatic conductor and impresario May Valentine (1890–1974), for whom Redpath's democratizing promotion proved both effective and lasting, received similar descriptions. Whereas Redpath management capitalized on Schumann-Heink's readymade egalitarian persona, it helped to create Valentine's public image as a socially motivated, national presenter of operas in English, one that lasted years after her successful chautauqua career. While on Redpath's rosters between 1917 and 1925, Valentine toured extensively throughout much of the United States with companies that presented English-language "light" operas, such as De Koven's *Robin Hood*, Gilbert and Sullivan's *The Mikado* and *The Gondoliers*, and Michael William Balfe's *The Bohemian Girl*.[56] However, in keeping with the spirit of mixed repertoires common to both chautauqua and its English-language companies, Valentine made it clear that, regardless of specific generic distinctions, her "business was to produce ... and entirely present operas—grand or light."[57] Notably, for Redpath-Harrison's "de-luxe" circuit season of 1925, Valentine's staged production of *Robin Hood*—with its season budget of nearly $30,000, widespread advertising partnership with dealers of Victor records, and private bus for a twenty-four-member company—was a substantial financial investment for Harrison, who was careful to quell potential audience uncertainties regarding her staged productions.[58]

Redpath's promotional tactics were crucial in creating Valentine's persona as an advocate for American musicianship nationwide. Though her Indiana upbringing and Chicago training belied common operatic associations with foreignness, Valentine's extensive democratizing press coverage betrays the extent to which Redpath went to ensure that her tours were considered democratic endeavors, publicizing her efforts to cultivate an ensemble composed entirely of American-born personnel. This proved to be an effective extension of English-language opera's egalitarian image and, in a hyper-nationalist postwar climate, prevented accusations of foreign leanings. Throughout her tours, Valentine advertised open auditions for "local singers with talent and ambition" so as "to assist many of them with advice regarding their careers."[59] One reporter noted, "Valentine stops long enough each day to hear and advise any singer who may call upon her," and another promised that she would hear "all young men or women who are interested in concert or operatic work."[60] Valentine's own goals for these practices were clearly stated: "We are no longer a protege of the old world and can stand in our own yard unassisted. . . . I want [audiences] to hear my American artists, born, reared and educated right here in this grand old country of ours."[61] For Harrison, this was an opportunity to reassert Redpath's commitment to the national importance of its operas: "The idea that opera can only be successfully presented by foreign singers is being definitely disposed of by what [Valentine] is accomplishing. . . . [She] is taking opera to many communities . . . [and] registering a definite step forward in American musical activities."[62]

The promise of national musical cultivation among audiences beyond those of the coasts was an expressed concern in the midwestern press, which at times espoused the cause of public cultural betterment via a democratic spread of operas in English. Valentine's tours were portrayed as harbingers of public cultural uplift, which ultimately helped to reinforce the perceived superiority of her productions over more popular forms of entertainment while also maintaining Redpath's democratizing appearances. In 1922, a Waterloo, Iowa, newspaper reported that Valentine's tours furnished "more than an opera"; rather, they were "an institution and a part of a liberal education."[63] A columnist in Belvidere, Illinois, claimed that Valentine's offerings were elevated alternatives to the "jingling Broadway tunes they are writing these days," which "bore" audiences.[64] In 1926, the *Green Bay Press-Gazette* remembered Valentine's Redpath seasons as having "struck the keynote to success" in providing "America something worthwhile" and inspiring a "taste for better things."[65]

Closing the Circuits

Following their peak in 1924, the chautauqua circuits declined rapidly. As fewer towns continued to hold annual chautauquas, circuit bureaus failed to sustain their operations. The Redpath-Vawter circuit closed in 1926, and by summer 1929, Redpath-Harrison had been completely dismantled and sold to competitors.[66] Harrison blamed the 1927 collapse of the real-estate market in the Midwest, which "distracted farmers ... the financial backbones of local Chautauqua committees," and more pithily remembered the end as a culmination of changing leisurely priorities and widespread economic uncertainties: chautauqua "died in 1932 under the hit-and-run wheels of a Model-A Ford on its way to the movies on a new paved road. Radio swept it into the ditch, and the Wall Street crash and the subsequent depression gave it the *coup de grâce*."[67] Indeed, as a result of new entertainment mediums, rampant urbanization, and, more directly, the lingering effects of declining crop prices that all coalesced in the latter half of the 1920s, the rural communities that once underwrote annual chautauquas increasingly turned away from such an expensive investment.[68] Thus, uninterrupted summer schedules of willing communities—the linchpins of circuit chautauqua's success—dwindled to the point of eventual fiscal impossibility, and the last of the formerly expansive circuit bureaus closed in 1932.[69]

A similar fate was not uncommon for touring opera troupes in a time of operatic institutionalization, as residential opera companies took hold in major cities and touring became an extension of urban cultural influence.[70] Valentine's career largely reflected this transition. Her touring company effectively ceased its operations at the end of 1928, but Valentine settled nicely into a four-decade career in Chicago, conducting opera choruses for the city's resident companies, managing the library of the eventual Lyric Opera of Chicago, and overseeing a regional operatic library.[71] Still committed to the nationwide spread of opera, in 1948, Valentine wrote that "between the West Coast and New York, no one can ever get [operatic productions]. If you're not on Broadway, you are a hick. So I started with the Chicago Opera music material and now can supply material for rental.... It is my idea for the Middle West."[72]

Much like the chautauqua movement itself, Redpath's touring opera companies traversed regional borders with their repertoires and middling promotional rhetoric. Their English-language productions were presented as a form of operatic democratization and sought to both reclaim opera from the domain of the northeastern elites and redeem its otherwise corrupting urban theatrical associations. For Schumann-Heink, whose maternal and egalitarian personas downplayed her position as a foreign-born diva, and Valentine, who was positioned as an advocate of local American performers and audiences alike, these promotional tactics were crucial to touring success in towns between the coasts. That Redpath marketed its operatic offerings as culturally beneficial to the rural midwestern audiences along its circuit route ultimately highlights the organization's consideration of national musical hierarchies inherent in the attempt to fashion a specifically midwestern musical sensibility within American musical culture writ large. In many ways, this case delays Levine's trajectory for total operatic sacralization, instead sustaining a nineteenth-century model of popular operatic itinerancy while catering to the middling demands of its rural chautauqua audiences and ultimately challenging the perceived cultural authority of the nation's industrialist tastemakers. The American cultural landscape may have been in the process of becoming "*more* sharply defined, *more* circumscribed, and *less* flexible than it had been," as Levine theorized, but amid chautauqua's transition from northeastern institution to midwestern phenomenon, its operatic acts of the 1910s and 1920s were neither solely highbrow nor entirely lowbrow.[73] Rather than delineating a clear musical division between regions, Redpath's programming underlines the flexible cultural boundaries and reveals the pervasiveness of art-music repertoires within the region's self-defining notions of musical taste. For the Midwest,

Redpath's chautauqua circuits provided a platform on which to stage and reassert the wider social utility of opera for rural, middling audiences, and as a result, opera again reached—if only temporarily—a significant portion of American audiences otherwise removed from its newly elite associations and changing social spheres.

Notes

I thank the volume's editors and reviewers for their assistance in preparing this research for publication, and I am grateful to Marian Wilson Kimber for her inspiration and ongoing support. Portions of this chapter were adapted from my PhD dissertation: "Opera in the Second City: Negotiating National Operatic Identities in and Around 1920s Chicago" (Univ. of Iowa, 2023).

1. "Opera Goes to Many Via Chautauqua," *Chicago Herald-Examiner*, Sept. 21, 1924, as reprinted in *Lyceum Magazine* 34, no. 6 (1924): 37.

2. For a roughly contemporaneous example of a movement for literary cultural diffusion between the East and Midwest, see Robert Loerzel, "'People Are Getting Tired of Broadway and Fifth Avenue': The Origins of the Society for Midland Authors," in *The Midwestern Moment: The Forgotten World of Early-Twentieth-Century Midwestern Regionalism, 1880–1940*, ed. Jon K. Lauck (Hastings, NE: Hastings College Press, 2017), 19–34.

3. Katherine K. Preston, *Opera for the People: English-Language Opera and Women Managers in Late 19th-Century America* (New York: Oxford Univ. Press, 2017), 243. The present research is, in many ways, an extension of Preston's prolific work. Some influential examples by Preston that are not directly cited include *Opera on the Road: Traveling Opera Troupes in the United States, 1825–60* (Urbana: Univ. of Illinois Press, 1993); "Between the Cracks: The Performance of English-Language Opera in Late Nineteenth-Century America," *American Music* 21, no. 3 (2003): 349–74; "Notes from (The Road to) the Stage," *Opera Quarterly* 23, no. 1 (2008): 103–19; and "Opera Is Elite / Opera Is Nationalist: Cosmopolitan Views of Opera Reception in the United States, 1870–90," *Journal of the American Musicological Society* 66, no. 2 (2013): 523–49.

4. Jacob Bruggeman and Eric Michael Rhodes take a similar tack in their chapter in this volume, examining the westward transmission of eastern cultural priorities in the establishment of Cleveland and its Cleveland Orchestra (215–37).

5. For more on the shifting social status of opera, see Lawrence W. Levine, *Highbrow/Lowbrow: The Emergence of Cultural Hierarchy in America* (Cambridge, MA: Harvard Univ. Press, 1988), 85–168; and Alexandra Wilson, *Opera in the Jazz Age: Cultural Politics in 1920s Britain* (Oxford: Oxford Univ. Press, 2019), 71–95.

6. Jeanette Wells, "A History of the Music Festival at the Chautauqua Institution from 1874 to 1957" (PhD diss., Catholic Univ. of America, 1958), 8.

7. John H. Vincent, *The Chautauqua Movement* (Boston: Chautauqua Press, 1886), v.

8. Vincent, *Chautauqua Movement*, 2.

9. Andrew Rieser, *The Chautauqua Movement: Protestants, Progressives, and the Culture of Modern Liberalism* (New York: Columbia Univ. Press, 2003), 126.

10. John E. Tapia, *Circuit Chautauqua: From Rural Education to Popular Entertainment in Early Twentieth Century America* (Jefferson, NC: McFarland, 1997), 12, 14–15.

11. Hugh A. Orchard, *Fifty Years of Chautauqua: Its Beginnings, Its Development, Its Message, and Its Life* (Cedar Rapids: Torch Press, 1923), 55.

12. Redpath Chautauqua, *Twenty Years of Chautauqua Progress, 1904–1923* (Cedar Rapids: Torch Press, 1924).

13. Tapia, *Circuit Chautauqua*, 29.

14. See Lauck, *Midwestern Moment*: Not only a time of self-conscious regionalist identity formation, the "Midwestern Moment" also proved to be a fruitful environment for the construction of arts institutions. For examples, see Michael J. Pfeifer, "A Symphonic Midwest: The Minneapolis Symphony Orchestra and Regionalist Identity, 1903–1922," in Lauck, *Midwestern Moment*, 101–12; Christa Adams, "Splendid and Remarkable Progress" in the Midwest: Assessing the Emergence and Impact of Regional Art Museums, 1875–1925," *Middle West Review* 7, no. 1 (2020): 85–92; and Jon K. Lauck, *The Good Country: A History of the American Midwest, 1800–1900* (Norman: Univ. of Oklahoma Press, 2022), 38–42, 109–11, 116–19.

15. "Who's Who in the Lyceum," *Lyceum Magazine* 32, no. 1 (1922): 46; and M. Sandra Manderson, "The Redpath Lyceum Bureau, An American Critic: Decision-Making and Programming Methods for Circuit Chautauquas, circa 1912 to 1930" (PhD diss., Univ. of Iowa, 1981).

16. "Current Tendencies in the Development of the Chautauqua Movement," *Current Opinion* 59 (Aug. 1915): 115; and Donald L. Graham, "Circuit Chautauqua, A Middle Western Institution" (PhD diss., Univ. of Iowa, 1953), 269.

17. Charlotte Canning, *The Most American Thing in America: Circuit Chautauqua as Performance* (Iowa City: Univ. of Iowa Press, 2005), 10.

18. Truman H. Talley, "The Chautauquas—An American Achievement," *Women's Work* 42 (1921): 175.

19. French Strother, "The Great American Forum," *World's Work* 24, no. 5 (1912): 553.

20. Harry P. Harrison and Karl Detzer, *Culture under Canvas: The Story of Tent Chautauqua* (New York: Hastings House, 1958), xviii.

21. Harrison and Detzer, *Culture under Canvas*, 261. For the May Valentine Opera Company, Harrison's 1925 route, managed from his offices within Chicago's Kimball Building, included stops in Illinois, Indiana, Michigan, and Wisconsin, as well as Kentucky, Tennessee, Georgia, and the Carolinas. "The Valentine Opera Company in De Koven's Masterpiece 'Robin Hood': Summer Season 1925," flier, Talent Correspondence and Brochures, Redpath Chautauqua Collection, Univ. of Iowa Libraries, Iowa City.

22. Sinclair Lewis, *Main Street* (New York: P. F. Collier & Son, 1920), 236.

23. Harrison and Detzer, *Culture under Canvas*, 97.

24. Paige Lush, *Music in the Chautauqua Movement: From 1874 to the 1930s* (Jefferson, NC: McFarland, 2013), 6, 93.

25. Louis O. Runner, "The Influence of the Lyceum and Chautauqua on Popular Music," in *The International Lyceum and Chautauqua Association, Year-Book* (Chicago: Executive Committee, 1920), 9:26–31.

26. Despite Redpath's promotional efforts to assure separation from vaudeville, numerous performers routinely appeared on both chautauqua and vaudeville stages. Ralph Dunbar, for example, supplied acts to both Redpath circuits and vaudeville syndicates. Lush, *Music in the Chautauqua Movement*, 29.

27. "The Woman's Column," *Henry (IL) Republican*, July 25, 1912.

28. Tapia, *Circuit Chautauqua*, 130–39; and Lush, *Music in the Chautauqua Movement*, 102–4. Additionally, Marian Wilson Kimber shows that the accompanied recitation of opera was not unfamiliar to period audiences, in "Reciting *Parsifal*: Opera as Spoken-Word Performance in America," *American Music* 38, no. 1 (2020): 7–9.

29. "The Harry Leiter Opera Company," pamphlet, Talent Correspondence and Brochures, Redpath Chautauqua Collection.

30. "The English Opera Singers," pamphlet, Talent Correspondence and Brochures, Redpath Chautauqua Collection; and "Mikado Tonight at Chautauqua," *Owensboro (KY) Inquirer*, June 28, 1917.

31. "The Great Creatore Coming," *Florence (AL) Herald*, Apr. 12, 1917.

32. Levine, *Highbrow/Lowbrow*, 102.

33. WOAW leaflet, Henry Field Seeds Catalogue, Autumn 1923, as cited by Kimberly K. Porter, "The Most Talked-About Personality in the Middle West: Henry Field's Struggle to Maintain the Midwestern Ideal on Iowa Radio," in Lauck, *Midwestern Moment*, 165.

34. Harrison and Detzer, *Culture under Canvas*, 98.

35. For Charlotte Canning, Redpath's continued investment in the defense of theater signaled the presence of lingering antitheatrical sentiments among its audiences. See her article "The Platform Versus the Stage: The Circuit Chautauqua's Antitheatrical Theatre," *Theatre Journal* 50, no. 3 (1998): 303–18. See also Gina Bombola and Kristen M. Turner on opera's ability to "project respectability" onto vaudeville programs and the early film industry: "Respectability, Prestige, and the Whiteness of Opera in American Popular Entertainment from 1890 to 1937," *Musical Quarterly* 105, nos. 3–4 (2022): 285.

36. Preston, *Opera for the People;* Kristen M. Turner, "'A Joyous Star-Spangled-Bannerism': Emma Juch, Opera in English Translation, and the American Cultural Landscape in the Gilded Age," *Journal of the Society for American Music* 8, no. 2 (2014): 219–52; and Jim McPherson, "The Savage Innocents, Part 2: On the Road with Parsifal, Butterfly, the Widow, and the Girl," *Opera Quarterly* 19, no. 1 (2003): 503–33.

37. Katherine K. Preston, "A Rarefied Art? Opera and Operatic Music as Popular Entertainment in Late Nineteenth-Century Washington City," in *Music, American*

Made: Essays in Honor of John Graziano, ed. John Koegel (Sterling Heights, MI: Harmonie Park Press, 2011), 3–46; and Kristen M. Turner, "Opera in English: Class and Culture in America, 1878–1910 " (PhD diss., Univ. of North Carolina at Chapel Hill, 2015).

38. Henry Savage, "Opera in English for America," *Independent* 52, no. 2684 (1900): 1109–10.

39. E. Douglas Bomberger, *Making Music American: 1917 and the Transformation of Culture* (New York: Oxford Univ. Press, 2018), 215. For more on period anti-foreign sentiments, see, among others, David E. Bennett, *The Party of Fear: The American Far Right from Nativism to the Militia Movement* (New York: Vantage, 1988), 183–98; and David M. Kennedy, *Over Here: The First World War and American Society* (New York: Oxford Univ. Press, 1980), 63–69.

40. "Anthem Slacker Stoop for Horn; Kick! Riot! Jail!" *Chicago Tribune*, Nov. 5, 1918. See also Edmund Bowles, "Karl Muck and His Compatriots: German Conductors in America during World War I (and How They Coped)," *American Music* 25, no. 4 (2007): 405–40; Matthew Mungmon, "Patriotism, Art, and 'The Star-Spangled Banner' in World War I: A New Look at the Karl Muck Episode," *Journal of Musicological Research* 33, no. 4 (2014): 4–26; Barbara Tischler, "One Hundred Percent Americanism and Music in Boston during World War I," *American Music* 4, no. 2 (1986): 164–76; and J. E. Vacha, "When Wagner Was Verboten: The Campaign against German Music in World War I," *New York History* 64, no. 2 (1983): 171–88.

41. "Thousands of Service Men Storm Theater as German Opera Is Given," *Lexington Herald*, Oct. 21, 1919; American Opera Society of Chicago (National), "Historical Data: Statement of Incorporation of Opera in Our Language Foundation," clipping, Scrapbooks of the American Opera Society of Chicago, Newbery Library. For more, see Norling, "Opera in the Second City," 113–22; Gwen D'Amico, "*Die Meistersinger*, New York City, and the Metropolitan Opera: The Intersection of Art and Politics during Two World Wars" (PhD diss., City Univ. of New York, 2016); and Sylvia M. Eversole, "Eleanor Everest Freer: Her Life and Music" (PhD diss., City Univ. of New York, 1992).

42. Erika Lee, *America for Americans: A History of Xenophobia in the United States* (New York: Basic Books, 2019), 143; David J. Goldberg, *Discontented America: The United States in the 1920s* (Baltimore: Johns Hopkins Univ. Press, 1999), 140–66.

43. Canning, *Most American Thing in America*, 49; Lush, *Music in the Chautauqua Movement*, 141–76; and Tapia, *Circuit Chautauqua*, 125–33.

44. Clay Smith, "What the Modern Chautauqua Is Doing for Music of All Kinds Everywhere in Our Country," *Etude* 40, no. 8 (1922): 514.

45. "The Tooley Opera Company," pamphlet, Talent Correspondence and Brochures, Redpath Chautauqua Collection.

46. "The Hinshaw Light Opera Singers," and "The People's Grand Opera Association: A Declaration," both pamphlets in Talent Correspondence and Brochures, Redpath Chautauqua Collection.

47. "Aborn Opera Company," pamphlet, Talent Correspondence and Brochures, Redpath Chautauqua Collection.

48. See Bomberger regarding Schumann-Heink's wartime activities, her efforts to assuage potential concerns regarding her Germanness, and the experiences of her contemporaries, in *Making Music American*, 164–99.

49. "Ernestine Schumann-Heink Says Hear America First," 6:24, YouTube video, from a performance directed by Com Hogan, *Pathé Audio Review* 2, no. 52, 1931, posted by "GCF9," July 6, 2017, https://www.youtube.com/watch?v=Rsw5XMKY2s0.

50. For more regarding the longstanding maternal and altruistic promotion of Schumann-Heink and other female opera singers, see Hilary Poriss, "Prima Donnas and the Performance of Altruism" in *The Arts of the Prima Donna in the Long Nineteenth Century*, edited by Rachel Cowgill and Hilary Poriss (Oxford: Oxford Univ. Press, 2012), 42–60; and Joy H. Calico, "Staging Scandal with *Salome and Elektra*," in *The Arts of the Prima Donna in the Long Nineteenth Century*, ed. Rachel Cowgill and Hilary Poriss (Oxford: Oxford Univ. Press, 2012), 61–82.

51. In addition to English songs, Schumann-Heink's programs included German-language folksongs, songs by Johannes Brahms, and arias from foreign-language operas. See "Madame Schumann-Heink: World Famous Contralto," program booklet, 1919, Talent Correspondence and Brochures, Redpath Chautauqua Collection.

52. Harrison and Detzer, *Culture under Canvas*, 113–14.

53. "Articles of Agreement" between Ernestine Schumann-Heink and Redpath-Chicago, performance contract, copy, 1914, Talent Correspondence and Brochures, Redpath Chautauqua Collection.

54. For perspective, the entire weekly salary of Ralph Dunbar's 1917 production of *The Mikado* totaled roughly $1,200. See "Dunbar Company Salaries," manuscript, 1917, Harrison to T. F. Graham, Feb. 20, 1919, and Hensel and Jones to Harrison, Dec. 14, 1922, all in Talent Correspondence and Brochures, Redpath Chautauqua Collection.

55. Treasury Department Secretary to Schumann-Heink, Apr. 17, 1919, Redpath Chautauqua Collection.

56. For more on Valentine's Redpath career and the operational details of chautauqua operas, see Cody A. Norling, "Operatic Egalitarianism: English-Language Opera, Redpath Chautauqua, and the May Valentine Opera Company" (MA thesis, Univ. of Iowa, 2018); and C. A. Norling, "Making an American Opera Career: Conductor May Valentine (1890–1974) and a Woman's Role(s) in the Business of Opera," *American Music* 40, no. 1 (2022): 116–25.

57. Valentine to Harry P. Harrison, Feb. 10, 1924, Redpath Chautauqua Collection.

58. Valentine to Harrison, 1925, and Redpath to The Elyea Talking Machine Co., Apr. 1, 1925, both in Talent Correspondence and Brochures, Redpath Chautauqua Collection.

59. "A Woman Director of Light Opera," *Billboard*, Dec. 8, 1928.

60. "May Valentine Asks Young Singers to Perform for Her," *Sunday Oregonian* (Portland), Nov. 7, 1926; and "Opera Conductor Seeks Talent for Robin Hood Tour," *Evening Courier and Reporter* (Waterloo, IA), Nov. 4, 1922.

61. "One of America's Most Popular Operas Coming," *Pensacola (FL) Journal*, Nov. 15, 1925.

62. Harrison to Eleanor Everest Freer, Oct. 7, 1925, Redpath Chautauqua Collection.

63. "Robin Hood," *Evening Courier and Reporter* (Waterloo, IA), Nov. 3, 1922.

64. "That Grand Old Opera Is Coming Back," *Daily Republican* (Belvidere, IL), Oct. 17, 1922.

65. "At the Theaters," *Green Bay Press-Gazette*, Sept. 11, 1926.

66. Canning, *Most American Thing in America*, 219.

67. Harrison and Detzer, *Culture under Canvas*, xvii, 261.

68. Michael Parish writes that the nation's farmers, feeling the effects of the wartime "agricultural boom," borrowed heavily to expand their annual yields but failed to foresee the sudden drop in crop prices that resulted from postwar overproduction. See his volume *The Anxious Decades: America in Prosperity and Depression, 1920–1941* (New York: W. W. Norton, 1994), 81–88.

69. Tapia, *Circuit Chautauqua*, 204.

70. Norling, "Opera in the Second City," 135–64. See also Bruggeman and Rhodes's contribution to this volume for a midcentury example of the Cleveland Orchestra's touring efforts and the implications for legitimizing the city's midwestern cultural identity (224–27).

71. For more on Valentine's career in Chicago, see Norling, "Making an American Opera Career," 126–33.

72. Valentine to Fritz Reiner, Mar. 16, 1948, Fritz Reiner Collection, Archival and Manuscript Collections, Northwestern Univ. Libraries, Evanston, IL.

73. Levine, *Highbrow/Lowbrow*, 234 (emphases added).

Chapter 11

From Crass Materialists to Missionaries of Culture

A Regional History of Cultural Ascendance and Economic Decline through the Cleveland Orchestra

JACOB BRUGGEMAN AND ERIC MICHAEL RHODES

The Midwest rose in economic and cultural stature during the early twentieth century. In this period, the region took pride in its "mature agricultural economy," which also boasted robust "railroads, steel mills, meat packers, and other industries," all of which made the region America's "cultural and economic mainstay." At the same time, "universities, libraries, art museums, and political reforms provided a feeling of intellectual accomplishment."[1] Midwestern replication of eastern symphony orchestras was one manifestation of this accomplishment. When Cleveland welcomed its own orchestra onto the scene in the early 1900s, the city's artists, boosters, and businessmen hoped to prove "to Easterners and Europeans that the heartland hubs were no longer a collection of bumpkins far removed from the cultural currents" of western—or, here, *eastern*—civilization.[2] However, as the twentieth century progressed, the feeling of accomplishment faded in Cleveland and across the Midwest as the industries that fueled their growth fell victim to economic restructuring and government policy.

Industrial decline ensued, but the Cleveland Orchestra remained on top. In the face of postwar economic decline, boosters turned to Cleveland's historic links to the East and to the cultural capital it had accrued during the early twentieth century through institutions such as the orchestra to "manage decline."[3] During the postwar years, Cleveland marked itself as a city of the postindustrial Midwest through its efforts to leverage old-world cultural capital to bolster its economic capital. Indeed, as Andrew Cayton and Peter Onuf observe about early Ohio, "political activity, narrowly understood, was itself the means of legitimating hegemonic values," especially those of bourgeois culture which defined Midwestern identity. Further, "territorial *politics*—even in an oppositionist mode—served to integrate scattered local elites and draw them into national political life."[4] Acknowledging the Western Reserve's historical ties to Connecticut, in this chapter we employ a similar logic: the Cleveland Orchestra's cultural pursuits worked to entrench and strengthen a cultural geography which prioritized old-world elegance as embodied by eastern cities. Its founding further integrated the city, and thus many of its business elites, into that national geography.[5] Later, during the mid-twentieth-century postindustrialization, the orchestra served as a reminder of the city's accomplishments in realms other than manufacturing.

We explain the orchestra's midcentury achievements within the context of the city's "struggle for memory" throughout postindustrialization.[6] Its accomplishments were not merely musical but functioned as a significant part of Cleveland's "constitutive narrative," the central image in the community's understanding of itself.[7] In fact, the orchestra assumed the status of that historically significant institution which simultaneously "express[ed] collective desires" and "impose[d] coherence" upon community experience.[8] As midwestern cities and their industrial strength faded following World War II, Cleveland joined other regional metros in its reclassification as the "geography of nowhere."[9] Yet, the city retained memories of economic and cultural glory, as symbolized by the Cleveland Orchestra.[10]

Missionaries of Culture (1796-1920)

Settled in 1796 by Moses Cleaveland, Cleveland quickly became the crown jewel of the Connecticut Western Reserve. The Reserve itself comprised 3 million acres Congress had set aside in the 1780s to fulfill Connecticut's claim to western lands.[11] When throngs of westbound travelers arrived at the close of the eighteenth century, surveyors took to shaping the settlement into a typical New England town, complete with a central commons today known as Public Square. Immigrants of "Yankee stock," as Frederick Jackson Turner described them, soon flocked to the Reserve in droves.[12] These immigrants embodied the region's earliest links to the East Coast.

Dreams of abundance, independence, and new beginnings flourished there and inspired Cleveland's settlers. Many New Englanders wagered that a chance out west was worth more than a lifetime of factory or wage work in the East. Writing on this dilemma, one contemporary commentator captured the appeal of the West's open horizons: "Ohio—with its rich soil, its mild climate, and its inviting prairies—was opened fully upon the alarmed and anxious vision. As was natural under the circumstances, a sort of stampede took place from the cold, desolate, worn-out New England, to this land of promise."[13] Such was the ballad to which New Englanders "carried their ideals and traditions into the wilderness."[14]

Once they arrived, Yankees took to the decades-long task of transforming the landscape from its natural, unfamiliar state into settlements that imitated the terra firma of their former homes in the East. Their communities, staked and cultivated in the newfound soil of the Ohio country, echoed those homes in name: the settlements of Norwich, Saybrook, New London, and Plymouth were centered around clusters of white clapboard houses, libraries, Congregationalist churches, and village greens, thus duplicating the designs and social functions New England's towns.[15] Equally telling, while many of the farmers in Ohio's middling and southern reaches raised pigs or grew corn, farmers in the Western Reserve focused on the traditional New England practice of dairying.[16]

By the mid-nineteenth century, more than three quarters of the Western Reserve's immigrants had come from New England or upstate and western New York, creating in Cleveland an "overwhelmingly Yankee" atmosphere.[17] Evidence from eastern outmigration appeared to some contemporary observers as a defining characteristic of the Western Reserve, and one scholar argued that the Reserve "became an extension of New England into the West."[18] Chief among those traditions was a "high estimation of the importance of literacy."[19]

Harlan Hatcher echoes this, describing how settlers established communities exhibiting "a most extraordinary amount of reading and thinking." "Outside of Massachusetts," he observed, "I do not believe that an equal average of intelligence could have been found among all sorts and conditions of men, who were there of an almost perfect social equality."[20] As Kenneth Lottich observed, soon "the Western Reserve was so impregnated with the Connecticut stock and the Connecticut spirit that it... furnished a good answer to that old conundrum, 'Connecticut, the nutmeg state! Where shall we find a greater?'"[21] In this fashion, as historian Burke Aaron Hinsdale argued about the significance of the Reserve, "no other five thousand square miles of territory in the United States lying in a body outside of New England ever had, to begin with, so pure a New England population."[22] As President James Garfield insisted, the Western Reserve's settlers "planted the institutions and opinions of Old Connecticut in their new wilderness homes."[23] The Western Reserve was, then, culturally eastern.

It was along these lines that the Western Reserve was transformed from a novel territory into a land whose mises-en-scène were constructed and maintained by eastern transplants. This change corresponded with the more extensive migratory process by which Yankee immigrants transported "Old World values" into "New World settings."[24] Meanwhile, a class of old-money Yankee elites emerged in the Reserve and exerted their influence on its economy and politics. They educated their children at both Oberlin and Western Reserve colleges, the latter established in 1826 and known as the "the Yale of the West."[25] The Yankee elite became so powerful that they "dominated social and political leadership" in the Reserve until the late nineteenth century, when European immigrants and the industrial nouveau riche came to rival them in power.[26]

Eventually, regional economic growth gave rise to an industrial class that contested the Yankee elite's hegemony by funding arts institutions modeled after those of the East. The nouveau riche thus launched new efforts to integrate their city into the nation's nascent cultural geography. Cleveland's up-and-coming status as a hub of commercial activity grounded the industrial elite's claim to power. Beginning in 1825, with the Erie Canal's opening, Cleveland became a center of manufacturing and metalworking on the Great Lakes. Connected by rail to booming capital markets in Chicago and along the East Coast, Cleveland accessed eastern capital and provisioned settlements along the Mississippi River. Since Cleveland was situated as such in a growing national economy, its commodities trades in grain, lumber, and coal grew further following the Civil War. Coupled with frequent cargoes of iron ore arriving from

Michigan's Upper Peninsula, Cleveland's proximity to the coal pits in Appalachia made it known as the "great Iron Mart of the West." Iron and steel production would produce even more wealth in the city after the advent of the automobile.[27] Yet, throughout its rapid industrialization, Cleveland maintained "a somewhat eastern persona."[28]

By the conclusion of World War I, Cleveland had joined other midwestern metros as a populous, multiethnic manufacturing hub with a wealthy elite.[29] By 1920, its population of nearly 800,000 made Cleveland the fifth-largest US city. Industrial magnates like John D. Rockefeller, empowered by the city's Chamber of Commerce—as was common throughout the Midwest—supplanted the Yankee elite as Cleveland's most powerful political entity.[30] Euclid Avenue, where Rockefeller and other industrial titans built their mansions, came to epitomize that industrial business elite's enormous wealth and power. Observers compared the street with Paris's Champs Elysees and Berlin's Unter den Linden. In 1860, writer John Fiske described it to a gathering of the Royal Society of Great Britain as reminiscent of "the nave and aisles of a huge cathedral."[31] Flush with liquid capital, Cleveland's nouveau riche began considering how their city compared with others. In fact, its boosters struggled with the perception that their city suffered from a lack of culture. Like other midwestern urban elites, they worried that their overgrown factory town was characterized by "crass materialism" and lacked the distinguished standing of the mature metropolises of the East Coast.[32]

Even if the heartland's industrial cities rivaled older eastern hubs in material wealth by 1900, popular perception held that the former lagged far behind the latter as cultural centers. Critic Robert Marsh admits as much in his 1967 history of the Cleveland Orchestra, writing, "Cleveland in 1901 was a dynamic city rather than a beautiful [city]."[33] Thus its industrial elite sought to replicate the arts institutions of the east and thereby "uplift the Midwest by making it more like Europe and the eastern seaboard."[34] Industrial elites "had seen what money and taste could do in Europe, and they had the means to endow their own city with culture and beauty." Crucially, "these refinements [were] not just for the elite but also for the masses."[35] Cleveland's cultural transformation along these lines was not that dissimilar from Cincinnati's. Indeed, as historian Karen Ahlquist has argued about the contemporary music scene in Cincinnati, as was the case in Cleveland, "urban civic elites drew on leadership skills, family and social connections, and financial resources to make music that could not only be heard, but heard *about* well beyond the city limits." Elites in both cities undertook cultural "reputation-building" so their cities would be seen as locales within the country's larger cultural geography.[36] If *both* local and national critics took note of their cities' musical accomplishments, elites would have succeeded in transforming their cities into countrywide bastions of high—read *European* or *East Coast*—culture.

To take a separate example, wealthy residents from the real estate, railroad, and manufacturing industries bequeathed millions for the construction of the Cleveland Museum of Art in 1913.[37] The museum's mission was to "import art rather than to nurture" a midwestern style, to "teach the styles of Europe and the East so that Midwesterners could keep up with artistic fashion."[38] Here again, the city's affiliation with high culture signified more than mere public access to cultural goods: nineteenth-century critics and elites alike believed that "a population willing to support high-cultural performances signaled a city with musical taste."[39] The operative word, *taste,* is telling. That midwestern urban elites in cities like Cleveland and Cincinnati consistently attempted to demonstrate their cultural merit is thus unsurprising. Cultural programming alone would not suffice: these cities had to prove their worth.

At this time, Adella Prentiss Hughes, whose family had moved from New England to Cleveland in the early 1800s, was the prime mover in Cleveland's music scene and the major force in founding the city's orchestra. In 1918, with Russian émigré and conductor Nikolai Sokoloff, Hughes inaugurated the first season of what was then called the Cleveland Symphony Orchestra.[40] The industrial elites, supplanting the Yankee elites as the newest self-appointed "missionaries of culture," thus set about transforming an economic boom town into a bastion of high culture.[41]

The Cleveland Orchestra and Cultural Ascendance

There is perhaps no better person to bridge the Cleveland Orchestra's deep-seated Western Reserve sensibilities and its connection to the country's geography of cultural capital than founder Adella Prentiss Hughes. After graduating from Vassar College, Hughes departed for a year of musical education in Europe. She studied piano in Berlin and accompanied

Austrian contralto Ernestine Schumann-Heink and violinist Fritz Kreisler, frequently regarded as one of history's greatest violinists.[42] When Hughes returned to Cleveland, her goal in founding the orchestra was to "bring good music within reach of every man, woman and child in Cleveland." Indeed, she returned from Europe "convinced she was one of the enlightened with a mandate to lift culture to a higher plane in her hometown."[43]

Whereas in 1915, Hughes was described simply as her husband Rubert's "charming" and "talented wife" who would "accompany him" in song, by 1920, she represented Cleveland among other "prominent musicians" in Ohio at an important conference at the Western College for Women, in Oxford.[44] There, Hughes rubbed shoulders with "prominent New York musicians" like Welsh tenor Dan Beddoe, an oratorio singer for more than five decades; composer Clarence Dickinson; and one of classical music's literary luminaries, John Christian Freund, the English cofounder and publisher of the *Music Trades*.[45] Hughes's success is also apparent in critics' initial impressions of her city's orchestra.

Indeed, following the Cleveland Orchestra's first performance, in Washington, DC, in February 1921, a critic in the *Evening Star* applauded its program as "brilliant and interesting" and praised Sokoloff as "a conductor of magnetism and force." However, the same critic candidly commented that the orchestra, "vigorous in tone," lacked "the mellowness that comes with maturity." Nevertheless, the audience thoroughly enjoyed the performance and made "up in enthusiasm what it lacked in numbers"—after all, the critic continued, "Washington is slow to patronize organizations or soloists who have not gained an unquestioned reputation."[46] Hughes's reputation-building would soon pay off. Within a year, when tickets for Cleveland's second DC concert were advertised in the *Star*, it was commended for its "richness of tone" *despite* its status as one of the country's youngest orchestras.[47] Soon thereafter, news of the Cleveland Orchestra started appearing more frequently in the *Star*.[48] A year later, in 1924, the *Star* celebrated one of its radio concerts as "a success almost unparalleled in the history of symphonic organizations."[49]

Hughes was central to this success. In 1922, New York's *Evening World Daily Magazine* praised her as the "Only Woman Manager of a Symphony Orchestra." Situated next to a piece on Mark Twain, the *World's* profile wrapped around a *Mona Lisa*–esque portrait of Hughes and a caption informing readers that she built the orchestra with "twenty-five years of hard work." Indeed, it already "rank[ed] in musical circles among the four best orchestras of the country" and thereby brought its superb renditions of the classics to "music lovers"—the "elite," *and* the "rank and file."[50] Further, Hughes had hosted numerous other notable artistic organizations, including Serge Diaghilev's Paris-based Ballets Russes, which collaborated with celebrated composers like Claude Debussy and Igor Stravinsky; commissioned costume designs from Coco Chanel, Pablo Picasso, and Henri Matisse; and is today regarded as one of the most influential troupes of the twentieth century.[51]

Hughes thus connected celebrated classical maestros, creators, and connoisseurs of high culture, all well-known among eastern and European elites, with the embryonic and malleable culture of the Midwest. In doing so, she connected the cultural geography of the East and the Old World to the country's interior. The Cleveland Orchestra was to be an outpost and outlet of high culture, introducing a new audience to its prized cultural goods—here, classical music—and incorporating the region as a new territory within the East's geography of cultural capital.

If the orchestra was to make world-class music, it needed a world-class home. To establish one, Hughes turned to John Severance, a member of an influential Yankee family whose ancestors included the Western Reserve's first physician and was a member of the industrial elite, having made his millions as the first treasurer of Standard Oil.[52] A missionary of culture, Severance had served as the president of the Cleveland Museum of Art and had donated generously to the Cleveland Musical Arts Association (CMAA, the city orchestra's forerunner).[53] In 1931, Hughes convinced Severance to donate some of his millions for the construction of the opulent Severance Hall on the north end of Wade Pond, across from the museum—in a neighborhood that would come to be known as University Circle. The hall's Georgian exterior sat princelike on Euclid Avenue, with a separate entrance for limousines. Its interior featured pink marble staircases and columns, Egyptian friezes, and terrazzo floors, while the auditorium's traditional red drapery replicated the finery of European concert halls.[54]

To inhabit its new home, the Cleveland Orchestra needed a new conductor. It found him in George Szell, appointed in 1946 after previously guest-conducting. Szell's reign marked the ascendancy of Cleveland's cultural capital. Previously, he had earned his reputation at New York's Metropolitan Opera, thus epitomizing the cultural connection to the

East.[55] What was once a province in the Old World's cultural geography had become one of its capitals. Unsurprisingly, then, the Cleveland Orchestra is the first thing cartoonist Harvey Pekar pointed to when recalling the "pro-Cleveland propaganda" of his childhood.[56] The exact contours of that propaganda and the orchestra's place within it reveals how deeply embedded the struggle for cultural capital was in Cleveland's history—and explains why members of the public continually associated the city's cultural standing with the orchestra's achievements.

Szell's Reign, Cleveland's Decline (1947-1970)

George Szell chose Cleveland because of the city's patrons, "whose great wealth enabled them to underwrite a costly cultural jewel."[57] Everyday Clevelanders, however, first felt the effects of economic decline in 1929.[58] Cleveland never recovered from the Great Depression's shock to its manufacturing capacity and national reputation. Population decline began in 1940. Midcentury business elites sought a solution to this by touting Cleveland, geographically proximate to most US industrial production, as the "best location in the nation." Part and parcel of the campaign to "manage decline" was its focus on high cultural achievement, beginning with Szell's 1947 arrival.[59]

During Szell's tenure, the Cleveland Orchestra accrued significant cultural capital.[60] Having promised the CMAA—an organization of wealthy donors drawn from Cleveland's booster class—to make the orchestra "second to none" in 1946, Szell had done so by 1966 and remained committed, telling the *New York Times* that he wanted to "keep on making progress in every possible direction."[61] Increasingly, that direction was east. Indeed, through its association with eastern and European symphonies, the orchestra joined the ranks of the world's best and transformed Cleveland's former economic base into cultural superstructure.

Under Szell, the Cleveland Orchestra solidified its reputation among eastern critics and entered the nation's most prestigious orchestral grouping: the "Big Five," measured by their achievement of "musical excellence, caliber of musicianship, total contract weeks, weekly basic wages, recording guarantees, and paid vacations."[62] It rose to meet each of those criteria from 1947 to 1970.

By Szell's arrival, America's orchestras were dominated by the country's oldest symphonies, "The Big Three": New York (1842), Boston (1881), and Philadelphia (1900), all cultural hubs.[63] Yet the Boston Symphony Orchestra and Philadelphia Orchestra played second and third chairs to the New York Philharmonic; their conductors accrued acclaim with annual performances at Carnegie Hall. In 1920, the Philharmonic became the first US orchestra to tour Europe, and by midcentury, Arturo Toscanini's thoroughly European repertoire led critics to conclude that it was "the principal centre of musical life in America."[64] Equally essential to elite musical status was the circulation of an orchestra's recordings; at a time when radio broadcasts emanated from East Coast cities, the Big Three held a monopoly. Before Szell's arrival, Cleveland paled in comparison, but by the 1960s, it had joined their ranks.

Perceptions of excellence were based on the extent of an orchestra's tours in New York and Europe. In Szell, Cleveland acquired a director with deep ties to both. Szell was born into Vienna's famed musical milieu and had conducted at Amsterdam's Concertgebouw Orchestra—one of Europe's own "Big Three."[65] In 1939, however, George and his wife, Helene, fled to New York City from Europe after the Nazis' rise to power (though raised Catholic, Szell was of Jewish heritage). Szell found success in New York and was appointed conductor of the New York Metropolitan Opera in 1942. The Szells retained a New York residence, allowing George to leverage conducting at Carnegie Hall throughout the 1950s.[66] In 1958, the Cleveland Orchestra secured what would become a longstanding series of subscription concerts at Carnegie. Journalists initially questioned the orchestra's reputation, but Szell retorted that he was bringing New York "what it doesn't get anymore, a high-level classical program such as it used to be able to count on . . . from the conducting of Toscanini."[67]

Indeed, Szell's repertoire was more consistently "standard" than that of the American Big Three's conductors, and Cleveland's players knew the "standard repertoire" (or the "teaching repertoire" consisting of composers of the Baroque, Classical, and Romantic movements) by heart.[68] Szell rarely ventured into American or twentieth-century composition and still less often into contemporary music—which he derided as "temporary music."[69] By focusing on the European and classical repertoire, Szell aimed to accrue cultural capital. He insisted that Carnegie audiences "should stop considering everything outside of New York as outlying," continuing,

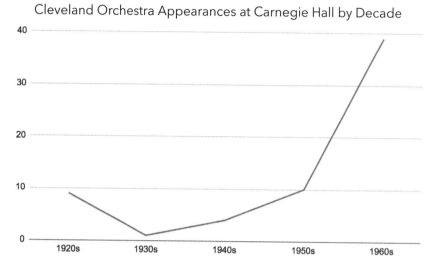

Cleveland Orchestra appearances at Carnegie Hall by decade. (Carnegie Hall, "Performance History Search," https://www.carnegiehall.org/About/History/Performance-History-Search?q=&dex=prod_PHS.)

"We are not provincial. . . . Cleveland has a very refined musical atmosphere."[70] In due course, the Carnegie performances led New York critics to contend that the Cleveland Orchestra was "one of the country's major concentrations of musical skill."[71]

Clevelanders admired Szell's European manners. He kissed audience members' hands. "I think she bought her clothes in Paris," one Clevelander remarked of Helene Szell.[72] All of this spoke to midwestern audiences' regard for bourgeois temperaments and tastes vis-à-vis audiences of eastern orchestras.[73] Yet attitudes alone would not suffice: neither Cleveland's boosters nor its public audiences could fully emulate New York's sophistication. One Cleveland player noted that Carnegie concerts ended with standing ovations, whereas "in Cleveland . . . the audiences take us for granted and applaud minimally." More experimental compositions such as Claude Debussy's *La Mer* "left Cleveland audiences confused," while New York roared.[74]

By the mid-1950s, the New York culturati had acknowledged Cleveland's excellence, but European audiences remained ignorant. However, Szell earned individual praise from the European press when he guest-conducted there in 1955. And Cleveland newspapers announced that summer that the Cleveland Orchestra would make its first European tour in 1957. It displayed its mastery of Mozart, Brahms, and Schumann even as European audiences expected a run of Gershwin. Szell explained that the tour must feature "the standard works ... to show the Europeans that their facile prejudice about Americans being able to play only loud and fast but not having any feeling, inwardness, or 'real musical culture,' is completely unjustified." Szell was right: European audiences applauded for "record lengths, even after several encores." Critics praised Cleveland in Madrid, Paris, Geneva, West Berlin, London, Brussels, Moscow, and Vienna. "No finer orchestral playing has yet been heard in the Festival Hall," wrote one London critic.[75] *Der Taggesspiegel* remarked, "The orchestra of the big American city on Lake Erie that was unknown in this country proved to be the equal of the star orchestras of New York, Boston and Philadelphia."[76]

This tour bolstered the Cleveland Orchestra's reputation abroad and at home, within the city and, crucially, along the East Coast. Szell was intent on capitalizing on the tour's success, writing that the CMAA should publish a brochure of foreign reviews to "impress upon the AMERICAN— not only the Cleveland—public ... that the C. O. has definitely been recognized internationally as one of the very very top ranking Orchestras of the world."[77] Clevelanders began to see their orchestra through the eyes of the world, as did New York's keepers of culture. The national press first referred to it as "second to none" in 1954, but it was not until 1958 that the *Times* mentioned it alongside the American Big Three: "Mr. Szell's tenure reached a climax last year with a European tour that drew overseas notices putting the Cleveland Orchestra at least on par with the American big three."[78] The *Nation* followed suit: "For decades we have all firmly believed that the principal American orchestras could be classified in a fixed order of merit ... it is time we revised our ideas ... [the Cleveland Orchestra plays] with the loving spontaneity of a fine European orchestra, as well as with the discipline, blend and unanimity characteristic of America."[79] Committed to the project of "reputation-building," Cleveland's boosters did their best to capitalize on its orchestra's renown.[80] University Circle— home to Severance Hall, Western Reserve University, the Museum of Art, and University Hospitals—should be transformed into a cultural hub to "stave off deindustrialization, rebrand Cleveland, and reverse or at least arrest the spread of urban decay." The Circle, a "brain worker's city within a city," would allow Cleveland to retain its numerous corporate headquarters and white-collar workers amid decline, in an early manifestation of what Patrick Leary has called "solutionism," or "the technocratic fantasy that systemic problems can be managed away" by a "creative class." Here, Cleveland's business elites pivoted toward the cultural industry as the traditional drivers of its economic prowess collapsed.[81]

To consolidate civic pride in the Cleveland Orchestra, the CMAA, Advertising Club, and Chamber of Commerce sponsored a luncheon honoring the 1957 European tour. Representatives of Columbia Broadcasting Service (CBS) attended.[82] Szell was now a "household word in all the musical circles of the United States." Cleveland's boosters mobilized the city's "growth coalition" to finance Szell's achievements through public funds and private philanthropy—for an important measurement of musical excellence was the size of an orchestra's endowment.[83] Cleveland's elites ensured that during the 1950s the city's orchestra had an annual operating budget of more than $100,000, matched in size by only the Big Three and the Chicago Symphony Orchestra.[84] By 1958, the Cleveland had "perhaps the largest endowment of any orchestra in the country," wrote the *Times*.[85] Thus endowed, it could compete with the Big Three to keep the nation's best players in pocket.[86]

In 1947, as the postwar mass culture industry rebounded after a slump during World War II, Szell signed his first recording contract with Columbia Records in. Despite his connections, Szell was unable to convince CBS to broadcast Cleveland Orchestra concerts by 1949. Columbia was pleased with the success of their first contract, though, and signed the orchestra again in 1952.[87] Consistent improvement in Cleveland's recordings was enough to convince CBS to syndicate and broadcast the orchestra's 1957 season to seventy-nine stations across the country. By 1965, it had recorded more than fifty albums.[88] In the same year, eighty American radio stations broadcast WCLV's Cleveland Orchestra program, and in 1966, NBC's *Bell Telephone Television Hour* featured the orchestra in a documentary.[89]

The syndication of Cleveland Orchestra recordings reinforced the city's international musical renown. In 1963, Szell graced the cover of *Time* in an issue on the new "Big Five": the Big Three plus Cleveland and Chicago.[90] The feature recounted that the orchestra's 1962 debut at the Lincoln Center, a new venue for the Philharmonic, garnered "astonishing international applause." Among the Big Five, it "fared the best ... because of the superb music-making under George Szell's direction."[91] Whereas the *Times* had

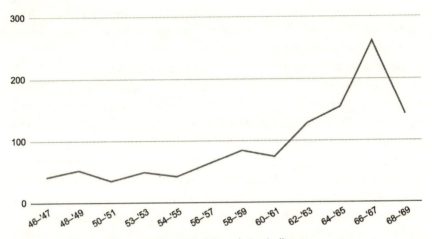

Mentions of Cleveland Orchestra in the *New York Times* during Szell's tenure.

mentioned the orchestra only around eighty times in 1960, a Proquest archive search of the middle of the decade saw it appear an average of more than 250 times annually. In a 1965 *New Yorker* feature on Szell, the Cleveland Orchestra was described as "the *Wunderkind* among American orchestras." By the mid-1960s, Szell had become guest conductor of the Philharmonic (which eventually courted him to replace Leonard Bernstein) and of two of Europe's Big Three (Amsterdam's Royal Concertgebouw Orchestra, and the Vienna Philharmonic).[92] In 1965, the Department of State selected the Cleveland Orchestra to serve as the nation's ambassador to the USSR, sponsoring the Soviet leg of its second European tour.[93] Russian and European presses hailed Szell's players.[94]

As the Steel Belt began to rust in the 1960s, Cleveland's reactions to its orchestra's second European tour, in 1965, exhibited how boosters and even everyday residents equated the fate of their orchestra with the fate of their city. As early as the 1940s, the *Times* reported, "Clevelanders display an exuberant enthusiasm for their town and their way of life . . . it really is remarkable, their town-boosting, their local pride."[95] The Chamber of Commerce and the Greater Cleveland Growth Corporation led the effort to roll out the red carpet for their returning heroes.[96] An "exultant crowd" of 5,500 Clevelanders gathered at Hopkins Airport with "banners welcoming the orchestra."[97] Mayor Ralph Locher lauded the orchestra in a speech over the loudspeakers. Competing with shouts from the crowd of "what music!" Locher presented it with notes from Cleveland politicians, Ohio congressmen, Governor James Rhodes, and Vice President Hubert Humphrey.[98] The next day, the *Plain Dealer* dedicated an editorial to Szell's players, thanking them for their service to a city "not known for its sophistication." The editorial reveled in the praise the orchestra had garnered: it "returned to the city with the enthusiastic, sometimes even frenzied, applause of sophisticated European audiences . . . ringing in their ears."[99] "Welcome home," the editorial concluded, "You're an unexcelled Cleveland institution . . . the city is grateful and proud."[100] As Robert Marsh wrote, "thousands . . . became aware of Cleveland as a metropolitan area with an audience and resources needed to sustain the highest type of musical culture."[101] Cleveland's civic pride was a welcome bit of optimism in the face of the decade's racial unrest, capital flight, and population decline.

Despite the Cleveland Orchestra's reputation, it remained a thoroughly midwestern institution compared to the rest of the Big Five. The self-conscious boosterism of the city's business elite marked Cleveland as a midwestern city.[102] Midwesterners' long-standing "heartland consciousness" and their attendant cultural (and economic) inferiority complex were evident in both Szell's and the CMAA's attitudes toward their orchestra.[103] Often, eastern music critics accused Szell's "characteristic precision" of what Pierre Bourdieu has called "hypercorrection," in this context playing *too perfectly* and marking the orchestra as a midwestern poseur.[104] "The tremendous control George Szell had over the Cleveland . . . tended to create a cold, clinical atmosphere," declared the *Musical Times* in 1965. In an echo of the 1920s *Evening Star* review, the *Times* continued, "The sound was very loud, but not free and full enough to make it as exciting" as its more established, eastern counterparts.[105]

The Cleveland Orchestra lagged behind in the wages it paid its players, too: salaries "never kept pace" with the other Big Five.[106] While the original Big Three boasted annual budgets in the millions during the 1960s, Cleveland's was around $500,000.[107] Further, it differed compared to the Big Five in that it did not offer year-round employment.[108] When orchestra players threatened to strike in 1967, failing a wage increase and year-round employment, the "wealthy businessmen and lawyers" comprising the CMAA balked.[109] The trustees kept their eyes on the bottom line, revealing their midwestern values of petit-bourgeois pragmatic thrift. Art was an investment for them, and it had a material benefit in the deindustrializing Midwest in contrast to the l'art pour l'art attitude of economically secure eastern elites. Trustees acceded to increasing wages and to building a summer venue only after reasoning that a larger budget was a sound investment in reputation-building and prestige. The orchestra's 1968 contract included raises and employment at both Severance Hall and the orchestra's new summer retreat, Blossom Music Center. Blossom was endowed by the business elites' in a bid to compete with Tanglewood and Ravinia and to showcase Greater Cleveland's historical ties to the East (as they had with the development of University Circle). The CMAA hired MIT-trained architect and Louis Kahn protégé Peter van Dijk to design the ultramodern summer venue.[110] The contract was the Cleveland growth coalition's final gambit to transform its economic capital into cultural capital, as it had been attempting since 1918. Converting "crass materialism" into higher pursuits in an effort to conquer their inferiority complex, while simultaneously forging postindustrial growth strategies based on the new arts economy, marked the Cleveland business elites as thoroughly midwestern.[111]

Both Chicago and Cleveland were industrial rather than cultural centers during the early twentieth century—"naturally less cosmopolitan . . . than the big eastern cities"—but Chicago elites were better established and less insecure than Clevelanders.[112] The Second City's booster elites were less stricken with the characteristically midwestern "interior mentality," or inferiority complex, than their Cleveland counterparts. While the Cleveland Orchestra and the Cleveland Museum of Art mimicked the Philharmonic and the Met, respectively, Chicago developed distinctive, self-consciously midwestern intellectual, artistic, and architectural styles that "momentarily at least made New York seem dull by comparison" during the "midwestern moment" of the late nineteenth and early twentieth centuries.[113] Indeed, in the early 1900s, under America's first great maestro, Theodore Thomas, the Chicago Symphony Orchestra earned a reputation for playing locally composed, homegrown works.[114] Cleveland, however, had always been an imitator of the East, a testament to the city's enduring "sense of cultural inferiority."[115] Before its efforts at reputation-building, the city "enjoyed the products of high culture primarily through visiting performers and touring organizations such as the Thomas orchestra" and Ballets Russes.[116]

Szell winced when eastern critics called the Cleveland Orchestra an upstart.[117] His rigid refusal to include American compositions in his heavily Austro-German repertoire contrasted with Chicago's embrace of local composers. Cleveland's laser focus on garnering good reviews in the eastern press was a manifestation of its business elites' aspirations and pride. Cleveland "remained focused on the world beyond the heartland and could see little merit in the works created ... within the shadow of their institutions," evidence of Cleveland's long-standing midwestern character as a "consumer of culture rather than a creator." More than Chicago, then, Cleveland exhibited an interior mentality, seen by locals as a "cultural port where cargoes of those valued commodities known as civilization and refinement regularly disembarked ... offering hope that the heartland might some day become as truly civilized as New York or Philadelphia."[118]

The Cleveland Orchestra's climb into the Big Five "wasn't an easy task—not for Szell, not for the Orchestra, and not for the community that had to pay the bill."[119] Toward the end of the 1960s, reports surfaced that increased touring, expanded seasons, full-time employment, inflation, and dwindling broadcasting revenue meant that one-third of the nation's major orchestras would be defunct by 1975.[120] The Big Five shared in "excellence, prestige and money troubles," wrote one critic, continuing: "Each loses money every season."[121] Tellingly, the two deindustrializing midwestern outposts of the Big Five were hardest hit: Chicago was at greatest risk of default, followed by Cleveland.[122] By 1969, the Cleveland Orchestra had to draw on its endowment to keep the lights on.[123] Suffering from an asymmetrical loss of metropolitan capital in the face of deindustrialization, the faltering economies in Chicago and Cleveland mirrored—or caused—their precipitous declines in orchestral revenues. Greater Cleveland's economy had gone into a tailspin, losing fifty thousand manufacturing jobs during the 1960s.[124]

After Szell died of a heart attack and bone cancer in 1970, Cleveland's business elite modified their reputation-building strategy. Having successfully converted Cleveland's economic capital into cultural capital through the orchestra's rise, the CMAA—buffeted by metropolitan economic decline and the economic rise of the Sunbelt—came to view the Cleveland Orchestra as "a high-status cultural amenity that enhanced Cleveland's reputation and attracted business."[125] Thus, during the 1970s, Cleveland's growth coalition again set about "orchestrating decline," now by mobilizing the orchestra's cultural capital to retain white collar workers and executives, reverse the flight of economic capital from the city, counter the decline in its national reputation, and combat the social decline it engendered.[126] Since the 1930s, when economic decline first set in, Cleveland's business elite had been engaging in a form of solutionism, hoping to cash in economic capital for cultural capital. In 1970, Cleveland was no longer "the best location in the nation"; rather the elite proclaimed that the "best things in life are here," including a world-renowned orchestra.

Notes

1. James Shortridge, *The Middle West: Its Meaning in American Culture* (Lawrence: Univ. Press of Kansas, 1989), 27.

2. Jon Teaford, *Cities of the Heartland: The Rise and Fall of the Industrial Midwest* (Bloomington: Indiana Univ. Press, 1994), 85.

3. J. Mark Souther, *Believing in Cleveland: Managing Decline in "The Best Location in the Nation"* (Philadelphia: Temple Univ. Press, 2017).

4. Andrew R. L. Cayton and Peter S. Onuf, *The Midwest and the Nation: Rethinking the History of an American Region* (Bloomington: Indiana Univ. Press, 1980), xvii, 20.

5. A note on terminology: throughout this chapter, we refer variously to *elites*, *boosters*, and *business elites*. We use them interchangeably to refer to what Brent Cebul has called "white business elites." Business elites were a powerful class of progressive, largely White Clevelanders, many of whom could trace their fortunes to the original white settlement of the Western Reserve but also to Cleveland's industrialization following the Civil War. These business elites and their families are the main actors in our story. For more on the class solidarity amongst these white business elites and their effect on Cleveland institutions and urban planning, see Brent Cebul, *Illusions of Progress: Business, Poverty, and Liberalism in the American Century* (Philadelphia: Univ. of Pennsylvania Press, 2023); Brent Cebul, Lily Geismer, and Mason B. Williams, *Shaped by the State: Toward a New Political History of the Twentieth Century* (Chicago: Univ. of Chicago Press, 2019).

6. Andreas Huyssen, *Twilight Memories: Marking Time in a Culture of Amnesia* (New York: Routledge, 1995), 5–7.

7. Robert Bellah et al., *Habits of the Heart: Individualism and Commitment in American Life* (Berkeley: Univ. of California Press, 1985), 153.

8. Henry Nash Smith, *Virgin Land: The American West as Symbol and Myth* (Cambridge, MA: Harvard Univ. Press, 1950), xi.

9. James Kunstler, *The Geography of Nowhere: The Rise and Decline of America's Man-Made Landscape* (New York: Touchstone, 1993), 180.

10. For other recent work on the history of high cultural institutions in the Midwest, see Michael Pfeifer, "A Symphonic Midwest: The Minneapolis Symphony Orchestra and Regionalist Identity, 1903–1922," in *The Midwestern Moment: The Forgotten World of Twentieth-Century Midwestern Regionalism, 1880–1940*, ed. Jon K. Lauck (Hastings, NE: Hastings College Press, 2017), 101–12; Christina Adams, "'Splendid and Remarkable Progress' in the Midwest: Assessing the Emergence and Social Impact of Regional Art Museums, 1875–1925," *Middle West Review* 7 (Fall 2020): 85–92.

11. Andrew Cayton, *Ohio: The History of a People* (Columbus: Ohio State Univ. Press, 2002), 29–30.

12. Frederick Jackson Turner, *The Frontier in American History* (New York: Henry Holt, 1920), 72.

13. Samuel Goodrich, *Recollections of a Lifetime*, 2 vols. (New York: Miller, Orton, & Mulligan, 1856), 1:79. Goodrich was known pseudonymously as Peter Parley.

14. Lois Kimball Matthews, *The Expansion of New England* (Boston: Houghton-Mifflin, 1909), 174–75.

15. "When Cleveland Belonged to Connecticut," last updated in 2023, New England Historical Society website, https://newenglandhistoricalsociety.com/when-cleveland-belonged-connecticut/

16. Gregory Rose, "The Western Reserve," in *The American Midwest: An Interpretive Encyclopedia*, ed. Andrew Cayton, Richard Sisson, and Chris Zacher (Bloomington: Indiana Univ. Press, 2007), 176–77.

17. Andrew Cayton, "On the Importance of Place, or, a Plea for Idiosyncrasy," *Journal of Urban History* 24 (Nov. 1997): 86.

18. Kenneth Lottich, *New England Transplanted* (Dallas: Royal, 1964), 38.

19. D. W. Brogan, *U.S.A.* (New York: Oxford Univ. Press, 1947), 83–84.

20. Harlan Hatcher, *The Western Reserve: The Story of New Connecticut in Ohio* (Kent: Kent State Univ. Press, 1991), 167.

21. Lottich, *New England Transplanted*, 48.

22. Burke Aaron Hinsdale, *The Old Northwest: With a View of the Thirteen Colonies as Constituted by the Royal Charters* (New York: MacCoun, 1888), 338.

23. James Garfield, "The Northwest Territory and the Western Reserve," in *Old South Leaflets* 2, no. 42 (1893): 20.

24. Garfield, "Northwest Territory and the Western Reserve," 26.

25. Rose, "Western Reserve"; "Marker #21–77 Western Reserve College and Academy," *Remarkable Ohio*, Ohio Historical Society, Columbus, https://remarkableohio.org/marker/21-77-western-reserve-college-and-academy/.

26. Rose, "Western Reserve," 175.

27. See Teaford, *Cities of the Heartland*.

28. John Grabowski, "Cleveland," in Cayton, Sisson, and Zacher, *American Midwest*, 1155.

29. Teaford, *Cities of the Heartland*, 52.

30. Grabowski, "Cleveland"; Teaford, *Cities of the Heartland*, 52.

31. Peter Jedick, *Cleveland: Where the East Coast Meets the Midwest* (Cleveland: Fine Line Litho, 1980), 19.

32. Teaford, *Cities of the Heartland*, 93.

33. Robert Marsh, *The Cleveland Orchestra* (Cleveland: World, 1967), 4.

34. Teaford, *Cities of the Heartland*, 249.

35. Marcia Kraus, *George Szell's Reign: Behind the Scenes with the Cleveland Orchestra* (Champaign: Univ. of Illinois Press, 2017), 10.

36. Karen Ahlquist, "Playing for the Big Time: Musicians, Concerts, and Reputation-Building in Cincinnati, 1872–82," *Journal of the Gilded Age and Progressive Era* 9 (Apr. 2010): 148.

37. "Cleveland Orchestra," in *Encyclopedia of Cleveland History* (Cleveland: Case Western Reserve Univ. Press, 2019).

38. Teaford, *Cities of the Heartland*, 249.

39. Ahlquist, "Playing for the Big Time," 150.

40. Kraus, *George Szell's Reign*, 10

41. Teaford, *Cities of the Heartland*, 249.

42. "A Woman Heads One of Nation's Famous Symphony Orchestras," *New Britain (CT) Herald*, June 20, 1930. For the significance of both artists mentioned, note the prominence of their obituaries in the *New York Times:* "Schumann-Heink, Great Singer, Dead," Nov. 18, 1936, and "Fritz Kreisler Dies Here at 86," Jan. 30, 1962.

43. Kraus, *George Szell's Reign*, 10.

44. "Recital Thursday Evening," *Daily Gate City* (Keokuk, IA), Feb. 22, 1915; "Dufau-Hughes Recital" in "Amusements," *Daily Gate City* (Keokuk, IA), Feb. 14, 1915; "Music Teachers Begin Thirty-Eighth Conclave; Artists of Note Attend," *Richmond Palladium and Sun-Telegram*, June 14, 1920.

45. "Dan Beddoe, Tenor, Is Dead Here at 74," *New York Times*, Dec. 28, 1937; "Clarence Dickinson, Composer of Church Music, Is Dead at 96," *New York Times*, Aug. 4, 1969; "Freund, John C.," in *Men and Women of America: A Biographical Dictionary of Contemporaries* (New York: L. R. Hamersly & Company, 1910), 659–60; "John C. Freund; Founder and Editor of Musical America Dies after Long Illness," *New York Times*, June 4, 1924.

46. "Amusements," *Evening Star* (Washington, DC), Feb. 2, 1921.

47. "Concerts—Lectures," *Evening Star* (Washington, DC), Jan. 14, 1923.

48. "Wagner to Be Director—Cleveland Chooses Son of Famous Composer for Opera," *Evening Star* (Washington, DC), Dec. 29, 1923.

49. "Famous Cleveland Orchestra on Air," *Evening Star* (Washington, DC), Dec. 5, 1924.

50. "Only Woman Manager of a Symphony Orchestra," *Evening World* (New York), Aug. 2, 1922.

51. For an insightful overview of the Russes' cultural significance, see Lynn Garafola, *Diaghilev's Ballets Russes* (Oxford: Oxford Univ. Press, 1989).

52. "John Long Severance," in *Encyclopedia of Cleveland History,* ed. John Grabowski, Case Western University Department of History, accessed Aug. 12, 2024, https://case.edu/ech/articles/s/severance-john-long.

53. "Musical Arts Assn.," in Grabowski, *Encyclopedia of Cleveland History,* accessed Aug. 12, 2024, https://case.edu/ech/articles/m/musical-arts-assn.

54. Kraus, *George Szell's Reign,* 11.

55. Michael Charry, *George Szell: A Life of Music* (Champaign: Univ. of Illinois Press, 2011), 2; Kraus, *George Szell's Reign,* 10–14.

56. Harvey Pekar and Joseph Remnant, *Harvey Pekar's Cleveland* (Marietta, GA: Top Shelf Productions, 2012), 10.

57. Kraus, *George Szell's Reign,* 131.

58. Carol Miller and Robert Wheeler, *Cleveland: A Concise History, 1796–1996* (Bloomington: Indiana Univ. Press, 1997), 146.

59. Souther, *Believing in Cleveland.*

60. Pierre Bourdieu, "The Forms of Capital," in *Readings in Economic Sociology,* ed. Nicole Woolsey Biggart (Oxford: Blackwell, 2002), 21.

61. Charry, *George Szell,* 87; Harold Schonberg, "After Forty Years: The Cleveland Orchestra Has Become Center of City's Musical Activity," *New York Times,* Feb. 2, 1958.

62. Robert Faulkiner, "Career Concerns and Mobility Motivations of Orchestra Musicians," *Sociological Quarterly* 14, no. 3 (1973): 336.

63. Marsh, *Cleveland Orchestra,* 101. Julie Schnepel, "The Critical Pursuit of the Great American Symphony, 1893–1950" (PhD diss., Indiana Univ., 1995), 355.

64. Schnepel, "Critical Pursuit of the Great American Symphony," 361–63.

65. Charry, *George Szell,* xxi; Harold Schonberg, "Cause for Pride," *New York Times,* Mar. 5, 1964.

66. Charry, *George Szell,* xxii, 101.

67. Marsh, *Cleveland Orchestra,* 100.

68. Charry, *Szell,* 198; Kraus, *George Szell's Reign,* 208; Marcia Citron, *Gender and the Musical Canon* (New York: Cambridge Univ. Press, 1993), 27.

69. Kraus, *George Szell's Reign,* 112.

70. Marsh, *Cleveland Orchestra,* 100–101.

71. Charry, *George Szell,* 160.

72. Kraus, *George Szell's Reign,* 86, 140.

73. Cayton and Onuf, introduction to *Midwest and the Nation,* xv–xix.

74. Kraus, *George Szell's Reign,* 50, 135, 118, 135.

75. Kraus, *George Szell's Reign,* 155, 165–66, 225.

76. Oscar Smith, "Cleveland Orchestra a Big Hit in Europe," *Akron Beacon Journal,* Feb. 6, 1957.

77. Charry, *George Szell,* 171

78. Schnepel, "Critical Pursuit of the Great American Symphony," 388; Schonberg, "After Forty Years."

79. Charry, *George Szell,* 166.

80. Ahlquist, "Playing for the Big Time," 145–65.

81. J. Mark Souther, "Acropolis of the Middle-West: Decay, Renewal, and Boosterism in Cleveland's University Circle," *Journal of Planning History* 10 (Feb. 2011): 3538; Dora Apel, *Beautiful Terrible Ruins: Detroit and the Anxiety of Decline* (New Brunswick: Rutgers Univ. Press, 2015), 35.

82. Charry, *George Szell*, 157.

83. A growth coalition is a coalition of metropolitan business and political elites invested in both population and economic growth. See Harvey Molotch, "The City as a Growth Machine: Toward a Political Economy of Place," *American Journal of Sociology* 82, no. 2 (1976): 309–32.

84. Schnepel, "Critical Pursuit of the Great American Symphony," 355.

85. Schonberg, "After Forty Years."

86. James Oestreich, "The Big Five Orchestras No Longer Add Up," *New York Times*, June 14, 2013.

87. Charry, *George Szell*, 101, 115, 122.

88. John Wechsberg, "The Grace of the Moment," *New Yorker*, Oct. 30, 1965.

89. "A Century of Excellence" Cleveland Orchestra website, 2024, https://www.clevelandorchestra.com/from-the-archives/soundwave/.

90. "The Glorious Instrument," *Time Magazine*, Feb. 22, 1963.

91. Charry, *George Szell*, 208.

92. Wechsberg, "Grace of the Moment," 80, 106.

93. Charry, *George Szell*, 218.

94. "Orchestra's Tour Brought Thaw to Cold War," *Cleveland Plain Dealer*, June 27, 1965.

95. Miller and Wheeler, *Cleveland*, 154.

96. "Cheers Welcome Orchestra," *Cleveland Plain Dealer*, June 27, 1965; "5,500 at Airport Greet Orchestra," *Cleveland Plain Dealer*, June 27, 1965; "Finding Aid for the Curtis Lee Smith Papers," Western Reserve Historical Society, Cleveland, available via OhioLink, accessed May 10, 2020, http://ead.ohiolink.edu/xtf-ead/view?docId=ead/OCLWHi2182.xml;query=;brand=default; John Gillis, *Commemorations: The Politics of National Identity* (Princeton: Princeton Univ. Press, 2018), 85.

97. "Crowd Parades," *Cleveland Plain Dealer*, June 27, 1965; "5,500 at Airport Greet Orchestra."

98. "Cheers Welcome Orchestra"; "5,500 at Airport Greet Orchestra"; "Crowd Parades."

99. Kraus, *George Szell's Reign*, 162; "A Bouquet for the Orchestra," *Cleveland Plain Dealer*, June 27, 1965.

100. "Century of Excellence."

101. Marsh, *Cleveland Orchestra*, 122.

102. William Cronon, *Nature's Metropolis: Chicago and the Great West* (New York: W. W. Norton, 1991), 23–55.

103. Teaford, *Cities of the Heartland*, ix, 249.

104. "Century of Excellence." Bourdieu describes hypercorrection in spoken language as a marker of social climbers, who adhere too perfectly to upper-class se-

mantics. See Pierre Bourdieu, *Language and Symbolic Power* (Cambridge: Polity Press, 2009), 63.
   105. "Festivals Abroad," *Musical Times*, Oct. 1965.
   106. Kraus, *George Szell's Reign*, 134, 157.
   107. "Top US Orchestras," *Time Magazine*, Feb. 22, 1963.
   108. Charry, *George Szell*, 218.
   109. Kraus, *George Szell's Reign*, 162; Cayton and Onuf, introduction.
   110. See Kraus, *George Szell's Reign*, 139.
   111. Teaford, *Cities of the Heartland*, 93.
   112. Schnepel, "Critical Pursuit of the Great American Symphony," 385, 378.
   113. Teaford, *Cities of the Heartland*, xi, 249, 164.
   114. Schnepel, "Critical Pursuit of the Great American Symphony," 378, 375.
   115. Teaford, *Cities of the Heartland*, x.
   116. Schnepel, "Critical Pursuit of the Great American Symphony," 385
   117. Wechsberg, "Grace of the Moment," 80.
   118. Teaford, *Cities of the Heartland*, 250, 224, ix.
   119. Wechsberg, "Grace of the moment," 96.
   120. Harry Neville, "Boston's, Nation's Orchestras in Financial Troubles," *Boston Globe*, June 23, 1969; "Tell Fight for Survival by Major Orchestras," *Chicago Tribune*, June 29, 1969.
   121. "Music: The Top U.S. Orchestras," *Time*, Feb. 24, 1963.
   122. "Tell Fight for Survival by Major Orchestras."
   123. "Boston's, Nation's Orchestras in Financial Troubles."
   124. Souther, *Believing in Cleveland*, loc. 3662 [Kindle edition].
   125. Kraus, *George Szell's Reign*, 163.
   126. See Souther, *Believing in Cleveland*.

Chapter 12

Locating Cleveland

Mapping Black Activism and Art in a "Way Post" City

STEPHANIE FORTADO

In the fall of 1964, in the midst of the civil rights movement, three working-class Cleveland Black activists, Lewis Robinson, Albert Ware-Bey, and Harllel "X" Jones, opened a new storefront youth center on Superior Avenue on the east side of Cleveland. The men founded the center as a safe space open to Black youth, run by the Black community, in response to police surveillance of city-run recreation sites and an alarming surge in the number of arrests of Black young people, especially teenage boys.[1] The new youth center stood along the northeastern edge of the Hough neighborhood, a predominantly Black enclave suffering from a deteriorating housing stock, median family incomes that were just 67 percent of the city average, and severely overcrowded schools.[2]

The three men named their new center the JFK House, a clever play on words. At first glance it paid homage to the recently assassinated president. And, indeed, a large photograph of John F. Kennedy hung just inside the center's entrance. But a second photograph—of Jomo Kenyatta, who helped lead the charge for Kenyan independence from British colonial rule—revealed the facility's official name: Jomo "Freedom" Kenyatta House. The word *freedom* sandwiched between the first and last names of a leading African anticolonialist unambiguously charted the purpose of the space—Black emancipation.

This naming also charted the location of Cleveland's JFK House in a broader Black US geography. Located near the northeastern edge of the Midwest, during the twentieth century Cleveland served as a vital and understudied site for the circulation of Black Nationalist ideas and a vibrant Black working-class culture, where community activists embraced a Pan-Africanist diasporic framework in their organizing for Black liberation. Historian Erik McDuffie has argued that we should approach Black midwestern history through the lens of what he has called the "diasporic Midwest" an area that "encompasses the American industrial heartland, a region that includes states north of the Ohio River between the Appalachians and Rocky Mountains, as a single yet complex geographic, political, historical and discursive formation linked to Africa, the black diaspora, and the world."[3] Cleveland's JFK House reflects such location. Founded to address issues of racism and oppression that were common across the midwestern urban spaces in the 1960s—anti-Black policing, segregation resulting in poor housing stock and severely overcrowded schools for Black families, and white backlash against Black assertion of equal rights to city spaces—the JFK House approached these issues through a Black Nationalist and Pan-Africanist framework of anticolonialism and solidarity with Black liberation efforts in both the US South and Africa.[4]

In his memoir, Lewis Robinson described the various figures who inspired his community organizing. They included men who gave their lives to the cause of Black liberation, including white Cleveland civil rights activist Reverend Bruce Klunder, who died when a bulldozer crushed him at a school segregation protest, Martin Luther King Jr., Malcolm X, Mississippi civil rights activist Medgar Evers, Congolese independence leader Patrice Lumumba, as well as President John F. Kennedy. Adorning the walls throughout the center, a photo of Lumumba joined those of Kenyatta and Kennedy and images of abolitionist Frederick Douglass, Malcolm X, and Marcus Garvey, who in 1914 founded the Black Nationalist Universal Negro Improvement Association.[5]

The programming at JFK further reflected Robinson's diasporic Black Nationalist consciousness. Teens entered the center "through a narrow plywood doorway" to attend a variety of recreational programs including dances and card games, or to hear from a slate of guest speakers that included then Carl Stokes, state representative for Cleveland, who would go on to become the first Black mayor of a major US city; Bernard Mandel, an activist with the Congress of Racial Equality; and Henry Austin, a member of the Black self-defense organization the Deacons for Defense, based out of Louisiana. While these speakers focused on conditions Black US residents faced, other programming connected participants to a wider Black diaspora. Don Freeman, the cofounder the Revolutionary Action Movement, volunteered giving lectures on African American and African history in the center's basement. In December 1964, the center held a party to celebrate Kenya's independence. The next summer, an art jamboree that featured African music showcased the creativity of local young people.[6]

Through these talks and other programs, JFK served as a space for the working out of the nascent rumblings of what would become the Black Power movement later in the decade. As historian Simon Wendt has observed in writing about Lewis and the center, "two years before Black Power activists began to call for political power, self defense, black pride and economic self help, these elements were already part of the Cleveland's black freedom movement."[7] James Smethurst, historian of the 1960s and 1970s Black Arts movement has described Cleveland as "an ideological and cultural way post between the Midwest and the East Coast" for the exchange of Black artistic expression.[8] Cleveland served as an important midwestern point for the development and circulation of ideas among grassroots Black organizers and artists, and a key connection point between the Midwest and East Coast Black freedom movement organizing.

Cleveland: A Midwestern City and Black Grassroots Organizing

This grassroots Black organizing took place in a city that prided itself as one of the "most progressive and attractive" cities in the nation, touting its abolitionist past and claims of racial liberalism.[9] In this, Cleveland followed what historian Ashley Howard has identified as a midwestern trend to ignore the "subtle yet powerful ways in which discrimination stalled black progress" as cities relied on tools such as human relations boards to address individual Black grievances instead of systemic structural and economic racism.[10] Historian Nicole Etcheson has described this as a regional penchant to engage in a "denial of very real class and race tensions."[11] Midwest civic leaders' refusal to acknowledge racial tensions in the region stemmed in part from their desire to differentiate the Midwest from the South, with its racial violence, in an effort to draw business investment. This rhetoric of racial liberalism served to mask the systemic racial oppression characteristic of the region.

Historians Sundiata Cha-Jua and Clarence Lang have argued for the importance attending to such "geographical differences" in the struggle for Black rights.[12] Lang has further called for "regional specificity in Black Freedom Movement histories," a specificity that does not elide the racism of any region but instead pursues a close analysis of regional differences in political economies, governmental processes, Black community institutions, migration patterns, and Black political development. In his analysis of what characterizes the Black Midwest, Lang has followed historian Joe William Trotter's lead and identified the Midwest as where a Black urban proletariat class emerged "earliest" and "most intensely." Lang also has argued that the presence of a small, but established Black professional class also led to class stratification and intra-racial class tensions in midwestern urban centers.[13]

In his book *Hostile Heartland*, Brent Campney traces anti-Black violence in the Midwest from 1830 through 1940. Campney identifies a thin veneer of racial liberalism in the region that occludes persistent anti-Black violence and Black community organizing in response to that violence. Differentiating the Midwest from the racialized violence in the South, Campney argues that in the postbellum period—especially in the Old Northwest states of Ohio, Indiana, and Illinois—state and local governments regularly intervened to stop white mob violence against Black residents, while at the same time police violence against Black residents remained persistent in the region.[14]

In many ways, Cleveland exemplified these markers of Black midwestern urban history identified by Lang and Campney—including an early, well-developed Black proletariat, or working-class, consciousness; a class-stratified local Black population that led to the development of a robust Black political class and interracial tensions; and a repressive, violent policing of Black residents that occurred at the same time the city celebrated its supposed racial liberalism. For decades, Cleveland city leaders sought to smooth over any accusations of racial inequality in their city, while they struggled to maintain the city as an industrial midwestern powerhouse. By 1900, Cleveland was established as "one of the world's preeminent manufacturing centers," and by World War I it was fifth largest city by population in the nation.[15] In the early part of the twentieth century, Cleveland became a national leader in manufacturing heavy equipment such as machine tools and production equipment and ranked only behind Detroit in car manufacturing, driving migration to the city from eastern Europe and the US South.

Yet in both Cleveland and Detroit, Black residents were largely left out of the economic gains of employment in this manufacturing boon. Therefore, it should come as little surprise that Cleveland joined Detroit and Chicago as f the most active sites for Marcus Garvey's Black Nationalist United Negro Improvement Association (UNIA), an organization dedicated to racial pride and economic self-sufficiency. Founded in 1919, Cleveland's UNIA division claimed fifteen thousand members at its peak, drawing predominantly from the ranks of the city's Black working class. This strong connection between Cleveland and the UNIA headquartered in Harlem and the circulation of UNIA activists between the two cities helped to establish Cleveland as a way post between the East Coast and Midwest for the organization. After Marcus Garvey's death in 1940, Clevelander James R. Steward succeeded the UNIA founder as president general and moved the organization's national headquarters to Cleveland.[16] The move made sense, given the rapid growth of Cleveland's Black population from 1920s, which reached eighty-five thousand, or roughly 10 percent of the city, by 1940, marking its rate of Black population growth second only to Detroit in the Midwest.[17]

Cleveland's reliance on heavy industry left the city susceptible to economic downturns, and the Great Depression ravaged the local economy as firms stopped ordering heavy equipment.[18] 1930 marked the peak of Cleveland's share of national industrial output. and The city entered its long slide into the Rust Belt. The Great Depression devastated the city's Black workforce, and in the 1930s one-third of black Clevelanders were unemployed.[19] In 1935, John O. Holly, a migrant from Alabama, founded the Future Outlook League, organizing campaigns against employment discrimination through boycotts and pickets and launched successful "don't buy where you can't work" campaigns.[20] In the 1930s, Black rights organizations in Cleveland—including the Communist League for Negro

Rights, NAACP, and National Negro Congress—also organized to confront white violence against African American swimmers at public pools in the city.[21] In addition to these locally focused campaigns, according to historian Melissa Ford, "outside of the South and Harlem, Cleveland in the mid-1930s had one of the most active communities in supporting the International Labor Defense and the Scottsboro Boys, and local black women were some of the most vocal and ardent supporters."[22] These organizations and activists represented a robust grassroots Black working-class organizing tradition in Cleveland.

Cleveland "Best Location in the Nation" for Black Residents?

As Cleveland failed to fully recover from the ravages of the Great Depression, business leaders cast about for a way to market their city to would-be investors. They decided that Cleveland's location, its very middle-ness in the national geography, would be the focus for their boosterism. In 1944, the Cleveland Electric Illuminating Company coined the slogan "The Best Location in the Nation" to promote the conversion of Cleveland's wartime industry to peacetime production and to encourage business and industrial investment in the city. The campaign boasted that Cleveland stood within five hundred miles of half of the population of the United States and Canada, was located at the intersection of several major shipping and rail lines, and had a large working-class labor force. The city's Chamber of Commerce soon picked up the slogan.[23] The marketing of Cleveland as the "Best Location" and especially the attempt to capitalize on the city's large skilled labor force attempted to smooth over both a rising labor militancy as well as the increasing tensions between the city's Black and white ethnic working classes to sell Cleveland as open and ready for business.

For many of Cleveland's Black residents, "Best Location in the Nation" was little more than a hollow slogan. Although the city touted its progressive values and skilled labor force, the lived experience of Black Clevelanders told a very different story. The city's organized labor movement controlled access to good paying skilled labor jobs and overt racism persisted in most unionized trades well into the 1960s.[24] In a city where residency was shaped by stringent de facto segregation, more than 98 percent of black residents lived in just a few neighborhoods on the east side, and Black Clevelanders were four times more likely to live in substandard housing than whites. Starting in the 1940s, urban renewal projects cleared more than six thousand acres, more than 10 percent of the city's total area, making it the largest clearance program by proportion in the nation. Housing for displaced residents did not keep pace with clearance, however, further exacerbating the tight housing market for Black residents.[25] This also led to severe overcrowding in schools in Black neighborhoods, in the city's highly segregated school system. Despite city boosters' efforts to market the city, the erosion of the industrial economy accelerated. Between 1953 and 1963, Cleveland lost eighty thousand blue-collar jobs. This hit African Americans particularly hard, and by 1960 Black unemployment rose above 30 percent.[26]

Black Clevelanders continued to organize against these conditions. In the 1940s the Cleveland chapter of the Congress of Racial Equality (CORE) led the charge to desegregate the city's public recreation spaces. In the early 1960s, a resurgent CORE chapter became one of the leaders in organizing around issues of policing and the Black community. In 1961, the chapter of CORE a "Fact Sheet on Police Brutality and Misconduct in the City." It listed six incidents that year in which police did not respond promptly to black residents' calls for assistance and, further, police shootings and beatings of black Clevelanders that had committed no crimes.[27] In a 1962 issue of its newsletter, the Afro-American Institute, a Black Nationalist organization led by activist Don Freeman, compared police tactics in Cleveland to those used in Birmingham, Alabama, and lambasted local Black councilmen and ministers for not being more vocal on the issue.[28] Of the 105 new police recruits who successfully completed training from December 1963 to December 1964, only six were African American, and policing of Black communities would remain one of the core issues of Black community organizing in Cleveland into the twenty-first century.[29] The city's Black activists also focused energy on the condition of schools that served Black communities. In 1963 Cleveland's CORE chapter was at the center of a coalition of some fifty community groups and civil rights organizations that joined together to form the United Freedom Movement, which launched an intensive campaign against school segregation in the 1963–64 school year—met by staunch white resistance and violence.[30]

During these campaigns against systemic racism, Black residents rejected Cleveland's marketing itself as "The Best Location in the Nation."

In the *Call and Post*, Cleveland's weekly Black newspaper, the slogan became a tongue-in-cheek reference in stories of discrimination and racism. Reporters and editorialists used the slogan repeatedly as a shorthand for the failed promise of racial equality, reporting on topics including unequal employment opportunities, housing discrimination, school segregation, and civil rights violations, referring to the slogan as a "guise" and a "myth."[31] Letters to the editor submitted to the newspaper also frequently questioned the truth of the slogan.[32] In 1968, *Call and Post* writer Charles Loeb described the problem in his "World on View" column, explaining that the city "for years had soothed its conscience by prating a slogan about the 'best location in the nation,' since there were many naïve enough to think that our Chamber of Commerce had reference to local customs rather than to location."[33]

Leaders of various local civil rights organizations also took the "Best Location" slogan to task. In a 1963 interview with the *Call and Post*, Clarence H. Holmes, president of the Cleveland branch of the NAACP explained, "But Cleveland is not the best location in the nation.... And this sloganeering is a substitute for action."[34] Three years later, Urban League leader Gerard Anderson declared in a speech to the City Club, "Cleveland is the best location, geographically only."[35] Lewis Robinson wrote in his memoir, "This was Cleveland, 'The Best Location in the Nation,' Not Mississippi. But it *was* Mississippi, and blacks like me had thought we had escaped Southern racism only to find it alive and growing north of the Ohio River."[36] In this reflection, Lewis dislodges Cleveland from its comfortable placement in the country's supposedly liberal Midwest and also disrupts the geographical imagination that maps racism as a southern problem. Examining how local Black community organizations emerged to confront this regional racism, and how these organizations connected to and diverged from broader national struggles for Black freedom, calls for further research by historians of the Midwest.

A Midwestern Way Post at Karamu House

While Cleveland was an important site of grassroots, working-class Black civil rights organizing, it also became an important site of exchange for Black arts and culture between the Midwest and East Coast, but that importance remains understudied. In his groundbreaking book on the formation of the US Black working class, historian Trotter has identified several urban spaces where Black migrants from the South contributed to the formation of a Black urban public sphere. He includes such vibrant Black midwestern corridors as the Stroll on Chicago's South Side, Hastings Street in Detroit, and Pittsburgh's Wylie Avenue—but no similar space in Cleveland made his analysis.[37] While historians Kenneth Kusmer and Kimberley Phillips have chronicled the history of Cleveland during the first Great Migration, the scholarship of Black life in the city post–World War II remains thin, compared to that of cities such as Detroit or Chicago, although there have been important recent contributions.[38] In his book on Black suburbanization around the city, historian Todd Michney declares Cleveland an "important but understudied locale."[39]

Perhaps no other site on Cleveland's landscape has functioned more as a site of cultural exchange between the East Coast and the Midwest than the Karamu House. Established in the Central neighborhood in 1915 by Russell and Rowena Jelliffe, a white couple, the Neighborhood Association Settlement House was part theater, part neighborhood center. By 1921, the theater was dubbed *Karamu*, a Swahili word meaning "banquet" or "place of joyful gathering," reflecting an effort to signify the space as welcoming to the neighborhood's growing Black population. Renowned Harlem Renaissance poet and playwright Langston Hughes helped fix Karamu on the nation's Black cultural landscape. Moving to Cleveland as a teenager, Hughes attended Central High School, where he wrote for the school newspaper and literary journal. He also took classes at the settlement house where the Jelliffes nurtured his creative voice. Hughes's relationship to Karamu was long lasting: he workshopped and premiered five of his plays at the theater in the late 1930s, featuring the interracial Gilpin Players theater troupe. Plays like Hughes's *Little Ham* gave Clevelanders a glimpse into the lives of Black Harlem.[40] Clevelanders responded with enthusiasm, and the theater was "filled to capacity for every performance" to see the "vivid portrayal of life in Harlem."[41] Scholar of the Black Arts movement James Smethurst has written that Hughes's works "in no small part maintained Harlem as an iconic Black landscape."[42] Cleveland was connected not merely to Harlem by the bridge of Hughes's writing, but, rather, the cultural meaning that the Black US diaspora attached to Harlem was partially created through Hughes's words—including through his depictions of Harlem in productions at Karamu, the publication of his "Simple" stories in the *Chicago Defender*, and the circulation of his poetry about the New York neighborhood in Black enclaves throughout the Midwest. Karamu gave midwesterners a glimpse of Harlem and in so doing helped to spread the idea of Harlem in the national Black public sphere.

Karamu and Cleveland served as a way post for Hughes who returned to the city often during his tours of the Midwest. He gave poetry readings and talks of his travels and civil rights activism at Karamu House as well at libraries, churches, and Cleveland's City Club.[43] Hughes spoke about the Black experience in the framework of a wider diaspora; for example, in 1938 he returned to the city to give a talk—"A Negro Poet Looks at the World"—that focused on his experiences reporting on the Spanish Civil War, where he served for three months as a columnist for the *Baltimore Afro-American*.[44]

Hughes also helped nurture Black creative voices in Cleveland. He was instrumental in starting the *Free Lance* literary journal. An interracial publication, it became "one of the few literary journals where African Americans set editorial policy during the 1950s and early 1960s," publishing Black experimental poets like Clevelander Russell Atkins. Langston Hughes penned the introduction to the first issue.[45]

Karamu has continued as a theater for more than a century, with a brief gap in 1939, when the center was destroyed by fire and was later rebuilt in a new location on Cleveland's east side after World War II with the help of the Rockefeller Foundation. One history of Black theater called Karamu "virtually the only stage on which black actors could receive professional training" during the 1940s and 1950s. Although it was not solely a Black space, Hughes explained in 1961, "It is a cultural shame that a great country like America, with twenty million people of color, has no primarily serious colored theater. There isn't. Karamu is the very nearest thing to it."[46] During the Black Power movement, Karamu's leadership shifted the operation to a more intentionally Black space.

Over the Christmas holidays of 1970, Karamu provided workshop space for the African People's Conference, bringing together two hundred attendees, including delegates from Boston, Nashville and Chicago. The schedule included poetry, music, and cultural programs such as the African People's Drummers and Dancers. Longtime Cleveland activist Don

Freeman led an education workshop while Gamell Shabazz, a teacher from Pittsburgh, led a workshop for women. Queen Mother (Audley) Moore, a renowned Black Nationalist activist based out of New York was among the conference speakers. The conference ended with the unanimous adoption of a ten-point platform of the African People's Party, "a Pan African Political Party dedicated totally to serving the needs of African Peoples."[47]

The Toll of Urban Renewal and Repression

While Karamu House continues to serve as place for the flourishing of Black art, Cleveland has not had other lasting, nationally significant institutions dedicated to Black cultural life on par with Chicago's *Jet* or *Ebony* magazines or Detroit's Motown. Although a significant local press organ, Cleveland's *Call and Post* did not achieve the same level of national influence as other midwestern Black weekly papers such as the *Chicago Defender* and the *Pittsburgh Courier*. Historian James Smethurst has argued that "failure to establish an infrastructure" and "out-migration of many of its most dynamic artists, particularly to Chicago," dampened Cleveland's Black artistic contribution.[48] The gutting of the city's oldest Black enclave, the Central neighborhood, under the banner of urban renewal certainly took its toll. An examination of the city's planning maps from the early 1950s reveals the extent of this impact. On one map, each renewal project under way in the Central neighborhood was marked alphabetically—beginning with A and continuing through to O. As a result of long construction delays and hoped-for private investment that failed to materialize, many of these projects never were finished. This alphabet soup of fifteen separate so-called slum clearance and renewal projects fragmented the Central landscape and permanently displaced thousands of Black residents, pushing them to neighborhoods further east in the city and into the eastern suburbs.[49] By 1968 by the city planners' own assessment the urban renewal project had failed, as they explained: "Today, to clear wide acreages of slums, and create new and decent housing for people, is no more unattainable than a trip the moon."[50] In the face of this devastating renewal program, it is perhaps not surprising that Black Clevelanders did not establish a more enduring Black cultural infrastructure on par with other midwestern cities.

While the city underwent a sweeping leveling of many predominantly Black neighborhoods, the city also engaged in more targeted demolition. On July 18, 1966, a white-owned neighborhood bar in the Hough neighborhood posted a sign with a racial epithet refusing to serve water to Black patrons. Angered at this refusal and at the deplorable living conditions in Hough, Black residents engaged in an urban rebellion. The rebellion resulted in four Black deaths and saw thirty to fifty people injured. The mayor called in the National Guard, which along with a rainstorm on July 24 quelled the uprising. In the aftermath of Hough, a grand jury convened to identify the causes of the rebellion. They blamed the uprising on "relatively small group of trained and disciplined professionals at this business" and with no evidence charged that the JFK House trained youth to make Molotov cocktails.[51] A photo of the doorway of the center went out over the United Press International (UPI) newswire service, labeling the center as a "fire bomb school" run by a "Negro extremist group."[52] Although Black Clevelanders led by the Urban League formed their own commission to challenge the findings of the Grand Jury report, blame had been firmly fixed on JFK. In April 1967, the city ruled the youth center building was not up to code, declared it a "health hazard," and bulldozed the building out of existence.[53] In an interview with the *Call and Post*, Lewis Robinson explained, "To the City's downtown establishment—which is their white Power—JFK is the despised symbol of Black Thinking, Black History, Black Action, Black Pride."[54] JFK was a space of Black midwestern organizing that linked Cleveland youth and activists to broader, national efforts for Black emancipation. Although JFK lasted only briefly, its influence in Cleveland was important, and the activists who contributed to the youth center would continue to work toward Black liberation. For example, Harllel "X" Jones founded the Black Cultural Nationalist organization Afro Set and continued to organize in Cleveland. Another longtime community activist remembered Jones as part of a "powerful and influential indigenous street leadership."[55] Don Freeman, who taught history courses for the center, would also continue his activism.

Don and Norma Freeman, *Vibration* and the Afro-American Institute

The destruction of the JFK House demonstrated the precariousness of revolutionary Black midwestern spaces. In the face of institutional oppression, small groups of Black activists developed and sustained creative ways to organize for Black liberation. Don Freeman and his wife, Norma, were two such activists. Don's community activism began when he joined the NAACP as a college student at Western Reserve University and then became involved in the Students for a Democratic Society. Attending a society conference in Madison, Wisconsin, Freeman met Max Stanford, a student a Central State University in Wilberforce, Ohio. When Stanford left school that summer to return to Philadelphia, Don Freeman visited him there over the Christmas holidays. Freeman had become particularly inspired by reading Harold Cruse's 1962 article in *Studies on the Left*—"Revolutionary Nationalism and the Afro-American"—which described the "domestic colonialism" of Black Americans, a framework that resonated with the conditions Freeman observed in Cleveland. Out of these readings and conversations came the idea to form the Revolutionary Action Movement (RAM).[56] According to Stanford, "by using mass direct action combined with the tactics of self-defense, it hoped to change the civil rights movement into a black revolution." In 1963, RAM activists from Chicago, New York, and Philadelphia gathered in Cleveland at a secret "Black Vanguard" conference to make plans.[57] In his memoir, Freeman describes his extensive traveling and visiting with Black activists, connecting the East Coast movement to Midwest cities such as Detroit and Chicago, an effort that places him as one of leading Black Nationalist thinkers and organizers of the past half century.

Between travels to build this network of Black radicals, back in Cleveland Freeman participated in various organizing efforts aimed at addressing structural racism. He also established the Afro-American Institute (AAI), what he described as "first Black Nationalist organization in Cleveland since the United Negro Improvement Association and the Nation of Islam."[58] The AAI held a triple motto of "Awareness, Agitation and Action," with the purpose of "fostering a concept of Pan Africanism that encompassed the entire African Diaspora."[59] Through the AAI, Freeman hosted a series of talks. In 1963, William Worthy, a Black journalist at the *Baltimore*

Afro-American, delivered a speech titled "The Plight of Black America—Where Do We Go from Here?" Two Nigerian graduate students attending university in Cleveland gave a talk: "The Relationship of the African Revolution to the Struggle of Black America."[60] Freeman's activism and writing on Black liberation took a personal toll: he lost his job as a junior high teacher in the Cleveland Public School System because of his organizing. In 1966, he was hired at the League Park Center, a Hough neighborhood center, where he would go on to hold the post of director and continue to work toward Black rights, especially in the area of education.

Don and Norma also established *Vibration,* a journal dedicated to "the Resurrection of the Mentally and Spiritually Dead," that provides a sharp analysis of the US and global political economy from a Black Nationalist perspective. For the inaugural issue, published on March 21, 1968, Don, who enjoys jazz music, wrote a tribute to John Coltrane and his "spiritual, aesthetic/musical, and cultural significance to Black America and the world."[61] Norman Jordan, a poet and playwright based out of Karamu House contributed to *Vibration.* Diasporic in its framework, the journal remains one of the longest running literary organs emerging from the Black Power era. Don Freeman continues to publish it, and he was assisted by his wife until she passed away in 2019.[62] The fiftieth anniversary edition included an article by Don that analyzed the recent Great Recession and the Occupy Wall Street movement and concluded, "Their endeavors must be renewed by potent and *radical* collective advocacy and activism."[63] For more than half a century, Don Freeman has sounded the call for such radical collective activism.

Only through heeding this call will Cleveland serve not only as a way post connecting Black artists and activists from the Midwest and East Coast but also as a way post on the road to Black liberation. As historians continue to situate Black Cleveland into midwestern history, we must further interrogate how individual activists and organizations responded to local conditions, imagined and realized Black visions for their city, and connected their activism and creativity to Black freedom struggles and Black artists in other regions of the United States and across the African diaspora.

Notes

1. Lewis G. Robinson, *The Making of a Man: An Autobiography* (Cleveland: Green & Sons, 1970), 71–92; "Police Chief Urges Playground Patrol," *Cleveland Call and Post,* June 27, 1964; Annual Report of Cleveland Police Department, 1964, 25, 453, box 12, file "Police-Community Relations in Cleveland Ohio (Publications and Reports)," National Archives, College Park, MD. In 1960 African Americans accounted for 48 percent of the arrests of juvenile boys in Cleveland; by 1964 that number had jumped to 61 percent.

2. 1960 US Censuses of Population and Housing, Cleveland Ohio, "Table P-1-General Characteristics of the Population by Census Tracts," 22–27; Carol Poh Miller and Robert A. Wheeler, *Cleveland: A Concise History, 1796–1996* (Cleveland: Case Western Univ. Press, 1997), 44; Don Freeman, interview by author, Cleveland, July 12, 2018.

3. Erik S. McDuffie, "'A New Day Has Dawned for the UNIA': Garveyism, the Diasporic Midwest and the West Africa," *Journal of West African History* 2 (Spring 2016): 76; and Erik S. McDuffie, "The Second Battle for Africa Has Begun: Rev. Clarence W. Harding Jr., Garveyism, Liberia and the Diasporic Midwest, 1966–1978," in *Global Garveyism,* ed. Ronald J. Stephens and Adam Ewing (Gainesville: Univ. Press of Florida, 2019), 90.

4. Historian Wendell Nii Laryea Adjetey has also recently made the call to consider how urban centers such as Cleveland in the Great Lakes region of the Midwest also should be considered in a Pan-African framework linking Canada to the region. Wendell Nii Laryea Adjetey, "Bridging Borders: African North Americans in Great Lakes Cities, 1920s–1940s," *Journal of American History* 11 (June 2023): 58–81.

5. Robinson, *Making of a Man,* 102.

6. Robinson, *Making of a Man,* 127; Alvin Ward, "Defense Deacons Raise Funds Here," *Cleveland Call and Post,* Nov. 27, 1965; "Troops Watch JFK House," *Chicago Tribune,* July 25, 1966; Don Freeman, interview by author, Cleveland, July 12, 2018.

7. Simon Wendt, *The Spirt and the Shotgun: Armed Resistance and the Struggle for Civil Rights* (Gainesville: Univ. Press of Florida, 2004), 163.

8. James Edward Smethurst, *The Black Arts Movement: Literary Nationalism in the 1960s and 1970s* (Chapel Hill: Univ. of North Carolina Press, 2005), 180.

9. Miller and Wheeler, *Cleveland,* 114.

10. Ashley Howard, "History for Black Lives: An American Tradition," Organization of American Historians website, accessed Aug. 15, 2024, https://www.oah.org/tah/history-for-black-lives/an-american-tradition/.

11. Nicole Etcheson, "Barbecued Kentuckians and Six-Foot Tall Rangers: The Construction of Midwestern Identity," in *The Identity of the American Midwest: Essays on Regional History,* ed. Andrew R. L. Cayton and Susan E. Gray (Bloomington: Indiana Univ. Press, 2001), 79.

12. Sundiata Keita Cha-Jua and Clarence Lang, "The 'Long Movement' as Vampire: Temporal and Spatial Fallacies in Recent Black Freedom Studies," *Journal of African American History* 92, no. 2 (2002): 265–88.

13. Clarence Lang, "Locating the Civil Rights Movement: An Essay on the Deep South, Midwest, and Border South in Black Freedom Studies," *Journal of Social History* 47 (Winter 2013): 380–83.

14. Brent M. S. Campney, *Hostile Heartland: Racism, Repression and Resistance in the Midwest* (Urbana: Univ. of Illinois Press, 2019), 157–59.

15. Miller and Wheeler, *Cleveland*, 40.

16. Frazier, *Harambee City*, 30; McDuffie, "New Day Has Dawned for the UNIA," 74, 81; McDuffie, "Second Battle for Africa Has Begun," 95; Kimberly L. Phillips, *Alabama North: African-American Migrants, Community, and Working-Class Activism in Cleveland, 1915–1945* (Urbana: Univ. of Illinois Press, 1999), 186–87.

17. Miller and Wheeler, *Cleveland*, 133; Melissa Ford, *A Brick and a Bible: Black Women's Radical Activism in the Midwest during the Great Depression* (Carbondale: Southern Illinois Univ. Press, 2022), 134.

18. Miller and Wheeler, *Cleveland*, 148; Edward W. Hill, "The Cleveland Economy: A Case Study for Economic Restructuring in *Cleveland: A Metropolitan Reader*, ed. W. Dennis Keating, Norman Krumholtz and David C. Perry (Kent: Kent State Univ. Press, 1995), 57–59.

19. Nishani Frazier, *Harambee City: The Congress of Racial Equality in Cleveland and the Rise of Black Power Populism* (Fayetteville: Univ. of Arkansas Press, 2017), 29.

20. Phillips, *Alabama North*, 190–225; Frazier, *Harambee City*, 28–29.

21. Todd Michney, *Surrogate Suburbs: Black Upward Mobility and Neighborhood Change in Cleveland, 1900–1980* (Chapel Hill: Univ. of North Carolina Press, 2017), 62–69.

22. Melissa Ford, *Brick and a Bible*, 131.

23. J. Mark Souther, *Believing in Cleveland: Managing Decline in the "Best Location in the Nation"* (Philadelphia: Temple Univ. Press, 2017), 74; Miller and Wheeler, *Cleveland*, 147–50; Christopher Wye, "Black Civil Rights," in *Cleveland: A Metropolitan Reader*, ed. Dennis Keating, Norman Krumholz, and David C. Perry (Kent: Kent State Univ. Press, 1995), 119.

24. Phillips, *Alabama North*, 60–76.

25. Miller and Wheeler, *Cleveland*, 43; David Stradling and Richard Stradling, *Where the River Burned: Carl Stokes and the Struggle to Save Cleveland* (Ithaca, NY: Cornell Univ. Press, 2015), 88.

26. Leonard More, "Carl Stokes: Mayor of Cleveland," in *African-American Mayors: Race Politics and the American City*, ed. David R. Colburn and Jeffrey S. Adler (Urbana: Univ. of Illinois Press, 2001), 82; *The Negro in Cleveland, 1950–1963: An Analysis of the Social and Economic Characteristics of the Negro Population: the Change between 1950 and 1963* (Cleveland: Urban League, 1964), 22, 35.

27. "Fact Sheet on Police Brutality and Misconduct in the City of Cleveland, Ohio," *The Papers of the Congress of Racial Equality, 1942–1967*, Microfilming Corp. of America, reel 23, 833.

28. Afro American Institute, *Afropinion*, undated, The Black Power Movement: part 3, Revolutionary Action Movement papers, 1962–96, UPA Collection from LexisNexis, reel 11.

29. Interview with Captain Lloyd Gary, Planning Officer, Police Academy, Cleveland, Ohio, Dec. 1, 1965, 53, box 7, file "Cleveland Ohio Interviews (2 of 3)," Records of the Commission on Civil Rights, Record Group 453, National Archives.

30. For a thorough review of CORE in Cleveland see Frazier, *Harambee City*.

31. See the following stories from the *Cleveland Call and Post*: "Tired, Jobless, Loses Faith in 'Best Location," Jan. 27, 1951; Al Sweeney, "City Desk: Best location in Nation . . . For What?" *Cleveland Call and Post*, July 2, 1960; "Join the March for Freedom," July 13, 1963; "Cleveland's March for Freedom," July 20, 1963; "'Economic Weakness' Seat of Negro Problem in Cleveland, Says McGhee," May 30, 1964; "After Ten Long Years," May 30, 1964; "Social Workers Urge Free Lunch Program," Jan. 23, 1965; "Open Confession Is Good for the Soul," Feb. 19, 1966; Bob Williams, "Rights Probers Bare City's Dirty Linen," Apr. 9, 1966; "Cleveland Presents a Poor Image," Apr. 9, 1966; E. Burrus Young, "U.S. Probe Airs Racial Injustice within Cleveland," Apr. 16, 1966; William O. Walker, "This Has Been a Sorry Story," Apr. 16, 1966; Daisy Craggett, "City Limits: What Price Glory," July 16, 1966; Daisy Craggett, "City Limits: Out of These Ashes," Aug. 27, 1966; "EEO Reports on Negro Jobs: Cleveland, Other Big Cities Ignore White Collar Workers," Aug. 12, 1967; Bob Williams, "Bobbing Along," Jan. 13, 1968.

32. See the following from the *Cleveland Call and Post*: letters to the editor, Feb. 22, 1964; Lois K. Dawson, "The Mistake on the Lake?" May 2, 1964; Martha Silver, "About Crime Epidemic," Feb. 27, 1965; Thomas Avery and Caroline Stoutemire, Kinsman Area Community Council, "A Letter to Locher," Feb. 18, 1967.

33. Charles H. Loeb, "Word View: White Racism on the Move," *Cleveland Call and Post*, Aug. 24, 1968.

34. "Holmes Undaunted in Civil Rights Fights," *Cleveland Call and Post*, August 10, 1963.

35. Bob Williams, "Violence Is Not the Answer City Club Forum Is Told," *Cleveland Call and Post*, Sept. 24, 1966.

36. Robinson, *Making of a Man*, 71.

37. Joe William Trotter Jr., *Workers on Arrival: Black Labor and the Making of America* (Oakland: Univ. of California Press, 2019), 125.

38. Kenneth L. Kusmer, *A Ghetto Takes Shape: Black Cleveland, 1870–1930* (Urbana: Univ. of Illinois Press, 1976); Phillips, *Alabama North*.

39. Michney, *Surrogate Suburbs*, 5. Michney's book is part of a recent spate of publishing on the history of Black Cleveland, which has begun to fill in this gap in Black urban scholarship. Other recent works include Frazier, *Harambee City*, and Stradling and Stradling, *Where the River Burned*, 2015.

40. Sharyn Emery, "The Philadelphia Harlem Story: Langston Hughes' Screwy Play *Little Ham*," *Modern Drama* 55 (Fall 2012): 374; Reuben Silver Reuben, "A History of the Karamu Theater" (PhD diss., Ohio State Univ., 1961), 3–5, 26, 194, 229–35; Smethurst, *Black Arts Movement*, 177.

41. Bud Douglass, "Gilpins Score in 'Little Ham,'" *Cleveland Call and Post*, Apr. 9, 1936.

42. James Smethurst, "'Don't Say Goodbye to the Porkpie Hat': Langston Hughes, the Left, and the Black Arts Movement," *Callaloo* 25 (Autumn 2002): 1228.

43. See the following *Cleveland Call and Post* stories: "The Vagabonds Entertain Langston Hughe[s]," Nov. 21, 1935; "Langston Hughes to Speak at Musical Tea," Nov. 28, 1935; Claire Davis, "The Arts," Aug. 20, 1936; "Langston Hughes to Speak at 2nd Baptist," Apr. 7, 1938; "Langston Hughes Speaks Here Sunday," Apr. 25, 1940; "Langston Hughes Here Easter Sun, for Dedication of Inter-Cultural Library," Apr. 24, 1943; "Langston Hughes to Address Forum at St. James Sunday," Mar. 30, 1946; "Langston Hughes Returns to Central Alumni Night, May 10," May 4, 1946; "Langston Hughes to Appear Here Sunday," Nov. 15, 1947, 8; "Festival Revives American Folklore," Feb. 2, 1952; "Langston Hughes Brings His 'Weary Blues' Home," Feb. 14, 1959; "Freedom's Not Free, Hughes Tells Group," Nov. 24, 1962.

44. "Langston Hughes Tells Experiences in Spain," *Cleveland Call and Post*, Mar. 31, 1938.

45. Smethurst, *Black Arts Movement*, 178.

46. Errol Hill and James Hatch, *A History of African American Theater* (New York: Cambridge Univ. Press, 2003), 228, 311. Later in the 1990s, the theater again allowed for more white artistic participation, in part due to the need to raise money.

47. Kathleen Johnson, "African People's Conference Held," *Black Liberator* 2, no. 2 (n.d.).

48. Smethurst, *Black Arts Movement*, 180.

49. "Report on Urban Renewal in Cleveland," Sept. 1955, 2–3, 10, subject file: Urban Renewal, 1950–1959, folder 2, and "Planning Cleveland," 4, subject file: "City Planning Cleveland, 1960–1969," Public Administration Section, Cleveland Public Library. See also Souther, *Believing in Cleveland*, 47–48.

50. "Planning Cleveland," 4.

51. Special Grand Jury report relating to Hough Riots, Judge Thomas J. Parrino, Criminal Branch Common Pleas Court of Cuyahoga County, Cleveland Public Library-Public Administration, file number 1738-66, 3–9, Cleveland County Archives; "Grand Jury Report: Robinson, Communists Keys in Hough Riots, *Cleveland Press*, Aug. 13, 1966.

52. UPI photograph, July 24, 1966, author's collection.

53. "J. F. K. House Is Torn Down," *Cleveland Call and Post*, Apr. 8, 1967. One of JFK's founders, Lewis Robinson, had previously worked for the city in building code enforcement and insisted the ruling was just an excuse to destroy the space.

54. "Robinson: Grand Jury Found Scapegoat," *Cleveland Call and Post*, Aug. 13, 1966.

55. "Longtime Cleveland Activist Harllel Jones Remembered for Leadership in the Community," *Cleveland Plain Dealer*, May 11, 2011.

56. Peniel E. Joseph, *Waiting to the Midnight Hour: A Narrative History of Black Power in America* (New York: Holt Paperbacks, 2006), 75–76. David M. Swiderski, "Approaches to Black Power: African American Grassroots Political Struggle in Cleveland, Ohio, 1960–1966" (PhD diss., Univ. of Massachusetts, Amherst, 2013), 120–21; Freeman interview.

57. Maxwell C. Stanford, "Revolutionary Action Movement (RAM): A Case Study of an Urban Revolutionary Movement in Western Capitalist Society" (MA thesis, Atlanta Univ., 1986), 67–77.

58. Freeman interview.

59. Don Freeman, *Resolutions of a Resolute Radical* (Scotts Valley, CA: Createspace, 2017), 61.

60. Freeman, *Resolutions of Resolute Radical*, 56–61; Freeman interview.

61. Freeman, *Resolutions of Resolute Radical*, 127.

62. Smethurst, *Black Arts Movement*, 179.

63. Don Freeman, "Inequality: The Arch Enemy of Democracy," *Vibration* 2 (Jan.–June 2018).

Chapter 13

Political Cultures in Conflict

Locating Ohio into a Region during and after the Era of the New Deal

KENNETH J. HEINEMAN

Defining a Region

Scholars who study American regional histories and politics often have a difficult time designating exactly what defines the Midwest. The South, in contrast, is relatively easy to define; slavery, rebellion, war, and poverty welded it into a cohesive, tragic region. As for the West, vicious conflict with Native Americans and among settlers became popular culture fodder for Hollywood. The West, as history, myth, and region, is clearly defined.

The Midwest, however, is more elusive. Historian Jon Lauck has argued that there is a discernable Midwest region that extends westward from the Great Lakes and the Mississippi River. His Midwest embodies the United States writ large. The region, after all, contains all of America's diverse cultural, ethnic, and racial groups and its economy is equally as diverse. Given such ethnocultural and economic diversity, the Midwest represents a national "template" for understanding American history and politics.[1]

We could set aside defining the Midwest as a geographic and political entity and instead embrace the idea of an "Industrial Heartland." Beginning in the 1930s, five northern states, each with a heavily unionized, significant eastern European Catholic and Jewish population, potentially formed a key, coveted electoral bloc for Democrats: Illinois, Michigan, New York, Ohio, and Pennsylvania. (Collectively, they had 157 votes of the then required 266 to win the Electoral College.) While a Democratic presidential candidate could lose three of the five and still win the presidential election (as Harry S Truman did in 1948), three was the normal minimum.

If uncomfortable with welding Michigan and New York together into an Industrial Heartland, we could set Pennsylvania and New York aside—designating them "Mid-Atlantic. Historian Howard Gillette has labelled Buffalo and Pittsburgh as "hinterlands," or dependencies, of New York and Philadelphia—rather than grouping them with Cleveland and Chicago. Students, however, might find Gillette's taxonomy unsatisfying, since Buffalo and Pittsburgh are, in demographic and economic terms, more like (and linked to) Chicago and Cleveland than either New York City or Philadelphia.[2]

One could follow political scientists David Morgan and Robert England's lead and designate two similar but geographically distinct regions: "Midwest Industrial" and "Northeast Industrial." There are, however, problems with such an approach, particularly in light of the conservative southern white cultural and political influence in some parts of Midwest Industrial and its relative absence in otherwise kindred states.[3]

Much of the problem with defining the Midwest is due to one state: Ohio. Regardless of whether we assign it to the Midwest, the Industrial Heartland, or some other region, Ohio remains politically elusive. Regions are, most generally, diverse and do not lack apparent contradictions. Ohio, though, while reflecting this reality, provides an especially complicated, confusing challenge in defining its political culture and regional location.

In this chapter, we will place the issue of regional "fit" in the context of the 1937 Little Steel Strike and its political fallout. In some ways, that strike became a Rosetta Stone with which to interpret Ohio's political culture for the balance of the twentieth century. The strike also underscored how much Ohio differed from such neighbors as Illinois, Michigan, and Pennsylvania

The Context

Philip Murray (1886–1952), the president of the Steel Workers' Organizing Committee (SWOC) and vice president of the Congress of Industrial Organizations (CIO), watched the late spring 1937 labor union drive with mounting frustration. In 1936, Murray had successfully unionized US Steel which controlled 60 percent of the market. The rest of the mills, collectively known as "Little Steel," were less cooperative. In Aliquippa, Pennsylvania, however, Jones & Laughlin had to back down in 1937. The US Supreme Court, in the *National Labor Relations Board vs. Jones & Laughlin,* ruled that the company had illegally prevented workers from voting on whether to choose SWOC as its collective bargaining agent. SWOC subsequently won the right to represent Jones & Laughlin workers.[4]

Overall, the CIO had enjoyed notable successes going into 1937, especially in Michigan, with the showdown between the United Automobile Workers' (UAW) union and the dominant car manufacturer, General Motors. Although it took the UAW longer to organize Chrysler and Ford, the union gained political momentum in Michigan. Wayne County, Detroit, accounted for two-thirds of Michigan's total Democratic vote and 57 percent of the state's CIO membership—a formidable power base with which the UAW used to assert control over the state Democratic Party.[5]

In Illinois, the 1937 Memorial Day Massacre outside Chicago's Republic Steel mill led to ten deaths at the hands of the city police. That demoralizing event, however, proved to be the figurative last shot in the anti-SWOC campaign in Illinois. The Cook County, Chicago, Democratic political machine, drawing on the reservoir of political strength that came with the fact that 45 percent of all Illinois voters lived in its territory, brought the CIO and a sympathetic Catholic Church leadership into its protective fold.[6]

Heading east to New York, while ethnocultural, religious, and racial tensions muddied the electoral waters, CIO affiliates in the garment industry were a political force. New York City, a bastion of unionism and support for Democratic president Franklin D. Roosevelt, claimed 51 percent of the state's voters. In Buffalo, the Catholic diocese and SWOC were allied with that city's dominant Democratic political machine. Unlike many of their New York City Irish Catholic counterparts, Buffalo's Irish built alliances with eastern European Catholics, Jews, and African Americans—

which meant that anti-CIO employers found it difficult to play various cultural groups against each other as part of a divide and conquer strategy.[7]

In Pennsylvania, the Allegheny County, Pittsburgh, Democratic political machine; the Catholic Church; and SWOC forged an "Iron City Trinity." Catholic parishes opened their doors to SWOC organizers, and clergy joined union picket lines. Murray welcomed whatever Catholic clerical assistance he could receive. As a devout Catholic, Murray kept the labor and social justice encyclicals of Popes Leo XIII (*On the Condition of Labor,* 1891) and Pius XI (*Reconstructing the Social Order,* 1931) at his office for ready reference. Both encyclicals, or letters to the clergy and laity, urged Catholics to pursue collective action through labor associations.[8]

Pittsburgh's Bishop Hugh Boyle (1873–1950) embraced SWOC, both at the local level and as a major player in the Washington, DC–based National Catholic Welfare Conference. Boyle's nephew was an adviser to Democratic machine leader David Lawrence (1889–1966) who, like Murray, was the son of impoverished Irish Catholic immigrants. The Pittsburgh bishop sought to build a pro-CIO alliance with his counterparts in Buffalo, Chicago, Cleveland, Detroit, Milwaukee, and Toledo. Tellingly, Lawrence's local allies—Paul Jones, the first African American elected to the city council, and Henry Ellenbogen and Samuel Weiss, the first Jewish Democrats sent to Congress from western Pennsylvania—were graduates of Duquesne University, Pittsburgh's leading Catholic institution of higher education.[9]

The 1936 presidential election, which had reelected Roosevelt in a historic landslide, revealed the contours of a Democratic Party electoral coalition that, though strained, remained unbroken for two generations. While the solid Democratic South embraced anti-CIO politics and racial segregation, it was wedded to federal agricultural subsidies and water projects. As long as the federal government did not push labor and civil rights on the South, Dixie reliably delivered 170 Electoral College votes to Democratic presidential nominees. In the North, twelve Democratically inclined urban-industrial counties, located mainly in the Industrial Heartland, greatly influenced which presidential candidate would receive 220 electoral votes. This meant that Roosevelt and subsequent Democratic presidential candidates potentially went into elections with 390 electoral votes—well above the minimum needed to win the presidency.[10]

In 1937, Murray and his allies noted that the bulk of the labor violence was taking place in Ohio. Of the several hundred strikers wounded and/or arrested, most were from Ohio's mill towns. (There were fewer fatalities in Ohio, however, with the Buckeye State claiming four of the eighteen strikers killed.) Given the concentration of Little Steel mills in Ohio, the state was bound to take center stage in the worst labor conflict of the New Deal era.[11]

By the summer of 1937, a bitter joke was wending its way around Pittsburgh's SWOC headquarters: the initials CIO actually stood for "Collapsed in Ohio." An electoral backlash in the 1938 midterm elections confirmed that Murray had reason to be fretful in 1937.[12]

The Clash

As soon as the Little Steel Strike commenced in Canton, Cleveland, Massillon, and Youngstown, Murray and his allies noticed worrisome trends. To begin with, the medium-sized Ohio industrial communities had a larger share of Protestants (white and Black) than was true in such cities as Cleveland and Pittsburgh. Nearly all the strikers were Catholic, while nearly all the workers who crossed picket lines were Protestants.

As a religious faith, Catholicism encouraged a collective response to moral and political issues. The CIO, according to labor activists like Murray, was a logical extension of Catholic faith. Protestantism, especially the socially and theologically conservative Baptist and Methodist denominations that dominated the mill towns and rural Ohio, emphasized individual action. One was saved or damned by individual effort or failing. Making the religious-ideological schism worse, many working- and lower-middle-class Protestants distrusted the Catholic Church, which they regarded as foreign and dictatorial.[13]

Since the early nineteenth century, the Ohio River counties in Illinois, Indiana, and Ohio boasted large populations of southern migrants who expressed a strong dislike of the federal government. (*Antebellum* southern whites did not typically migrate to Michigan or Wisconsin.) During the Civil War and Reconstruction eras, Ohio Democrats were more vocal than most northerners in denouncing President Abraham Lincoln, opposing the emancipation of slaves, and voting against giving African Americans the constitutional right to vote.[14]

By the 1930s, as the ideologies of the two major parties evolved, Ohio's southern, or "Dixie," Democrats had become Republicans. If big-city Catholics joined the CIO and voted for New Deal Democrats, then it was near gospel that Ohio's farming and working-class white Protestants would do the opposite. Nationally, only 40 percent of Protestants voted Democratic—and most such voters were white southerners. In contrast, the overwhelming majority of Catholics voted Democratic and accounted for one-quarter of the national Democratic vote. Ohio fit the national religious voting patterns nearly perfectly, though, at least until the end of the 1930s, the Buckeye State had a sufficient number of white Protestant Democrats to exercise control over their party.[15]

While southern Illinois had a demographic history similar to Ohio's, and later political analysts joked that Pennsylvania was "two cities with Alabama in between," Ohio's white Protestant population grew more than its counterparts in either state. The influx of poor white Appalachian Protestants into Akron, for instance, was so great in the 1920s that a gubernatorial candidate from West Virginia went there to encourage to them go "home" and cast a ballot for him. Such migrants often brought with them a suspicion of labor unions, Catholics, Blacks, and federal activism. Their critics dismissed them as snake-eaters who practiced bizarre religious rituals.[16]

Racial antagonism proved just as crippling as Ohio's religious-political divisions in staging SWOC's defeat in 1937. The *Pittsburgh Courier*, which in the 1930s was among the nation's largest and most influential African American newspapers, provided extensive coverage of Ohio's Little Steel Strike. In communities such as Canton, Massillon, and Youngstown, mill operators mobilized African Americans to cross picket lines. As the *Courier* reported, the Ohio mills had recruited thousands of southern Blacks as strikebreakers during the 1919 unrest. After 1919, mill owners had fired their Black labor forces—but reactivated them in 1937.[17]

CIO organizers warned Blacks that the mills were exploiting them. The problem for SWOC was that though its leaders embraced equal rights, the white rank and file generally did not. Catholic strikers clashed frequently with white Protestants, but nonetheless, they fixated on the African Americans. Screams of "Black bastards!" reverberated in picket lines. The *Courier* predicted that race relations in Ohio's mill towns would be poisoned for at least another generation.[18]

In Cleveland's streets, armed company guards and CIO organizers had been fighting each other since December 1936 at the local General Motors' Fisher Body plant. The May 1937 Little Steel Strike was just one more battle in a continuous labor war. As steel workers and company guards beat and shot each other, Bishop Joseph Schrembs (1866–1945) announced, "It is both a privilege and a duty to champion the cause of labor."[19]

His words having little effect, Schrembs sought help from Pittsburgh. Although Schrembs had established "labor schools" to train workers in union organizing and Catholic social thought, he lacked the support network Boyle enjoyed in western Pennsylvania. Schrembs had few allies in a municipal government that remained in Republican hands, and he faced an array of local law enforcement agencies that regarded the CIO as an un-American threat to public order. Additionally, Cleveland's Catholics and African Americans often resented each other more than they despised the leadership of Republic Steel. Boyle sent priests to Schrembs, but their efforts proved futile.[20]

Complicating matters for Schrembs and SWOC was the role of the Communist Party and its relationship with anti-Communist Catholics. As historian Patrick McNamara has insightfully observed: "Catholic anticommunism had a doctrinal basis. In a broad sense, every Catholic was a *de facto* anti-communist." Given this reality, it was not surprising that Murray worked quietly behind the scenes to minimize communist influence in SWOC and the CIO. Len DeCaux, the CIO publicity director and a secret Communist, complained that Murray's SWOC was "a setup—a Catholic setup.... In national CIO and most other new unions, religion didn't stick out as it did in SWOC."[21]

Pittsburgh's terrain proved inhospitable to the Communist Party, in large part because Catholic activists had built inclusive alliances across ethnic and racial lines. Within a few years, the demoralized leadership of the western Pennsylvania Communist Party transferred its Pittsburgh Slovenian and Jewish section organizers to Cleveland. Pennsylvania communists believed Cleveland offered better prospects for success.[22]

In 1937, Ohio's Communist CIO organizers took advantage of not being under Murray's direct supervision. CIO president John L. Lewis (1880–1969) had brought Communists into the union because he appreciated their willingness to work for little pay, as well as their militant idealism. They also did not back down from a fight. That trait, however, turned out to be a problem. Ohio SWOC organizer Gus Hall (1910–2000), later a perennial Communist Party presidential candidate, coordinated a plot to dynamite steel mills, bridges, and the homes of workers in the Niles–Warren area who had refused to join the strike.[23]

CIO general counsel Lee Pressman, secretly a Communist Party member, visited with Hall and his half-dozen coconspirators—but hastily departed without offering to defend them. To staunch the flow of negative national publicity surrounding Hall, Murray quickly expelled him from SWOC. Neither Murray's nor Pressman's efforts to disassociate the union from Hall, however, succeeded. A Youngstown grand jury, seeing an opportunity to exploit SWOC's vulnerability, indicted two hundred labor organizers for alleged rioting and weapons' possession. Demoralized Catholic workers, increasingly convinced that the CIO might, as the mill owners charged, be a Communist front, refused to support the Ohio SWOC.[24]

Perhaps most detrimental to the Ohio SWOC was a comparative lack of political protection relative to the rest of the Industrial Heartland. Keystone State Democrats had enacted a labor and social welfare program known as "Pennsylvania's Little New Deal." Senator Robert Wagner of New York authored the New Deal's legacy labor and welfare programs. The Chicago political machine reliably delivered Illinois electoral votes to Roosevelt. In Michigan, Democratic governor Frank Murphy (1890–1949), who, like Murray, embraced the papal encyclicals on social justice, sided with the UAW in the 1936–37 GM strike. Murphy mobilized the Michigan National Guard in early 1937, placing his troops between strikers and hostile local law enforcement. Unable to battle the UAW in the streets, GM capitulated to the CIO.

Although Ohio had a Democratic governor, Martin Davey (1884–1946), who had been elected in 1934 (and reelected in the 1936 Roosevelt landslide), he did not resemble his Industrial Heartland counterparts. A small businessman from Kent, Davey was a conservative Protestant Democrat. He had once staged a boisterous press conference at which he threatened to arrest Roosevelt's relief program director for corruption. Davey warned against encroaching federal power and regarded labor unions as communist.

Davey was the product of an Ohio Democratic Party that had not made the cultural transition from the small town to the big city. The reasons for this were interconnected. Cleveland Democrats, unlike those in Chicago or Pittsburgh, failed to unite their voters beyond the cause of electing Roosevelt. At the city level, Republicans exercised power in the 1930s even as Pittsburgh's Republican officeholders became extinct. Further, Ohio's numerous medium-sized industrial centers did not cohere. Meanwhile, Cincinnati's home county, Hamilton, typically gave Roosevelt tight winning margins—unlike Cleveland's Cuyahoga County, which gave the president lopsided wins.

As Ohio had many medium-sized urban settlements, so too it had a variety of industrial activities and, consequently, a number of different unions. Ohio's SWOC, UAW, United Mine Workers, United Rubber Workers, Teamsters, and American Flint Glass Workers' Union, to list a few, largely operated as independent fiefdoms. There was no great urban political machine on a par with Chicago's to force unions to collaborate, just as no one union dominated the state Democratic Party as was true in Michigan and Pennsylvania. The Ohio Democratic Party leadership understandably believed it could safely ignore or oppose labor unions.

In eastern Ohio's mill towns municipal and county police officers, along with private security in the employ of Republic and Youngstown Sheet & Tube, beat and shot strikers—often without provocation. Businessmen formed "law and order leagues" to identify "professional agitators" to the police. Local law enforcement officers drove by SWOC headquarters in Canton and Massillon, opening fire. Subsequently, three SWOC supporters died in Massillon and one in Canton. In Niles and Warren, Republic Steel security men and SWOC organizers took to small aircraft, firing shotguns and pistols at each other and at people on the ground.[25]

Youngstown's *Democratic* mayor urged Davey to deploy the Ohio National Guard to break up picket lines. Citing the violence that he blamed on SWOC and communist agitators, Davey agreed to use the Ohio National Guard to end the strike. The guard brandished rifles in the mill towns to intimidate strikers and assist company agents and local police in the capture of "rioters." To Davey's surprise, his bold action successfully galvanized Ohio's New Deal Democrats to deny him renomination. He would not, however, be counted out for long, and Davey reasserted his control of the party's gubernatorial primary machinery.[26]

The Fallout

A backlash against 1937 labor unrest, along with an economic downturn which reversed most of the New Deal's employment gains, boosted the morale of conservative Republicans and Democrats. Democratic representative Martin Dies of Texas, a fierce foe of unions, established the House Committee on Un-American Activities in 1938. Dies held one-sided hearings in Michigan and Washington, DC, arguing that the CIO was a violent communist enterprise. Gus Hall's activities in Ohio a year earlier took the media's center stage once again. At the same time, tens of thousands of working-class Catholics, many of them thrown out of work in the automobile and steel industries, suspected that Dies might have a point. Many decided not to vote in the 1938 midterm elections. Conversely, anti-CIO small-town white Protestants were fully mobilized for the elections.[27]

Nationally, Republicans wrested seventy-two seats from Democrats in the US House and gained eight in the Senate. The contours of the 1938 midterm elections showed a disproportionate Democratic loss in the Industrial Heartland. Of the Democrats' loses in the House, 35 percent came from just Ohio and Pennsylvania, where a depressed Catholic turnout and a mobilized Protestant electorate benefitted Republicans. Both states' congressional delegations flipped from Democratic to Republican, with Ohio claiming a decisive Republican majority. Michigan went from a nearly evenly split congressional delegation to being Republican dominated. In contrast, House Democrats in Illinois and New York retained clear majorities.

Republican gubernatorial candidates defeated Democrats across the Industrial Heartland. (Illinois did not have a gubernatorial election and the Democratic incumbent in New York won a close election.) The loss of the governorships in Michigan, Ohio, and Pennsylvania alarmed the Roosevelt White House. As was true for both major parties, presidential candidates often came from gubernatorial ranks—as did New York's Roosevelt. Moreover, a gubernatorial ally could greatly assist a presidential candidate in winning a state's electoral votes. In 1938, the Democrats' presidential bench evaporated, along with the political influence to lock in a victory in the 1940 presidential election. That was a major problem since few pundits expected Roosevelt to run for an unprecedented third term.

Ohio's gubernatorial and US Senate elections caused great consternation in national CIO and Democratic Party ranks. Big-city Democrats may have been able to prevent Governor Davey from winning the party primary, but it was a hollow victory. An anti-CIO Democratic gubernatorial candidate was better positioned to win the general election than a pro-CIO Democrat. The victorious Republican gubernatorial candidate, Ohio attorney general John Bricker, touted his credentials as a champion of law and order in the battle against purported CIO thuggery and federal political corruption.

The Senate election in Ohio had national political consequences—more so than any other contest in the Industrial Heartland or the country at large. In 1938, Robert A. Taft (1889–1953) defeated the Democratic incumbent. A scion of a Cincinnati Republican political dynasty (his father was President William H. Taft), Robert Taft ran a shrewd campaign.

Although his natural constituency was small-town white Protestants, Taft saw an opening to Black Protestants who had overwhelmingly switched to the Democrats in the 1936 presidential election. Taft and his allies addressed Black audiences and leaders, insisting that the 1937 strike had shown that the CIO's supporters were racists. The strategy paid off, leading Taft to launch a career as the most conservative, anti-New Deal member of Congress. He also emerged as a national Republican leader. There were no Republican senators elsewhere in the Industrial Heartland who possessed Taft's national profile as a conservative leader.[28]

At least one urban Ohio Democrat learned a lesson from the 1937–38 unrest and backlash: Frank Lausche (1895–1990). The son of Slovenian immigrants, Lausche obtained a law degree and won Cleveland's mayoral election during World War II. As a mayoral candidate, and then as the Democratic gubernatorial nominee in 1944, when Bricker set his sights on a Senate seat, Lausche castigated greedy government workers and expressed his independence from labor unions and the Ohio Democratic Party. Working-class eastern European Catholics regarded Lausche as one of their own, while white Protestants viewed him as a friend inside, yet apart from, the enemy camp.[29]

The rise of the Lausche cult of personality was not the only development during World War II that shaped Ohio politics. Half of the postwar southern Black migration to the North went largely to Illinois, Michigan, and

Ohio. Indeed, tens of thousands of southern African Americans moved into Ohio during and immediately after World War II in search of industrial jobs. Their numbers were sufficient in Cleveland to influence Ohio's presidential choice in a close election. Similar developments occurred in Illinois, Michigan, Pennsylvania, and New York. Given this new reality, Democratic president Harry Truman embraced civil rights, in the hope of appealing to northern Blacks while not alienating southern whites.[30]

There was, however, another southern migration—which received less media attention and understanding. Enormous numbers of southern whites moved to the North between 1940 and 1970, some going on to Detroit and 950,000 settling in Ohio. (Of Appalachian whites who moved to the North came, 70 percent from Ohio's neighbors Kentucky and West Virginia.) No other Industrial Heartland state received such an influx of white southerners. Indeed, so many southern whites relocated to Ohio that by the 1950s the fastest growing religious denomination in the Buckeye State was the economically and socially conservative Southern Baptist Church.[31]

If these impoverished southern whites had voted Democratic in their homeland (as long as they had paid their poll taxes), their political leanings in Ohio increasingly favored Republicans. The new southern white migrants, like the majority of Ohio's white Protestants, had little use for Blacks, Catholics, and unions. Their growing numbers further pulled Ohio from the voting patterns of comparable urban-industrial states.

Ten years after the Little Steel Strike, Senator Taft scored his payback. In the 1946 midterm elections, Republicans took control of Congress for the first time since 1932. Their numbers, and support from southern Democrats, were sufficient to override presidential vetoes. Senator Taft drafted what became known as the Taft-Hartley Act. The legislation, which survived Truman's veto, allowed employers to oppose union drives with speakers and literature, prohibit the CIO from directly giving money to political candidates, and compelled labor leaders to sign an affidavit that they were not communists. Moreover, the federal government could force unions to call off a strike and return to the negotiating table. Critics aptly described Taft-Hartley as the most anti-union legislation enacted after World War II. It was almost inconceivable that a senator from any other industrial state would have authored such legislation.[32]

Meanwhile in Pittsburgh, machine leader and mayor David Lawrence joined forces with Richard King Mellon to revitalize the region and clean up its industrial waste. Mellon owned, among other enterprises, Gulf Oil and ALCOA. This cooperation soon extended to the political and labor arenas. Unlike such giants in other industrial cities, notably Cleveland and Buffalo, the Mellon family remained in its hometown and worked to bring about what became known as the Pittsburgh Renaissance. If improving their home meant accommodating the heirs of the New Deal, so be it; this attitude dumbfounded conservative Republicans and was largely alien to Ohio's political culture.

It was telling that while Ohio's Taft drove what he hoped would be the final nail in the New Deal's coffin, a vastly different kind of Republican rose to power elsewhere in the region. Like President Dwight Eisenhower, such Republicans made peace with the Roosevelt legacy. They also championed civil rights. Governors George Romney of Michigan, Nelson Rockefeller of New York, and William Scranton of Pennsylvania embodied what Eisenhower called Modern Republicanism. Each, in turn, was a credible candidate for president. Meanwhile in Illinois, Charles Percy, an Eisenhower disciple, rose through Republican ranks to win a US Senate seat and become an important player in Congress.

Ohio's political culture did not tend to produce influential Modern Republicans. As for reconciling with the New Deal, it was anathema to the party's leadership. Of course, many Ohio Democratic figures placed distance between themselves and labor unions. They billed themselves as independent Democrats; less often they claimed the label New Deal Democrat. Given how Ohio's elections frequently shook out, and possessing a fractured political landscape, both parties pursued strategies that would have likely not worked in other industrial states. Whether in 1937, or years after, Ohio went its own way.

So, Ohio Is What?

Ohio's demography and economy in the 1930s seemed to make it an important part of the New Deal's Industrial Heartland electoral bloc. The reality, though, was more complicated. Organized labor struggled and fractured in Ohio even as it gained power in Illinois, Michigan, New York, and Pennsylvania.

Eastern Ohio's steel region most closely resembled western Pennsylvania's, creating something that looked like a coherent borderland. However, even if eastern Ohio Democrats had a cultural kinship with Pittsburgh's political, religious, and labor leaders, it mattered relatively little. State political boundaries placed the Buckeye steel belt outside the authority of its natural western Pennsylvania allies. Moreover, the rest of Ohio did not share Pittsburgh's political culture. Ohio and Pennsylvania claimed variants of what might be considered the Midwest or the Industrial Heartland but did not have a common political culture.

Illinois and Michigan resembled Ohio with its big cities and small towns, Protestant farmers, and Catholic industrial workers. All three states also had their racial tensions. At the same time, before, during, and after the Little Steel Strike, Ohio responded very differently to unions and Democratic political machines than was the case with Illinois and Michigan. If we were to incorporate the New Deal and CIO bastions of Minnesota and Wisconsin into Morgan and England's Midwest Industrial framework, Ohio's political culture would appear even more atypical of the region. Clearly, the state often failed to act politically in concert with Lauck's conceptional Midwest.[33]

Given the consistent and large migration of white Protestants from the Upper South over a great portion of the nineteenth and twentieth centuries, a case could be made that Ohio is "Dixie North." Ohio's white Protestant Democrats, like white Protestant Republicans, largely opposed the CIO, disliked Blacks and Catholics, and were increasingly leery of Roosevelt. By the late 1930s, southern white Protestants, like their Ohio counterparts, also rejected the CIO and expressed displeasure with Roosevelt. Most southern white Protestants, however, would not consider voting Republican until the 1970s. Moreover, the actual, as opposed to fanciful, Dixie of the New Deal era had little in the way of major urban-industrial centers and union-joining descendants of eastern European immigrants. Ohio, then, is not "southern," though it has frequently acted as if it were.

If Ohio is not comfortably southern, Midwest, Midwest Industrial, or Industrial Heartland, then what is it? Perhaps Ohio is an amalgamation of the four regions. That would mean it has all of these regional constructions and, in its sum, none of them. Ohio is its own entity, set apart from its neighbors and possessing a singular and chaotic political culture. Conflict and violence were ever present in a political and social environment that spawned personality cults, hardline Republicans, and dysfunctional Democrats. The 1937 Little Steel Strike and its aftermath revealed all these characteristics.

Ohio's chaotic political culture as it evolved in the 1930s had enduring electoral consequences far beyond its borders. Neither national Democrats nor Republicans could depend on receiving Ohio's electoral votes. Both parties had to compete fiercely, hoping to mobilize sympathetic slices of the electorate without provoking other slices to mobilize against them. This was a difficult, frustrating, and often financially draining challenge, but in close elections the path to the White House ran through Ohio—whether in the New Deal era or in the twenty-first century.

Notes

1. Jon K. Lauck, *The Lost Region: Toward a Revival of Midwestern History* (Iowa City: Univ. of Iowa Press, 2013), 23, 39.

2. Howard Gillette Jr., "Defining a Mid-Atlantic Region," *Pennsylvania History* 82 (Summer 2015): 373–80.

3. David R. Morgan and Robert E. England, "Classifying the American States: An Update," *Social Science Quarterly* 68 (June 1987): 405–17.

4. Robert H. Zieger, *The CIO: 1935–1955* (Chapel Hill: Univ. of North Carolina Press, 1995), 60.

5. Kenneth J. Heineman, "Catholics, Communists, and Conservatives: The Making of Cold War Democrats on the Pittsburgh Front," *U.S. Catholic Historian* 34 (Fall 2016): 25–54; Fay Calkins, *The CIO and the Democratic Party* (Chicago: Univ. of Chicago Press, 1952), 137.

6. Kristi Anderson, *The Creation of a Democratic Majority, 1928–1936* (Chicago: Univ. of Chicago Press, 1979), 29–34, 41–42.

7. Steven P. Erie, *Rainbow's End: Irish-Americans and the Dilemmas of Urban Machine Politics, 1840–1985* (Berkeley: Univ. of California Press, 1988), 99–100, 114, 119, 137.

8. Kenneth J. Heineman, *A Catholic New Deal: Religion and Reform in Depression Pittsburgh* (University Park: Pennsylvania State Univ. Press, 1999), 121; Kenneth J. Heineman, "Iron City Trinity: The Triumph and the Trials of Catholic Social Activism in Pittsburgh, 1932–1972," *U.S. Catholic Historian* 22 (Spring 2004): 121–45.

9. Heineman, *Catholic New Deal*, 104–6; Heineman, "Iron City Trinity," 121–45.

10. Erie, *Rainbow's End*, 137.

11. The most recent scholarly account of the Little Steel Strike is Ahmed White's *The Last Great Strike: Little Steel, the CIO, and the Struggle for Labor Rights in New Deal America* (Berkeley: Univ. of California Press, 2016).

12. George W. Knepper, *Ohio and Its People* (Kent: Kent State Univ. Press, 1989), 375–76.

13. Hadley Cantril, "Educational and Economic Composition of Religious Groups: An Analysis of Poll Data," *American Journal of Sociology* 48 (Mar. 1943): 574–79; John J. Kane, "The Social Structure of American Catholics," *American Catholic Sociological Review* 16 (Mar. 1955): 23–30.

14. Gregory S. Rose, "American-European Immigrant Groups in the Midwest by the Mid-Nineteenth Century, " in *Finding the New Midwestern History*, ed. Jon K. Lauck, Gleaves Whitney, and Joseph Hogan (Lincoln: Univ. of Nebraska Press, 2018), 73–95. See also Christine Dee, ed., *Ohio's War: The Civil War in Documents* (Athens: Ohio Univ. Press, 2006), and Kenneth J. Heineman, *Civil War Dynasty: The Ewing Family of Ohio* (New York: New York Univ. Press, 2012).

15. Anderson, *Creation of a Democratic Majority*, 30, 41–42; Liston Pope, "Religion and the Class Structure," *Annals of the American Academy of Political and Social Science* 256 (Mar. 1948): 84–95.

16. Jon C. Teaford, *Cities of the Heartland: The Rise and Fall of the Industrial Midwest* (Bloomington: Indiana Univ. Press, 1994), 108; Phillip J. Obermiller and Robert Olendick, "Political Activity among Appalachian Migrants," *Social Science Quarterly* 65 (Dec. 1984): 1058–64.

17. Heineman, *Catholic New Deal*, 124–27.

18. Heineman, *Catholic New Deal*, 124–27.

19. Heineman, *Catholic New Deal*, 135–36.

20. Paul Lubienecki, "From Parish Hall to the Union Hall: Catholic Labor Education in Cleveland," *Ohio History* 124 (2017): 49–84.

21. Patrick McNamara, *A Catholic Cold War: Edmund Walsh, S.J., and the Politics of American Anticommunism* (New York: Fordham Univ. Press, 2005), xviii, 108; Len DeCaux, *Labor Radical: From the Wobblies to the CIO* (Boston: Beacon Press, 1970), 115.

22. Heineman, "Catholics, Communists, and Conservatives," 25–54.

23. "Hunt CIO Leader as Bombing Chief," *New York Times*, June 30, 1937.

24. "CIO Aide Surrenders," *New York Times*, July 2, 1937; "200 Men Indicted at Youngstown," *New York Times*, July 7, 1937.

25. Zieger, *CIO*, 61–63; Heineman, *Catholic New Deal*, 124–25.

26. Donald Gene Sofchalk, "The Little Steel Strike of 1937" (PhD diss., Ohio State Univ., 1961).

27. "Testify Reds Led Ohio Steel Strike," *New York Times*, Nov. 5, 1938; Heineman, "Catholics, Communists, and Conservatives," 25–54; Michael Barone, *Our Country: The Shaping of America from Roosevelt to Reagan* (New York: Free Press, 1990), 115; M. Stephen Weatherford and Boris Sergeyev, "Thinking about Economic Interests: Class and Recession in the New Deal," *Political Behavior* 22 (Dec. 2000):

311–39; Milton Plesur, "The Republican Congressional Comeback of 1938," *Review of Politics* 24 (Oct. 1962): 655–62.

28. Charles R. Michael, "Ohio Republicans in Close Contest," *New York Times*, July 17, 1938; Clarence E. Wunderlein Jr., "Text and Context in Ohio's 1938 Senate Campaign: Race, Republican Party Ideology, and Robert A. Taft's Firestone Memorial Oration," *Northeast Ohio Journal of History* 6 (2010), https://blogs.uakron.edu/nojh/2010/04/22/text-and-context/.

29. Frederick S. Tisdale, "Strong Man of Columbus," *Saturday Evening Post*, July 7, 1945, 17, 90, 92. The definitive biography of Frank Lausche is James E. Odenkirk, *Frank J. Lausche: Ohio's Great Political Maverick* (Wilmington, OH: Orange Frazer Books, 2005).

30. Jeffrey Helgeson, "Politics in the Promised Land: How the Great Migration Shaped the American Midwest," in Lauck, Whitney, and Hogan, *Finding the New Midwestern History*, 111–26.

31. See Kevin F. Kern and Gregory S. Wilson, *Ohio: A History of the Buckeye State* (Hoboken, NJ: John Wiley & Sons, 2013); J. Trent Alexander, "Defining the Diaspora: Appalachians in the Great Migration," *Journal of Interdisciplinary History* 37 (Aug. 2006): 219–47.

32. Richard C. Cornter, "Liberals, Conservatives, and Labor," *Annals of the American Academy of Political and Social Sciences* 344 (Nov. 1962): 44–54.

33. Morgan and England, "Classifying the American States," 405–17.

Chapter 14

The Divided Battleground

Presidential Voting in Ohio and the Midwest in the Twenty-First Century

A. LEE HANNAH AND CHRISTOPHER J. DEVINE

The Midwest has been the principal battleground in American electoral politics for more than a century. Here, more than any other region in the United States, is where presidential candidates are born and raised, political parties hold their national conventions, and presidential campaigns schedule rallies. At the heart of it all—as Buckeyes proudly describe their home—is Ohio, the nation's quintessential battleground state. Indeed, from 1980 to 2016, media coverage described Ohio more often than any other state as a presidential battleground in eight out of ten elections, and from 1988 to 2016, Ohio hosted more presidential campaign visits than any other state twice while in all but one year ranking among the top three most-visited states.[1] Ohio, therefore, may be fairly described as the linchpin of the midwestern battleground. But this raises the question: politically speaking, is Ohio—or, to put a finer point on it, *all of Ohio*—truly part of the Midwest? That is to say, does the midwestern battleground begin at Ohio's eastern and southern borders—and if not there, then where, exactly?

This chapter complements others in the present volume that examine where the Midwest begins, in general, and within Ohio, specifically. Ours is distinctive because it focuses on electoral politics. In particular, we examine voting patterns in recent presidential elections. Drawing on previous work, we divide Ohio into six regions—or, the "Six Ohios"—to evaluate partisan voting patterns in twenty-first-century presidential elections and compare these results to the Midwest as a whole. In short, our objective is to determine which parts of Ohio have voted in accordance with the Midwest, in such a way as to warrant their inclusion in that region, politically speaking.

Our results indicate that regional political alignments within Ohio have shifted in recent elections, particularly in response to the presidential candidacies of Donald Trump. Prior to Trump, the most midwestern regions of Ohio—in terms of their presidential voting patterns—were in the Southeast (i.e., Appalachia) and Northwest (i.e., Toledo). With Trump on the ballot, both regions (particularly, the latter) diverged, in the Republicans' direction. At the same time, Northeast Ohio (i.e., Cleveland) and Central Ohio (i.e., Columbus)—which had previously skewed in favor of Democrats and Republicans, respectively—became most closely aligned with the Midwest as a whole. Only Central Ohio has consistently voted with the Midwest since 2000.

Simply put, when it comes to presidential voting, we cannot draw the Midwest's border at the Ohio River—nor can we locate it along any single line within Ohio. The midwestern border instead seems to be something of a moving target when it comes to politics. Trump's candidacy has spun Ohio's midwestern border on its axis, from a Northwest–Southeast orientation to Northeast–Central. This shift is hardly random. Rather, our analysis indicates that Trump's appeal within Ohio—relative to the Midwest as a whole—has been concentrated in more rural, white, and evangelical, as well as less-educated, counties. Trump's populism, we conclude, has redefined Ohio's relationship to the broader Midwest; rural Ohio has become a Republican outlier, while suburban Ohio has become essentially midwestern.

Ohio as Battleground *and* Bellwether

For many years, Ohio has been the quintessential battleground *and* bellwether state. To be clear, there is a difference. To say that Ohio is a *battleground* is to say that it is electorally competitive; in other words, the state typically could be won by either party's presidential candidate in a given election. Indeed, as noted, Ohio has been more likely than any other state to be treated by the news media and presidential candidates as a battleground in recent elections. But in a landslide election, a competitive state may not represent the nation as a whole; rather, that it remains competitive might suggest that it skews toward supporting the losing candidate's party. To say that Ohio is a *bellwether* is to say that it tracks closely with the national popular vote. Thus, in a close election Ohio will be competitive, while in a lopsided election it will favor the winning candidate by about as much as he or she wins the vote nationwide.

Fig. 14.1 shows that the Midwest in general and Ohio in particular are electoral bellwethers. That is to say, presidential voting in the Midwest has closely matched the national popular vote over time, as has voting in Ohio. Indeed, from 1964 to 2012, two-party vote share in the Midwest as well as Ohio differed from the United States as a whole by no more than about two percentage points in each election. Winning Ohio typically meant winning the Midwest, and winning the Midwest typically meant winning nationally. Such a track record is truly exceptional; from 1896 to 2012, Kondik finds, Ohio's average deviation from the national popular vote (2.2 percentage points) was smaller than for any other state, and

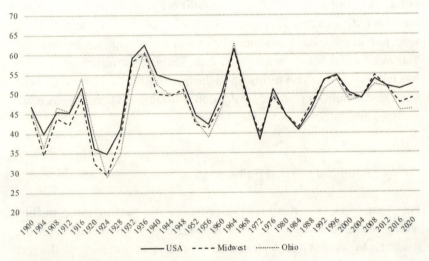

Fig. 14.1. Democratic presidential vote share, 1900–2020.

from 1964 to 2012, it deviated by no more than two percentage points in each election, while always voting for the winning candidate.[2]

But these patterns began to change in 2016. With Donald Trump on the ballot, the Midwest voted more Republican than the United States did, by 3.41 percentage points, as did Ohio, by 5.37. In 2020, with Trump running for reelection, the gap remained about the same in the Midwest (3.36 percentage points) but widened in Ohio (6.34). These results, therefore, cast doubt on the Midwest's enduring status as an electoral bellwether, and all the more so for Ohio.[3] For that matter, they cast doubt on Ohio's status as a *midwestern* bellwether.

However, Ohio is not monolithic; in recent elections some parts of the state have shifted further toward the Republican Party and away from the Midwest. For instance, Trump seems to have won over many voters to the Republican Party in rural Appalachian Ohio while alienating many previously Republican voters in the Columbus suburbs. We must ask, then: how have voting patterns changed within Ohio, particularly in relation to the Midwest, over recent elections? And how should this evidence influence our determination of where the Midwest begins within the Buckeye State? But first: where might we draw the potential border lines within Ohio?

The Six Ohios

Political analysts and scholars often divide Ohio into five or six regions. The authors of *Buckeye Battleground*, for instance, analyze political attitudes and behaviors across the "Five Ohios."[4] Each region, they argue, is distinguished by demographic commonalities and a unique sense of identity—respectively, providing "compositional" and "contextual" explanations for differences in political attitudes and voting behavior across the regions. Each region also includes a relatively large population center. The Five Ohios are designated as Northeast (including Cleveland), Northwest (Toledo), Central (Columbus), Southwest (Cincinnati), and Southeast (Zanesville).

The "Six Ohios" model, depicted in Fig. 14.2, is more commonly used. To the five regions identified above, it adds West Ohio (including Dayton). Former *Columbus Dispatch* editor and state legislator Mike Curtin, creator of the "Six Ohios" model, organized the regions according to media markets.

Fig. 14.2. The Six Ohios.

He notes, "Any attempt to divide Ohio into political regions requires some subjective judgments as to which region should get certain counties."[5] Indeed, while both models identify a Cleveland-based "Northeast" region, in the "Five Ohios" it includes twelve counties, versus twenty in the "Six Ohios." Meanwhile, Southeast Ohio includes twenty-seven counties, versus seventeen in the "Six Ohios." We agree with Kondik: "Whether one prefers to use five or six regions to divide the state, both methods do a good job of explaining the state's different areas."[6] To streamline the present analysis, however, we must choose one or the other. In this chapter, we use the "Six Ohios" model. This is more appropriate for an analysis of presidential voting patterns, we believe, because presidential campaigns typically allocate strategic resources intended to influence voting behavior, including candidate visits and television advertisements, based on media market designations.[7]

The Six Ohio regions are unique, demographically and politically. They also vary in size, with the Northeast comprising nearly 40 percent of the state's total votes, albeit decreasing from 39.6 percent in the Bush elections (2000 and 2004) to 37.6 percent in the Trump elections (2016 and 2020). Central Ohio has grown the fastest, comprising 17.5 percent of the total votes in the former time period versus 20.3 percent in the latter. The Southwest is the next largest region, consistently contributing 15 percent of the state's total vote. In twenty-first-century elections, the West has made up about 12 percent, the Northwest about 9 percent, and the Southeast just 6 percent.

How do the Six Ohios vote—and how has this changed over time? Fig. 14.3 shows the two-party vote share (i.e., percentage of votes cast for the Democrat or Republican, excluding all other candidates) won by the Democratic presidential candidate in each region from 2000 to 2020. To simplify such comparisons, here and throughout this chapter we analyze the vote in three different sets of elections, defined by the initial winner who then ran for reelection: George W. Bush (2000 and 2004), Barack Obama (2008 and 2012), and Donald Trump (2016 and 2020).[8] Subsequently, we refer to these as the Bush, Obama, and Trump elections. In each case, we average Democratic two-party vote share across the two elections.[9] Because the Six Ohios—like Ohio, as a whole—are not monoliths, Fig. 14.4 also depicts Democratic two-party vote share in the same elections at the county level. This enables us to provide a more nuanced analysis of the voting patterns underlying changes within Ohio's regions.

Fig. 14.3 shows that the Northeast, anchored by Cuyahoga County (Cleveland), has been the most Democratic region of Ohio—albeit less so in the two most recent elections, which had Donald Trump on the ballot. Indeed, in 2016 and 2020, the average Democratic two-party vote share dropped to about 50 percent in Northeast Ohio, putting it in a tie with increasingly Democratic Central Ohio. While Cuyahoga is known as the Democratic stronghold of the Northeast, Democrats could expect similar margins in the Mahoning Valley (Mahoning and Trumbull Counties) in the Bush elections. There, Democrats typically earned about two-thirds of the vote (see Fig. 14.4). In 2016, Mahoning and Trumbull counties swung thirteen and fifteen points respectively toward Republicans. Cuyahoga has remained deep "blue" (pro-Democratic), but the working-class counties in the region have all been turning "red" (Republican).

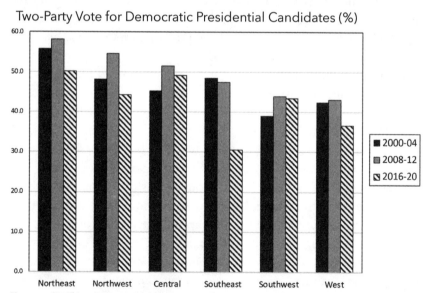

Fig. 14.3. Six Ohios: Democratic vote, 2000–2020.

Northwest Ohio slightly favored Republicans in the Bush elections, then voted for Democrats by nine-point margins in the Obama elections, only to swing back to Republicans by ten-point margins in the Trump elections. Much like Northeast Ohio, Lucas County (Toledo) has consistently voted for Democratic presidential candidates by twenty-point margins, but each of the neighboring counties moved toward the Republican Party, by seven to fifteen percentage points, during the Trump elections.

Central Ohio, once a Republican stronghold, has been competitive over the last six elections. Much of this dynamic is driven by Franklin County (Columbus), which surpassed Cuyahoga as the most populous county in the Buckeye State in 2017 and accounts for a majority of the total votes in the region.[10] Franklin and its neighboring high-growth counties look more like the nation's Sun Belt than any other Ohio region; politically, its younger and more college-educated residents are pushing the area in the opposite direction of statewide trends. Franklin is the only county in which the Democratic presidential candidate performed better in each successive election represented in Fig. 14.4, from winning a bare majority in the Bush elections (52 percent) to decisive victories in the Obama (61 percent) and Trump (65 percent) elections. This trend, combined with increased Democratic voting in Franklin's neighboring suburban counties, has transformed Central Ohio from a competitive but Republican-leaning region to a competitive but Democratic-leaning one. Fast-growing Delaware County, directly north of Franklin, exemplifies this shift. Its share of the statewide vote has increased from 7.5 percent in the Bush elections to 8.9 percent in the Obama elections and 9.9 percent in the Trump elections. At the same time, its support for Republican presidential candidates has steadily dropped, from 67 percent (Bush) to 61 (McCain, Romney) to 56 (Trump).

The starkest changes, in terms of party voting, have occurred in Southeast Ohio. From 2000 to 2012, this Appalachian region was consistently the most competitive of the Six Ohios. Bush carried thirteen of Southeast Ohio's seventeen counties in 2000 and 2004, but Gore and Kerry still averaged 48 percent of the vote. Similarly, Obama captured 48 percent of the region's votes while winning four counties in 2008 and 47 percent in 2012 even though Romney flipped Jefferson and Monroe Counties. But with Donald Trump on the ballot, Democratic support in Southeast Ohio cratered. Between 2000 and 2012, no Democrat had earned less than 36 percent of

Average Democratic Presidential Vote by County, 2000-2004

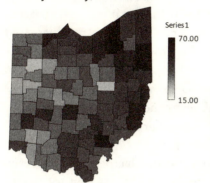

Average Democratic Presidential Vote by County, 2008-2012

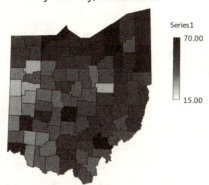

Average Democratic Presidential Vote by County, 2016-2020

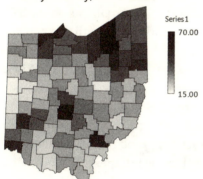

Fig. 14.4. Democratic presidential vote share (two-party) in Ohio's counties, 2000-2020.

the vote in any county within this region. In 2016 and 2020, the Democratic candidates won less than 36 percent of the vote in *sixteen of seventeen* counties there.[11] While Southeast Ohio represents only 5 percent of the state's population, its rapid move toward the Republican Party combined with a shrinking and slightly more Republican population in the Northeast has contributed to Ohio losing its bellwether status over the past decade.

Southwest Ohio has trended similarly to Central Ohio, but from a starting point that was more favorable to Republicans. Just as Democrats have relied on piling up victory margins in Northeast Ohio, Republicans have viewed Hamilton County (Cincinnati) as critical to their electoral fate. For example, in 2016, Republican strategists openly questioned the Trump campaign's lack of effort in Hamilton County and argued the state was unwinnable for Republicans without Hamilton.[12] Over the last six elections, Hamilton has become more Democratic; after Bush carried 54 percent of the vote in that county, Obama flipped it with a 53 percent victory, and with Trump running in 2016 and 2020, Democrats increased their advantage to 56 percent. While the rural counties such as Adams and Highland became about 15 percentage points more Republican in the Trump elections, the suburban-ring counties (Butler and Warren) have consistently voted for the Republican candidates with at least 60 or 65 percent of the vote, respectively. Unlike other suburban counties, they barely budged during the Trump elections.

West Ohio is a Republican-leaning region that has been trending even more Republican in recent elections. In the twenty-first century, Democrats have captured only one West Ohio county: Montgomery (including Dayton). They did so by a narrow margin in the Bush elections (50.5 percent, on average) and a bit more comfortably with Obama on the ballot (52.7 percent). Donald Trump won the county in 2016 with 50.4 percent of the vote. In 2020, Montgomery was one of about sixty counties nationwide that Biden flipped back to the Democrats, with 51.1 percent.[13] While Montgomery has remained competitive across these elections, surrounding rural counties have become much more Republican. Clark County (Springfield), also known as one of Ohio's bellwethers, had been decided by no more than 2.1 percentage points between 2000 and 2012. But in 2016 and 2020, Trump carried it by more than twenty percentage points. Meanwhile, the rural counties have voted much like heavily Republican Southeast Ohio.

Where in Ohio Does the Midwest Begin?

Fig. 14.5 provides the most direct evidence for categorizing the Six Ohios as "midwestern" (or not) based on presidential election results. It shows the difference in voting between the Midwest as a whole (minus Ohio) and each of the Six Ohio regions, across the Bush, Obama, and Trump elections.[14] That is to say, it shows how much better or worse Democrats performed in the Six Ohios, relative to the entire Midwest, in a given set of elections. If, for example, at one point Democrats won 51 percent of the two-party vote in the Midwest *and* in Northeast Ohio, the difference pre-

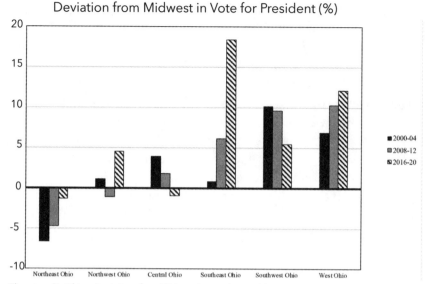

Fig. 14.5. Six Ohios: Deviations from Midwest in vote for president, 2000–2020.

sented in Fig. 14.5 would be zero. This would clearly suggest that Northeast Ohio is midwestern in its voting behavior. If, however, Northeast Ohio deviated by 10 percentage points, with Democrats winning 61 percent of the vote in a given set of elections, we would have reason to question whether this part of Ohio belongs to the Midwest, politically speaking.

Where, then, does the Midwest begin in Ohio? Judging by the evidence presented in Fig. 14.5, the border has shifted over recent elections. First, in the Bush elections of 2000 and 2004, only Northwest and Southeast Ohio closely matched voting patterns within the broader Midwest—with both being slightly more favorable to Republicans, by 1.1 and 1.2 percentage points. Central Ohio also voted similarly to the Midwest, favoring Republicans by an additional 4 percentage points. The other regions diverged by quite a bit more, favoring Democrats in the Northeast (6.6 percentage points) and Republicans in the West (6.9 percentage points) and Southwest (10.1 percentage points). Only the latter deviated by more than 10 percentage points. Perhaps this is a fair cutoff for drawing the region outside of the Midwest. Or perhaps 5 percentage points is enough—thereby excluding Northeast and West Ohio, too. Frankly, there are no precise answers to be had here. Suffice it to say that at the beginning of the twenty-first century

Northwest and Southeast Ohio clearly voted as if they were part of the Midwest, while Southwest Ohio was the most divergent.

Barack Obama's elections, in 2008 and 2012, seem to mark a transition point in Ohio's relation to the Midwest. We see some evidence of stability, with Northwest Ohio again closely matching the Midwest but now slightly favoring the Democratic ticket, by 1.1 percentage points. Central Ohio also remained something of a bellwether, now favoring Republicans by only 1.7 percentage points more than the Midwest as a whole. But, as indicated above, Southeast Ohio began to diverge from past voting patterns at this point, now favoring Republicans by a much greater margin than the rest of the Midwest (5.9 percentage points). At the same time, West Ohio's divergence from the Midwest now slightly exceeded Southwest Ohio's, both favoring Republicans by about an additional ten percentage points. Northeast Ohio voted a bit more similarly to the Midwest in these elections than before, with a pro-Democratic deviation of 4.7 percentage points. In short, in 2008 and 2012, Northwest and Central Ohio were most clearly midwestern in their voting, Northeast and Southeast Ohio less so, and Southwest and West Ohio least of all.

With Trump's elections, Ohio's midwestern border seemed to spin on its axis. Whereas Southeast Ohio had been one of the two regions most clearly aligned with midwestern voting patterns during the Bush years, now it diverged sharply (in the Republicans' direction), by nearly 20 percentage points. Northwest Ohio, the other most midwestern region from that period (as well as in the Obama years), also started to diverge, but only by 4.5 percentage points. Southwest Ohio's deviation, by a similar margin, of 5.4 percentage points, brought it into closer alignment with the Midwest than in previous elections. West Ohio moved in the opposite direction, away from the Midwest, as it supported Republicans by an even greater margin, of 12.1 percentage points. Only two regions voted quite similarly to the Midwest as a whole. Central Ohio remained a regional bellwether, deviating only slightly from the Midwest and now in favor of Democrats. by 1.3 percentage points. Northeast Ohio, in contrast, supported Democrats by quite a bit less than in previous elections. But in doing so, it began to closely mirror the Midwest, deviating by only 1.3 percentage points.

If one were to draw the Midwest's border within Ohio based on presidential election results, then, clearly it would have to include the Northeast and Central regions. Northwest and Southwest Ohio probably belong there, as well. West Ohio's inclusion is less certain, given that it has come to deviate from midwestern voting patterns by more than ten percentage points. Most clearly falling outside of midwestern political boundaries is Southeast Ohio—until recently, a bellwether for the Midwest, and now, in the Donald Trump era, so heavily Republican that it is anything but. Rather, Southeast Ohio has much more in common with Appalachian states, such as West Virginia and Kentucky, that have been attracted to Trump's populism. Whether this means Southeast Ohio belongs to the US South, politically speaking, as do those states, or to a subregion such as Appalachia or even the Deep South would require analysis outside the scope of this work.[15] Here, we can only conclude that the Midwest—wherever it begins in Ohio, exactly—does not include Southeast Ohio.

Why Have Some Parts of Ohio Moved Away from the Midwest?

We conclude our analysis by addressing a separate but related question: what explains the correspondence, or lack thereof, between voting behavior in Ohio and the broader Midwest? That is to say, why have some parts of Ohio become more or less politically midwestern than others over time? In pursuing this line of inquiry, we build on the distinction made by Coffey and his colleagues between the role of compositional and contextual factors in explaining voting behavior within Ohio. Compositional factors include demographic characteristics—such as race, religion, and education—that are closely linked to voting behavior nationwide. Contextual factors implicate geographic identity or political culture, both of which might moderate or overcome the influence of compositional factors in comparison to the rest of the United States or other regions within a state. Coffey and his colleagues find that compositional variables are quite predictive of voting behavior in Ohio, but their effects vary across regions within the state. They conclude, "The Buckeye State's diverse regions arise in part from demography and in part from geography, and they help explain why the state is a perennial battleground."[16] Given that when these authors conducted their analysis, Ohio was also a bellwether for the Midwest and the United States, the same factors might help to explain why some parts of Ohio have remained or become midwestern bellwethers while others have sharply diverged.

Testing for causal relationships—that is, whether some factors (independent variables) have caused changes in a specified outcome such as presidential voting (a dependent variable)—requires more sophisticated methods of analysis than the descriptive evidence thus far presented. Specifically, in this section we estimate linear regression models based on election results from each of Ohio's eighty-eight counties in the Bush, Obama, and Trump elections. The dependent variable in each model is the difference between Democratic two-party vote share in the Midwest and a given county in the relevant set of elections (i.e., $Democratic\_vote_{Midwest} - Democratic\_vote_{County}$). In other words, we seek to determine the factors that explain why a county voted very similarly to, or differently than, the Midwest. If the dependent variable equals zero, this means that Democrats won the same vote share in the Midwest as in a given county. A negative (positive) value means that Democrats won more votes in the county than in the Midwest as a whole and a positive value indicates that Democrats won fewer votes in the county than in the Midwest (i.e., the county is "more Republican" than the Midwest average).[17]

Linear regression allows us to estimate which factors, or independent variables, were associated with changes in the dependent variable, while statistically controlling for the effects of other variables included in the model. An independent variable's effect is deemed statistically significant if we can estimate with 95 percent confidence that a change in its values was associated with a change in our dependent variable, the gap between midwestern and county-level voting in Ohio. Otherwise, we conclude that the independent variable had no effect, at least in a particular set of elections. Also, linear regression reports the direction of such effects. Thus, we can determine not only whether a given compositional or contextual factor influenced relative vote share in Ohio but also whether it increased or decreased the gap between Midwest and county voting—that is, whether the factor led to more Republican outcomes than the Midwest or more Democratic outcomes.

Table 14.1 reports the results from two linear regression models. The first model (Compositional) controls for demographic and economic factors that might affect presidential vote choice. The second model (Combined) adds the Six Ohios as contextual controls. In cases where the independent variable's effect on the dependent variable is statistically significant, we include a plus (+) or minus (−) sign to indicate whether the direction of that effect was positive or negative. A negative effect means that the variable accounts for the county being more Democratic than the Midwest and a positive effect means that the variable accounts for the county being more Republican than the Midwest. Finally, Table 14.1 reports the Adjusted R-Squared for each model. Adjusted R-Squared is a statistic ranging from 0 to 1 that estimates how well the dependent variable (i.e., Midwest deviation) can be predicted based on all of the independent variables included in a given model, with higher scores indicating greater predictive power.[18] Table 14.1 therefore indicates not only which factors have influenced Ohio's deviation from midwestern voting patterns, and in what direction, but also the comprehensiveness of our empirical models in relation to the outcome that we are trying to predict.

Compositional Models

The Compositional models use variables that are often predictive of electoral outcomes: whether the county is rural, the share of its population that is Black, the share of its population that is Hispanic, the percent of college educated people in the county, the rate of evangelical Christians, and median household income.[19] Again, the model is predicting whether these factors lead counties to *deviate* from the Midwest (and if so, in which direction).

In the 2000 and 2004 elections (column 1), rural counties were more Republican than the Midwest, even after controlling for other factors. Pro-Republican deviations also resulted from counties having wealthier and more evangelical populations. Counties with higher percentages of college-educated residents and Hispanic residents, in contrast, favored Democrats by greater margins than in the broader Midwest. Black population percentages, according to this model, had no independent effect on the dependent variable. Altogether, the model explains about 59 percent of the variance in Midwest deviation. The same is true in the Obama elections (column 3), although rural classification is no longer a significant predictor. The results for 2016 and 2020 (column 5) are similar in terms of significant factors, but, notably, the R-Squared jumps to 0.87, indicating that the variables in our Compositional model, as a whole, explain 87 percent of the variation in Midwest deviations. In short, these are the factors that we think affect deviation from the Midwest in each of these elections, but much more so in the Trump elections-in comparison to the model's performance in the Bush and Obama elections.

Combined Models

The Combined models for the Bush (column 2) and Obama (column 4) elections show that—as Coffey and colleagues' analysis would suggest—both compositional and contextual factors influence voting behavior in Ohio.[20] With respect to the Bush and Obama elections, the effects of several compositional factors remain statistically significant, even when controlling for regional context in the Combined models where the Northwest, Central, Southwest, and West all account for a Republican deviation. The additional regional information increases the R-Squared values in both models by 0.17 and 0.13, respectively. Out of six compositional independent variables, four (Hispanic, college, Evangelical, and household income) have the same effect in terms of statistical significance and direction in each of the models. It is clear from these models what explains Ohio's deviation from midwestern voting patterns: geography, race, education, and religion. Specifically, Ohio counties that are rural and have more white and evangelical residents and fewer college graduates vote for Republicans by a greater margin than in the Midwest generally. To the extent that Ohio's divergence from the Midwest—to say nothing of the nation—along such demographic lines continues into the future, so should its voting patterns. As Ohio's demographics go, one might say, so goes its bellwether status.

But we also see in Table 14.1 that context—that is, which region of Ohio voters live in—matters. Even when controlling for major demographic factors such as race, religion, and education, Ohio's regions are distinctive in their voting behavior. For example, counties in Southwest and West Ohio were significantly more likely to deviate from midwestern voting patterns, in favor of Republicans, in all three sets of elections, independent of the demographic controls. The same can be said for Northwest and Central Ohio in the Bush and Obama elections.

The results presented in Table 14.1, therefore, are remarkably consistent: we see that composition and context influence election results, with

Table 14.1: Predicting Deviations from Midwestern Presidential Voting in Ohio's Counties, 2000-2020

	2000-2004 Compositional (1)	2000-2004 Combined (2)	2008-2012 Compositional (3)	2008-2012 Combined (4)	2016-2020 Compositional (5)	2016-2020 Combined (6)
Rural	+	+		+		+
Percent Black	-	-	-	-	-	-
Percent College Educated	-	-	-	-	-	-
Evangelical	+	+	-	+	+	+
Median HH Income	+	+	+	+	+	
Six Ohios (Ref=Northeast)						
Northwest	NA	+	NA		NA	
Central	NA	+	NA	+	NA	
Southeast	NA		NA	+	NA	+
Southwest	NA	+	NA	+	NA	+
West	NA	+	NA	+	NA	+
Adj. R^2	0.55	0.72	0.53	0.73	0.86	0.89
N	88	88	88	88	88	88

Note: Results are from linear regression models. The dependent variable is calculated as the difference between Democratic two-party vote across two elections (averaged) in the Midwest and a given Ohio county. Statistically significant effects are indicated by the presence of a plus (+) or minus (-) sign, respectively indicating whether the independent variable is associated with an increase or decrease in the dependent variable's values. The absence of a sign indicates that the independent variable's effect is not statistically significant.

many of the same variables predicting Midwest deviations from one election to the next. Also, it is clear that our models, in general, are quite effective at predicting changes in the dependent variable. This is evident in the Adjusted R-Squared statistic, which in the Bush and Obama elections exceeds 0.50 in the Compositional model and then—further demonstrating the empirical value of accounting for regional context—improves considerably to above 0.70 in the Combined models. We do, however, observe an important change in the Trump elections. Compositional factors alone explain 86 percent of the variance in county-level deviation from midwestern voting. This is remarkably high and creates something of a ceiling effect when adding in the contextual (i.e., regional) variables. Indeed, the Combined model's Adjusted R-Squared values increase, but only slightly, to 0.89.

What should we make of this apparent increase in the explanatory power of demographics, and the muting of regional distinctions within Ohio, corresponding to the Trump elections? While we cannot reach definitive conclusions based on only two elections, it must be said that these results are consistent with scholars' observations regarding the increasing nationalization of American politics.[21] That is to say, Americans have become increasingly likely to identify with broad social groups that converge in their support for one political party rather than maintaining more complex social identities whereby, for instance, individuals might be cross-pressured to support one party versus another based on conflicting group loyalties. To the extent that living in a particular geographic region, state, or region within a state (e.g., the Six Ohios) with a clear partisan preference cross-pressures individuals who also identify with demographic groups that support a different party, geographic identities may moderate the effects of compositional factors. But if, as our data suggest, compositional factors are coming to overwhelm the voting decision, it might be the case that regional identities—within Ohio, and perhaps within the Midwest as a whole—are becoming less powerful and at some point could become nearly irrelevant.

To be clear, our data do not yet warrant such a sweeping conclusion. In many cases, however, knowing which region of the state a county is located in still helps to predict election results. But in terms of overall predictive power, this matters much less than in previous elections. We could do nearly as well at predicting how Ohio counties voted relative to the Midwest based on demographic factors, alone—namely rural designation, race, education, religion, and income.

What might account for such a dramatic change in regional influence starting in 2016? Perhaps this is attributable to Trump building a unique identity-based coalition—one that particularly resonated with non-college–educated white voters. Lauck has noted that across the Midwest, Trump outperformed previous Republican presidential candidates in the "outstates."[22] In short, a white person in rural Ohio without a college degree was much more likely to vote for Trump (than say, for Romney, McCain, or Bush), regardless of whether they owned a farm in Darke

County (West Ohio), held down a union railroad job in Ottawa County (Northwest Ohio), or worked on a natural gas well in Belmont County (Southeast Ohio). Whether this dynamic is unique to Trump, and thus temporary, or a glimpse into a future in which politics becomes increasingly nationalized while regional distinctions fade is something that we may speculate about but cannot determine at this time.

Conclusion

The Midwest has long been the battleground of American politics—with Ohio, as far as presidential campaigns are concerned, at the heart of it all. The borders of that battleground, however, seemed to shift with Donald Trump's election in 2016. While the Midwest once again proved decisive, this time the election came down to voters in Michigan and Wisconsin (as well as in Pennsylvania). Ohio was hardly competitive; it gave Trump a lopsided eight-point victory at the same time he lost the national popular vote, apparently making it no longer a battleground *or* bellwether state. The 2020 election only reinforced this conclusion. Such a dramatic change makes it worthwhile, even necessary, for scholars to document and investigate Ohio's shifting place within the electoral landscape. The present analysis focuses on Ohio's identity as the quintessential midwestern, let alone American, electoral battleground. We ask which parts of Ohio—specifically in terms of the "Six Ohios"—are in political alignment with the broader Midwest and which factors might explain deviations from it.

Our analysis indicates that—in political terms, at least—the Midwest does not encompass all of Ohio, and its borders within the state have shifted in recent years. Most notably, Southeast Ohio, once the state's preeminent battleground and bellwether, can no longer be classified as midwestern in its voting behavior. While the Midwest voted somewhat more Republican with Donald Trump on the ballot, Southeast Ohio—like other Appalachian states or regions—became overwhelmingly Republican, with Trump's victory margins in 2016 and 2020 exceeding those in the Midwest by more than 18 percentage points. West Ohio, including Dayton, also has become increasingly Republican and increasingly divergent from the Midwest, favoring Trump by an additional 12 percentage points. The rest of Ohio may be fairly included within the political Midwest. Central

Ohio, in particular, stands out as consistently midwestern in its voting behavior. Northeast Ohio, once a heavily Democratic region, also became something of a midwestern bellwether starting in 2016.

What further shifts might we expect in the future? If present trends, as displayed in Fig. 14.5, continue, we might well anticipate Northwest Ohio drifting further toward the Republican Party, and perhaps outside the Midwest's borders, much like Southeast and West Ohio already have done. Only Central and Southwest Ohio have become increasingly Democratic, with the latter still voting more Republican than the broader Midwest. Perhaps in the near future, it will join Central and Northeast Ohio as midwestern bellwethers, in something of an increasingly suburban axis encompassing the state's major population centers, from greater Cleveland to Columbus to Cincinnati. To the extent that rural areas in Ohio and nationwide continue to develop a distinct sense of cultural and political identity, in close alignment with the Republican Party, the rest of the state might cease to be clearly identifiable as part of the Midwest.[23] But at that point, as regional lines blur, making visible only the singular images of a national Democratic Party and a national Republican Party, how much sense would it make to speak of a political entity called the Midwest, anyway?

Notes

1. Daniel R. Birdsong and Christopher Devine, "Fly-To Country: The Midwest as Presidential Battleground, 1946–2016," in *The Conservative Heartland: A Political History of the Postwar American Midwest,* ed. Jon Lauck and Catherine McNicol (Lawrence: Univ. Press of Kansas, 2020).

2. Kyle Kondik, *The Bellwether: Why Ohio Picks the President* (Athens: Ohio Univ. Press, 2016). Ohio's bellwether status is limited to presidential elections; it is not nearly as predictive of national trends in congressional and gubernatorial voting. See Daniel J. Coffey et al., *Buckeye Battleground: Ohio, Campaigns, and Elections in the Twenty-First Century* (Akron: Univ. of Akron Press, 2011), 18–21. This is one reason we focus only on presidential elections in this chapter. The other major reason is methodological: a presidential election is the only one in which Ohio and the rest of the Midwest choose among the same candidates running for the same office at the same time. This enables us to directly compare voting behavior. We cannot do this for congressional elections, for instance; not only do different candidates run for the House and Senate in different states, but some of these

elections are uncontested and one-third of the states do not hold Senate elections in a given year. Gubernatorial elections also feature different candidates in different states, and while most states elect governors in the midterm between presidential elections, three in the Midwest (Indiana, Missouri, and North Dakota) hold them in presidential election years.

3. Jo Ingles, "Political Scientist Says Ohio Is No Longer A Bellwether, Swing, Or Battleground State," *Statehouse News Bureau,* Nov. 5, 2020, https://www.statenews.org/government-politics/2020-11-05/political-scientist-says-ohio-is-no-longer-a-bellwether-swing-or-battleground-state; Jim Gaines, "Bellwether No More: Ohio's Republican Strength Falls Out of Step with Nation," *Dayton Daily News,* Nov. 13, 2022.

4. Coffey et al., *Buckeye Battleground.*

5. "In cases where a media market is too small to be considered a political region unto itself, it is grouped with an adjacent media market," Michael Curtin clarifies. See Michael F. Curtin, *The Ohio Politics Almanac* (Kent: Kent State Univ. Press, 1996), 93. This explains why the counties within Lima's media market, the smallest in the state, are included in the West region, along with other counties in the larger Dayton media market.

6. Kondik, *Bellwether,* 37

7. Christopher Devine, *I'm Here to Ask for Your Vote: How Presidential Campaign Visits Influence Voters* (New York: Columbia Univ. Press, 2024); Daron R. Shaw, *The Race to 270: The Electoral College and the Campaign Strategies of 2000 and 2004* (Chicago: Univ. of Chicago Press, 2006).

8. County-level vote share is relatively constant when the same candidate runs in consecutive elections (Bush, Obama, Trump), on average varying by only 0.82 percentage points. This makes it reasonable to group elections accordingly, as we do here. Changes in county voting patterns are much more likely to occur when new candidates appear on the ballot—by 7.14 percentage points, on average, according to our data.

9. For example, if Obama had won 55 percent of the two-party vote in Central Ohio in 2008, and 45 percent there in 2012, we would average the two and report the Democratic vote in Central Ohio across the Obama elections as 50 percent.

10. Rick Exner, "Franklin County Now Tops Cuyahoga County in Population, Census Estimates Say," *Cleveland Plain Dealer,* Mar. 23, 2017.

11. The lone Democratic outlier in Southeast Ohio is Athens County, home to Ohio University. The college town of Athens makes this county one of the most reliably Democratic in the state. Since 1972 it has voted for a Republican presidential candidate only once (in 1984).

12. Paula Christian, "Local Republicans Wonder Why Donald Trump Isn't Campaigning in Battleground Hamilton County," *WCPO,* Aug. 22, 2016, https://www.wcpo.com/news/insider/local-republicans-wonder-why-donald-trump-isnt-campaigning-in-battleground-hamilton-county.

13. Thomas Beaumont, "Counties That Flipped from Donald Trump to Joe Biden in the 2020 Presidential Election," *MassLive*, Mar. 17, 2021, https://www.masslive.com/politics/2021/03/counties-that-flipped-from-donald-trump-to-joe-biden-in-the-2020-presidential-election.html.

14. We summed the total Democratic vote across all of the midwestern states and divided by the total Democratic and Republican votes in those states. We did not sum up vote averages in each state as that would drive down the influence of more populous states.

15. Coffey et al., *Buckeye Battleground*.

16. Coffey et al., *Buckeye Battleground*, 161

17. The median county in Ohio was 8.8 percentage points more Republican than the Midwest in 2000–04, versus 11.1 in 2008–12 and 19.4 in 2016–20. Deviations across all counties ranged from 16.9 to 25.5 percentage points more Republican in 2000–04, 16.5 to 28.3 in 2008–12, and 19.0 to 32.5 in 2016–20.

18. Paul D. Allison, *Multiple Regression: A Primer* (Thousand Oaks, CA: Sage, 1998).

19. Election data comes from Carlos Algara and Sharif Amlani, "Replication Data for: Partisanship Nationalization in American Elections: Evidence from Presidential, Senatorial, Gubernatorial Elections in the U. S. Counties, 1872–2020," Harvard Dataverse, 2021), https://doi.org/10.7910/DVN/DGUMFI.; educational attainment, from the US Department of Agriculture, Economic Research Service, County-Level Data Sets, accessed July 23, 2023, https://www.ers.usda.gov/data-products/county-level-data-sets/county-level-data-sets-download-data/; median household income, from Federal Reserve Bank of St. Louis's GeoFRED website, accessed June 1, 2022, https://geofred.stlouisfed.org/map; Black and Latino percentages for 2008, from "County Intercensal Datasets, 2000–2010," US Census Bureau website, https://www.census.gov/data/datasets/time-series/demo/popest/intercensal-2000-2010-counties.html), 2012, and 2016 (https://www.census.gov/data/tables/time-series/demo/popest/2010s-counties-detail.html), derived from state-level population estimates made available on the Census Bureau website; evangelical population, from C. Grammich et al., Longitudinal Religious Congregations and Membership File, 1980–2010 (County Level), Association of Religion Data Archives, accessed June 15, 2023, https://www.thearda.com/data-archive?fid=RCMSMGCY; and *2020 PRRI Census of American Religion: County-Level Data on Religious Identity and Diversity,* Public Religion Research Institute, July 8, 2021, https://www.prri.org/research/2020-census-of-american-religion; Urban-rural classification scheme from US Department of Health and Human Services, *2013 NCHS Urban–Rural Classification Scheme for Counties*, Apr. 2014, https://www.cdc.gov/nchs/data/series/sr_02/sr02_166.pdf.

20. Coffey et al., *Buckeye Battleground*.

21. Daniel J. Hopkins, *The Increasingly United States: How and Why American Political Behavior Nationalized* (Chicago: Univ. of Chicago Press, 2018); Lilliana Mason, *Uncivil Agreement: How Politics Became Our Identity* (Chicago: Univ. of Chicago Press, 2018).

22. Jon K. Lauck, "Trump and the Midwest: The 2016 Presidential Election and the Avenues of Midwestern Historiography," *Studies in Midwestern History* 3, no. 1 (2017): 1–24.

23. See Katherine J. Cramer, *The Politics of Resentment: Rural Consciousness in Wisconsin and the Rise of Scott Walker* (Chicago: Univ. of Chicago Press, 2016).

Contributors

Jacob Bruggeman studies modern political economy and intellectual history with a focus on technology, policy, and professional culture in the twentieth-century United States at Johns Hopkins University. His dissertation, "Securing the System," explores how regulation, professionalization, and technological change reshaped the practice and significance of hacking in the twentieth-century United States and world. Bruggeman is the editor-at-large of the *Cleveland Review of Books*.

Mary Kupiec Cayton is Professor Emerita of history at Miami University. She has also served as visiting professor of history and visiting scholar at the Ohio State University. Coeditor of *The Encyclopedia of American Social History* (1993) and *The Encyclopedia of Cultural and Intellectual History* (2001), she has written on the social contexts of American intellectual and religious history, on the history of print communication, and on the teaching of writing.

Donna M. DeBlasio is Professor Emerita of history and former director of the Center for Applied History and the Oral History Program at Youngstown State University. DeBlasio has also published both scholarly and popular works, most of which focus on the history of Youngstown and the Mahoning Valley. These include five books, scholarly articles in *Rethinking History*, the *International Journal of Local and Regional History*, and *Ohio History*, and the coauthored *Catching Stories: A Practical Guide to Oral History* (2009). DeBlasio is currently editor of the *Ohio History* journal.

Christopher J. Devine is associate professor of political science at the University of Dayton. Devine earned his PhD in political science from the Ohio State University. His research and teaching focus on American politics, particularly the American presidency and vice presidency, campaigns and elections, political parties, and constitutional law. He is the author of several books, including *Do Running Mates Matter? The Influence of Vice Presidential Candidates in Presidential Elections* (with Kyle C. Kopko, 2020) and *I'm Here to Ask for Your Vote: How Presidential Campaign Visits Influence Voters* (2024).

Stephanie Fortado is teaching assistant professor at the University of Illinois Labor Education Program, where she teaches courses in their global labor studies minor and provides classes and extension programming for union members throughout Illinois. Stephanie is the codirector of the Regina V. Polk Women's Labor Leadership programs. She is coeditor of *Histories of a Radical Book: E. P. Thompson and the Making of the English Working Class* (2020) with Antoinette Burton. In 2022, she received the American Council of Learned Societies Fellowship to support her research and writing of a monograph about Black community organizing in Cleveland, Ohio.

Randall S. Gooden is professor of history at Clayton State University in Morrow, Georgia. His interest in the Midwest stems from his experiences as a project historian with the National Park Service's Historic American Engineering Record in documenting historic bridges in Ohio. He was also head of the archives and library at Ohio Historical Society's Youngstown Historical Center of Industry, and then executive director of Geauga County Historical Society in Burton, Ohio, before settling in Georgia. He is the author of *The Governor's Pawns: Hostages and Hostage-Taking in Civil War West Virginia* (2023).

A. Lee Hannah is professor of political science at Wright State University in Dayton, Ohio. He has written in popular and academic forums on drug policy, education policy, and electoral politics. He is coauthor of *Green Rush: The Rise of Medical Marijuana in the American States* (2024), with Daniel J. Mallinson. His work on electoral politics has been published in

Political Research Quarterly, Party Politics, and *Research and Politics.* He holds a PhD from Penn State University.

Kenneth J. Heineman is professor of history and global security studies at Angelo State University, in Texas. He is the author of seven books, including *A Catholic New Deal: Religion and Reform in Depression Pittsburgh* (1999). His other work includes *Civil War Dynasty: The Ewing Family of Ohio* (2013). Currently Heineman is writing a monograph titled "Bourbon, Cigars, and a Bucket of Warm Spit: Cactus Jack Garner and the Rise of Texas Political Power."

Timothy C. Hemmis is associate professor of history, with a specialization in early American history, at Texas A&M University–Central Texas, in Killeen. His research focuses on empire, identity, the frontier, war, and society in Revolutionary America (1750–1815). His anthology, coedited with David Head, *A Republic of Scoundrels: The Schemers, Intriguers, and Adventurers Who Made a New American Nation,* was released in 2023. He is currently working on a biography of Captain Thomas Hutchins, the only Geographer of the United States.

Kevin F. Kern is associate professor of history at the University of Akron, specializing in Ohio history and late-nineteenth- and early-twentieth-century US history. He currently serves as the chair of the University of Akron Press Editorial Board and is editor of the Press's Ohio History and Culture series. He is cofounder and former editor of the *Northeast Ohio Journal of History.* Kern is the coauthor of *Ohio: A History of the Buckeye State* (2013), now in its second edition.

Jon K. Lauck is the author of *The Lost Region: Toward a Revival of Midwestern History* (2013); *From Warm Center to Ragged Edge: The Erosion of Midwestern Regionalism, 1920–1965* (2017); and *The Good Country: A History of the American Midwest* (2022). Lauck currently serves as adjunct professor of history and political science at the University of South Dakota, editor in chief of *Middle West Review,* and president of the Society for the Study of Midwestern Literature. He earned his PhD in history from the University of Iowa and his law degree from the University of Minnesota. Lauck has served as the editor of several collections, including this one, that are designed to advance and promote the study of the American Midwest.

Jeanne Gillespie McDonald is professor of English at Waubonsee Community College, in Sugar Grove and Aurora, Illinois, where she was honored with the 2019 Outstanding Faculty Member. She holds a PhD in English studies. She has been teaching, presenting, and writing for over thirty-five years on writing, assessment, service learning, learning communities, leadership, literature, religion, labor, and Illinois history. Valuing a cross-disciplinary approach to history, she currently researches antislavery and abolition movements and is working on a book about Zebina Eastman, editor of the antislavery newspaper *Western Citizen*.

Cody A. Norling holds a PhD in musicology from the University of Iowa, where he completed a dissertation exploring the ethos of progress and nation-building that characterized the civic density of Chicago's operatic cultures in the 1920s. His work on American opera histories can be found in *American Music*, the *Opera Journal*, and an in-progress volume on Black American operatic identities, and he was the 2016 recipient of the National Opera Association's Leland Fox Scholarly Paper Award. Norling currently serves as faculty affairs officer at the University of Rochester's Eastman School of Music.

Martha I. Pallante, professor of history, holds the Charles Darling Endowed Chair in American History at Youngstown State University and specializes in Early America, ethnicity, and material culture. She received her BA from Youngstown State University and her MA in history and historic archaeology from the College of William and Mary. She completed her PhD in early American history at the University of Pennsylvania. Her most recent publications include articles in *Italian Americana* and *Ohio History*.

Eric Michael Rhodes is a PhD student at Northwestern University. He writes about the sociocultural history of inequality in the urban industrial Midwest and the ways global history ties into the history of the region's midsized cities. Eric has published chapters on segregation and inequality in Jacksonian-era Cincinnati and late-twentieth century Dayton in *The Making of the Midwest: Essays on the Formation of Midwestern Identity*,

1787 to 1900 (2020) and in *The Dayton Anthology* (2020). His essays and reviews have appeared in numerous journals.

Gregory S. Rose is a recently retired dean and director of the Ohio State University at Marion and Associate Professor Emeritus of geography. His received bachelor's degrees in geography and history from Valparaiso University in Indiana and master's and doctorate degrees in geography from Michigan State University. His primary research area is the nineteenth-century Midwest, particularly the Old Northwest.

Mary Stockwell received her PhD in history from the University of Toledo and later served as a professor of history and department chair at Lourdes University. She has been awarded research fellowships at the New York Public Library and the William L. Clements Library at the University of Michigan. She is the author of nine books, most recently *Unlikely General: "Mad" Anthony Wayne and the Battle for America* (2018) and *Interrupted Odyssey: Ulysses S. Grant and the American Indians* (2018).

Gleaves Whitney has written or edited eighteen books, four of them with Jon Lauck. The Texas native has served as the executive director of the Gerald R. Ford Presidential Foundation since 2020. Before that, he established and led the Hauenstein Center for Presidential Studies (2003–17), and prior to that he served on the staff of Governor John Engler of Michigan (1992–2002). A historian by training, Gleaves did graduate work at the University of Michigan, was a Fulbright Scholar to then West Germany, and graduated Phi Beta Kappa from Colorado State University.

Andrew W. Wiley is assistant professor of history and the editor for the Papers of Martin Van Buren at Cumberland University. He specializes in the history of conservatism, the Midwest, the Civil War, and Reconstruction. His manuscript, "White Man's Liberalism, American Conservatism: Race, Economics, and the Origins of Popular Conservatism in Nineteenth-Century Indiana," is currently under revision with an academic press. Wiley has several forthcoming publications and has presented at many academic conferences.

Gregory S. Wilson is Distinguished Professor of History at the University of Akron. His research and teaching includes Ohio history, public history, labor, and the environment in recent US history. He is a coprincipal investigator for "Deindustrialization and the Politics of Our Time," a transnational research project examining the historical roots, lived experiences, and responses to deindustrialization. He is the author or coauthor of four books, including *Ohio: A History of the Buckeye State* (with Kevin F. Kern, 2013), and most recently *Poison Powder: The Kepone Disaster in Virginia and Its Legacy* (2023).

Index

Page numbers in *italics* refer to illustrations.

Abbott, Emma, 202
abolitionism: in Illinois, 46, 51, 53–59, 61; law and, 48; Lincoln and, 60–61; in the Midwest, 45–47, 50–51, 53–55, 61, 63; in Ohio, 47–48, 54–56, 77–78, 147–49; politics and, 9–10, 50–51, 56–59, 126–28
Achilles, 113
Adams, Bluford, 152–54
Adams, John, 7–8, 16, 112
Adams, John Quincy, 8, 112, 132
Adams County, OH, 282
Adena people, 10, 69, 71
Aeneid (Virgil), 112–13
Africa, 239–40, 251
African Americans: abolitionism and, 46, 51, 53–54, 57–58, 63; activism by, 15, 45, 83, 238–44, 249–51; arts and, 245–48; discrimination against, 53, 57–59, 244, 249; education and, 77; election of, 260; enslavement of, 48; labor movement and, 259, 261–63; liberation of, 50; in the Mahoning Valley, 176, 186; migration of, 6, 10, 51–52, 186, 246, 267–68; news coverage of, 28; in Ohio, 69, 76, 83, 241–46, 248, 251, 267–68; politics of, 287; racism against, 34, 51–53, 62–63, 83, 123–24, 239–41, 245, 249–50, 262–63; rights of, 47, 51–52, 59–60, 83, 262
African Methodist Episcopal Church, 53
African People's Party, 248
Afro-American Institute (AAI), 244, 250
agriculture: Midwest and, xiv, 4, 164–68, 170, 207, 215; in Ohio, 68, 71, 76, 140, 153, 165–68, 170, 217; slavery and, 53; subsidies for, 260
Ahlquist, Karen, 219–20
Akron, IA, xxiii
Akron, OH, xxiii, 80, 82, 84, 262
Alabama, 242, 262
Albany, NY, 28, 30, 35, 40
Albemarle County, VA, 52
Alger, Horatio, viii
Algonquian peoples, 31
Aliquippa, PA, 259
Allan, William T., 55–56, 58
Allegheny (proposed state), 161
Allegheny County, PA, 260
Allegheny Mountains, 101, 179
Allegheny Plateau, 1–2, 4, 6–7, 16, *162*, 168
Allegheny River, xvii, 5
American Anti-Slavery Society, 46–47, 53–55
American Colonization Society, 53
American Federation of Labor, 81
American Party. *See* Know-Nothing Party
American Revolution, xii–xiii, 28, 75, 90, 94–95, 100, 115, 134; Ohio and, xvii, 6–7, 16, 74; veterans of, 50–51, 103
American Temperance Society, 77
Amish, xv
Amsterdam, 224, 228
Anderson, Benedict, 28
Anderson, Gerard, 245
Anderson, Sherwood, 81
Anglicanism, xiii
animals, xi, 78, 94, 115, 153, 176, 217
Annapolis, MD, 24, *29*, *33*, 34, *34*
anticolonialism, 239. *See also* colonialism
Anti-Nebraska Party, 57

302

INDEX

Anti-Saloon League, 80
Appalachia, xi; borders of, 6; history of, xiii–xiv; industry in, xix; influence of, 3; Ohio and, 15, 163, 169, 219; Ohio River and, xiii, xx; migration from, 262, 268; Pittsburgh and, 5–6; politics of, 16, 275, 277, 280, 285, 291; Presbyterianism in, xxi–xxii; reputation of, xv–xvi; topography of, ix, xxiii
AppalachiaFest (conference), xii
Appalachian Mountains, xiv, xvi, 4, 11, 70, 76, 123; frontier and, 27; Midwest and, 1, 16–17, 103, 109, 135, 239; migration to, xiv–xv; topography of, ix, xvii
Appalachian Plateau, 70, 76, 168–69; borders of, ix–x; forests of, xii
Appalachian studies, xii
apple trees, ix
archaeology, 71
Aristotle, 112, 119
Armstrong, Neil, 83
Articles of Confederation, 93, 96
arts, 81, 230, 240, 245–48, 251. *See also* epics; literature; music
Ashley, James, 79
Ashtabula, OH, 148
Asia. *See* Eurasia
astronauts, x, 83
Athens, OH, xi–xii, xvi–xvii
Atkins, Russell, 247
Atlantic Ocean, 1, 24, 27, 71, 108, 182
atomic weapons, 82
Augusta, GA, 29, 35, 38, 40
Augusta County, VA, 27, 30
Augustana University, ix
Austin, Henry, 240
Austin, Stephen F., 93
Austria, 231
automobiles, 219, 242, 266

Bailey, Gamaliel, 47, 57
Baker, O. E., 165–66
Balfe, Michael William, 205
"Ballad of East and West, The" (Kipling), 2
Ballets Russes, 222, 231
Baltimore, 13, 106
Baltimore, Priscilla "Mother," 53
Baltimore Afro-American, 247, 250–51
Baltimore Convention, Old Tippecanoe, a Patriotic Song (James Fuller Queen), 117
Baltimore Republican, 107
Baptist churches, 53, 56, 146, 261, 268

Barilla, Jerry, xvii–xviii, xx
Barlow, Joel, 112
Barquet, Joseph H., 57
Barron, Hal, 177
baseball, xxii, 82
basketball, xi, xxii–xxiii
Baton Rouge, LA, 102
Bay City, MI, 3
Bear, John, 115
Beaver River, xviii, 143–44
Beaver Valley, 142, 144
Beaver Wars, 72
Beddoe, Dan, 221
Beecher, Edward, 54
Beecher, Henry Ward, 47, 126
Beecher, Lyman, 77
Beecher Stowe, Harriet, 47, 54, 77–78
Belmont County, OH, 291
Belvidere, Illinois, 207
Bennett, Franklin, 140
Benton, Thomas Hart, 107
Berks County, PA, 27, 30
Berlin, 219–20, 226
Bernard, Francis, 37
Bernstein, Leonard, 228
Bethlehem, PA, 30, 177
Bibb, Henry, 58
Bible, viii, 48–50, 58, 61
Big Sioux River, xxiii
Bilbro, Jeff, xxi–xxii
Bingham, John, 79
Birmingham, AL, 244
Birney, James G., 47–49, 55
Black Americans. *See* African Americans
Black Arts movement, 15, 240, 245–46
Black Nationalism, 15, 239, 242, 248, 250–51
Black Power movement, 240, 247, 251
Blanchard, Jonathan, 54
Bomberger, E. Douglas, 202
Bonner, James D., 57
Boone, Daniel, vii–viii, xvi
borderlands, 1, 3, 163, 270; of the Midwest, vii, xxiii, 6, 8, 13–14, 158–59; of the United States, 9–10, 27, 93. *See also* frontier
boreal forest, 3
Boston, 55, 108, 196, 247; newspapers in, 22–25, 22, 29, 33, 34
Boston News-Letter, 22, 23
Boston Symphony Orchestra, 14, 202, 224, 226
Bourdieu, Pierre, 229
Boyle, Hugh (Bishop), 260, 263

INDEX

Boy Scouts, xv
Bradford, David, 102
Bradford, Henry, 57
Brahms, Johannes, 226
Brandywine, Battle of, xiii
bread, 181, 183
Breckinridge, John C., 132–34
Brethren, Church of the, 146, 148
Bricker, John, 267
bridges, ix, 264
Britain, xvi–xvii, 6, 22–23, 26–28, 37–38, 97, 219; government of, 47; Native Americans and, 31, 35–36, 38, 72–74; settlers from, 37; in the Seven Years' War, xvi, 7, 20–21, 73; United States and, 92, 94; in the War of 1812, 11, 110
British Empire, 6, 8, 21, 22, 25–27, 29, 40, 72, 238
British North America, 7–8, 20, 22, 26, 32, 34, 37
Broadway, 207–8
Bronner, Simon J., 152
Brooklyn, IL, 53
Brooklyn, NY, 55
Brooks, Corey M., 51
Brooks, James, 115
Brooks, Preston, 128
Brown, Asa B., 50
Brown, Hallie Quinn, 81
Brown, John, 55, 62, 78
Bruggeman, Jacob, 14
Buchanan, James, 11, 62, 132–35
buckeye (tree), xii
Buckeye Battleground (Coffey et al.), 277, 285, 288
Buffalo, NY, 176, 181, 258–60, 269
Buffum, Arnold, 48
Burr, Aaron, 10, 90, 92–93, 101–3
Bush, George W., 16, 278–80, 282–84, 286, 288–90
Butler, Andrew P., 128
Butler, Jon, vii–viii, xxiii
Butler, Joseph G., Jr., 145
Butler County, OH, 282
Butler Institute of American Art, xxi

Cairo, IL, 99
California, 84
Call and Post (Cleveland), 245, 248–49
Cambridge, MA, 107
Campbell, Robert, 36
Campney, Brent, 241

Canada, 20, 28, 47, 71, 78–79, 110, 243
Canfield Fair, 140
Canfield, OH, 12, 153
Canning, Charlotte, 203
Canonsburg, PA, 90, *91*, 101
Canton, OH, 81–82, 84, 261–62, 265
Caribbean region, 20, 29. *See also* West Indies
Carnegie Hall (New York), 224–25, *225*
Carpenter, Philo, 56
Cass, Douglas, 128
Cass, Lewis, 128
Castor, Annie, x
Catawba people, 31
Catholicism, xiii, 224, 259–63; education and, 95; politics and, 257, 262–64, 266–68, 270; prejudice against, 46, 185–87
cattle, 176
Cave, Alfred, 109
Cayton, Andrew, 68–69, 86, 92, 216
Cayton, Mary Kupiec, 7–9
Cedar Rapids, IA, 196
Centerburg, OH, viii
Central Lowlands (geologic region), 168–69
Central Region Humanities Center, xii
Central State University, 250
Cha-Jua, Sundiata, 241
Chalcedony, 71
Chanel, Coco, 222
Chapman, Johnathan. *See* Johnny Appleseed
Charles City, VA, 109–10
Charleston, SC, *22*, 23, 25, 28, *33*, 34
Chase, Salmon P., 49, 77, 79
Chautauqua, NY, 195
Chautauqua Institute, 14, 195
Chautauquas, 14, *197*, *199*; history of, 194–96, 198, 207; opera and, 193–94, 199, 200–201, 203–6, 208–9
Cherokee people, 31
cherry trees, xii, 113
Chicago, 53, 198, 218; abolitionism in, 50, 56–58; activism in, 242, 246–48, 250, 260; culture of, 193, 202, 206, 208, 230–31; geography of, 13, 177, 258; politics of, 61–62, 81, 259, 264–65
Chicago, University of, x
Chicago Defender, 247–48
Chicago Symphony Orchestra, 227, 230–31
Chicago Theological Seminary, 54
Chickasaw people, 31
Choctaw people, 31

Christianity, 35, 39, 74, 77, 186, 195, 287; abolitionism and, 53–54; place-names and, viii
Ciarniello, Dominic, 179, 184–85
Cincinnati, xvii, 49, 76–77, 109, 112, 219–20; abolitionism in, 47, 50, 55, 78; geography of, 4, 13, *162*, 170; politics of, 57, 265, 267, 277, 281, 292; sports in, 82
Cincinnati, Society of, xvii
City University of New York, 108
civil rights movement, 83, 238–39, 244–45, 247, 250, 260, 268–69
Civil War, 54, 159, 185; Midwest and, 80, 123–24; Ohio and, xii, 12, 78–79, 149–50, 155, 179, 218, 261–62; politics and, 9, 11, 76–77, 149–51, 261–62; regionalism and, 45; slavery and, 62
Clark, Caitlin, xxii
Clark, George Rogers, viii, 74
Clark County, OH, 282
class, 240–41, 243, 246
Clay, Henry, 131–32
Clay, James B., 131, 133
Cleaveland, Moses, 216
Cleveland, xxii–xxiii, 184; activism in, 238–40, 242–45, 249–51; African Americans in, 15, 83, 238–48, 251; culture of, 14–15, 215–17, 219–22, 230–32, 245–48; demographics of, 80; economy of, 82, 218–19, 223, 226–27, 231–32, 242, 244; geography of, 3–4, 13, 170, 177, 245–46, 258, 278; labor in, 260, 263; music in, 82, 219–32; politics of, 81, 265, 268, 275, 277, 292; settlement of, xv, 216–17
Cleveland Browns, xxii, 5, 83
Cleveland Guardians, xxii
Cleveland Morning Leader, 149–50
Cleveland Museum of Art, xxii, 220, 222, 226, 230
Cleveland Musical Arts Association (CMAA), 222–23, 226–27, 229–32
Cleveland Orchestra, 14, 215–16, 219–32, *225*, *228*
Cleveland Plain Dealer, xxii, 229
climate, 13, 164, 166–67, 217. *See also* weather
coal, 182; industry and, 80, 179, 219; mining of, xi, xiv
Codding, Ichabod, 57–58, 60
Coffey, Daniel J., 277, 285, 288
Coffin, Levi, 78
Colden, Cadwallader, 37

Cold War, viii
Coles, Edward, 52, 56
Colley, Linda, 37
Collins, Gail, 11, 108–9
colonialism, 6, 32, 72–73, 238, 250. *See also* anticolonialism
Columbia Broadcasting Service (CBS), 227
Columbiana, OH, 154
Columbiana County, OH, 12, 139, 143, *144*, 146, 149, *150*, 154
Columbus, Christopher, 186
Columbus, OH, 115, 198; airport in, xi; economy of, 84; location of, vii, xiv, xx–xxii, *162*, 170; people from, 80, 82–83; politics of, 275, 277, 280, 292
Columbus Dispatch, x, 277
communism, 81, 263–66, 268
Communist League for Negro Rights, 242–43
Communist Party, 81, 263–64
Compromise of 1850, 148
Concord, MA, 106–7
Conestoga, PA, 39
Confederacy (US Civil War), xii, 134
Congo, Democratic Republic of, 239
Congregationalism, 53–54, 77–78, 145–46, 217
Congress of Industrial Organizations (CIO), 259–64, 266–68, 270
Congress of Racial Equality (CORE), 240, 244
Connecticut, xv, 32, 141–42, 144, 152, 159, 216, 218; abolitionism in, 128; migration from, 164
Connecticut Land Company, 141–42
Connecticut Missionary Society, 145
Connecticut Western Reserve, xvii, 12–13, 141–49, *144*, 153, 176, 222; abolitionism in, 47; culture of, 152, 154–55, 216–18, 220
Connelly, John, 97
conservatism, 17, 49–50, 60–61, 258, 261, 264, 266–69
Conti, Dominic, 185
Conzen, Katherine Neils, 154
Cook County, IL, 259
Coolidge, Calvin, 203
Cooper, James Fenimore, viii, 113
Cooper Guasco, Suzanne, 52–53
copper, 7
Copperheads (political faction), 12, 79
corn, 176; in ancient agriculture, 71; geography of, x, 13, 164–68, 170, 217
Corn Belt, 1, 3–4, 13, *162*, 164–69
Cox, James M., 81
Cox, John Rogers, xxii

Coxey, Jacob, 81
Creek people, 31
Croatian Americans, 185
Crocetti, Dino, xviii
Cross, John, 55
Cruse, Harold, 250
Cumberland, Duke of, xvi
Cumberland, MD, 39
Cumberland County, PA, 27
Cumberland Gap, xvi
Cumberland Road, xvi, 142
Curtin, Mike, 277
Cutler, Manasseh, 75
Cuyahoga County, OH, 265, 279–80. *See also* Cleveland
Cuyahoga River, xxii, 2, 83

dairy farming, 176, 217
Dakotas, vii, 71. *See also* North Dakota; South Dakota
Darke County, OH, 290–91
Davey, Martin, 264–65, 267
Davies, Robert, 36
Davis, Harry P., 143
Dawson, Moses, 112, 114
Dayton, OH, xiv, 79–80, 82, 84, 116, 277, 282, 291
DeBlasio, Clotilda DiLullo, 180, 185
DeBlasio, Donna M., 13–14
Debs, Eugene, 81
Debussy, Claude, 222, 225
DeCaux, Len, 263
Declaration of Independence (USA), 7, 48–50, 61–62, 109
De Koven, Reginald, 200, 205
Delaware, 22, 159
Delaware County, OH, 280
Delaware people, 31, 74
Delaware River, 159
democracy, 59, 203; freedom and, 45, 47–49, 63; Jacksonian, 12, 148; in the Midwest, 46
Democratic Party: in the 1840 elections, 107–8, 114; in the 1854 elections, 125, 127; in the 1856 elections, 123–24, 131–35; abolitionism and, 9, 50, 57–59; Civil War and, 150–51; Kansas-Nebraska Act and, 62, 130; labor and, 259–60, 264–67; in the Mahoning Valley, xxi, 140; media and, 17; in the Midwest, 258, 286–87; in Ohio, 70, 79, 81, 85–86, 149, 261–62, 264–70, 278–86, *279*, *281*, 291–92; primaries of, xiv; slavery and, 11–12, 125–27
Denison University, x

Denver, John, xvii
DeRogatis, Amy, 145
Des Moines, IA, xxii
Detroit, 13, 30, 35, 242, 246, 248, 250, 259–60; migration to, 268. *See also* Fort Detroit
Devine, Christopher, 15
DeWine, Mike, vii, xi
DeWolf, Calvin, 56
Diaghilev, Serge, 222
Dickinson, Clarence, 221
Dies, Martin, 266
Dillon, Merton, 62
Dilullo, Gaetano, 181
Dilullo, Pasquale, 181
Dodd, William E., 61
Donofrio, Rudy, 180, 182–83
Donofrio, Vito, 180
doughfaces (political faction), 50, 59, 62
Douglas, H. Ford, 57–58
Douglas, Stephen A., 46, 50, 52, 59, 61–62, 124, 126, 128; presidential campaign of, 132–33, 135
Douglass, Frederick, 58, 239
Drake, Benjamin, 119
Dred Scott decision, 59
Dunbar, Ralph, 201
Duncan Falls, OH, xi, xvi
Dunmore, Lord (Virginia governor), 75
Duquesne University, 260
Duval, Peter S., *111*
Dwight, Timothy, 112
Dyer, Charles V., 56

East (USA): abolitionism and, 46, 54–55, 128; borders of, xxiii, 1–2, 7–8, 155, 163, 169–70; Britain and, 72; Cleveland and, 215–16, 218–20, 222, 230–31, 240, 242, 245; culture of, 14–15, 202, 208, 223, 225; democracy in, 60; Midwest and, 17, 68–69, 92–93, 129, 170, 176–77, 215, 250; migrants from, 12; Ohio and, 80, 86, 163, 170, 176, 217–18; Pittsburgh and, 5; politics and, 10, 108; regionalism and, 100–103. *See also* Mid-Atlantic (USA); New England
East Liverpool, OH, 141
Eastman, Zebina, 54, 56–58, 60–61
Easton, Treaty of, 73
East Palestine, OH, xx, xxiii
Edison, Thomas, 80
education, 14, 77, 85, 152, 178, 184–85, 188, 260; in Cleveland, 244, 251; voting and, 287–88, 290
Eels, Richard, 55

eighty-second meridian, viii
Eisenhower, Dwight D., viii, 269
elections: of 1840, 76, 106–9, *111*, 113–16, 118; of 1854, 125, 127; of 1856, 123, 131–35; of 1860, 135; of 1936, 260; of 1938, 261, 266–67; of 1946, 268; of 2008, 284; of 2012, 284; of 2016, 277, 281–82; of 2020, 277, 281–82; abolitionism and, 61–62; charts of, *276, 279, 283;* congressional, xxi, 46, 110, 134, 266, 268, 124–25; in the Mahoning Valley, xxi; maps of, *281;* models of, 286–90, *289;* in Ohio, 15–16, 79, 81, 85, 266, 268–69, 274–86, 288–92; presidential, xiv, 76, 106–9, 274–85, 278–79; to the Senate, 46, 266–67; in West Virginia, xiii, 262
Electoral College, 76
Ellenbogen, Henry, 260
Emancipation Proclamation, 150
Emerson, Ralph Waldo, 11, 106, 109
England, xiii, 37
England, Robert E., 270
English, William Hayden, 124–25
English language, 14, 193–94, 201–6, 208
environmentalism, 83–84
epics, 112–13, 118. *See also* literature
Equal Rights Amendment, 83
Erie, PA, 4
Erie Canal, xvi, 218
Etcheson, Nicole, 240–41
ethanol, xxiii
Eurasia, 2
Europe: culture of, 14, 202–4, 215, 219–29; immigrants from, 10, 32, 80, 140, 154, 175, 178–79, 185–86, 218, 242, 270; news from, 23–25
Europeans: migration of, 163–64; Native Americans and, 21, 27, 30–32, 72–73; Seven Years' War and, 8, 20, 35. *See also* white Americans
Evangelical Christianity, 47, 275, 287–88, *289*
Evening Star (Washington, DC), 221, 229
Evening World (New York), 221–22
Evers, Medgar, 239

Fallen Timbers, Battle of, 74, 110, 115, 118
Falmouth, 25
Faneuil Hall, Boston, 55
Fargo, ND, 3
feminism, 83. *See also* women's rights
ferries, ix
Field, Henry, 201
Findlay, Hugh, 25
Finney, Charles Grandison, 77

Fire-Eaters (political faction), 47, 62
Fire Lands, xvii
Fiske, John, 219
flooding, vii, ix, xi, xiv–xv
Florida, 27, 29. *See also* West Florida
food, x, viii, 178, 181, 183
football, x, xix, xxiii, 5, 82–83
Forbes Road, 142–43
Ford, Barney L., 57
Ford, Melissa, 243
forests, xii, 3, 164–67; border surveys and, 160; in Ohio, x, xvii, 167; in West Virginia, xiv
Fortado, Stephanie, 15
Fort Ancient culture, 71
Fort Augusta, 30
Fort Detroit, 36, 73
Fort Meigs, 110, 115–16; siege of, 11, 112–14, 116, 118–19
Fort Pitt, 27, 73, 90, 96. *See also* Pittsburgh
Fort St. Augustine, 25
Fort Steuben, xvii
Fort William Henry, 113
Fosdick, Charles, viii
Foucher, Pedro, 99
Fowler, Jonathan, 142
Fox Creek (OH), ix
France, xvi, 6, 72–73; in the American Revolution, xiii; Pontiac's Rebellion and, 35; settlers from, 93–94; in the Seven Years' War, xvi, 7, 20, 31, 35, 73
Franciscan University of Steubenville, xviii
Franklin (proposed state), 94, 98
Franklin, Benjamin, 23–25, 75
Franklin County, OH, 280. *See also* Columbus, OH
Fredericka, Marie, 187
Frederick County, VA, 27
Frederick-Town, MD, 30
Freed, Alan "Moondog," 82
freedom, 50–58, 62, 75, 100, 152; for African Americans, 238, 240–41, 245, 251; democracy and, 45, 47–49, 63; economic, 99; slavery and, 4, 9, 45–46, 50, 59–61; of speech, 128; Underground Railroad and, 78
Freedom Summer, 83
Free Lance (journal), 247
Freeman, Don, 15, 240, 244, 247–51
Freeman, Norma, 250–51
Freer, L. C. P., 56
Free-Soil Party, 48–49, 59, 76–77, 119
Frémont, John C., 134

308 INDEX

French and Indian War. *See* Seven Years' War
Freund, John Christian, 221
frontier: history of, 21, 32, 92, 96–98, 100, 114, 119; news from, 27–28, *29*, 30, 32, *33*, 34–37, *34;* in Ohio, 68, 143. *See also* borderlands
fugitive slave laws, 48, 53, 59, 78. *See also* slavery
Future Outlook League, 242

Gable, Clark, 82
Gaetano, Carmella, 182–83, 185
Gaines, Edmund P., 102
Gale, George W., 54
Galvez, Bernardo, 94
gardens, 14, 181, 183, 188, 201
Gardoqui, Don Diego de, 93–98, 100
Garfield, James, 79, 81, 218
Garrison, William Lloyd, 46–48, 55–56, 61
Garvey, Marcus, 239, 242
Gaysport, OH, xi
Gaza war, viii
Georgia, 9, 25, 28, 71, 185
Georgia Gazette, 22, 25
German Americans: discrimination against, 46, 202; on the frontier, 32, 37; in the Mahoning Valley, 13, 140, 143, 149, 176, 185; migration of, xv–xvi, xviii, 12; in Ohio, 77, 144–45, 154; politics of, 147–49, 151; religion of, 146–47; reputation of, xvi, 145. *See also* Pennsylvania Dutch
German Flats, NY, 35
German language, 26, 147, 151, 202
German Reformed Church, xv, 146–47
Germany, 231
Gershwin, George, 226
Gilbert, W. S., 200, 205
Gillette, Howard, 258
Gist, Christopher, xvii–xviii
glaciation, ix–x, xii, xviii, 4, 168; effects on soils, viii, x, xvii–xviii, 167–68; maps of, *162*
Glenn, John, Jr., x–xi, xiv, 83
Glenn, John, Sr., x
Gnadenhutten, OH, 74
gold, 96
Goodell, William, 48
Gooden, Randall, 12
Gore, Al, 280
Grand Rapids, MI, 2
Grant, Ulysses S., 78, 81

Granville, OH, x
Gratiot, OH, ix
Gray, Susan, 68–70
Gray and Gold (Cox painting), xxii
Great Britain. *See* Britain
Great Depression, 82, 185, 207, 223, 242–43
Great Lakes, xvi, 68, 70–71, 76, 158, 218; history of, 6, 9–10, 28, 30, 72; Midwest and, 1, 3, 16, 160–61, 257
Great Migration, 6, 186, 246, 267–68. *See also* migration
Great Plains, 3, 119, 167
Great Valley of the Appalachians, xvi
Green Bay, WI, 3
Green Bay Press-Gazette, 207
Greene County, OH, 74
Greenville, Treaty of, 110
Grey, Zane, viii, xv, xvii, 81
Grove City, PA, xxi
Groza, Lou, xix
Guglielmo, Thomas, 177
Gulf of Mexico, 1, 27, 71, 76
Gulf Oil, 269
Gunderson, Robert Grey, 109
Gunn, Glenn Dillard, 193

Hall, Abraham T., 57
Hall, Gus, 264, 266
Hall, James, 112
Hamilton, Alexander, 7, 100
Hamilton County, OH, 265, 281–82. *See also* Cincinnati
Hammond, Jeffrey, 86
Hammond, John Craig, 51
Hampshire County, VA, 27
Hannah, Lee, 15
Hannegan, Edward Aleen, 127–28
Harding, Warren, 81
Harlem, 15, 242–43, 246–47
Harmar, Josiah, 74, 97
Harper, William Rainey, x
Harpers Ferry, WV, 62, 78
Harrisburg, PA, 177
Harrison, Benjamin (US president), 81
Harrison, Benjamin, V, 109
Harrison, Harry P., 196, 198, 200–201, 205–7
Harrison, William Henry, 10–11, 109–10, 120; campaign of, 106–9, *111*, 113–16, 118; election of, 76; historiography of, 107–9, 112, 119–20; writings of, 113–14
Harrold, Stanley, 60
Hartford, CT, 35, 40, 128

Hartford Convention, 128–29
Harvard University, 107
Hasseler, Sue, ix
Hatcher, Harlan, 217–18
Haudenosaunee Confederation, 6, 31, 72–73
Havana, Cuba, 20
Hayes, Max, 81
Hayes, Rutherford B., 81
Heaton, Daniel, 179
Heaton, James, 179
Heaver, Jefferson Davis, 151
Heaver, Solomon, 151
Heaver, Susanna, 151
Hebron (biblical city), viii
Hebron, CT, viii
Hebron, OH, viii–ix
Hector (of Troy), 113
Hector, MN, vii
Heerman, M. Scott, 52
Heineman, Kenneth, 15
Hemmis, Timothy, 10, *91*
Herndon, William, 60
Highland County, OH, 282
Hinsdale, Burke Aaron, 218
Hinshaw, William, 203
Hispanics, 176, 287–88
Hocking Hills State Park, xiv, xvii
Holl, John O., 242
Holmes, Clarence H., 245
Holmes County, OH, 151, 154
Homer, 112, 118
Hopewell people, 10, 69, 71
Horner, Charles F., 196
horses, 78, 115
Hough (Cleveland neighborhood), 238, 249, 251
House Committee on Un-American Activities, 266
housing, 181–84, 188, 244–45
Howard, Ashley, 240
Howells, William Deal, xx, 81
Hudson, OH, 78
Hudson River, 109, 113
Hughes, Adella Prentiss, 220–22
Hughes, Langston, 15, 246–47
Hughes, Rubert, 221
Humphrey, Hubert, 229
hundredth meridian, viii
Hungarian Americans, xix
Hunter, William, 24
Huron people. *See* Wendat Confederacy
Hutchins, Thomas, 95

Iliad (Homer), 112
Illinois: abolitionism in, 46, 51, 53–59, 61; African Americans in, 53, 241; agriculture in, 165–66; constitution of, 52; culture of, 198; elections in, 62; history of, 63; Midwest and, 177; Morgan in, 93, 95; Native Americans in, 38; politics of, 124, 132, 135, 258–59, 261, 264, 266, 269–70; soils of, 167–68; statehood of, 7
Illinois College, 54–55
immigration: democracy and, 45; from Europe, 10, 32, 80, 140, 154, 175, 178–79, 185–86, 218, 242, 270; from Ireland, 260; from Italy, 177–78, 180–82, 186; Ku Klux Klan and, 185, 187; to the Mahoning Valley, 176, 178, 180–82, 186, 188; to Ohio, 80, 140, 151, 154, 163–64, 218; politics and, 131, 203. *See also* migration
indentured servitude, 9, 51–53. *See also* slavery
India, 20
Indiana, 7, 9, 11, 99, 194, 206, 241, 261; abolitionism in, 48, 56, 62; geography of, 165, 167–68, 177; newspapers in, 126–27; politics of, 62, 86, 108–10, 113, 124–26, 129–30, 132, 134–35
Indiana Land Company, 99
Indian Removal Act, 47
Insurrection Act, 103
internet, 23–24, 160, 163
Interstate 80, 2, 139
Iowa, xxiii, 165–68, 177, 196, 198, 201; abolitionism in, 56, 62; politics of, 62, 133–34
Iowa, University of, xxiii
Ireland, xiii
Irish Americans, 46, 176, 186–87, 259–60
Irish Sea, xiii
iron, 55, 95, 218–19; in the Mahoning Valley, xvii–xix, 13, 153, 176, 179
Iroquois Confederation, 6, 31, 72–73
Iroquois County, IL, 55
Italian Americans, xviii; historiography of, 13, 177; in the Mahoning Valley, xviii, 13–14, 140, 178–88
Ithaca, NY, 177

Jackson, Andrew, 47, 107–9, 130–32
Jacksonianism, 12, 46, 58, 107, 148
Jacobs Bond, Carrie, 200
Jacobson, Matthew Frye, 177
Japan, 82
jazz, 201, 251

Jefferson, Thomas, 7, 52, 75, 90, 102–3, 131, 157, 159, 170
Jefferson County, OH, x, 141, 280
Jeffersonianism, 59
Jelliffe, Rowena, 246
Jelliffe, Russell, 246
Jennings, Joe, 187
Jewish Americans, 185–86, 224, 257, 260, 263
JFK House. *See* Jomo Freedom Kenyatta House
John Glenn International Airport, xi
Johnny Appleseed, ix
Johnson, Allan, 60
Johnson, Andrew, 79
Johnson, Bill, xxi
Johnson, Reinhard O., 58–59
Johnson, Richard Mentor, 115
Johnson, Tom, 80
Johnston, John, 116
Jomo Freedom Kenyatta House, 15, 238–40, 249–50
Jones, Harllel "X," 238, 250
Jones, John, 57
Jones, Paul, 260
Jones, Sam "Golden Rule," 80
Jones & Laughlin, 259
Jordan, Norman, 251
Jortner, Adam, 109
Josephy, Alvin, 11, 119–20
Juch, Emma, 202

Kahn, Albert, xxi
Kahn, Louis, 230
Kansas, viii, 165–66, 168, 195; conflict about slavery in, 78, 124–27, 129–30, 133–35
Kansas City, 196
Kansas-Nebraska Act, 59, 62, 124, 129, 133
Karamu House (theater), 245–48, 251
Kaskaskia, IL, 93
Kellogg, Clara Louise, 202
Kennedy, John F., xiv, 238–39
Kent, OH, xxii, 264
Kent State University, 2, 84
Kentucky, xvi, 5, 51, 78, 97, 131–33, 166, 285; geography of, 159, 161; migration from, xv, 6, 268
Kenya, 238, 240
Kenyatta, Jomo, 238–39
Kern, Kevin F., 10
Kerry, John, 280
Kessner, Thomas, 177
Kettering, Charles, 80

King, Martin Luther, Jr., 83, 239
Kipling, Rudyard, 2
Kirtland, OH, 77
Kirtland, Turhand, 142
Kistler, Harvey, 187
Klunder, Bruce, 239
Knapp, Heloise, xix
Knepper, George W., 69, 154
Know-Nothing Party, 49, 60, 124–25, 129, 131–34
Knox, Henry, 92, 97
Knox College, 54
Knox County, OH, viii, 154
Kohler, Lee, 140
Kondik, Kyle, 276, 278
Kreisler, Fritz, 221
Ku Klux Klan, 185–87
Kurtz, Henry, 148
Kusmer, Kenneth, 246

labor, 259–60; elections and, 266–67, 270; in Ohio, 10, 15, 81, 258, 261–65, 269–70
Lafayette, Marquis de, xiii
Lake Chautauqua, NY, 194–95
Lake Erie, xxii, 1, 3, 70, 75, 141–42, 164, 166, 226
Lake Erie, Battle of, 74–75, 110, 116
Lancaster, PA, 30, 39
Lane Seminary, 47, 54–55, 77
Lang, Clarence, 241
Lariccia, Michael, 185
Last of the Mohicans, The (Cooper), 113. See also *Leatherstocking Tales* (Cooper)
Latin language, xix
Latinos, 176, 287–88
Latter-Day Saints, 77, 164
Lauck, Jon, 2, 46, 70, 257, 270, 290
Lausche, Frank, 267
Lawrence, David, 260, 269
Lawrence, Jerome, 81
Lawrence, KS, 126, 130
Leary, Patrick, 227
Leatherstocking Tales (Cooper), viii, 113
Leavitt, Joshua, 46
Lefoer, Annette, 183
Leiter, Harry, 200
Lenape people, 31, 74
Leo XIII (Pope), 260
Levine, Lawrence, 201, 208
Lewis, John L., 263–64
Lewis, Sinclair, 198
Lexington, KY, 131

INDEX

liberty. *See* freedom
Liberty Party, 48–50, 56–59
libraries, 208, 215, 217, 247
Licking County, OH, viii
Licking River, ix
Life magazine, xix
light, satellite photography of, 3–4
Lincoln, Abraham, xxi, 46, 49–50, 54, 59–62, 79, 150, 159, 261; election of, 135
Lincoln, Nebraska, 198
Lincoln Center, 227
Lincoln-Douglas debates, 46, 61–62
Lincoln the Railsplitter (Rockwell painting), xxi
Liste, Louise, 187
literacy, 217–18
literature, xx, 78, 163, 247. *See also* epics; poetry
Little Rock, AR, 83
Little Steel Strike (1937), 15, 258, 261–63, 268, 270–71
livestock, 94, 153, 217
Local Culture (journal), xxii
Locher, Ralph, 229
Loeb, Charles, 245
Loess Hills, xxiii
logging, xiv
London, 25, 226
Lord Dunmore's War, 74
Lottich, Kenneth, 152, 218
Louisiana, 27, 93, 133–34, 240
Louisiana (proposed state in Illinois), 93–94
Louisville, KY, 4
Lovejoy, Elijah Parish, 54–56, 58
Lovejoy, Owen, 57–58, 60
Lowell, IL, 56
Lowellville, OH, 154, 179
Lucas County, OH, 280
Lucius Quinctius Cincinnatus, xvii
Lumumba, Patrice, 239
Lundy, Benjamin, 56–57, 77
Lush, Paige, 200
Lutheranism, xv, 146

Mably, Abbé de, 8
Macali, Anna Marie, 183–84
Madison, James, 52
Madison, WI, 250
Madrid, 226
Mahoning County, OH, 12, 139, 149, 150, 151, 153, 155, 279
Mahoning Register, 151

Mahoning River, xviii, 143–44, 152, 179
Mahoning Valley: economy of, xvii–xix, xxi, 13, 153, 176, 178–79, 188; geography of, 14, 176–77, 187; German Americans in, 13, 140, 143, 149, 176, 185; Italian Americans in, xviii, 13–14, 140, 178–88; migration to, 142, 176, 178, 180–82, 186, 188; politics of, xxi, 279
mail, 9, 24–25
Main Street (Lewis), 198
maize. *See* corn
Malcolm X, 83, 239
Malta, OH, xii
Mandel, Bernard, 240
Manhattan Project, 82
Marietta, OH, ix, xi–xvii, 1, 4, 16, 141
Marietta College, xiii–xv
Marine Corps, x, xxiii
Markley, Stephen, x
Marsh, Robert, 219, 229
Martin, Dean. *See* Crocetti, Dino
Martins Ferry, OH, xviii–xx
Maryland, 9, 25–26, 28, 30, 32, 101, 115, 143
Maryland Gazette, 22, 26, 28, 35–36
Mason-Dixon Line, 5, 92, 159–60
Massachusetts, 27, 37, 127–28, 217
Massachusetts Emigrant Aid Company, 125. *See also* New England Emigrant Aid Company
Massillon, OH, 81, 261–62, 265
Mastropietro, Dominic, 180, 185
Mather, William, xxii
Matisse, Henri, 222
Maumee (proposed state), 161
Maumee River, 110
Mayflower (flatboat), xvi–xvii
Maysville, Kentucky, ix
McCain, John, 290
McConnelsville, OH, xi
McDonald, Jeanne Gillespie, 9
McDuffie, Erik, 239
McGuffey, William Holmes, 77
McIntosh, AL, 102
McKinley, William, 81, 152
McNamara, Patrick, 263
Meinig, D. W., 169
Mellon, Richard King, 269
Mennonites, xv
Mercer County, OH, x
Methodism, 53, 194–95, 261
Metropolitan Opera (New York), 193, 201, 204, 222, 224

Metropotamia (proposed state), 158, 170
Metzka, Reed, 140
Mexico, 47, 119. *See also* New Spain
Miami people, 6–7, 31
Miami rivers, 165
Miami University, 83
Michigan, xxi, 7, 9, 11, 58, 69, 177, 219, 261; agriculture in, 165; labor in, 15, 259, 264; politics of, 130–31, 134, 258–59, 264–70, 291
Michney, Todd, 246
Mid-Atlantic (USA), xvi, 5, 13, 15, 39, 76, 160, 258; frontier in, 30. *See also* East (USA)
Middle Ground (historical region), 2, 5–6, 10, 69, 72–75
Midwest (USA): abolitionism in, 45–47, 50–51, 53–55, 61, 63; African Americans in, 239–42, 245, 247, 250–51; agriculture and, xiv, 4, 164–68, 170, 207, 215; borders of, 1–4, 12–14, 16–17, 155, 158–65, *162*, 169, 282–85, 291; cities in, 76; civil rights movement in, 83, 239; Columbus in, vii, xxiii; culture of, 14–15, 194–96, 198, 201–2, 208–9, 219–20; democracy in, 46; economy of, 85, 188, 207, 215, 219, 230; elections in, 274–77, *276*, *283*, 284–86, 289–92; geography of, ix, xi, xiv, xx, 161–62; history of, 7, 69; housing in, 181–83, 188; identity of, 14, 123–24, 135, 145, 176–77, 216, 257; industry in, 80, 187–88; Italian Americans in, 178, 188; migration to, xvi, 12, 217; Ohio in, 68–70, 75, 79–80, 86, 158, 160–64, 169–70, 258, 270, 282–88, 291–92; Ohio River and, xiii, 1, 4, 6–8, 16–17, 109, 158–59, 161–63, 239, 275; orchestras in, 215, 222, 225, 229; politicians from, 108; politics of, 11, 15, 45, 123–27, 130–35, 260, 269–70; racism in, 185; regionalism and, 91–93, 98, 100–103, 128–29; reputation of, 10, 79–80; Spain and, 94, 98; wars in, xii, 11, 109, 112, 114, 116, 119–20. *See also* Old Northwest (USA)
migration, xii–xvi, xviii, 53, 59, 142, 268; of African Americans, 6, 10, 186, 246; from Appalachia, 262, 268; from New England, 8, 12, 16, 141–42, 144–48, 164, 176, 217–18; to Ohio, 12, 142, 155, 217–18, 246; regions and, 2–3. *See also* Great Migration; immigration
Mikado, The (Gilbert and Sullivan), 200–201, 205
Milan, OH, 80
Miller, Lewis, 195

Milwaukee, WI, 260
Minnesota, vii, 71, 165, 177, 195–96, 270
Miro, Esteban, 97, 99
Mississippi, 239, 245
Mississippi River, 7, 11, 27, 72, 92–97, 100, 103, 119; Cleveland and, 218; Midwest and, 109, 158, 257; watershed of, 70
Mississippi Valley, 4, 31, 71, 94, 123, 135
Missouri, 53, 90, 92, 107, 125–27, 165–66, 195–96
Missouri Compromise, 47, 59, 124
Missouri River, xxiii
Monongahela River, xvi, 5
Monongahela Woodland culture, 71
Monroe County, OH, 280
Montgomery bus boycott, 83
Montgomery County, OH, 282
Moore, Queen Mother (Audley), 248
Moravian Church, xv, 37
Morgan, David, 258
Morgan, George, 10, 90–91; Burr and, 92–93, 101–3; monument to, 90, *91*, 103; New Madrid and, 93–99
Morgan, George, Jr., 101
Morgan, John, 101–3
Morgan, Thomas, 103
Morganza (estate), 90, 100, 102
Mormonism, 77, 164
Morrison, Michael A., 45–46
Morrison, Toni, 81
Moses, Robert (civil rights activist), 83
Mount Pleasant, OH, xv
Muck, Karl, 202
Murphy, Frank, 264
Murray, Philip, 259–61, 263–64
music, 82, 198, 200–201, 206, 224, 219, 240, 251. *See also* opera; orchestras
Musical Times, 229
muskellunge (fish), ix
Muskingum County, OH, ix
Muskingum River, ix, xi, xiii, 71
Muskingum University, ix, xiv
Musser, Margaret, 143–44
Musser, Peter, 143–44

NAACP, 243, 245, 250
NASA, 3
Nashville, TN, 247
Nation, The, 226
National Guard, 84, 249, 264–65
nationalism, 194, 202–6, 250
National Negro Congress, 243

National Origins Act (1924), 180
National Road, viii, 164
National Road and Zane Grey Museum, xi
Native Americans: Britain and, 31–32, 73; diplomacy with, 90, 93; in the Midwest, 6–7; news coverage of, 28–30, *29*, 35–36, 40; in Ohio, 10, 71–75, 163–64; in Pontiac's Rebellion, 27, 29–31, 35–38; racism against, 9, 32, 34–35, 37–40; Scots-Irish and, xiv; in the Seven Years' War, 20–21; in the War of 1812, 11, 109–10, 112, 119–20; in the West, 257
natural gas, xxi, 80, 291
Nazism, 224
Nazzarini, Nicholas, 185
Nebraska, xxiii, 124, 165–66, 196
Nelli, Humbert, 177
Nelson, Daniel, 177, 185, 187–88
New Albany, OH, 84
New Concord, OH, ix–xi
New Deal, xxi, 15, 261–62, 264–67, 269–71
New England, 69, 75; abolitionism and, 47–48, 59, 77, 125–28, 134; economy of, 187; migration from, xii, xv–xvi, 8, 12, 16, 141–42, 144–48, 152–54, 164, 176, 217–18; religion in, 146–47. *See also* East (USA)
New England Emigrant Aid Company, 125–26, 130
New Haven, CT, vii, *22, 29, 33*
New Jersey, *22*, 27, 48, 159
New Jersey Land Society, 93–94, 101
New Lisbon Anti-Slavery Bugle, 148–49
New London, OH, 217
New Madrid, MO, 10, 90, 92–100, 103
New Middletown, OH, 139, 146–47, 153–54
New Orleans, 94–96, 98–99
New Philadelphia, IL, 53
New Philadelphia, OH, xv
Newport, RI, *22, 29, 33,* 39
New Spain, 97. *See also* Mexico
newspapers, 9, 21–24, *22,* 56–57, 112, 126, 207, 248; coverage of the frontier, 26–30, 32, *33,* 34–40, *34;* geography of, 24–25; orchestras and, 226, *228*
New Springfield, OH, 148–49, 151, 153
New York, xvi, xix, 4, 37, 93, 159, 168, 194; abolitionism in, 47–48; frontier in, 27; labor in, 15; migration from, 53, 59, 142, 217; migration to, 268; newspapers in, 28; politics of, 108, 258, 264, 266; regional identity of, 177
New York City, 13, 55, 76, 101, 108, 112, 198, 248; activism in, 250; culture of, 201–2, 204, 208, 230–31, 247; hinterlands of, 258; music and, 14–15, 221–22, 224–26; newspapers in, 23–25, 39; politics of, 259
New Yorker (magazine), 228
New-York Gazette, 36
New York Philharmonic, 224, 227–28, 230
New York Times, 108, 223, 226–29, *228*
NFL, xix, 5. *See also* football
Nicklaus, Jack, 83
Nigeria, 251
Niles Fire Brick (company), 179–81, 183–84
Niles, OH, 112, 179–81, 183–84, 186–87, 264–65
Niles, William Ogden, 114
NOAA, 3
Norling, Cody, 14
North (USA), 7, 103, 268. *See also* East (USA); Mid-Atlantic (USA); Midwest (USA); New England
North America, 31–32; history of, 6, 10, 69–72, 86, 98; newspapers in, 21, *22,* 23, 25–27, 30, 32, 34, 37; regions of, 2–3, 161, 163; Seven Years' War in, 7–9, 20, 24, 73
North Bend, OH, 108, 116, *117,* 118
North Carolina, *22,* 25–26
North Dakota, viii, 165, 168. *See also* Dakotas
Northwest Indian Confederacy, 74
Northwest Ordinance, xvi, 1, 8, 16, 75, 158, 169; slavery and, 48, 52, 77
Northwest Territory (USA), xii, 9, 141–42, 158, 160, 169–70; Ohio and, 13
Norwich, OH, 217

Oakes, James, 51
Obama, Barack, xxi, 16, 278–80, 282–84, 286–89
Oberlin College, 47, 54–55, 77–78, 218
Oberlin-Wellington Rescue Cases, 78
obsidian, 71
Occupy Wall Street movement, 251
Odyssey (Homer), 112
Ohio: abolitionism in, 47–48, 54–56, 77–78, 147–49; activism in, 80–81, 83; agriculture in, 68, 71, 76, 140, 153, 165–68, 170, 217; borders of, xxi, 1, 12–13, 140, 143, 159–61; center of, vii–viii, x; in the Civil War, xii, 12, 78–79, 149–50, 155, 179, 218, 261–62; culture of, 14, 69, 81–83, 140–42, 145, 154–55, 216; demographics of, 69, 75–76, 85, 141–42; economy of, 70, 76, 82, 84–85; elections in, 15–16, 79, 81, 85, 266, 268–69, 271, 274–86, 288–92; electoral geography

Ohio (*cont.*)
of, *276, 279, 281, 283, 289;* environment of, 166–67; forests in, x, xvii, 167; geography of, ix–x, xxiii, 4, 6, 8, 12–13, 76, 143–44, 151; historical role of, 10, 68–70, 75–80, 84, 86; immigration to, 80, 140, 151, 154, 163–64, 218; labor in, 10, 15, 81, 258, 261–65, 269–70; land schemes in, 100; local government in, 143, 149; maps of, *144, 162, 278, 281;* Midwest and, 68–70, 75, 79–80, 86, 158, 160–64, 169–70, 258, 270, 282–88, 291–92; migration to, xv–xvii, 3, 76, 141–42, 148, 155, 217, 268; Native Americans in, 10, 71–75, 163–64; news from, 27; opera in, 205; politics of, 12, 56, 76–77, 80–81, 85–86, 110, 126–27, 130, 261–62, 269–71; Pontiac's Rebellion in, 31–32, 38; racism in, 83, 185–87, 241, 249, 262–63, 270; regions of, xiv, xviii, 16, 176–77, 275, 277–80, *278,* 282–85, *283,* 288–91, *289;* religion in, 76; Tocqueville on, 5; topography of, xvii–xviii, 164, 167–68; wars in, xii, 72–75; William Henry Harrison in, 115
Ohio Agricultural Research and Development Center, 168
Ohio Company of Associates, xii, xvii, 75
Ohio & Erie Canal, viii
Ohio River, xi, 5, 11, 27, 70, 75, 99, 108, 245; flooding of, xv; geology and, 168; industry and, xix–xx; Midwest and, xiii, 1, 4, 6–8, 16–17, 109, 158–59, 161–63, 239, 275; migration and, 143, 164, 261; Pontiac's Rebellion and, 30, 32; Seven Years' War and, 73; slavery and, 4–5, 7, 123–25, 130, 133; surveys and, 141; trade and, 96; tributaries of, xvi, xviii; War of 1812 and, 110; watershed of, 1, 20
Ohio Supreme Court, 85
Ohio University, xii, xvii–xviii
Ohio Valley, xiv, 4, 20, 32, 142, 161, 169; Native Americans in, 6, 38, 72
oil, 80
Ojibwe people, 31
Old Chillicothe, OH, 74
Old Northwest (USA), 92, 123–24, 160; abolitionism in, 45, 50–51, 58–59, 124–25; politics in, 124–30, 132–35, 153; racism in, 63, 241. *See also* Midwest (USA)
Old Springfield, OH, 146
"Old Tippecanoe" (song), *117,* 118
Oldtown, OH, 74

Omaha, NB, xxiii
Onuf, Peter, 92, 216
opera, 14, 193–94, 200–209
orchestras, 14–15, 215, 221–32
Ottawa, IL, 129
Ottawa County, OH, 291
Ottawa people, 31
Our Western Border (book), viii
Owens, Robert, 109
Oxford, OH, 83, 221

Pacific Ocean, x, 46
Paducah, KY, 4
Pallante, Donald, 185, 187
Pallante, Lorenzo, 179–80
Pallante, Martha I., 13–14
Papillion, NB, xxiii
Paris, 219, 222, 225
Paris, Peace of, 7–8, 16, 19
Parker, James, 23
Parker, Theodore, 60
Parkinson, Robert, 28, 34
Patrone, Michael, 179–81, 183–84
Patterson, James, 80
Paul, Ella, x
Paxton Boys, 39
Pease, Theodore Calvin, 63
Peck, Gunther, 177
Peck, John Mason, 53
Pekar, Harvey, 223
Pennsylvania, xv, xviii; borders of, xxi, 1, 12–13, 140–41, 143, *144,* 149, 155, 159–60; elections in, 266; geography of, 4–5, 13, 162, 177; labor in, 15, 260, 263, 270; migration from, 142, 144, 164; migration to, 268; militia of, 74; Native Americans in, 9, 32, 39; politics of, 132, 135, 258, 262, 264, 269–70, 291; Pontiac's Rebellion in, 28–30; Seven Years' War in, 7, 9; travel through, 145; Whiskey Rebellion in, 100–101
Pennsylvania Dutch, 140, 143, 145–46, 148–49, 151–52, 154; migration of, xv, 12. *See also* German Americans
Pennsylvania Gazette, 22, 24, 28–29
Pensacola, FL, 25
Pepper Pike, OH, xxii
Percy, Charles, 269
Perry, Oliver Hazard, 74
Petersburg, OH, 144, 146, 149, 155
Philadelphia, xv, 8, 99–100, 112, 231, 250, 258; geography of, 5; newspapers in, 22, 23–25, *29, 33,* 34, *34,* 39

INDEX   315

Philadelphia Orchestra, 15, 224, 226
Phillips, Kimberly, 246
Phillips, Wendell, 55
Phillips, William, 129
Picasso, Pablo, 222
Pierce, Franklin, 135
pigs, 217
Pinckney's Treaty, 95–96
Pinkerton, Allan, 56
Pittsburgh, xvi, xix, 97, 100, 246, 248; geography of, xx, 1, 3–6, 176–77, 258; labor movement in, 260–61, 263; politics of, 263, 265, 269–70. *See also* Fort Pitt
Pittsburgh Courier, 248, 262
Pittsburgh Steelers, 5
Pius XI (pope), 260
pizza, x, viii, 178, 181, 183
Plymouth, OH, 217
Poetics (Aristotle), 112, 119
poetry, xix, 2, 112, 134, 247. *See also* literature
Pogue, James, xxi
Poland, OH, 139–40, 142–44, 154
Poland Township, OH, 12, 139–49, 151–55
Poland Union Seminary, 152
policing, 238–39, 241, 244, 259, 265
Pollock, Oliver, 94
pollution, xix–xx, xxiii, 83, 269
Pontiac, 36
Pontiac's Rebellion, 9, 21, 27–31, 34, 37, 73
Porfirio family, 183
Port Huron, MI, 3
Potomac River, xvi, 101
Pottawatomi people, 31
Powell, John Wesley, viii
Prairie du Rocher, IL, 93
Prairie Peninsula, 167
prairies, xxiii, 3, 165, 167, 217
Presbyterianism, x–xi, xiii–xiv, xxi–xxii, 37, 53–54, 77, 145
Pressman, Lee, 264
Preston, Katherine, 193–94
Proclamation of 1763, xvi, 73–74
Proctor, Henry, 110
progressive movement, 10, 17, 80–81
prohibition movement, 12, 80, 153. *See also* temperance movement
Prophet's Town, 110. *See also* Tippecanoe, Battle of
Prospect, NJ, 100
Protestantism, xv, 176, 196, 261–62, 264, 266–68, 270
Puccini, Giacomo, 200

Putnam County, IL, 53
Putnam, Rufus, xiii, xvii

Quakerism, xv–xvi, xvii–xviii, 37, 39; abolitionism and, 48, 53, 56, 77–78
Quebec, Battle of, 73
Quebec Act, 73–74
Queen, James Fuller, *117*
Quincy, IL, 53, 55
Quincy County, IL, 53
Quinn, Paul, 53

racism: against Black Americans, 34, 51–53, 62–63, 83, 123–24, 239–41, 245, 249–50, 262–63; against immigrants, 185–87; against Native Americans, 9, 32, 34–35, 37–40; in Ohio, 83, 185–87, 241, 249, 262–63, 270. *See also* segregation; slavery
radio, 82, 201, 207, 221, 224, 227
railroads, xvi, 154, 179, 183, 196, 215, 220; employees of, 291; in Ohio, 76, 80
Rankin, John, 47
Ray, Joseph, 77
Reconstruction, 78–79, 261
redbud (tree), xii
Redpath Chautauqua Bureau, 14, 196; opera and, 193–94, 200–209
Redpath Lyceum Bureau, 193–94, 196
regionalism, xii, xxiii, 10, 45, 91–93, 98, 100–103, 177, 196, 290–91; culture and, 194, 196; literary, xx; in Ohio, 176–77; slavery and, 123, 125, 128–29
Republican Party: in the 1856 elections, 123–25, 127, 134–35; in the 1938 elections, 266; abolitionism and, 9, 57, 59, 61; in Cleveland, 265; in the Mahoning Valley, xxi, 140, 148; media and, 17; in the Midwest, 129, 269, 277, 287, 290; in Ohio, 70, 77, 79, 81, 85–86, 130, 149, 262–63, 267–71, 277–85, 288, 291–92; slavery and, 11–12, 123–25, 127, 135
Republic Iron & Steel (company), 179–80, 265
Ress, David, 52
Revolutionary Action Movement, 15, 240, 250
rhinoceroses, xi
Rhode Island, xiii, *22*, 48
Rhodes, Eric Michael, 14
Rhodes, James, 229
Richmond, VA, 102
Right Stuff, The (Wolfe), xi
Riley, James Whitcomb, xx
roads, vii, 2, 139, 155, 164

Robin Hood (De Koven), 200, 205–6
Robinson, Lewis, 238–39, 245, 249
Rockefeller, John D., 219
Rockefeller, Nelson, 269
Rockefeller foundation, 247
Rock & Roll, 82
Rockwell, Norman, xxi
Rocky Mountains, 27, 70, 119, 239
Rome, xvii, 113, 115
Romney, George, 269
Romney, Mitt, 280, 290
Roosevelt, Franklin D., 259–60, 264–66, 269–70
Rose, Gregory, 4, 12–13
Rose, Pete, 82
Ross, Chappy, 187
rubber, 80, 82
Ruberto, Pasquale, 187
Rulli, Michael, xxi
Runner, Louis, 200
Russia, 220, 228
Rust Belt, xviii, xxii–xxiii, 5, 68, 84, 86, 161, 177, 242
Rust Belt Studies (journal), xxiii
Ruthenberg, Charles, 81

Saint Lawrence River, 72
Sandow, Robert M., 151
Sandusky, OH, 36, 73
Sandusky culture, 71
Sangamon County, IL, 54
San Lorenzo, Treaty of, 95
San Pietro Avellana, Italy, 181
Saratoga (proposed state), 158, 170
satellite photography, 3–4
Savage, Henry, 202
Savannah, GA, 22, 28, *29*, *33*, *34*
Saybrook, OH, 217
Schillinger, Jonathan, 153
Schlesinger, Arthur, Jr., 11, 107–9
Schrembs, Joseph (Bishop), 263
Schumann, Robert, 226
Schumann-Heink, Ernestine, 194, 204–5, 208, 221
Scioto River, 165
Scotland, xiii
Scots-Irish, xiv–xvi, xviii, xxii, 12, 32, 37, 142, 145–46; dialect of, 6
Scott, Abraham, 146
Scottsboro Boys, 243
Scranton, William, 269
secessionism, 62, 78, 128, 150

Second Great Awakening, 12, 77, 147, 155
Second Industrial Revolution, 80, 82, 85
segregation, 83, 239, 243–45, 260. *See also* racism
Seneca people, 31, 38, 73
Seven Ranges, 12, 141–45, 149, 154–55
Seventy-Eighth Ohio Volunteer Infantry, xii
Seven Years' War, xvi, 7–8, 20–21, 24, 27, 31, 37, 73, 113
Severance, John, 222
Shabazz, Gamell, 248
Shafer, Ronald G., 109
Shawnee people, xvi, 31, 72; wars with the United States, 6, 11, 74, 109–10, 116, 119
Shawneetown, IL, 53
Shay's Rebellion, 95
Sheehan, Grace, 183
Shelby, IA, *197*, *199*
Sheridan, Philip, 78
Sherman, John, 79
Sherman, William Tecumseh, 78–79
silver, 71, 96
Silver, Peter, 37
Sinatra, Frank, xviii
Sioux City, IA, xxiii
Sioux Falls, SD, ix, xxiii
slavery: abolition of, 10, 262; Civil War and, 62; debates about, 9, 11, 46–52, 59–62, 147–49, 155; escape from, 76, 78; New Madrid and, 96; Northwest Ordinance and, 48, 52, 77; Ohio River and, 4–5, 7, 123–25, 130, *133*; politics and, 11–12, 115, 123–30, 132–35; resistance to, 53
Slovakian Americans, 185
Slovenian Americans, 263, 267
Smethurst, James, 15, 240, 246, 248
Smith, Alexander, 57
Smith, Clay, 203
Smith, Gerrit, 48, 56, 61
Smith, Hannah, 142
Smoky Hollow, OH, 178–86
soils, vii, x, xvii–xviii, 165, 167–68
Sokoloff, Nikolai, 220–21
"Soldier of Tippecanoe, The" (song), 118
"Song of an Old Soldier," 118
South (USA), 7, 69, 163, 185; abolitionism in, 55; civil rights movement in, 83, 239, 243; Civil War and, 150; definition of, 257; Midwest and, 4–5, 258; migration from, 6, 80, 164, 186, 188, 242, 246, 261, 267–68, 270; Native Americans in, 9, 28, 38, 40; news in, 28–29, 40; politics of, 50,

260, 285; racism in, 241, 245; regionalism in, 103; secessionism in, 78; slavery in, 11, 125, 133–34
South Carolina, 9, 25–26, 28, 128
South-Carolina Gazette, 25
South Dakota, viii, 165, 196; topography of, x. *See also* Dakotas
South Dakota, University of, xxiii
Southern Baptist Church, 268
Soviet Union, 228
Spain, 20, 27, 90, 92–103
Spanish Civil War, 247
sports, 82–83, 164. *See also* baseball; basketball; football
Springfield, IL, 60
Springfield Township, OH, 12, 139–40, *150*; history of, 141–45, 147–54; religion in, 146–47
Stanford, Max, 250
Stanton, Elizabeth Cady, 47
Stanton, Henry, 47
Stark County, OH, 154
State Route 170 (Ohio), 139, 155
steel, 80, 228, 259, 263, 266; in Cleveland, 219; in the Mahoning Valley, 13–14, 153, 176, 178–79, 186. *See also* Little Steel Strike (1937)
Steel Workers' Organizing Committee (SWOC), 259–65
Steinem, Gloria, 83
Steuben, Friedrich Wilhelm von, xvii
Steubenville, OH, x, xv–xviii, xx, 141, 143, *144*
Steubenville District, *144*
Steward, James R., 242
St. Louis Democrat, 129
Stockwell, Mary, 11
Stokes, Carl, 83, 240
Stravinsky, Igor, 222
Strickland, Ted, 85
strikes: of musicians, 229–30; in Ohio, 261–65, 270–71; Taft-Hartley Act and, 268. *See also* Little Steel Strike (1937)
Struthers, OH, 139, 153, 179
Students for a Democratic Society, 250
suburbs, 82–83, 140, 154, 246, 248; politics of, 275, 277, 280, 282, 292
Sullivan, Arthur, 200, 205
Sumner, Charles, 128
Sun Belt, 84, 231, 280
Sussex County, NJ, 27
Swahili language, 246
Swartz, Joel, 146–47

Szell, George, 222–29, *228*, 231
Szell, Helene, 224–25

Taft, Robert A., 267–69
Taft, William H., 81, 267
Taft-Hartley Act, 268
Taggesspiegel, Der, 226
Tanaghrisson, 73
Tarbell, Ida M., 152
Teaford, Jon, 14, 177, 181–83, 187–88
Tecumseh, 11, 74, 109–10, 112–16, 118–20
temperance movement, 12, 46, 80–81, 147–49, 153, 155. *See also* prohibition movement
Tennessee, 55, 98, 161, 166
Tenskwatawa, 74, 110, 114
Terre Haute, IN, xxii
Texas, 47, 71, 84, 93, 119, 266
Thames River, Battle of, 11, 110, 112–16, 118–19
Thayer, Eli, 125, 127
theater, 201, 246–47
Thomas, John R., 181
Thomas, T. E., 184
Thomas, Theodore, 230–31
Thompson, Richard Wigginton, 129
Tibetts, Paul, 82
Time (magazine), 227
Tippecanoe, Battle of, 11, 107, 109–10, *111*, 112–16, 118–19, 132–33
Tippecanoe battlefield, 115, 132–33
Tippecanoe Creek, 107, 110, 116
Tocqueville, Alexis de, 4–5, 7–8, 16–17, 46
Tod, David, 149–50
Toledo, OH, 79, 81, 84, 260, 275, 277, 280
Tooley, Howard, 203
Toronto, OH, xviii
Toscanini, Arturo, 224
trees, ix, xii, xiv, xvii, 113, 160, 167
Trotter, Joe William, 241, 246
Troy, 113
Truman, Harry S., 258, 268
Trumbull, John, 112
Trumbull County, OH, 12, 142–43, *144*, 149, 179, 279
Trump, Donald, xxi, 16, 85, 275, 277–82, 284–86, 288–91
Truth, Sojourner, 58
Turner, Frederick Jackson, 21, 92, 217
Twain, Mark, 221

Ulster, xiii
Uncle Tom's Cabin (Beecher Stowe), 78

INDEX

Underground Railroad, 47, 55, 58, 78, 148
Union Army (US Civil War), 78
unions, 259–60, 266, 268, 270; in Ohio, 81, 261–65, 267, 269. *See also* labor
United Automobile Workers (UAW), 259, 264–65
United Freedom Movement, 244
United Kingdom. *See* Britain
United Mine Workers, 81
United Negro Improvement Association (UNIA), 15, 239, 242, 250
United Press International (UPI), 249
United Rubber Workers, 81, 265
United States: abolitionism in, 52, 59, 63; African Americans in, 246–47, 251; Cleveland in, 243; culture of, 193–94, 196, 198, 201–6, 208–9, 247; democracy in, 45; elections in, 11, 86, 276, 276, 290–91; ethnicity in, 186; geology of, 168; history of, 95; housing in, 182, 188; immigration to, 181, 188; independence of, 40; industry in, 80, 223; literature of, 112–14; Native Americans and, 6, 11, 74–75, 109–10, 112, 116, 119; Ohio in, 68–70, 75, 79–80, 86, 274, 276, 291; orchestras in, 224, 226–27, 231; regionalism in, 10, 45, 48, 51, 91–93, 100–103; regions of, 1–4, 17, 257; slavery in, 48, 51; Spain and, 94, 97–98, 100; in the War of 1812, 11; Tocqueville on, 7–8
United Steel Workers, 81
Upper Peninsula (Michigan), 219
Upton, Harriet Taylor, 81, 142
Urban League, 245, 249
Urban renewal, 244, 248
Ursuline College, xxii–xxiii
US Army, 74, 149
US Census, 49, 112, 160, 164–66, 183, 186
US Congress, 79, 93–94, 96, 99, 101–2, 216, 260, 269; elections to, xxi, 46, 110, 134, 266, 268, 124–25; Kansas-Nebraska Act and, 124; Northwest Ordinance and, xii, 7; Ohio representatives in, 76, 85, 110, 229, 267; slavery and, 45, 47, 52, 127
US Constitution, 47–50, 54, 62–63, 74, 95, 99, 262
US Department of Agriculture (USDA), 4, 166
US Department of the Treasury, 205
US Senate, x–xi, 62, 79, 126, 128, 269; elections to, 46, 266–67
US Steel (company), 179, 259
US Supreme Court, 57, 79, 259

Valentine, May, 194, 204–8
Vallandigham, Clement, 79
Van Buren County, MI, 128
Van Buren, Martin, 107
Van Buskirk, Judith L., 50
van Dijk, Peter, 230
Vassar College, 220
Vawter, Keith, 196, 198
Vechiarelli, Donetta Clemente, 185
Verdi, Giuseppe, 200
Vermillion, SD, xxiii
Vermont, 56, 58
veterans, xii–xiii, 50–51, 103, 115; land grants to, xvii
Vibration (journal), 251
Vienna, 224, 226
Vietnam War, 84
Vincennes, IN, 110, 118
Vincent, John Heyl, 195
Virgil, 112
Virginia, xiv, 51–52, 73, 99–101, 108, 113–15, 127, 164; borders of, 159; frontier in, 7, 9, 27–28, 30, 32; mail in, 25
Virginia Gazette, 22, 26

Wade, Benjamin F., 57, 79
Wade Pond, 222
Wagner, Richard, 200
Wagner, Robert, 264
Wagoner, Henry O., 57
Walker, William, 126
Wall Street Journal, xxii
War Department, 113
Ware-Bey, Albert, 238
War of 1812, 11, 51, 74–75, 110, 112, 115, 128
Warren, Hooper, 56
Warren, OH, 177, 179, 264–65
Warren County, OH, 282
Washington (proposed state), 158, 170
Washington, DC, 47, 54, 57, 81, 221, 260, 266
Washington, George, xii, xvii, 7, 16, 73–75, 92, 100–101, 113
Washington, PA, 102
Washington County, NJ, 101
Washington County, OH, 141
Waterloo, IA, 207
Wayne, Anthony, xii, 110, 118
Wayne County, MI, 259. *See also* Detroit
Wayne County, OH, 154
Wayne National Forest, xii
weather, vii–viii, ix, xi. *See also* climate

Weaver, Glenn, 146–47
Webster, Daniel, 115
Weld, Theodore, 47, 54–55, 58
Welsh Americans, 180, 221
Weems, Parson, 113
Weiss, Samuel, 260
Wendat Confederacy, 72
Wendt, Simon, 240
Wenger, Dianna, 152
West (USA): borders of, viii; British Empire and, 40; definition of, 257; Midwest and, 92; news from, 26–27; Ohio and, 86; politics and, 10, 119; publications from, 109; slavery and, 124–25; Spain and, 94, 98. *See also* Midwest (USA); Old Northwest (USA)
West Erie Basin culture, 71
Western Antislavery Society, 47
Western Citizen (newspaper), 50, 54–56, 60
Western College for Women, 83, 221
Western Reserve. *See* Connecticut Western Reserve
Western Reserve University, 184, 226, 250
West Florida, 27, 29, 94
West Indies, 25–26. *See also* Caribbean region
West Virginia, xiii–xiv, xvii–xviii, xx–xxi, 5–6, 163, 262, 268, 285; borders of, 159; Midwest and, 161; Rust Belt and, 177
Wheaton College, 54
Wheeler, Kenneth H., 151
Wheeling, West Virginia, ix, xv
Whig Party, 9, 49–50, 56–57, 59, 76, 124–25, 131–33, 148–49; William Henry Harrison and, 106–8, 114, 116
Whiskey Rebellion, 74, 100–102
white Americans: abolitionism and, 51, 56, 63; in cities, 177; ethnicities of, 185; labor movement and, 261–62, 266, 268; Native Americans and, 28, 30–32, 34–35, 37–38, 40, 109; in Ohio, 69, 85–86, 243, 249, 270; politics of, 258, 267–68, 270, 275, 288, 290–921. *See also* Europeans
Whitman, Walt, 8, 16
Whittlesey culture, 71
Wichita, KS, 3
Wiecek, William, 48–49, 57
Wieck, Carl F., 60
Wilberforce, OH, 250
Wilds, the (zoo), xi
Wiley, Andrew, 11

Wilkes, Ruth, 139–40
Wilkinson, James, 94, 97, 99, 102
Willard, J. P., *150*
William G. Mather (ship), xxii
Williamsburg, VA, 22, 24–26
Williamstown, WV, xiii
Wilson, Gregory S., 10
Wilson, Hiram, 47
Wisconsin, ix, 7, 9, 11, 56, 165, 177, 196, 250; migration to, 261; politics of, 134, 270, 291
Wolfe, Tom, xi
women: abolitionism and, 46; activism by, 243; economy and, 14, 188; education of, 152, 185; in the Mahoning Valley, 178, 180, 185, 188
Women's Christian Temperance Union, 80
women's rights, 81, 83–84. *See also* feminism
Woodard, Colin, 2–3
Wooster, OH, 168
World War I, xviii, 186, 202–3, 219, 242
World War II, x, 82–84, 140, 178, 180, 186, 188, 246–47; economy and, 216, 227; politics and, 267–68
Worthy, William, 250–51
Wright, Gwendolyn, 182
Wright, James, vii, xix–xx, 81
Wright, Wilbur, 80
Wright Brothers, 80

Yans-McGlaughlin, Virginia, 181
Yellowstone region, 71
York County, Pennsylvania, 143
Yorktown, Battle of, xiii, 74
Yost, Jean, xiv
Youngstown, OH, xxi, 12–13, 139, 145, 149, 151–53; demographics of, 186; economy of, 80, 82, 84, 153–54, 179; geography of, 177; Italian Americans in, 179–80, 186; strike in, 261–62, 264–65; Underground Railroad in, 148
Youngstown Sheet & Tube, xxi, 179, 265
Youngstown State University, xxi

Zane, Ebenezer, viii
Zane family, viii
Zane's Trace, viii–ix
Zanesville, OH, viii–ix, xi, xx, 277
zebras, xi
Zoar, OH, 77
zoos, xi